T0396669

Italy and Australia

Gabriele Abbondanza · Simone Battiston
Editors

Italy and Australia

Redefining Bilateral Relations for the Twenty-First
Century

Editors
Gabriele Abbondanza
Discipline of Government
and International Relations
University of Sydney
Sydney, NSW, Australia

Complutense University of Madrid
Madrid, Spain

Istituto Affari Internazionali (IAI)
Rome, Italy

Simone Battiston
Department of Humanities and Social
Sciences
Swinburne University of Technology
McKinnon, VIC, Australia

ISBN 978-981-99-3215-3   ISBN 978-981-99-3216-0   (eBook)
https://doi.org/10.1007/978-981-99-3216-0

To H.E. Francesca Tardioli, Italian ambassador to Australia from 2019 to 2022

CONTENTS

NOTES ON CONTRIBUTORS

Dr. Gabriele Abbondanza is Marie Curie Fellow (a leading EU position) at the Complutense University of Madrid (Spain); Associate Researcher at the School of Social and Political Sciences of the University of Sydney (Australia); and Associate Fellow at the Italian Institute of International Affairs—IAI (Italy). He specialises in Australian and Italian foreign and security policy; irregular migration; the Indo-Pacific; and middle power and great power theory. He has published widely on these subjects, including articles in leading journals such as *International Affairs, International Political Science Review, European Political Science*, and *History of Political Thought*, and is co-editor, with Thomas Wilkins, of "Awkward Powers" (Palgrave Macmillan, 2021). Dr. Abbondanza currently teaches a number of courses related to international relations, security studies, and irregular migration, and frequently contributes to media and public debates concerning his fields of expertise.

Dr. Francesco Bailo is a Lecturer in data analytics for the social sciences at the University of Sydney. His research focuses on the impact of media and internet technologies on politics.

Prof. Loretta Baldassar is Professor in Anthropology and Sociology, Vice Chancellor Professorial Research Fellow, and Director of the Social Ageing (SAGE) Futures Lab, Edith Cowan University. Baldassar is one of Australia's leading and most highly cited social scientists. She was named Australian Research Field Leader in Migration Studies as well as Ethnic and Cultural Studies in 2020, 2021, and 2022, (The Australian Research Magazine 10/11/2022). Baldassar is Vice President of the International Sociological Association Migration Research Committee and Regional Editor for the journal, Global Networks. Baldassar has been a Chief Investigator on over 50 research projects, 20 as Lead. She is a highly regarded supervisor, with 26 Ph.D. completions and 7 international postdoctoral fellowships. Her career has been devoted to better understanding the impact of migration on families and communities, with a focus on social care and the role of social support networks, intergenerational relations, the ageing process, and the social uses of new technologies.

Dr. Simone Battiston is Senior Lecturer in History and Politics at the Department of Humanities and Social Sciences, Swinburne University of Technology. His research examines different aspects of post-war Italian emigration, with a particular attention to the Australian context: external voting behaviour, history and memory of radical migrants, and migrant media history. Battiston has published widely; his monograph, *Immigrants Turned Activists: Italians in 1970s Melbourne*, was published by Troubador Publishing (Italian Studies Series) in 2012. He co-edited, with Stefano Luconi and Marco Valbruzzi, *Cittadini oltre confine. Storia, opinioni e rappresentanza degli italiani all'estero*, published by Il Mulino in 2022. Battiston is the recipient of the 2001 Honours Thesis Award (Friuli-Venetia Julia Regional Government) and the 2007 PhD Thesis Award (Giovanni Agnelli Foundation-Altreitalie Research Centre). He is an executive member of the Australian Migration History Network, and a member of the Australian Historical Society and of the Australian Society for the Study of Labour History.

A/Prof. Andrea Benvenuti is Associate Professor in Politics and International Relations at the School of Social Sciences, University of New South Wales, Australia. He currently teaches twentieth-century history and diplomacy at both undergraduate and postgraduate levels. His research interests lie in post-1945 international history with a strong focus on the Cold War in both Asia and Europe. He recently published Cold War and Decolonisation: Australia's Policy towards Britain's End of Empire in Southeast Asia (NUS Press, 2017) and China's Policy: The Emergence of a Great Power (Routledge, 2022) with Chung, Khoo, and Tan. He is currently completing two books—a co-authored two-volume monograph on the role of western powers in Asia from the end of the First World War to the end of the Cold War (Bloomsbury) and a single-authored book on Nehru's non-alignment in the 1950s (Hurst). He has a D.Phil. in International Relations from Oxford University, an M.A. in research from Monash University, and a B.A. Hons from the University of Florence.

Dr. Matteo Dutto leads the research group of the Monash University European Research Foundation, overseeing the identification of funding opportunities across local, national, and European grant schemes, and stakeholder engagement with academics, industry partners, and policymakers. Before joining the Monash University European Research Foundation, he was a postdoctoral researcher on the *Youth in the City* research project. Matteo is an Associate Research Fellow in the School of Languages, Literatures, Cultures and Linguistics at Monash University. His research employs decolonial, digital, and participatory action methodologies to explore how cultural producers collaborate with Indigenous, migrant, and multi-ethnic communities to produce transmedia and transcultural counter-narratives of belonging and identity. His monograph *Legacies of Indigenous Resistance* was published in 2019 and shortlisted in 2021 for the ASAL Alvie Egan award.

Dr. Giulia Marchetti is a Research Associate for the YMAP Project, a longitudinal, mixed-method study on youth mobilities to and from Australia originating from 5 countries (the UK, Italy, India, China, and Australia). She has recently completed her Ph.D. in Anthropology and Sociology on the Australian Research Council funded project, YMAP— Youth Mobilities Aspirations and Pathways—led by Prof. Anita Harris (Deakin University), Prof. Loretta Baldassar (Edith Cowan University), and Prof. Shanthi Robertson (Western Sydney University). Her thesis explored how transnational mobility impacts the identity and youth-to-adulthood transitions of young Italians who have moved to Australia and those who have returned to Italy.

Dr. Ilaria Stefania Pagani is a cancer researcher at the South Australian Health and Medical Research Institute, Adelaide, and affiliated senior lecturer in health and medical science at The University of Adelaide. She is leading her programme of research as Cancer Council fellow investigating new targeted therapies for blood cancer patients. She is a proud and active member of the Italian community in Australia where she contributes as President of the Association of Italian Researchers in Australasia, and treasurer of Com.It.Es South Australia. Funder of

Chronic Myeloid Leukaemia Australia Patient's Association, she is advocating for health equity ensuring a better care for cancer patients in Australia and worldwide.

Dr. Cristiana Palmieri is research affiliate at the School of Languages and Cultures, University of Sydney, where she completed her doctorate in Sociolinguistics and Adult Education, conducting research in Italian Studies on the motivations to learn Italian as a second language in Australia. She has been working in education since 1992, and has designed and delivered training programmes, workshops, and seminars on a variety of professional development subjects. Her main research interests are motivation for language learning in multicultural and multilingual contexts, language learning and identity, adult learning, and migration studies. She has presented at several national and international conferences on second language learning motivation and her research has been published in several academic journals and as a monograph by Multilingual Matters in 2018. She currently is the Head of Member Learning and Development at the Royal Australasian College of Physicians.

Prof. Robert Pascoe is Dean Laureate and Professor of History at Victoria University, Melbourne. He is the author or editor of three dozen books and technical reports in social history, Italian migration, and tertiary education.

A/Prof. Francesco Ricatti is Associate Professor and convenor of Italian Studies at the Australian National University. He has published extensively of the history of Italian migration to Australia, including his most recent book, *Italians in Australia: History, Memory, identity* (Palgrave 2018). His current research focuses on decolonial and transcultural approaches to migration and ethnic history—including a special forum in the journal Altreitalie on decolonising Italian migration to Australia, and the articles *Migrant Lives on First Nation Land: Greek-Australian Memories of Titjikala in the 1960s* (with Maria Pallotta-Chiarolli; Journal of Intercultural Studies 43.5 2022); *Mio figlio è color pesca: vita, attivismo e ricerca antirazzista* (Voci XIX 2022), and *Mapping transnational lives: patterns of dislocation and reorientation in contemporary carto-graphic memoirs* (with Barbara Pezzotti, Journal of Graphic Novels and Comics 2023). He also conducts participatory research projects on the role of art and sport in informal processes of transculturation within superdiverse cities.

Dr. Kurt Sengul is a sessional lecturer and tutor at the University of Sydney, Australia. His research focuses on the communication and discourse of the populist far-right in Australia.

Dr. Tiziana Torresi is Senior Lecturer in Political Theory at the University of Adelaide. She holds a B.A. Honours, First class and the University Medal, from the University of New South Wales, and a D.Phil. in Politics and International Relations, from the University of Oxford. Her research interests are mainly in normative international theory. She writes on migration and temporary labour migration, migrants' voting rights, the role of cities in migration, citizenship, and populism. She has published on state policies about women's bodies, especially in relation to health and development policy and theories of well-being more in general. She has an interest in the philosophy of love, both in interpersonal relations and as a public and political value. She is a founding member of the Global Justice Network and the Vice-president of ARIA—Associazione Ricercatori Italiani in Australasia.

LIST OF FIGURES

LIST OF TABLES

Italy and Australia in the Twenty-First Century: Distant Connections or Close Partners?

Gabriele Abbondanza and Simone Battiston

INTRODUCTION

In a global order in flux, marked by unprecedented power shifts, multiple regional crises, and additional uncertainty caused by the COVID-19 pandemic, the role of cooperation between liberal democracies is increasingly significant, and is regarded as such by both policymakers and scholars.[1] Italy and Australia represent two telling case studies in this

---

[1] Hal Brands and Francis J. Gavin, Eds., *COVID-19 and World Order: The Future of Conflict, Competition, and Cooperation* (Baltimore: Johns Hopkins University Press, 2020).

G. Abbondanza (✉)
Complutense University of Madrid, Madrid, Spain
e-mail: gabriabb@ucm.es

School of Social and Political Sciences, University of Sydney, Sydney, NSW, Australia

Istituto Affari Internazionali (IAI), Rome, Italy

1

respect, for a number of reasons. First, they are both highly developed countries that play a substantial role internationally: the former in Europe, the Mediterranean, the Horn of Africa, and the Middle East[2]; and the latter in the Indo-Pacific, especially in the South Pacific.[3] Second, they actively uphold the same understanding of "rules-based" international order, centred on the prominence of the international law, cooperation, and interdependence, and with the United States (US) as the country with informal leadership within it. Third, as a consequence of their shared worldviews, they are highly embedded in the multi-layered diplomatic, security, economic, scientific, and cultural networks that support such interdependence. As members of numerous international organisations and as co-signatories of multiple agreements, they regularly cooperate in international forums, also thanks to the benefits of evolving practices in digital diplomacy. Fourth, as established nations, they face the same major challenges that are affecting the international system as a whole,[4] in addition to many that are specific to their regional contexts.

As a result of this, Italy and Australia have enjoyed increasingly cordial bilateral relations since the 1970s, which are currently driven by shared values and strategic interests. Such relations are set to become even stronger in the future, should a comprehensive and ambitious Australia-European Union Free Trade Agreement be finally struck.[5] However,

---

S. Battiston
History and Politics, Department of Humanities and Social Sciences, Swinburne University of Technology, Hawthorn, NSW, Australia
e-mail: sbattiston@swin.edu.au

[2] Elisabetta Brighi, *Foreign Policy, Domestic Politics and International Relations: The Case of Italy* (London: Routledge, 2013); Gabriele Abbondanza, "The West's Policeman? Assessing Italy's Status in Global Peacekeeping", *The International Spectator* 55, no. 2 (2020): 127–141.

[3] Allan Patience, *Australian Foreign Policy in Asia: Middle Power or Awkward Partner?* (London: Palgrave Macmillan, 2018); Dennis Rumley, Vivian Louis Forbes, and Christopher Griffin, eds., *Australia's Arc of Instability: The Political and Cultural Dynamics of Regional Security* (Berlin: Springer, 2006).

[4] For a comprehensive discussion on global security challenges see Peter Hough, *Understanding Global Security* (London: Routledge: 2018).

[5] Jane Drake-Brockman and Patrick Messerlin, eds. *Potential Benefits of an Australia-EU Free Trade Agreement: Key Issues and Options* (Adelaide: Adelaide University Press, 2018).

scholars and practitioners have seldom examined these relations comprehensively, or beyond specific frames such as immigration or tourism. Indeed, even a cursory glance at the available literature would provide a more than sobering image of the current state of bilateral relations, which can be exemplified with two illustrations drawn from academic and diplomatic circles. The first one is provided by Bruno Mascitelli, a well-known scholar in this niche field, who defined bilateral relations as essentially "made and unmade by immigration".[6] The second one comes from former Australian Ambassador to Italy David Ritchie, who simply described them as "non-existent" at the end of his tenure, in December 2013.[7] Conversely, the appointment of Anthony Albanese as the first Australian Prime Minister with Italian-Australian heritage, in May 2022, is a remarkably significant development, although it is also a recent one and has consequently not captured yet the full attention of scholars focusing on relations between the two countries.

The extant literature is emblematic of this context and focuses predominantly on migration studies, broadly defined and chiefly understood as Italian immigration to Australia. To that end, relevant research efforts offer a substantial, multifaceted, inclusive, and decades-long scholarship on the presence of Italians in Australia, from wealthy adventurers, Catholic missionaries, and politically active émigrés and early settlers in the nineteenth century,[8] to a broader array of emigrants, including a significant presence of working and peasant class background labourers, throughout the twentieth century.[9] These are accounts of hardship,[10]

---

[6] Bruno Mascitelli, "Italy and Australia: A Relationship Made and Unmade by Immigration", *Australian Journal of International Affairs* 69, no. 3 (2015): 339–355.

[7] Gabriele Abbondanza, "Italy and Australia: Time for a Strategic Partnership", *IAI Commentaries* 20, no. 87 (2020): 1–5.

[8] Gianfranco Cresciani, *The Italians in Australia* (Cambridge: Cambridge University Press, 2003), 26–50.

[9] Loretta V. Baldassar, "Italians in Australia", in *Encyclopedia of Diasporas: Immigrant and Refugee Cultures Around the World*, eds. M. Ember, C. R. Ember, and I. Skoggard (Berlin: Springer, 2005), 850–864.

[10] Bruno Mascitelli, "Italian Immigration to Australia: The Way It Was", in *Australia's New Wave of Italian Migration: Paradise or Illusion?*, eds. B. Mascitelli and R. Armillei (Melbourne: Australian Scholarly Publishing, 2017), 34–52.

racism (received and inflicted),[11] (geo)political antagonism,[12] success,[13] socio-cultural liminality,[14] and a remarkably positive and constructive role in shaping Australia's evolving society.[15] More recent research has studied the contemporary effects of the above, and has subsequently investigated issues such as Italian expatriate voting in Australia,[16] the attractiveness of Italian culture in Australia,[17] and the highly educated and skilled Italians who in recent years have made Australia home, albeit temporarily, while learning or further mastering English as a second language.[18]

Notwithstanding this rich tapestry of scholarship, such focus on migration has left other fields of study on Italian–Australian relations deficient of contributions. This edited volume seeks to rectify this substantial gap in the literature by undertaking a comprehensive and multidisciplinary review of contemporary bilateral relations. Building from previous works, it expands the scope of analysis by encompassing and critically reviewing cultural, social, migratory, political, international relations, economic, and scientific research avenues that have been understudied so far. Subsequently, the leitmotif of this book is twofold: on the one hand the investigation of fields that—albeit overlooked in the literature—provide a remarkable contribution to the two countries' "non-official relations"; on

[11] Francesco Ricatti, *Italians in Australia: History, Memory, Identity* (London: Palgrave Macmillan, 2018), 53–74.

[12] Gianfranco Cresciani, *Fascism, Anti-fascism, and Italians in Australia 1922–1945* (Canberra: Australian National University Press, 1980).

[13] Laura Hougaz, *Entrepreneurs in Family Business Dynasties: Stories of Italian-Australian Family Businesses Over 100 Years* (Berlin: Springer, 2015).

[14] Simone Marino, *Intergenerational Ethnic Identity Construction and Transmission Among Italian-Australians: Absence, Ambivalence and Revival* (London: Palgrave Macmillan, 2020).

[15] Stephen Castles, "Italians in Australia: The Impact of a Recent Migration on the Culture and Society of a Postcolonial Nation", *Center for Migration Studies special issues* 11, no. 3 (1994): 342–367.

[16] Simone Battiston, "Il voto degli italiani in Australia fra continuità e segnali di cambiamento", in *Autopsia di un diritto politico. Il voto degli italiani all'estero nelle elezioni del 2018*, eds. S. Battiston and S. Luconi (Turin: Accademia University Press, 2018), 145–161.

[17] Cristiana Palmieri, *Identity Trajectories of Adult Second Language Learners: Learning Italian in Australia* (Bristol: Multilingual Matters, 2019).

[18] Chiara De Lazzari, "New Italian Emigration Globally: Who They Are and Where They Go", in *Australia's New Wave of Italian Migration: Paradise or Illusion?*, eds. B. Mascitelli and R. Armillei (Melbourne: Australian Scholarly Publishing, 2017), 14–33.

the other, a subsequent focus on how such cooperation could be strengthened and elevated to the status of formal cooperation between Italy and
Australia.

With such premises, this introductory chapter provides a guide to both
the volume's rationale, means, goals, and chapters, and a review of the
relevant literature. First, the next section explores the latter, and thus
examines in depth the corpus of Italian-Australian scholarship, which
is mostly focused on migration. While making no pretence to comprehensiveness,[19] we argue that a solid grounding in the extant literature
is necessary not only as an essential starting point for any academic
endeavour, but also to better trace the contours of the related gaps in
the literature that this book seeks to address. Second, an overview of
the understudied facets of Italian–Australian relations is presented. By
showing the limited amount of literature that is available on specific
aspects of bilateral relations—or even the absence thereof—we argue that
a sufficient understanding of the scope for potential cooperation between
the two countries can be achieved. In doing so, we also introduce the
book's chapters and their authors—who directly engage with the gaps
in the literature that have been previously highlighted—and we outline
the nature of the editorial guidance that has been applied throughout
this volume. The volume's chapters are divided into 4 sections,[20] with
the goal of arranging together works from the same disciplines and thus
enhancing the logical cohesion and readability of the whole book. Lastly,
we concisely summarise this chapter's premises, goals, and findings, which
are then revisited in Chapter 11 in the light of the insights from the rest
of the volume.[21]

---

[19] For additional sources on Italians in Australia, see Matteo Pretelli, "Gli Italiani in
Australia: lo stato dei lavori", *Studi Emigrazione* 46, no. 176 (2009): 779–792, and
Francesco Ricatti, *Italians in Australia: History, Memory, Identity* (London: Palgrave
Macmillan, 2018). For Australian perspectives on Italy at the end of the 1980s, see Camilla
Bettoni and Joseph Lo Bianco, eds., *Understanding Italy: Language, Culture, Commerce:
An Australian Perspective* (Sydney: Frederick May Foundation for Italian Studies, 1989).

[20] They are: (1) introduction; (2) history, migration, and culture; (3) international
relations, politics, trade, and science; and (4) conclusion.

[21] Simone Battiston and Gabriele Abbondanza, "Where to from Here? The Need for
a Long-Term Strategy in Italian-Australian Relations", in *Italy and Australia: Redefining
Bilateral Relations for the Twenty-First Century*, eds. Gabriele Abbondanza and Simone
Battiston (London: Palgrave Macmillan, 2024), pp. 269–280.

THE LITERATURE ON ITALIAN–AUSTRALIAN
RELATIONS: A CRITIQUE

As mentioned previously, a large proportion of the extant literature focuses on migration studies, understood as Italian migration to Australia, generally divided into five distinct periods of time by scholars. During the first one—ranging from early British settlement to the end of the nineteenth century—Italians who reached Australia were explorers, naturalists, wealthy adventurers, artists, missionaries, and both professional and unskilled workers.[22] With reference to the latter, and specifically during the second migration period (first half of the twentieth century), authors such as Langfield, Andreoni, and Dewhirst recount the attitudes to European migration in Australia, tracing the relative ease with which migrants from Northern and Central Italy were accepted into the Australian society due to their "whiteness", and the wariness or openly racist attitudes faced by Southern Italians on account of their "olive" complexion.[23] Additionally, while Ricatti emphasises the struggles of many Italians due to racial prejudice, he also points out that Italians themselves were not immune from such behaviours—it is appropriate to remind that Italy remained a *de facto* colonial power until 1960[24]—and therefore engaged in racial discrimination too, especially with Indigenous Australians and other minorities.[25]

Exploring the events that took place in those years, scholars draw attention to the social, cultural, and political heritage that all migrants bring with them, and explain that the chasm between fascists and anti-fascists

[22] Gianfranco Cresciani, *The Italians in Australia* (Cambridge: Cambridge University Press, 2003), 26–50.

[23] Michele Langfield, "Attitudes to European immigration to Australia in the Early twentieth Century", *Journal of Intercultural Studies* 12, no. 1 (1991): 1–15; Helen Andreoni, "Olive or White? The Colour of Italians in Australia", *Journal of Australian Studies* 27, no. 77 (2003): 81–92; Catherine Dewhirst, "Collaborating on Whiteness: Representing Italians in Early White Australia", *Journal of Australian Studies* 32, no. 1 (2008): 33–49.

[24] Mohamed Aden, "Italy: Cultural Identity and Spatial Opportunism from a Postcolonial Perspective", in *Revisioning Italy: National Identity and Global Culture*, eds. B. Allen and M. Russo (Minneapolis: University of Minnesota Press, 1997), 101–115.

[25] Francesco Ricatti, *Italians in Australia: History, Memory, Identity* (London: Palgrave Macmillan, 2018), 53–74.

eventually reached Australia because of this.[26] Consequently, at a time when fascist propaganda was being systematically employed in Australia and was able to allure a number of Australians,[27] fascist Italy successfully gathered strategic information on the country's military weaknesses,[28] however it did not succeed in exploiting Italian migrants' communities for colonial purposes.[29] Closely related, the difficult issue of Italian prisoners of war—mostly captured by the Allies during the African campaigns in World War II—further nuanced the image of Italians in Australia. Specifically, Borrie, Moore, and Fedorowich remind us that their good behaviour and hard-working attitude led them to be better accepted than their German and Japanese counterparts, and were therefore often free to wander during the day.[30]

A significant part of the literature on Italian–Australian relations investigates the 1950s and 1960s (the third migration period), which is not surprising given that these were the years of European mass immigration to Australia. Like many other European countries, Italy too encouraged emigration as a means with which to control unemployment while rebuilding its war-crippled economy,[31] to such an extent that between 1947 and 1974 almost 360,000 Italians settled in Australia, second only to the British who amounted to almost four times that.[32]

[26] Gianfranco Cresciani, *Fascism, Anti-fascism, and Italians in Australia 1922–1945* (Canberra: Australian National University Press, 1980).

[27] Richard J. B. Bosworth, *Mussolini's Italy: Life Under the Dictatorship, 1915–1945* (London: Penguin Books, 2006), 317.

[28] Gerardo Papalia, "Mussolini's Australian campaign of 1935–1936", in *Italy and Australia: An Asymmetrical Relationship*, eds. G. Cresciani and B. Mascitelli (Ballarat: Connor Court Publishing, 2014), 145–176; Gianfranco Cresciani, "Refractory Migrants. Fascist Surveillance on Italians in Australia, 1922–1943", *Altreitalie* 28 (2004): 6–47.

[29] Catherine Dewhirst, "Colonising Italians: Italian Imperialism and Agricultural 'Colonies' in Australia, 1881–1914", *The Journal of Imperial and Commonwealth History* 44, no. 1 (2016): 23–47.

[30] Wilfrid D. Borrie, *Italians and Germans in Australia: A Study of Assimilation* (Canberra: Australian National University Press, 1954); Bob Moore and Kent Fedorowich, *The British Empire and Its Italian Prisoners of War, 1940–1947* (London: Palgrave Macmillan, 2002).

[31] Donna R. Gabaccia, *Italy's Many Diasporas* (London: Routledge, 2003).

[32] Loretta V. Baldassar, "Italians in Australia", in *Encyclopedia of Diasporas: Immigrant and Refugee Cultures Around the World*, eds. M. Ember, C. R. Ember, and I. Skoggard (Berlin: Springer, 2005), 850–864.

Bosworth's vivid description of Italian migrants' extremely diverse cultural heritages—strongly linked to their regions, provinces, cities, and towns of origin[33]—is an effective reminder of the complex process with which they inadvertently spurred a socio-cultural transformation of the Australian society, until then still heavily influenced by older British and Irish roots. Battiston underlines that such process also had political implications, which led to a direct interaction between Italian and Australian communist parties.[34] Additionally, Cresciani provides a compelling account of the disparate and diverse situations involving Italians in Australia in those years. On the one hand, many suffered from legal and political problems, as well as from the wariness of numerous Australians. On the other, however, stories of economic success, social integration, and newfound Australian interest in Italian culture were increasingly common, and Cresciani highlights the substantial Italian contribution to the development of the Australian society as a whole, as a result of these evolving social dynamics.[35]

The process of integration of Italian settlers into Australia's society—however generally considered successful—was neither easy nor swift, as it also challenged the regional cultures and identities of migrants and their offspring. Rubino, for instance, provides an apt description of the intersectional role of language and dialect with regard to Sicilian migrants, explaining that the original Italian-Sicilian bilingualism had to evolve into an unusual trilingualism (Italian–Sicilian–English) once in Australia, which adds to the complexity of adapting to new environments abroad and cater for intergenerational needs.[36] Kinder and Scotellaro emphasise that comparable instances of linguistic intersectionality concerned a large number of Italians, although this was more marked in the past

---

[33] Richard J. B. Bosworth, *Italy and the Wider World 1860–1960* (London: Routledge, 1996), 137–158.

[34] Simone Battiston, "Migrants, Identity and Radical Politics: Meaning and Ramifications of the Visits of Italian Communist Party Officials to Australia", *Australian Journal of Politics and History* 63, no. 2 (2017): 187–205.

[35] Gianfranco Cresciani, *The Italians in Australia* (Cambridge: Cambridge University Press, 2003), 119–150.

[36] Antonia Rubino, *Trilingual Talk in Sicilian-Australian Migrant Families: Playing Out Identities Through Language Alternation* (London: Palgrave Macmillan, 2014).

compared to recent years.[37] As Marino attests, older first-generation (overseas-born) migrants tended to feel often undesired in Australia, while their Australian-born sons and daughters felt the indescribable tensions of a liminal identity. Yet, so-called third-generation Australians of Italian heritage are often proud of their ancestry in modern-day Australia, thus tracing the evolution of multi-layered identities through multiple generations, as affected by the changing nature of the Australian society.[38]

Despite these difficulties, what is usually identified as the fourth migration period (1970s–1990s) represented a watershed in the history of Italians in Australia, for a number of reasons. Firstly, Italians and Australian-Italians were enjoying the fruits of hard labour and inventive entrepreneurship: indeed, many of them had become well off, and some had established thriving enterprises of national and international relevance, as Hougaz reminds us, which reinforced the collective imagery of Italians as productive and beneficial members of the Australian society.[39] Secondly, in the early 1970s migration trends shifted, and Italy became a migrant-receiving rather than a migrant-sending country.[40] Thirdly, by virtue of its post-war "economic miracle", Italy had become an industrial powerhouse and the 5th largest economy in the world, with strategic, political, and cultural influence to match. Such a transformation—from the war-torn country of the two previous decades—could not go unnoticed, and Italian–Australian relations evolved accordingly.

The renewed climate of friendship and cooperation between the two countries is perhaps best illustrated by former Australian Prime Minister Gough Whitlam, who in his "Italian notebook" wrote not only of his fascination with Italy, but also the country's "new" standing in Australia once its post-war economic recovery had been achieved. In one passage, he recalls a ceremonial speech he made during his tenure as Leader of

---

[37] John J. Kinder and Grazia Scotellaro, *A Linguistic History of Italy: Storia linguistica d'Italia* (Canberra: Australian National University Press, 2020).

[38] Simone Marino, *Intergenerational Ethnic Identity Construction and Transmission among Italian-Australians: Absence, Ambivalence and Revival* (London: Palgrave Macmillan, 2020).

[39] Laura Hougaz, *Entrepreneurs in Family Business Dynasties: Stories of Italian-Australian Family Businesses Over 100 Years* (Berlin: Springer, 2015).

[40] Gabriele Abbondanza, "Italy's Migration Policies Combating Irregular Immigration: From the Early Days to the Present Times", *The International Spectator* 52, no. 4 (2017): 76–92.

the Opposition. Despite the somewhat emphatic tone, it shows that bilateral relations could benefit from steady cooperation between like-minded politicians:

> What people in all history have contributed so much to civilisation over so many centuries and from so many cities and in so many fields? Rome established law and order around the Mediterranean and as far as the North Sea and the Black Sea. Rome transmitted Christianity throughout Western Europe and to the European possessions across the seas. Italy pioneered navigation, revived the arts and set the forms of drama and poetry. Italian, the most musical of languages, became the language of music. Today, Italy leads in fashion and films, in electrical and highway engineering, and helps to found the new Europe through the Treaties of Rome.[41]

Reflecting the broad migration trends that have been mentioned previously, Baldassar and Pesman note that throughout the 1980s and the 1990s the number of Italian-born residents in Australia kept declining, although second and third-generation Australian-Italians increased in number.[42] Moreover, thanks to the internet, new communication technologies, and advancements in the travel industry, Baldassar applies the concept of "circularity" to Italian migrants in Australia, arguing that it supports a continuing connection between the two countries, a condition that helps transnational caregiving.[43] Despite a decrease in Italian migration to Australia—and an unavoidable demographic decline—Cresciani writes of a "cultural renewal" concerning Italian–Australian relations. He mentions the many official visits paid by both governments, the ongoing impact of Italian culture in every major Australian city—including film festivals, university departments of Italian Studies, Italian Cultural Institutes, Dante Alighieri Societies, cultural associations, and major Italian construction projects—and both the Italians' and the Australians' fascination with each other's country, as attested by the growing number of

---

[41] Gough Whitlam, *My Italian Notebook* (Crows Nest: Allen and Unwin, 2002), 5–6.

[42] Loretta Baldassar and Ros Pesman, *From Paesani to Global Italians: Veneto migrants in Australia* (Perth: University of Western Australia Press, 2005).

[43] Loretta Baldassar, "Italian Migrants in Australia and Their Relationship to Italy: Return Visits, Transnational Caregiving and the Second Generation", *Journal of Mediterranean Studies* 20, no. 2 (2011): 255–282.

two-way tourist flows.[44] Additionally, the solid cultural interactions of these years were unwaveringly supported by the Frederick May Foundation for Italian Studies, active between 1976 and 1999, which organised a long series of high-profile initiatives.[45] The broader, far-reaching but less explicit role of the Italians in Australia is effectively summarised by Castles, who writes:

> Mass immigration of Italians and other Europeans undermined Anglo-Australian narrowness, showing not only that there were other ways of doing things, but also that these ways were often more successful, dynamic and rewarding. [...] the Italians who migrated to the Pacific Rim not only helped to open Australia to a greater diversity of European cultures, but they also paved the way for Anglo-Australian awareness of new geo-political realities, and in the long run for the opening to Asia.[46]

As the official data collated by Cavallaro show, at the end of the 1990s the Italian community in Australia was well-integrated and "comfortably well of", as the home-ownership rate among Italian-Australians was "the highest of all the ethnic groups in Australia".[47] However, the Italian community was ageing and started declining in the same years, a downward trend that scholars also detected in the use of the Italian language by Australians with Italian heritage.[48] The decline in Italian immigration to Australia continued up until the fifth and ongoing migration period, starting in 2004 and partially due to the many negative repercussions of the 2007–2008 global financial crisis. On this, Mascitelli aptly writes that "Much has been said about the Italian immigration of

[44] Gianfranco Cresciani, "The Italians in Sydney", *Sydney Journal* 1, no. 1 (2008): 73–79.

[45] Gianfranco Cresciani, "Italo-Australian Cultural Relations after the Second World War: The Case of Frederick May Foundation for Italian Studies", in *Italy and Australia: And Asymmetrical Relationship*, eds. G. Cresciani and B. Mascitelli (Ballarat: Connor Court Publishing, 2014), 39–80.

[46] Stephen Castles, "Italians in Australia: The Impact of a Recent Migration on the Culture and Society of a Postcolonial Nation", *Center for Migration Studies special issues* 11, no. 3 (1994): 342–367.

[47] Francesco Cavallaro, "Italians in Australia: Migration and Profile", *Altreitalie* 26 (2003): 65–90.

[48] Antonia Rubino, "Immigrant minorities: Australia", in *Handbook of Language and Communication: Diversity and Change*, eds. M. Hellinger and A. Pauwels (Berlin: De Gruyter, 2007), 87–122.

the 1950s and 1960s but little is known or understood of the new, young, skilled and educated migrants of the current period".[49] De Lazzari further clarifies that younger generations of Italians show a globalist attitude and tend to temporarily relocate abroad once their studies are completed, both to learn English as a second language and to make a formative international experience.[50] Armillei refutes the idea of a "new wave" of Italian migration to Australia through the use of official statistics, which show that Italy does not figure in the top-10 list of net migration source countries, and that even when Working Holiday Visas (WHV, the most popular option for citizens of industrialised countries) are concerned, the number of Italian migrants is smaller than that of Canadians, Japanese, Taiwanese, French, Irish, Germans, South Koreans, and British (in ascending order).[51] Moreover, recent data show that WHV applications keep declining due to a number of reasons, including the lack of an appropriate mechanism for the recognition of overseas qualifications and skills.[52] Lastly, Mares contributes to this discussion by shedding light on "Australia's permanent shift to temporary migration", which affects migrants of all nationalities through a series of progressively restrictive migration policies making permanent migration unattainable for most of them.[53]

It should be noted that there are additional insights expanding this niche of migration studies, such as Pascoe's and Caffarella's sociological

[49] Bruno Mascitelli, "A New Exodus of Italians to Australia?", in *Australia's New Wave of Italian Migration: Paradise or Illusion?*, eds. B. Mascitelli and R. Armillei (Melbourne: Australian Scholarly Publishing, 2017), 1–13.

[50] Chiara De Lazzari, "New Italian Emigration Globally: Who They Are and Where They Go", in *Australia's New Wave of Italian Migration: Paradise or Illusion?*, eds. B. Mascitelli and R. Armillei (Melbourne: Australian Scholarly Publishing, 2017), 14–33.

[51] Riccardo Armillei, "A Statistical Analysis of the 'New Italian Migration' to Australia: Redressing Recent Overstatements", in *Australia's New Wave of Italian Migration: Paradise or Illusion?*, eds. B. Mascitelli and R. Armillei (Melbourne: Australian Scholarly Publishing, 2017), 53–78.

[52] Bruno Mascitelli and Riccardo Armillei, "Nuovi sviluppi, riflessioni e scoperte sugli italiani che migrano in Australia", in *Gli italiani in Australia: Memoria storica e nuovi modelli di mobilità*, eds. B. Mascitelli and R. Armillei (Perugia Stranieri University Press, 2018), 253–281.

[53] Peter Mares, "Australia's Permanent Shift to Temporary Migration", in *Australia's New Wave of Italian Migration: Paradise or Illusion?*, eds. B. Mascitelli and R. Armillei (Melbourne: Australian Scholarly Publishing, 2017), 110–135.

understanding of contemporary Italian migrants as "*globalisti*" (globe-trotters)[54]; Davis' research on their use of social media to gather information on Australia and form realistic expectations[55]; Battiston's political analysis of Italian expatriate voting[56]; Jupp's and Pietsch's acknowledgement that older, first-generation Italians in Australia still form a "pro-Labor bloc" and engage in a range of social activities that also comprise political debates[57]; and Palmieri's account of why Australians are attracted to Italy—its culture, lifestyle, land, people—which helps explaining why "Italian is one of the most widely studied languages at all educational levels" in Australia.[58] In essence, however, as can be seen from this review of the literature on Italian–Australian relations, much of the existing scholarship is focused exclusively on Italian migration to Australia over time. A few authors have provided interesting but sporadic investigations that address different topics and thus engage in different fields, and some of these publications are reviewed in the following section, which outlines what aspects of Italian–Australian relations have been neglected so far, or, alternatively, only partially dealt with.

[54] Robert Pascoe and Caterina Cafarella, "The Latest Wave of Italians in Australia", *Altreitalie* 59 (2019): 101–117.

[55] Catherine Davis, "The role of social media: 'New Italian Migrants' on Facebook Groups", in *Australia's New Wave of Italian Migration: Paradise or Illusion?*, eds. B. Mascitelli and R. Armillei (Melbourne: Australian Scholarly Publishing, 2017), 136–161.

[56] Simone Battiston, "Il voto degli italiani in Australia fra continuità e segnali di cambiamento", in *Autopsia di un diritto politico. Il voto degli italiani all'estero nelle elezioni del 2018*, eds. S. Battiston and S. Luconi (Turin: Accademia University Press, 2018), 145–161.

[57] James Jupp and Juliet Pietsch, "Migrant and Ethnic Politics in the 2016 Election", in *Double Disillusion: The 2016 Australian Federal Election*, eds. A. Gauja, P. Chen, J. Curtin, and J. Pietsch (Canberra: Australian National University Press, 2018), 668.

[58] Cristiana Palmieri, *Identity Trajectories of Adult Second Language Learners: Learning Italian in Australia* (Bristol: Multilingual Matters, 2019), 2. There are additional reasons for the steady interest in the Italian language in Australia, including different curriculum priorities in Australian states and territories, and the number of Australians with Italian heritage.

THE GAPS IN THE LITERATURE
AND THE STRUCTURE OF THIS BOOK

As mentioned previously, while this chapter's literature review on Italian–Australian relations makes no pretence to comprehensiveness, it is arguably sufficient to depict both the main strength and weakness of this niche field. The former is certainly a well-focused and multifaceted approach to Italian migration to Australia, and the latter is its highly circumscribed dimension, which very rarely operates outside the boundaries of migration studies. Consequently, this deficiency also emphasises the gaps in the available scholarship, which we believe concern a number of facets of Italian–Australian relations, including: history, migration (more broadly understood), culture, politics, international relations, trade, and science. After all, even children's books hint at the multiple benefits in the fields of "business, culture, food, and government" when Italy and Australia are concerned, but these are not appropriately explored in the scholarship on bilateral relations.[59] The paucity—or absence—of literature in these seven fields therefore provides the rationale behind this book, which we have structured to directly address such issues.

With the goal of providing a comprehensive account of Italian–Australian relations in the twenty-first century—thus addressing the aforementioned gaps in the literature—this volume relies on a combination of Italian, Australian, and international sources, written both in English and Italian. Additionally, mindful of the wide scope and multidisciplinarity of this innovative research, the editors oversee a careful balance of both different theoretical and methodological approaches and qualitative and quantitative data, in accordance with the conventions of each discipline employed in this volume. These premises grant the volume's authors latitude in terms of their research, though they interpret and engage with the key themes raised in this document throughout, and they all provide an innovative contribution to a new, more comprehensive understanding of Italian–Australian bilateral relations and cooperation in the twenty-first century. Each contributor has been chosen on the basis of his/her expertise in the proposed topic they work on, experience in producing high-quality research publications, and capacity to provide

---

[59] See Carmen Reilly, *Finding a Place: Italian Migration to Australia* (Melbourne: Cengage Australia, 2007).

original insights on understudied facets of bilateral relations, broadly defined.

With reference to the history of Italian–Australian bilateral relations, the works by Steele and Mascitelli provide a solid foundation, although both were published some time ago and therefore do not cover more recent developments.[60] In Chapter 2, Robert Pascoe addresses this short-coming by outlining a comprehensive and up-to-date review of diplomatic bilateral relations. He outlines the key moments in Italian-Australian from the 1940s to the present day, and argues that recent waves of temporary migration and increased defence and trade links do not appear to be able to compensate a lack of "ballast" in bilateral relations.[61] Academic discussions concerning migration, on the other hand, are abundant and deal with a number of aspects that have been discussed in the previous section. Yet more can be said about the current flow of skilled, educated, and temporary Italian migrants in Australia, a task that Simone Battiston undertakes in Chapter 3. His account engages with different datasets as well as the recent scholarship in order to provide a nuanced picture of Italians in twenty-first-century Australia.[62] The opposite phenomenon of Australian migration to Italy, however, remains little-known in the study of bilateral relations, and has so far been examined only by two interesting volumes, both of which published more than 10 years ago.[63] Giulia Marchetti and Loretta Baldassar shed light on this interesting but under-studied topic in Chapter 4, where they present an overview of research

[60] Rory Steele, "Twentieth-Century Diplomatic and Trade Relations", in *Australians in Italy: Contemporary Lives and Impressions*, eds. B. Kent, R. Pesman, and C. Troup (Melbourne: Monash University Publishing, 2008), 02.1–02.7; Bruno Mascitelli, "Italy and Australia: Different Origins—Different Strategies", in *Italy and Australia: And Asymmetrical Relationship*, eds. G. Cresciani and B. Mascitelli (Ballarat: Connor Court Publishing, 2014), 1–38.

[61] Robert Pascoe, "A Historical Overview of Italian-Australian Bilateral Relations", in *Italy and Australia: Redefining Bilateral Relations for the Twenty-First Century*, eds. Gabriele Abbondanza and Simone Battiston (London: Palgrave Macmillan, 2023), pp. 25–48.

[62] Simone Battiston, "Italians in Australia in the Twenty-First Century", in *Italy and Australia: Redefining Bilateral Relations for the Twenty-First Century*, eds. Gabriele Abbondanza and Simone Battiston (London: Palgrave Macmillan, 2023), pp. 49–80.

[63] Bill Kent, Ros Pesman, and Cynthia Troup, eds. *Australians in Italy: Contemporary Lives and Impressions* (Melbourne: Monash University Publishing, 2008); Roberta Trapè, *Imaging Italy Through the Eyes of Contemporary Australian Travellers (1990–2010)* (Newcastle upon Tyne: Cambridge Scholars Publishing, 2011).

and writing on Australians in Italy, and identify the main types of migration and mobility that characterise the contemporary Australian diaspora in Italy.[64]

Despite the scholarship's substantial focus on migration, related cultural implications remain surprisingly and largely understudied. Italian relations with Indigenous Australians represent one such aspect, and Francesco Ricatti and Matteo Dutto draw from the very limited literature on this[65] to investigate past and present issues in Chapter 5. They first provide a historical overview of such relations, and then suggest a number of ways to further promote decolonial and transcultural relations between Italy and Indigenous Australia.[66] In Chapter 6, Cristiana Palmieri expands on her previous works to provide a study on why and how Italians learn English in Australia, and why and how Australians choose to learn Italian. In doing so, she focuses on the role played by language in fostering closer bilateral relations, and therefore interprets linguistic, societal, and emotional elements in an innovative manner.[67]

The following four contributions focus on the fields of international relations, politics, trade, and science, which have seldom analysed Italy and Australia together.[68] In Chapter 7, Gabriele Abbondanza builds on

[64] Giulia Marchetti and Loretta Baldassar, "Australians in Italy in the Twenty-First Century", in *Italy and Australia: Redefining Bilateral Relations for the Twenty-First Century*, eds. Gabriele Abbondanza and Simone Battiston (London: Palgrave Macmillan, 2024), pp. 81–111.

[65] See Francesco Ricatti, "Forum. Towards a Decolonial History of Italian Migration to Australia: Introduction", *Altreitalie* 59 (2019): 8–15. See also the other five contributions published Open Source in the Forum section of *Altreitalie* 59.

[66] Francesco Ricatti and Matteo Dutto, "Italians' Relations with Indigenous Australia", in *Italy and Australia: Redefining Bilateral Relations for the Twenty-First Century*, eds. Gabriele Abbondanza and Simone Battiston (London: Palgrave Macmillan, 2024), pp. 113–136.

[67] Cristiana Palmieri, "Connecting Australia and Italy Through Language", in *Italy and Australia: Redefining Bilateral Relations for the Twenty-First Century*, eds. Gabriele Abbondanza and Simone Battiston (London: Palgrave Macmillan, 2024), pp. 137–154.

[68] For a rare exception, specifically focusing on seaborne asylum seekers, see Irial Glynn, *Asylum Policy, Boat People and Political Discourse: Boats, Votes and Asylum in Australia and Italy* (London: Palgrave Macmillan, 2016).

previous calls for greater bilateral cooperation and undertakes a theo-retical analysis of both countries' global status and behaviour.[69] This complements his subsequent empirical analysis concerning how a strategic partnership would benefit Italian-Australian cooperation in a number of fields, including international relations and trade, while also arguing that digital diplomacy and the Prime Ministership of Anthony Albanese could further reinvigorate relations between Rome and Canberra.[70] In Chapter 8, Andrea Benvenuti examines Italy's and Australia's economic and strategic interests in each other's regions, thus focusing on how Italy could promote Australian interests in the European Union, and how Australia could support Italian interests in the Asia/Indo-Pacific.[71] In Chapter 9, Kurt Sengul and Francesco Bailo provide the first comparative analysis of populism and political instability in Italy and Australia. They investigate the interaction between different forces—the media system, the party and electoral system, and long-term decline in political trust—to explain why the expression of populism in Australia has been remark-ably different from that of Italy.[72] In Chapter 10, Ilaria S. Pagani and Tiziana Torresi further nuance the image of bilateral cooperation this volume seeks to update. They explore how closer bilateral relations can be fostered through significant scientific cooperation, and then outline the impressive list of scientific projects currently pioneered by both Italy and Australia.[73] Lastly, Chapter 11 assesses the multifaceted nature of Italian–

[69] For a discussion on the two countries' complicated global status, with migration policies as case studies, see Gabriele Abbondanza, "A Sea of Difference? Australian and Italian approaches to Irregular Migration and Seaborne Asylum Seekers", *Contemporary Politics* 29, no. 1 (2023): 93–113.

[70] Gabriele Abbondanza, "Time for a Strategic Partnership: The Scope for International Cooperation Between Italy and Australia", in *Italy and Australia: Redefining Bilateral Relations for the Twenty-First Century*, eds. Gabriele Abbondanza and Simone Battiston (London: Palgrave Macmillan, 2024), pp. 155–187.

[71] Andrea Benvenuti, "The Australian Interest in the European Union and the Italian Interest in the Asia-Pacific", in *Italy and Australia: Redefining Bilateral Relations for the Twenty-First Century*, eds. Gabriele Abbondanza and Simone Battiston (London: Palgrave Macmillan, 2024), pp. 189–212.

[72] Kurt Sengul and Francesco Bailo, "Twenty-First Century Populism in Australia and Italy: A Comparative Analysis", in *Italy and Australia: Redefining Bilateral Relations for the Twenty-First Century*, eds. Gabriele Abbondanza and Simone Battiston (London: Palgrave Macmillan, 2024), pp. 215–241.

[73] In this respect, the Association for Research between Italy and Australasia (ARIA) represents an innovative new platform for bilateral scientific cooperation. See Ilaria S.

Australian relations in the twenty-first century in the light of this volume's chapters, and summarises the objectives and findings of the whole book.[74]

CONCLUSION

This volume seeks to provide a broader and more comprehensive understanding of Italian–Australian relations in the twenty-first century, with a focus on bilateral cooperation. Reviewing and drawing from the abundant scholarship on Italian migration to Australia, it acknowledges that contemporary relations are more multifaceted and complex, and thus identifies several aspects of them that have been understudied or neglected over the years. These gaps in the literature concern history, migration (more broadly understood), culture, politics, international relations, trade, and science, which have shaped the very structure of the book that seeks to address them.[75] The latter's contributors are experts in a variety of fields that are relevant to this endeavour, and are therefore instrumental in reaching these ambitious goals. Given its purpose, this volume engages with a wide range of topics and disciplines, while pursuing an equally wide scope of research methods and traditions, as well as a combination of Italian, Australian, and international sources, written in both English and Italian. This versatile approach reflects the multidisciplinary rationale of this book, and is carefully overseen by the editors. With such premises, we present the following chapters which provide a diverse and yet cohesive set of innovative contributions, whose aspiration is to produce a long-overdue and comprehensive image of Italian–Australian relations in the twenty-first century.

Pagani and Tiziana Torresi, "Italian-Australian Scientific and Research Cooperation", in *Italy and Australia: Redefining Bilateral Relations for the Twenty-First Century*, eds. Gabriele Abbondanza and Simone Battiston (London: Palgrave Macmillan, 2024), pp. 243–267.

[74] Simone Battiston and Gabriele Abbondanza, "Where to from Here? The Need for a Long-Term Strategy in Italian-Australian Relations", in *Italy and Australia: Redefining Bilateral Relations for the Twenty-First Century*, eds. Gabriele Abbondanza and Simone Battiston (London: Palgrave Macmillan, 2024), pp. 269–280.

[75] There are additional under-examined elements that would benefit from novel research, including the two countries' media systems, their environmental policies, and their attitudes and policies concerning religion, ethnicity, and irregular migration. These significant but understudied aspects of Italian–Australian relations are therefore left for future research.

BIBLIOGRAPHY

Abbondanza, Gabriele. "Italy's Migration policies combating irregular immigration: From the Early days to the present times". *The International Spectator* 52, no. 4 (2017): 76–92.

Abbondanza, Gabriele. "The West's Policeman? Assessing Italy's Status in Global Peacekeeping". *The International Spectator* 55, no. 2 (2020): 127–141.

Abbondanza, Gabriele. "Italy and Australia: Time for a strategic partnership". *IAI Commentaries* 20, no. 87 (2020): 1–5.

Abbondanza, Gabriele. "Time for a strategic partnership: the scope for international cooperation between Italy and Australia". In *Italy and Australia: Redefining bilateral relations for the twenty-first century*, edited by G. Abbondanza and S. Battiston, pp. 155–187. London: Palgrave Macmillan, 2024.

Abbondanza, Gabriele. "A sea of difference? Australian and Italian approaches to irregular migration and seaborne asylum seekers". *Contemporary Politics* 29, no. 1 (2023): 93–113.

Aden, Mohamed. "Italy: Cultural identity and spatial opportunism from a postcolonial perspective". In *Revisioning Italy: National identity and global culture*, edited by B. Allen and M. Russo, 101–115. Minneapolis: University of Minnesota Press, 1997.

Andreoni, Helen. "Olive or white? The colour of Italians in Australia". *Journal of Australian Studies* 27, no. 77 (2003): 81–92.

Armillei, Riccardo. "A statistical analysis of the 'new Italian migration' to Australia: Redressing recent overstatements". In *Australia's new wave of Italian migration: Paradise or illusion?*, edited by B. Mascitelli and R. Armillei, 53–78. Melbourne: Australian Scholarly Publishing, 2017.

Baldassar, Loretta V. "Italians in Australia". In *Encyclopedia of diasporas: Immigrant and Refugee cultures around the world*, edited by M. Ember, C. R. Ember, and I. Skoggard, 850–864. Berlin: Springer, 2005.

Baldassar, Loretta V. "Italian migrants in Australia and their relationship to Italy: Return visits, transnational caregiving and the second generation". *Journal of Mediterranean Studies* 20, no. 2 (2011): 255–282.

Baldassar, Loretta V., and Ros Pesman. *From paesani to global Italians: Veneto migrants in Australia*. Perth: University of Western Australia Press, 2005.

Battiston, Simone. "Migrants, identity and radical politics: Meaning and ramifications of the visits of Italian Communist party officials to Australia". *Australian Journal of Politics and History* 63, no. 2 (2017): 187–205.

Battiston, Simone. "Il voto degli italiani in Australia fra continuità e segnali di cambiamento". In *Autopsia di un diritto politico. Il voto degli italiani all'estero nelle elezioni del 2018*, edited by S. Battiston and S. Luconi, 145–161. Turin: Accademia University Press, 2018.

Battiston, Simone. "Italians in Australia in the twenty-first century". In *Italy and Australia: Redefining bilateral relations for the twenty-first century*, edited by

G. Abbondanza and S. Battiston, pp. 49–80. London: Palgrave Macmillan, 2024.

Battiston, Simone, and Gabriele Abbondanza. "Where to from here? The need for a long-term strategy in Italian-Australian relations". In *Italy and Australia: redefining bilateral relations for the twenty-first century*, edited by G. Abbondanza and S. Battiston, pp. 269–280. London: Palgrave Macmillan, 2024.

Benvenuti, Andrea. "The Australian interest in the European Union and the Italian interest in the Asia-Pacific". In *Italy and Australia: Redefining bilateral relations for the twenty-first century*, edited by G. Abbondanza and S. Battiston, pp. 189–212. London: Palgrave Macmillan, 2024.

Bettoni, Camilla, and Joseph Lo Bianco, editors. *Understanding Italy: Language, culture, commerce: an Australian perspective*. Sydney: Frederick May Foundation for Italian Studies, 1989.

Borrie, Wilfrid D. *Italians and Germans in Australia: A study of assimilation*. Canberra: Australian National University Press, 1954.

Bosworth, Richard J. B. *Italy and the wider world 1860–1960*. London: Routledge, 1996.

Bosworth, Richard J. B. *Mussolini's Italy: Life under the dictatorship, 1915–1945*. London: Penguin Books, 2006.

Brands, Hal, and Francis J. Gavin, eds. *COVID-19 and world order: The future of conflict, competition, and cooperation*. Baltimore: Johns Hopkins University Press, 2020.

Brighi, Elisabetta. *Foreign policy, domestic politics and international relations: The case of Italy*. London: Routledge, 2013.

Castles, Stephen. "Italians in Australia: The impact of a recent migration on the culture and society of a postcolonial nation". *Center for Migration Studies special issues* 11, no. 3 (1994): 342–367.

Cavallaro, Francesco. "Italians in Australia: Migration and profile". *Altreitalie* 26 (2003): 65–90.

Cresciani, Gianfranco. *Fascism, anti-fascism, and Italians in Australia 1922–1945*. Canberra: Australian National University Press, 1980.

Cresciani, Gianfranco. *The Italians in Australia*. Cambridge: Cambridge University Press, 2003.

Cresciani, Gianfranco. "Refractory migrants. Fascist surveillance on Italians in Australia, 1922–1943". *Altreitalie* 28 (2004): 6–47.

Cresciani, Gianfranco. "The Italians in Sydney". *Sydney Journal* 1, no. 1 (2008): 73–79.

Cresciani, Gianfranco. "Italo-Australian cultural relations after the Second World War: The case of Frederick May Foundation for Italian studies". In *Italy and Australia: And asymmetrical relationship*, edited by G. Cresciani and B. Mascitelli, 39–80. Ballarat: Connor Court Publishing, 2014.

Davis, Catherine. "The role of social media: 'New Italian migrants' on Facebook groups". In *Australia's new wave of Italian migration: Paradise or illusion?*, edited by B. Mascitelli and R. Armillei, 136–161. Melbourne: Australian Scholarly Publishing, 2017.

De Lazzari, Chiara. "New Italian emigration globally: Who they are and where they go". In *Australia's new wave of Italian migration: Paradise or illusion?*, edited by B. Mascitelli and R. Armillei, 14–33. Melbourne: Australian Scholarly Publishing, 2017.

Dewhirst, Catherine. "Collaborating on whiteness: Representing Italians in early White Australia". *Journal of Australian Studies* 32, no. 1 (2008): 33–49.

Dewhirst, Catherine. "Colonising Italians: Italian imperialism and agricultural 'Colonies' in Australia, 1881–1914". *The Journal of Imperial and Commonwealth History* 44, no. 1 (2016): 23–47.

Drake-Brockman, Jane, and Patrick Messerlin, eds. *Potential benefits of an Australia-EU free Trade Agreement: Key issues and options.* Adelaide: Adelaide University Press, 2018.

Gabaccia, Donna R. *Italy's many diasporas.* London: Routledge, 2003.

Glynn, Irial. *Asylum policy, boat people and political discourse: Boats, votes and asylum in Australia and Italy.* London: Palgrave Macmillan, 2016.

Hougaz, Laura. *Entrepreneurs in family business dynasties: Stories of Italian-Australian family businesses over 100 years.* Berlin: Springer, 2015.

Hough, Peter. *Understanding global security.* London: Routledge: 2018.

Jupp, James, and Juliet Pietsch. "Migrant and ethnic politics in the 2016 election". In *Double disillusion: The 2016 Australian federal election*, edited by A. Gauja, P. Chen, J. Curtin, and J. Pietsch, 661–679. Canberra: Australian National University Press, 2018.

Kent, Bill, Ros Pesman, and Cynthia Troup, eds. *Australians in Italy: Contemporary lives and impressions.* Melbourne: Monash University Publishing, 2008.

Kinder, John J., and Grazia Scotellaro. *A linguistic history of Italy: Storia linguistica d'Italia.* Canberra: Australian National University Press, 2020.

Langfield, Michele. "Attitudes to European immigration to Australia in the early twentieth century". *Journal of Intercultural Studies* 12, no. 1 (1991): 1–15.

Marchetti, Giulia, and Loretta Baldassar. "Australians in Italy in the twenty-first century". In *Italy and Australia: redefining bilateral relations for the twenty-first century*, edited by G. Abbondanza and S. Battiston, pp. 81–111. London: Palgrave Macmillan, 2024.

Mares, Peter. "Australia's permanent shift to temporary migration". In *Australia's new wave of Italian migration: Paradise or illusion?*, edited by B. Mascitelli and R. Armillei, 110–135. Melbourne: Australian Scholarly Publishing, 2017.

Marino, Simone. *Intergenerational ethnic identity construction and transmission among Italian-Australians: Absence, ambivalence and revival*. London: Palgrave Macmillan, 2020.

Mascitelli, Bruno. "Italy and Australia: Different origins—Different strategies". In *Italy and Australia: And asymmetrical relationship*, edited by G. Cresciani and B. Mascitelli, 1–38. Ballarat: Connor Court Publishing, 2014.

Mascitelli, Bruno. "Italy and Australia: A relationship made and unmade by immigration". *Australian Journal of International Affairs* 69, no. 3 (2015): 339–355.

Mascitelli, Bruno. "A new exodus of Italians to Australia?". In *Australia's new wave of Italian migration: Paradise or illusion?*, edited by B. Mascitelli and R. Armillei, 1–13. Melbourne: Australian Scholarly Publishing, 2017.

Mascitelli, Bruno. "Italian immigration to Australia: The way it was". In *Australia's new wave of Italian migration: paradise or illusion?*, edited by B. Mascitelli and R. Armillei, 34–52. Melbourne: Australian Scholarly Publishing, 2017.

Mascitelli, Bruno, and Riccardo Armillei. "Nuovi sviluppi, riflessioni e scoperte sugli italiani che migrano in Australia". In *Gli italiani in Australia: Memoria storica e nuovi modelli di mobilità*, edited by B. Mascitelli and R. Armillei, 253–281. Perugia Stranieri University Press, 2018.

Moore, Bob, and Kent Fedorowich. *The British empire and its Italian prisoners of war, 1940–1947*. London: Palgrave Macmillan, 2002.

Pagani, Ilaria S. and Tiziana Torresi. "Italian-Australian scientific and research cooperation". In *Italy and Australia: Redefining bilateral relations for the twenty-first century*, edited by G. Abbondanza and S. Battiston, pp. 243–267. London: Palgrave Macmillan, 2024.

Palmieri, Cristiana. *Identity trajectories of adult second language learners: Learning Italian in Australia*. Bristol: Multilingual Matters, 2019.

Palmieri, Cristiana. "Connecting Australia and Italy through language". In *Italy and Australia: Redefining bilateral relations for the twenty-first century*, edited by G. Abbondanza and S. Battiston, pp. 137–154. London: Palgrave Macmillan, 2024.

Papalia, Gerardo. "Mussolini's Australian campaign of 1935–1936". In *Italy and Australia: An asymmetrical relationship*, edited by G. Cresciani and B. Mascitelli, 145–176. Ballarat: Connor Court Publishing, 2014.

Pascoe, Robert. "A historical overview of Italian-Australian bilateral relations". In *Italy and Australia: Redefining bilateral relations for the twenty-first century*, edited by G. Abbondanza and S. Battiston, pp. 25–48. London: Palgrave Macmillan, 2024.

Pascoe, Robert, and Caterina Cafarella. "The latest wave of Italians in Australia". *Altreitalie* 59 (2019): 101–117.

Patience, Allan. *Australian foreign policy in Asia: Middle power or awkward partner?*. London: Palgrave Macmillan, 2018.

Pretelli, Matteo. "Gli Italiani in Australia: lo stato dei lavori". *Studi Emigrazione* 46, no. 176 (2009): 779–792.

Reilly, Carmen. *Finding a place: Italian migration to Australia*. Melbourne: Cengage Australia, 2007.

Ricatti, Francesco. *Italians in Australia: History, memory, identity*. London: Palgrave Macmillan, 2018.

Ricatti, Francesco. "Forum. Towards a decolonial history of Italian migration to Australia: Introduction", *Altreitalie* 59 (2019): 8–15.

Ricatti, Francesco, and Matteo Dutto. "First Nations sovereignty: Towards a decolonial approach to Italy-Australia relations". In *Italy and Australia: Redefining bilateral relations for the twenty-first century*, edited by G. Abbondanza and S. Battiston, pp. 113–136. London: Palgrave Macmillan, 2024.

Rubino, Antonia. "Immigrant minorities: Australia". In *Handbook of language and communication: Diversity and change*, edited by M. Hellinger and A. Pauwels, 87–122. Berlin: De Gruyter, 2007.

Rubino, Antonia. *Trilingual talk in Sicilian-Australian migrant families: Playing out identities through language alternation*. London: Palgrave Macmillan, 2014.

Rumley, Dennis, Vivian Louis Forbes, and Christopher Griffin, eds. *Australia's arc of instability: The political and cultural dynamics of regional security*. Berlin: Springer, 2006.

Sengul, Kurt, and Francesco Bailo. "Twenty-first century populism in Australia and Italy: A comparative analysis". In *Italy and Australia: Redefining bilateral relations for the twenty-first century*, edited by G. Abbondanza and S. Battiston, pp. 215–241. London: Palgrave Macmillan, 2024.

Steele, Rory. "Twentieth-century diplomatic and trade relations". In *Australians in Italy: Contemporary lives and impressions*, edited by B. Kent, R. Pesman, and C. Troup, 02.1–02.7. Melbourne: Monash University Publishing, 2008.

Trapè, Roberta. *Imaging Italy through the eyes of contemporary Australian travellers (1990–2010)*. Newcastle upon Tyne: Cambridge Scholars Publishing, 2011.

Whitlam, Gough. *My Italian notebook*. Crows Nest: Allen and Unwin, 2002.

CHAPTER 2

A Historical Overview of Italian–Australian Bilateral Relations

Robert Pascoe

AN ELABORATE INTERPLAY

Italy and Australia provide a compelling example of diplomatic relations and migratory patterns between two nations that at times have run along separate but parallel tracks, or one ahead of the other, or even orthogonal to the other.[1] It is the story of an elaborate interplay of ideas, of people and of national interests. The story can be told as diplomatic history, threaded by social, economic, political and cultural intersections. Our method here is to analyse from a variety of historical sources how diplomats and political leaders from both nations understood the political developments, economic opportunities and labour needs of the other. It is a complex jigsaw of shifting perspectives over a dozen decades, with the

---

[1] Thanks to Rosemary Clerehan, Mark Considine, the editors, and the Italian Embassy in Canberra for their help with this chapter.

R. Pascoe (✉)
Institute for Sustainable Industries & Liveable Cities, Victoria University, Melbourne, VIC, Australia
e-mail: robert.pascoe@vu.edu.au

© The Author(s), under exclusive license to Springer Nature Singapore Pte Ltd. 2023
G. Abbondanza and S. Battiston (eds.), *Italy and Australia*,
https://doi.org/10.1007/978-981-99-3216-0_2

added complication of the role played by the Vatican in world affairs and the increased significance of the Catholic Church in Australia.

Diplomatic connections between the newly emerging nation of Italy and the pre-federated Australian colonies were modest. In 1864 Giuseppe Biagi was appointed as Italian Consul in Melbourne, but such appointments required the approval of the British Government and were listed as 'Foreign Consulates in British Colonies'. While Biagi sent the Italian Ministry of Foreign Affairs its first report on Italians in the colonies in 1869,[2] the Anglo-Italian Treaty of Commerce and Navigation in 1883 made it clear that Britain controlled the foreign affairs of their Australian colonies.[3] By 1910 the Italian Government was advocating Italian settlement in Australia, but the proposal was scotched by the burgeoning Australian labour movement as part of its historic 'settlement' with capital.[4] In 1914 Bonaventura Cerretti was appointed the first Apostolic Delegate to Australasia, the beginning of a continuous connection between the Vatican and the (then largely Irish) Australian Catholic Church.[5]

Relations between Italy and Australia were strengthened when Italy joined the Allies in the Great War. A total of 800 Italians in Australia were conscripted to serve in the Italian army; however, at war's end these men were entitled to war pensions from neither Italy nor Australia.[6] Because the uniforms of Italian *alpini* soldiers closely resembled those of the Australians, they served as models for many Anzac monuments.[7] The Italian shipping line Lloyd Sabaudo began bimonthly trips to Australia

---

[2] Nino Randazzo and Michael Cigler, *The Italians in Australia* (Melbourne: AE Press, 1987), 68, 70.

[3] Rory Steele, 'Twentieth-Century diplomatic and trade relations', in Bill Kent, Ros Pesman and Cynthia Troup, eds, *Australians in Italy: Contemporary Lives and Impressions* (Melbourne: Monash University ePress, 2008), 2.1–2.7, p. 1.

[4] Randazzo and Cigler, *The Italians*, 94–96; the 1909 report by Professor Giuseppe Capra had provided the argument for this proposal. Refer to his report in published form: Giuseppe Capra, *L'Italiano in Australia e Nuova Zelanda: guida practica* (Ivrea: Ditta Francesco Viassone, 1914).

[5] Cerretti subsequently represented the Holy See at the 1919 Paris Peace Conference, but died quite young in 1933, aged 60.

[6] Randazzo and Cigler, *The Italians*, 96.

[7] Robert Pascoe, *Buongiorno Australia: Our Italian Heritage* (Melbourne: Greenhouse Publications, in association with the Vaccari Italian Historical Trust, 1987) 86.

in 1919, a service that increased to 15 per year during the 1920s.[8] This limited flow of Italians was cut after 1927, following the speech given by Dino Grandi in the Chamber of Deputies in Rome on 1 March that enunciated the Fascist policy on emigration: 'For the Fascist State emigration was a wealth to defend'.[9] Italians abroad were directed to see themselves as colonies that would advance the interests of Fascist Italy.[10] In 1937, Italian-Australian importer Gualtiero Vaccari controversially offered to donate money for a Melbourne Casa d'Italia (Fascist-leaning club), as a means of protecting his business, but the then Consul, Ernesto Arrighi, ended his term without the project starting, and this pledged donation, condemned by both sides of Australian politics, triggered a 30-year dispute within the Italian community of Melbourne.[11]

By 1935 the Australian Government had created its own External Affairs Department and had begun to develop its own national foreign policy outlook, and had started to strengthen its own domestic intelligence capacity. When in June 1940 Italy entered the Second World War on the Axis side, this new interior ministry flexed its muscles and interned 3631 Italians, even brothers of men serving in the Australian military and others who were naturalised British subjects. Unfounded accusations of a 'Fifth Column' were commonplace, especially in Queensland.[12] It was ironic that it was the Italians rather than the Germans who inspired talk of a Fifth Column. The antagonisms towards the Italians in this period might signal the beginnings of a multicultural society, precisely because

[8] Steele, 'Twentieth-Century relations', p. 1.

[9] Salvo Mastellone, 'Emigration as an ideological problem for the Fascist State', in Richard Bosworth and Romano Ugolini, eds, *War, Internment and Mass Migration: The Italo-Australian Experience, 1940–1990* (Rome: Gruppo Editoriale Internazionale, 1992) 117–23: 117.

[10] Mastellone, 'Emigration as an ideological problem for the Fascist State'.

[11] Geoff Easdown, *Gualtiero Vaccari: A Man of Quality* (Melbourne: Wilkinson Publishing, 2006), 37–40.

[12] Randazzo and Cigler, *The Italians*, 138; Gerardo Papalia, 'The Italian "Fifth Column" in Australia: Fascist propaganda, Italian-Australians and internment', *Australian Journal of Politics & History*, vol. 66, issue 2, 2020, 214–31.

they were now seen as 'a serious community'.[13] Vaccari was spared internment because he was already supplying information on Fascist activities in
Australia.[14]

In Fremantle, Western Australia, Italian fishermen were interned
because of the port's military and naval role. As elsewhere across
the continent before the Second World War, Western Australia was a
society divided between Italians and the majority population. This shared
experience of internment might, ironically enough, have fostered the
development of the commercially very successful, and predominantly
Italian, Fremantle Fishing Co-operative in the late 1940s.[15] As the war
progressed, a total of 18,432 Italian Prisoners of War were held in
Australia. These POWs carried out exactly the kind of work a previous
generation of Italian labourers had been denied entry to undertake. They
were found to be hard-working and allowed much more liberty than
the Japanese and German POWs at the time. Nonetheless—and as an
indication of their value as workers—these Italian POWs were held long
after September 1943, with their release delayed until 1947.[16] As with
the internees, the Australian authorities were blissfully oblivious to the
profound cultural, social and political differences among the Italians in
their care.[17]

RELATIONS RESUMED AFTER 1947

Australia was still a deeply sectarian nation in 1945, when the Labor
Government appointed Arthur Calwell its Minister for Immigration, with
the aim of building an ambitious programme of 'populate or perish'. In

[13] Gianfranco Cresciani, 'The bogey of the Italian Fifth Column: Internment and the
making of Italo-Australia', in Richard Bosworth and Romano Ugolini, eds, *War, Internment and Mass Migration: The Italo-Australian Experience, 1940–1990* (Rome: Gruppo
Editoriale Internazionale, 1992), 11–32: 11–12, 30.

[14] Easdown, *Vaccari*, 54.

[15] Michal Bosworth, 'Fremantle interned: The Italian experience', in Richard Bosworth
and Romano Ugolini, eds, *War, Internment and Mass Migration: The Italo-Australian
Experience, 1940–1990* (Rome: Gruppo Editoriale Internazionale, 1992), 75–88.

[16] Randazzo and Cigler, *The Italians*, 139–45.

[17] Gabriele Abbondanza and Simone Battiston, 'Italy and Australia in the twenty-first
century: Distant connections or close partners?', in Gabriele Abbondanza and Simone
Battiston, eds, *Italy and Australia: Redefining Bilateral Relations for the Twenty-first
Century* (London: Palgrave Macmillan, 2024), pp. 1–23.

other words, 'it was the failure of Anglo-Saxon Australia to accommodate the Irish which opened the way for the demolition of that monoculture'.[18] On the other side, after 1946 emigration once again seemed to be a solution for the economic woes of Italy (and for other European nations in that era). American investment in large-scale emigration programmes from Italy to other destinations across the world suited that country's unwillingness to restore its Italian immigration to pre-1921 levels.[19] In February 1947, Prime Minister, Alcide De Gasperi, faced a frosty reception in Paris when he arrived to sign the peace treaty, except from the Australian delegate present.[20] That year Australian diplomatic relations with Italy resumed,[21] but Calwell's tour of European capitals to publicise Australia's new immigration scheme did not include Rome.[22] Events were moving faster in Australia's mining industry. In July 1947 the Lakewood Firewood Co Pty Ltd in Western Australia received permission to introduce 150 Italians to work on the 'woodline' ferrying timber to Kalgoorlie's Golden Mile.[23] Under the Contract Immigrants Act of 1905, not repealed until 1950, employers could recruit and transport foreign workers into Australia to fill vacancies for which there were no local applicants.[24] Other projects in Western Australia, such as the notoriously dangerous Wittenoom asbestos mines, were staffed under the terms of these quasi-legal contracts that trapped immigrant Italian workers in 'a temporary no-man's land'.[25]

[18] Pascoe, *Buongiorno Australia*, 221–22.

[19] Richard Bosworth, 'Post-War Italian immigration', in James Jupp, ed., *The Australian People: An Encyclopedia of the Nation, its People and Their Origins* (Cambridge, UK: Cambridge University Press, 2001 [1988]), 500–05: 505.

[20] Romano Ugolini, 'From POW to emigrant: The post-war migrant experience', in Richard Bosworth and Romano Ugolini, eds, *War, Internment and Mass Migration: The Italo-Australian Experience, 1940–1990* (Rome: Gruppo Editoriale Internazionale, 1992), 125–37: 134–35.

[21] Steele, 'Twentieth-Century relations', 2.

[22] Richard Bosworth, 'Post-War Italian immigration', 505–06.

[23] Lenore Layman, 'Migrant labour contract: The first years of post-war migration, 1947–1952', in Richard Bosworth and Romano Ugolini, eds, *War, Internment and Mass Migration: The Italo-Australian Experience, 1940–1990* (Rome: Gruppo Editoriale Internazionale, 1992) 173–89: 181.

[24] Layman, 'Migrant labour contract', 176.

[25] Layman, 'Migrant labour contract', 189.

The following year, in 1948, the US infamously interfered in Italy's national elections to prevent a Communist victory, using its Marshall Plan as the carrot.[26] Giulio Del Balzo di Presenzano was appointed Italian Ambassador to Australia on 4 February 1949,[27] while the Australian Legation in Rome opened in July, with C. V. ('Ced') Kellway as Minister.[28] He arrived in Italy in November.[29] Kellway was an outstanding diplomat who was skilled at analysing Italian politics, and, as a Catholic, worked well with the Vatican. He helped set up the new post-war migration programme.[30] Kellway's term as Australian Minister to Italy ended in 1954, and by 30 June 1950 a further 33,280 Italians had migrated to Australia (from 1 July 1947), using the time-honoured method of family nomination known as 'chain migration'.[31]

During the northern summer of 1950 Sir John Storey, chairman of Australia's Immigration Planning Council, toured north Italy.[32] In July the new Prime Minister Robert Menzies travelled via Cairo and then Rome when he flew to London. In Rome, he met with Prime Minister, De Gasperi, and Foreign Minister Carlo Sforza. Among other issues discussed, De Gasperi explained that unemployment in Italy was running at 1.5 million.[33] Subsequently, the Legation reported to Canberra on these discussions of the potential emigration of Italians. Kellway wrote that 'questions are constantly being directed at the Legation in regard to the possibility of increasing the intake of Italian migrants into Australia'.[34] By the end of 1950 the terms of the migration agreement were reached. It would last for five years and 20,000 migrants would be assisted annually,

---

[26] Greg Behrman, *The Most Noble Adventure: The Marshall Plan and the Time When America Helped Save Europe* (New York: Free Press, 2007), 175–77.

[27] The Del Balzo di Presenzano family are Italian aristocrats with a lineage dating back to the ninth century: Berardo Candida-Gonzaga, *Memorie delle famiglie nobili delle province meridionali d'Italia* (Bologna: Forni Editore, 1875), 8–14.

[28] Steele, 'Twentieth-Century relations', 2.

[29] Richard Bosworth, 'Post-War Italian immigration', 506.

[30] Jenny Newell, 'Kellway, Cedric Vernon (1892–1963)', *Australian Dictionary of Biography* (https://adb.anu.edu.au/biography/kellway-cedric-vernon-10673/text1891, published in first in hardcopy 1966, accessed 31 January 2022).

[31] Richard Bosworth, 'Post-War Italian immigration', 506.

[32] Richard Bosworth, 'Post-War Italian immigration', 506.

[33] Steele, 'Twentieth-Century relations', 2.

[34] Steele, 'Twentieth-Century relations', 2.

with each government providing 25 per cent of the cost and the immigrants able to borrow from ICLE (Instituto nazionale di Credito per il Lavoro italiano all'Estero) on 30-month terms. Article 10 in this agreement was interpreted by the Italians as promising two years of guaranteed work.[35]

In these negotiations, many aspects of Italian civic and diplomatic life were foreign to their Australian counterparts. Fundamental to the Italian definition of citizenship, as elsewhere in Europe, is the notion of 'blood', ancestry. Living in Italy for many years is in itself insufficient to qualify for citizenship. One's place of birth is immutable. For example, every Italian resident or citizen has since 1976 been assigned a tax file number (*codice fiscale*), an alphanumeric code of 16 characters that embeds not only their name, gender, and date of birth, but also their township (or foreign country) of origin.[36]

In a similar vein the Italians found it mysterious that Australian citizenship, originally defined as being 'a subject' of the British, for two-thirds of the twentieth century explicitly excluded people of colour, including Aboriginal Australians, even if these people were born in Australia.[37]

Australia's External Affairs Department was of very recent creation. Although Australian politicians were prominent at key moments of twentieth-century international diplomacy, such as Paris in 1919 and San Francisco in 1945, the reality was that Australian diplomacy was still in its infancy. In the negotiations of the late 1940s, Australia's relative inexperience in treaty-making was evident in the framing of the 1951 Migration Agreement. The Australians carefully inserted clauses that itemised and

---

[35] Richard Bosworth, 'Post-War Italian immigration', 506; Australia. Department of External Affairs. 'Agreement between the Government of Australia and the Government of Italy for Assisted Migration, Melbourne, 29 March 1951', *Australian Treaty Series* No. 1951 No. 12 (http://www.austlii.edu.au/au/other/dfat/treaties/1951/12. html, accessed 12 January 2022).

[36] As an example, a Matteo Moretti born in Milan on 8 April 1991 would be identified as MRTMTT 1D08 F205 J. The Italian tax file number was first legislated by the Presidential degree no. 605 of 29 September 1973 (see: https://www.normattiva.it/uri-res/N2Ls?urn:nir:stato:decreto.del.presidente.della.repubblica:1973-09-29;605!vig=). On how the Italian tax file number is composed, refer the Italian Taxation Office website: https://www.agenziaentrate.gov.it/portale/web/guest/schede/istanze/richiesta-ts_cf/informazioni-codificazione-pf.

[37] Gwenda Tavan, *The Long, Slow Death of White Australia* (Melbourne: Scribe, 2005); on the 1967 Referendum, see Frank Brennan, *No Small Change: The Road to Recognition for Indigenous Australia* (Brisbane: University of Queensland Press, 2015).

measured each cost and contingency in the process of marshalling the Italian labour force they required, whereas the Italians crafted Article 10, when read in conjunction with other aspects of the Agreement, as a means of promising for the immigrant Italians two years of guaranteed work in Australia.

On 29 March 1951 the Migration Agreement was promulgated. On 1 August 1951 the migration scheme formally began. Menzies promised De Gasperi the immigrants would be made welcome. The Italian Minister in Australia, Don Giulio De Balzo, asserted that 'the bonds of friendships between our countries are being strengthened...'.[38] Now that Italy was beginning on its road to economy recovery, returning to the eighth place in global rankings it had occupied in 1940, it was enjoying a subtle shift in the balance of power vis-à-vis Australia. When, in 1951, Australian Foreign Minister R. G. Casey visited Rome, he was informed by Under-Secretary of State for Foreign Affairs, Francesco Dominedò, that the Australian officials were not processing the applicants quickly enough.[39] In this new friendlier environment, floods in Italy during November 1951 prompted a more generous Australian Government response (although so as not to stir up xenophobia among Australians, the Menzies Government recommended donations via the Red Cross).[40]

Riots took place in July 1952 at Bonegilla in north-eastern Victoria during the unemployment crisis caused by the Korean War.[41] Subsequent public protests took place in Brisbane, Melbourne, and Sydney, and there was talk of taking Australia to the International Court of Justice at The Hague for breaches of Article 10.[42] This changing mood was reflected at the diplomatic level. Silvio Daneo was appointed Italian Ambassador to Australia on 5 June 1952, arriving in August. He reported to Rome on the 'rustic democracy' he encountered.[43] He remained in Australia

[38] 'Italian migration plan begins: 15,000 here soon', *Daily Advertiser* (Wagga Wagga), Thursday 2 August 1951, 3ef.

[39] Richard Bosworth, 'Post-War Italian immigration', 506.

[40] Steele, 'Twentieth-Century relations', 3.

[41] Pascoe, *Buongiorno Australia*, 229; Richard Bosworth, 'Post-War Italian immigration', 506–07; Alexandra Dellios, *Histories of Controversies: Bonegilla Migrant Centre* (Melbourne: Melbourne University Press, 2017).

[42] Richard Bosworth, 'Post-War Italian immigration', 507.

[43] Richard Bosworth, 'Post-War Italian immigration', 507.

during the unemployment crisis that forced the suspension of the migration programme from 1952 to 1954. Daneo also intervened in the Mario Abbiezzi case: Abbiezzi was a decorated *partigiano* (Resistance fighter) whom Menzies, as part of his campaign to ban the Communists in Australia, naively threatened with deportation.[44]

In August 1952 Pope Pius XII issued *Exsul Familia* (The Émigré Family'), comprising guidelines for how bishops in countries of immigration should care for families in exile, taking as their model the flight of the Holy Family into Egypt. The Vatican's attitude towards overall emigration to Australia was reflected in the work of the two main orders ministering to Italian migrants—the Capuchins and the Scalabrinians; the latter arrived in Australia in 1952.[45] The Vatican adroitly distanced itself from B. A. Santamaria's notorious right-wing Movement in 1957.[46]

In 1953, Giorgio Mangiamele directed his first Australian film, *Il Contratto* (92 mins, silent, black and white). The opening scene shows an Italian politician selling the virtues of emigration to a group of enthusiastic young Italian men.[47] The film goes on to depict the alienation and bitterness of the reality of life in inner-suburban Melbourne, as these young men struggle to find employment—'the contract' into which they had entered proves worthless.[48]

Relations between Italy and Australia were more promising during the second half of the 1950s. In 1954 Paul McGuire was named Australia's second Minister to Italy, with his title changed to Ambassador in 1958, following McGuire's argument that Australia upgrade its Legation to

[44] V. G. Venturini, *Never Give In: Three Italian Antifascist Exiles in Australia, 1924–1956* (Sydney: Search Foundation, 2007), 784, claims somewhat churlishly that Daneo urged Abbiezzi's supporters to keep quiet. See also Evan Smith, 'Shifting undesirability: Italian migration, political activism and the Australian authorities from the 1920s to the 1950s', *Immigrants and Minorities: Historical Studies in Ethnicity, Migration and Diaspora*, 2021 (published online 21 September).

[45] Richard Bosworth, 'Post-War Italian immigration', 507–08.

[46] Richard Bosworth, 'Post-War Italian immigration', 508.

[47] Giorgio Mangiamele, dir., *Il Contratto*, 92 mins, b/w, Ronin Films and National Film and Sound Archive, 2011 [1953].

[48] Gaetano Rando, 'Liminality, temporality and marginalization in Giorgio Mangiamele's migrant movies', *Studies in Australasian Cinema*, vol. 1, no. 2, 2014, 209–21.

an Embassy.[49] This change reflected Italy's newly won status as a vital Australian ally in Europe. In December 1954, as the Australian economy improved, the Migration Agreement was revived. Italy's new confidence in world affairs was reflected in Daneo's description of Australia as a place of 'golden mediocrity'.[50] After Daneo was re-appointed in March 1958 for a few months, Eugenio Prato was appointed the third post-war Italian Ambassador to Australia on 2 December 1958.[51] 1957 was the year the apex of Italian emigration was reached, with an outflow of 400,000 people.[52] McGuire was followed as Ambassador later in 1958 by Hugh McClure Smith. McClure Smith was not a career diplomat, but Associate Editor of the influential *Sydney Morning Herald*. McClure Smith died of a heart attack in Florence on 8 October 1961.[53]

Some of Australia's renowned intellectuals were taking more interest in Italy. In 1959 Shirley Hazzard's first work of fiction was published, 'Harold', a short story set in Siena.[54] Having first visited Italy in 1951, with a trip to Naples, it was there that Hazzard, the daughter of an Australian diplomat, discovered her ability to write. She was one of many post-war Australian writers, artists and historians inspired by Italy and Italian people, strengthening cultural relations between the two countries. That same year *Il Globo* was launched in Melbourne, eventually becoming

---

[49] A South Australian Catholic, McGuire wrote non-fiction, detective stories, and poetry. His best-known book was *There's Freedom for the Brave: An Approach to World Order* (1949), a call for an 'open society' in preference to communism.

[50] Richard Bosworth, 'Post-War Italian immigration', 507. Daneo's use of the term 'golden mediocrity' is witty, as Horace intended *aurea mediocratis* to carry the meaning (lost in English) to mean 'safely in-between', which of course anticipates Donald Horne's famously ironic description of Australia as a 'lucky country', or the injunction on Australian beaches to 'swim between the flags'. Rosa Cappiello (see below) will use the same metaphor in her trenchant novel of 1981.

[51] Prato was a career diplomat whose wartime service included the rescue of Jews in Athens.

[52] Pascoe, *Buongiorno Australia*, 229; Gabriele Abbondanza, 'Italy's migration policies combating irregular immigration: From the early days to the present times', *The International Spectator*, vol. 52, issue 4, 2017, 76–92.

[53] Jenny Newell, 'McClure Smith, Hugh Alexander (1902–1961), *Australian Dictionary of Biography* (https://adb.anu.edu/biography/mcclure-smith-hugh-alexander-10914/text19387, published first in hard copy 2000, accessed 31 January 2022).

[54] Shirley Hazzard, *Collected Stories* (London: Virago Press, 2020).

the most successful Italian-language newspaper outside Italy, as its American equivalents gradually reverted to English. There were still limits to bilateral harmony, of course: Australian trade unions were mostly still not persuaded of the benefits of international migration. The Italian seamen's strike in July 1959 was a rare example of cross-national solidarity between Italian and Australian trade unions.[55]

Towards Symmetry During
the 1960s and Early 1970s

Relations between the two governments became even more symmetrical during the 1960s. Remittances from overseas Italians and the repatriation back home of many Italians contributed to Italy's economic resurgence.[56] In 1961, treatment of Italian immigrants on a par with those from Britain was demanded by the Amintore Fanfani Government.[57] Some of these demands were met by 1967, including the right to leave Australia if conscripted for military service in the Vietnam War.[58]

There were other signs of positive change in 1961. November saw the retirement of the inaugural Secretary of the Australian Immigration Department, Tasman Heyes, reluctant in his support of non-British immigration. Then the term 'New Australian' was formally dropped from government publications.[59] A second set of riots at Bonegilla took place with unemployment levels rising owing to the government's ill-advised 1961 'credit squeeze'. That same year saw the publication of *La Bora*, a novel by Philip M. Jones, which examined the life of an Australian immigration official in Trieste trying to adjudicate who were genuine

---

[55] Pascoe, *Buongiorno Australia*, 225.

[56] Pascoe, *Buongiorno Australia*, 230.

[57] Pascoe, *Buongiorno Australia*, 220, 229.

[58] Pascoe, *Buongiorno Australia*, 231. Italo-Australians who did serve in this war have been interviewed by Annamaria Davine, published as *Italo-Australians in the Vietnam War: A Migrant Perspective* (Melbourne: Italian Australian Institute, 2021), examining the family backgrounds of these men, their experience serving in the Australian forces, and their return to civilian life in the aftermath of what became in Australia a deeply unpopular war.

[59] Pascoe, *Buongiorno Australia*, 220. The term 'New Australian' had been invented years earlier by Arthur Calwell in preference to 'reffo' or 'Balt', but by the late 1950s had come to be seen as patronising.

refugees.[60] In 1961 the Italian Cultural Institute opened in Melbourne, providing opportunities for more Australians to learn Italian language and culture.[61] At the same time the Italian Trade Commission opened an office in St Kilda Road, Melbourne, in the hope of deepening commercial connections between the two nations. By 1964, approval ratings for Italians among Australians had reached 47 per cent, up from only 21 per cent in 1948.[62] Like the hard-working internees and POWs of the Second World War, the outdoor labourers of the 1950s, with handkerchiefs knotted on their heads, had earned grudging respect.

A posting to Rome or Canberra became more prestigious in each country's diplomatic pecking order. A Piedmontese, Mario Tonarelli was appointed the head of the Italian mission in Australia on 1 December 1961, and in 1962 Alfred Stirling was appointed Ambassador to Italy. A career diplomat, Stirling continued in the role until 1967.[63] The following month Renato Della Chiesa d'Isasca was appointed Italian Ambassador to Australia on 3 August, bringing to the role considerable knowledge of the English-speaking world.[64] Mario Majioli, a seasoned diplomat with UN experience, became Italy's sixth post-war Ambassador to Australia on 31 January 1967.

This new level of inter-governmental cooperation reached new heights in 1967, with the official visit to Australia of President Giuseppe Saragat during the last week in September. He was accompanied by the Italian Minister for Foreign Affairs, the former PM Amintore Fanfani. The Australian PM, Harold Holt, stated that 'the warm friendship between

[60] Philip M. Jones, *La Bora* (Sydney: Angus & Robertson, 1961) was reviewed by Dorothy Auchterlonie in *Quadrant*, vol. 6, no. 2, March 1962, 86. Jones later became a journalist on *The Australian*.

[61] Pascoe, *Buongiorno Australia*, 230.

[62] Approval ratings for the Irish in Australia rose accordingly, from 65 to 89 per cent, as the non-British immigrants filled the social space they had formerly occupied: Pascoe, *Buongiorno Australia*, 222–23.

[63] In retirement Stirling wrote several books, including *The Italian Diplomat: and, Italy and Scotland* (Melbourne: Hawthorn Press, 1971), and *A Distant View of the Vatican* (Melbourne: Hawthorn Press, 1975).

[64] Born in Livorno in 1903, Dr. Della Chiesa d'Isasca had emigrated to the US in 1929.

Australia and Italy has been strengthened by the many thousands of Italians who have made their homes in this country'.[65] The Italo-Australian committee entrusted with this visit formed the nucleus of a group of Italo-Australian leaders that over time helped to foster a true sense of *italianità*.[66] That year the RAAF purchased Macchi jet trainers from Italy, whose arms exports rank seventh in the world (while Australia is the third-largest importer of arms). The following year Austrade set up an office in Milan.[67] Stirling was succeeded as Australian Ambassador in Rome by another career diplomat, Walter Crocker, whose term ran from 1968 to 1970.[68] These were all promising indications of a stronger relationship between the two nations.

Australian knowledge and understanding of Italian history and culture deepened during the 1970s. In 1970 Malcolm Booker followed Crocker as Australia's Ambassador to Italy.[69] Booker's term in Rome ended in 1974. His career as a diplomat ended in 1976 when he published a book, *The Last Domino*, arguing that the Whitlam Dismissal had diminished Australia's international standing.[70] The year 1971 was the high-water mark of Italian migration to Australia, with 290,000 Italians counted in the census of that year.[71] Paolo Canali was appointed Italy's Ambassador to Australia on 10 June. This was a significant appointment, as Canali, a British voice actor, entered Italian politics as a Christian Democrat with Prime Minister De Gasperi, bridging the post-war diplomatic gap between Rome and London. He was re-appointed to Canberra on 22 December 1972.

---

[65] Australia. Department of the Prime Minister and Cabinet. Press release, 23 July 1967 (https://pmtranscripts.pmc.gov.au/release/transcript-1630, accessed 3 January 2022).

[66] Pascoe, *Buongiorno Australia*, 232.

[67] Steele, 'Twentieth-Century relations', 3, 4.

[68] Walter Crocker, *Australian Ambassador: International Relations at First Hand* (Melbourne: Melbourne University Press, 1971).

[69] Booker had been the private secretary to Australian prime minister Billy Hughes and wrote a biography of him in 1980.

[70] 'Diplomat without post is puzzled', *Sydney Morning Herald*, 2 December 1976. The full title of his book was *The Last Domino: Aspects of Australia's Foreign Relations* (Collins, 1976).

[71] Richard Bosworth, 'Post-War Italian immigration', 509. For the Italian perspective, see Gabriele Abbondanza, 'Italy's migration policies combating irregular immigration: From the early days to the present times', *The International Spectator*, vol. 52, issue 4 (2017), 76–92.

To the dozens of Australian intellectuals who had followed in the path of Shirley Hazard, academic Bernard Hickey and journalist Desmond O'Grady, were added the hundreds and then thousands of Australian travellers attracted to explore Italy by cheaper air fares and improved tourism infrastructure. They learned that Italy was richer in its traditions and lifestyle than they had earlier imagined. The film *Bello, onesto, emigrato Australia sposerebbe compaesana illibata* was released in December 1971. This Italian film, one of very few featuring Italians in Australia, demonstrated an attempt to bridge the cultural gap between the two countries. In one crucial scene, Carmela (Claudia Cardinale) overhears a conversation on a train with three Italian men: 'In that mine there were 47 of us from Bergamo. You know what they called it? The cemetery of the *Bergamaschi*!' 'That may be true', replied another man, 'but we could get our revenge by having our children university educated'.[72] In December 1972 the Whitlam Government was elected, ending 23 years of conservative rule in Canberra. With the new higher education policy, university was free of charge. The Canadian policy of 'multiculturalism' was adopted by Australia, and Italy was one of Whitlam's favourite allies.

Expatriate Italians were receiving new attention from all quarters. On 15 August 1969 Paul IV had issued *Pastoralis Migratorum Cura*. The 1952 *Exsul Familia* had presumed that only first- and second-generation emigrants from Italy needed pastoral support; now the emergence of 'guest-workers' demanded longer-term support.[73] On the Left there were also new initiatives for migrant workers. In 1972, a branch of FILEF (*Federazione Italiana Lavoratori Emigrati e Famiglie*) was launched in Australia. It was linked to the Italian Communist Party. Its Australian patron was the Labor parliamentarian, Giovanni Sgrò.[74]

The ties between Australian Catholics and the Vatican were strengthening, in the aftermath of Vatican II. The post-conciliar Church in Australia was demonstrably less Irish, and greater numbers of priests, nuns

---

[72] Luigi Zampa, dir. *Bello, onesto, emigrato Australia sposerebbe compaesana illibata*, 1 hr 53 m, 1971, 1:21:20. The title translates literally as 'Handsome, honest emigrant in Australia would marry chaste fellow-countrywoman', but the film was given the simpler English-language title, *A Girl in Australia*.

[73] Sylvan [Silvano] M. Tomasi, 'Pastoral and canonical implications of *Pastoralis Migratorum Cura*', *The Jurist*, vol. 31, no. 2, Spring 1971, 332–41.

[74] Simone Battiston, *Immigrants turned Activists: Italians in 1970s Melbourne* (Kibworth Beauchamp, UK: Troubador Italian Studies, 2012).

and laypeople were attracted to Rome for pilgrimage, studies and work. The Whitlam Government decided in 1973 to strengthen its diplomatic ties with the Vatican. Unfortunately, Australia's nominee as Ambassador to the Holy See, Tobruk veteran and military historian Dudley McCarthy, was rejected by the Vatican on the grounds he was a divorcee. The appointment then became an attachment to the work of ambassadors in other European nations, especially Ireland, until Tim Fischer's appointment in 2008.

RELATIONS STALL AFTER WHITLAM

The pace of cooperation in secular relations between Australia and Italy during the latter half of the 1970s also stalled. During the term of the next Australian Ambassador, John Ryan, who served from 1974 to 1977,[75] Australia and Italy signed an Agreement of Cultural Cooperation, a framework for cooperation, but not a stimulus to action.[76] Whitlam's successor, the conservative Malcolm Fraser, made a state visit to Italy in 1977. That same year the FILEF organiser in Australia, Ignazio Salemi, was abruptly deported to Italy for reasons that were never made clear.[77] Career diplomat Paolo Molajoni became the Italian Ambassador to Australia on 21 June 1977 while, in 1978, Robert (R. H.) Robertson was appointed Ambassador to Italy, a role he held until 1980. In 1980 Dr. Sergio Angeletti became the Italian Ambassador to Australia on 15 March, and in 1981 career diplomat Keith Douglas-Scott was appointed the Australian ambassador to Rome. Despite the warmth between the two governments, little progress was made on deeper economic cooperation. Government-to-government relations were not frosty, merely lukewarm.

Cultural links did, however, continue to develop. In 1981 Rosa Cappiello published her autobiographical *Paese fortunato/Oh Lucky Country*. Born in Naples in 1942, Cappiello had migrated to Australia

---

[75] Ryan resigned from the Australian Secret Intelligence Service after the bungled Sheraton Hotel incident of 1983, which occurred under his watch as acting head of ASIS.

[76] Steele, 'Twentieth-Century relations', 4.

[77] Pascoe, *Buongiorno Australia*, 226; Battiston, *Immigrants turned Activists*, 76–93, highlights the role played by Giovanni Sgrò. An earlier version of Battiston's argument appeared as 'Salemi v MacKellar revisited: Drawing together the threads of a controversial deportation case', *Journal of Australian Studies*, vol. 28, issue 84, 2005, 1–10.

in 1971, without any knowledge of English. The novel is a gritty account of her experience as a manual labourer in the so-called 'lucky country'. It was translated into English by Gaetano Rando. For a half century from 1976, dozens of cultural tours to Italy were organised under the auspice of Australians Studying Abroad, the brainchild of Melbourne art historian Chris Wood. In 1982 Senator Libero Della Briotta became the first European socialist to address the biennial conference of the Australian Labor party (the ALP).[78]

In 1984, with the return of Labor to Government in Canberra, the two deputy PMs, Lionel Bowen and Arnaldo Forlani, signed an Economic and Commercial Cooperation Agreement. This was the first of several attempts to broaden bilateral trade and cooperation. Australian scholars attempted to weave forecasts of a stronger economic relationship with considerations of the literary and cultural connections between the two nations.[79] In 1985 Gerald (Gerry) Nutter was appointed ambassador. Nutter was senior in Australia's intelligence community; his term in Rome ended in 1987. In 1986 Eric Da Rin was appointed Italy's Ambassador to Australia on 2 January, having just spent five years as the Deputy Secretary General of NATO. The general secretaries of Italy's three main union organisations (CGIL, CILS and UIL) took part in an Australian trade union conference. That year the new Labor PM, Bob Hawke, visited Italy.[80] His Government introduced portable pensions, a long-awaited reform allowing migrants to return home with an Australian pension.[81] In 1988, the year of Australia's bicentenary, President Francesco Cossiga visited Australia in October; in greeting him, Hawke said Australia owed a 'great historical debt' to Italy.[82] In 1988 A.D. (Duncan) Campbell,

[78] Pascoe, *Buongiorno Australia*, 231.

[79] Camilla Bettoni and Joseph Lo Bianco, eds, *Understanding Italy: Language, Culture, Commerce: An Australian Perspective* (Sydney: Frederick May Foundation for Italian Studies, Sydney, 1989).

[80] Steele, 'Twentieth-Century relations', 4.

[81] Pascoe, *Buongiorno Australia*, 232. The Bilateral Social Security Agreement was revised and ratified in 2000.

[82] Steele, 'Twentieth-Century relations', 4.

another career diplomat, with a special interest in decolonisation, took Australia's posting in Rome, his term ending in 1993.[83]

During the 1990s Italy changed fundamentally, with consequences for its bilateral relations with Australia. Although Italy was proceeding far more cautiously towards a neo-liberal economy than Australia,[84] its economy was growing so fast—famously overtaking the UK in 1992—that it reached fifth place, a remarkable achievement. From 1992 Italian civic life was reshaped by the *tangentopoli* ('kickback city') scandal. The post-war political parties, so confident in their position, lost the good will of Italian voters, and the Berlusconi era was the much-debated result. In 1993 Lance Joseph was appointed Australian ambassador to Italy, where he continued until 1996. The same year Marcello Spatafora was appointed Italian Ambassador to Australia on 28 October 1993.[85] Australia's PM from 1993 to 1996, Paul Keating, was the one of the few post-war leaders not to make a state visit to Italy, partly because he devoted more of his time to cementing Australia's relations with Asia.

IN THE AFTERMATH OF *TANGENTOPOLI*

Part of the shake-up of Italian politics involved renewed calls for diasporic Italians to vote in the national elections. Australia indicated its nervousness about expatriate votes in foreign electorates.[86] In 1997 Rory Steele began his term as Australian Ambassador. Born in Western Australia in 1943, Steele lived and taught in Italy before entering the Australian diplomatic service. The end of his term in 2001 marked the completion of his career in diplomacy. He continued to write about Italian history and culture, and in 2006 published an award-winning novel about the anti-Fascist *partigiani* entitled *Ghosts in the Helmet Trees*.

---

[83] Upon retirement from the foreign service, Campbell continued to write about decolonisation, including a trenchant critique of Australia's concession of East Timor to Indonesia in 1975.

[84] Richard Bosworth, 'Post-War Italian immigration', 505.

[85] Spatafora represented Italy at the UN from 2003 to 2008.

[86] Bruno Mascitelli, Rory Steele and Simone Battiston, *Diaspora Parliaments: How Australia Faced the Italian Challenge* (Ballan, VIC: Connor Court Publishing, 2010), 59.

In 1997 the trade ministers Tim Fischer and Augusto Fantozzi created a Business Leaders' Forum, the second attempt to strengthen bilateral economic relations.[87] In 1998 Giovanni Castellaneta was appointed Italy's Ambassador to Australia on 22 January. He became the Italian Ambassador to the US from 2005 to 2009; later he represented the Italian government on its public entity, the defence company Finmeccanica (subsequently renamed Leonardo). In 1998 President Oscar Luigi Scalfaro became the third Italian head of state to visit Australia.[88] Italy's entry into the Eurozone that same year further diminished its trading interests with Australia,[89] but in other respects the links were stronger than ever. In 1999 Ambassador Steele reported that Australia was now isolated in international opinion on expatriate voting via overseas electorates.[90] That same year, in a significant gesture of solidarity with Canberra, Italy contributed 640 personnel to the Australian-led Internet Force East Timor (Interfet) operation that liberated the East Timor province from Indonesian rule.[91]

In 2001, on 17 June, Dino Volpicelli was appointed the Italian Ambassador to Australia.[92] Not long afterwards, Murray Alexander Cobban's term as Ambassador began; Cobban's term ended in 2004. In 2001 foreign ministers Alexander Downer and Lamberto Dini set up an Australia-Italy Economic and Cultural Council. Again, despite the best intentions of both governments, economic links between the two countries were not appreciably stronger as a result.[93] In 2002, conservative PM John Howard visited Italy.[94] In a clear signal of Italy's waning importance to Australia, as a consequence of stronger links with Asia, Qantas cancelled its direct flights to Italy in 2003.[95]

---

[87] Steele, 'Twentieth-Century relations', 5.

[88] Steele, 'Twentieth-Century relations', 4.

[89] Gianfranco Cresciani and Bruno Mascitelli, eds, *Italy and Australia: An Asymmetrical Relationship* (Ballarat, VIC: Connor Court Publishing, 2014), 25.

[90] Mascitelli, Steele, Battiston, *Diaspora Parliaments*, 74. FOI requests during the 2000s made it possible to publish the diplomatic correspondence relating to this policy change.

[91] Steele, 'Twentieth-Century relations', 4.

[92] Having entered the diplomatic service in 1969, his previous postings had included Japan and South Korea.

[93] Steele, 'Twentieth-Century relations', 5–6.

[94] Steele, 'Twentieth-Century relations', 4.

[95] Steele, 'Twentieth-Century relations', 6.

In 2004 Peter Woolcott was appointed the Australian Ambassador to Italy.[96] Woolcott's term ended in 2007. A Memorandum adding Italy to Australia's Working Holiday Visa scheme was signed in January 2004. The scheme proved popular, taken up by 83,462 Italians (or 4.2 per cent of the total) between 2004 and 2015. Italian diplomats in Australia helped in setting up an organisation, NOMIT, to advance their interests.[97] It was a sign of improving relationships, once more built on migration.[98] In 2005, Stefano Starace Janfolla was appointed Italy's Ambassador to Australia on 15 June.[99] In April 2006, the former *Il Globo* editor Nino Randazzo successfully stood for election in Italy as a centre-left senator representing 'Africa, Asia, Oceania and Antarctica'. In 2007 Randazzo refused Berlusconi's blandishments to support him.[100] In 2007 Amanda Vanstone became Ambassador after her retirement from Australian politics; her term ended in 2010. In 2008 Tim Fischer was appointed Australian Ambassador to the Holy See. Fischer was the first permanent resident ambassador; his term concluded in 2012.

During the second Italian election in which expatriates were permitted to vote, in 2008, Berlusconi was returned to power. The expatriate vote

[96] He was the son of distinguished Australian diplomat Richard Woolcott. He subsequently provided significant leadership at the United Nations on climate change and on arms trade.

[97] Robert Pascoe and Caterina Cafarella, 'The latest wave of Italians in Australia', *Altreitalie* 59, July-December 2019, 101–17; Marco Maria Cerbo and Francesca Basso, 'The Consular approach towards incoming Italians in Victoria and Tasmania', in Bruno Mascitelli and Riccardo Armillei, eds, *Australia's New Wave of Italian Migration: Paradise or Illusion?* (Melbourne: Australian Scholarly Publishing, 2017), 249–62.

[98] See Simone Battiston, 'Italians in Australia in the twenty-first century', in Gabriele Abbondanza and Simone Battiston, eds, *Italy and Australia: Redefining Bilateral Relations for the Twenty-first Century* (London: Palgrave Macmillan, 2024), pp. 49–80; and Loretta Baldassar and Giulia Marchetti, 'Australians in Italy in the twenty-first century', in Gabriele Abbondanza and Simone Battiston, eds, *Italy and Australia: Redefining Bilateral Relations for the Twenty-first Century* (London: Palgrave Macmillan, 2024), pp. 81–111.

[99] With his considerable experience in diplomatic work, Janfolla later offered Italian-funded programmes in diplomatic protocol for emerging countries such as Palestine.

[100] Carlo Carli, 'A community paper for a changing community', in Bruno Mascitelli and Simone Battiston, eds, *Il Globo: Fifty Years of an Italian Newspaper in Australia* (Ballan, VIC: Connor Court Publishing, 2009), 96–117: 115.

had become less significant.[101] In 2009, on 21 February Gian Ludovico de Martino di Montegiordano became Italy's Ambassador to Australia.[102] In 2010 David Ritchie was appointed Australia's Ambassador to Italy. During his term the Australian Sports Commission's European Training Centre was opened in the Lombard city of Varese. The Centre is a facility for elite Australian athletes needing to train or compete in Europe.

A series of high-profile people were chosen for diplomatic roles in Rome, the Vatican and Canberra during the 2010s. In 2012 the prominent QC John McCarthy was appointed Australia's second permanent resident ambassador to the Holy See.[103] His term finished on 29 January 2016. Pier Francesco Zazo served as the Italian Ambassador to Australia from 15 October 2013 to 2018. In May 2014 South Australian politician Mike Rann was appointed Ambassador to Italy. Rann had become an Italophile, supporting, for example, the cultural ambassadorial work of Bernard Hickey.[104] His term ended on 8 January 2016, with Jo Tarnawsky appointed *Chargé d'Affaires* between January and May 2016. On 17 February 2015 Adolfo Tito Ylana was appointed the sixteenth papal delegate to Australia; his term ended in July 2020.

[101] Bruno Mascitelli and Simone Battiston, *The Italian Expatriate Vote in Australia: Democratic Right, Democratic Wrong, or Political Opportunism?* (Ballan, VIC: Connor Court Publishing, 2008).

[102] His wife Camilla Thompson is a noted sculptor. In retirement the couple offer art classes at their restored palace in the Calabrian port city of Amantea.

[103] Alluding to his predecessor, McCarthy said, with characteristic dry wit: 'There are some challenges I will not take up. I will never compete with Tim about trains and about the range of hats that I may have. However, I do hope to follow him in being able to put to the dicasteries [departments] and congregations of the Holy See, positions that Australia has on human rights, inter-faith dialogue, food security, peace in our world and region, all areas in which the Holy See has influence'.

[104] Maria Renata Dolce and Antonella Riem Natale, eds, *Bernard Hickey, A Roving Cultural Ambassador: Essays in His Memory* (Udine: Forum, University of Udine, 2009).

A FRESH START, POST-BREXIT

With the Brexit vote of 2016, Italy seemed poised to assume a stronger role for Australia as a gateway into Europe.[105] From May 2016 to July 2020, Greg French served as the Australian Ambassador in Rome. From 18 July 2016 to 2020 Melissa Hitchman was in the role of Australian Ambassador to the Holy See. On 26 March 2018 Stefano Gatti took up Italy's post in Canberra. There were high hopes of major inter-governmental contracts. In February 2019, frustrated by Canberra's reluctance to enter into a major contract, Gatti cut short his term and returned to Italy. He was replaced on 16 September 2019 by the first woman, Francesca Tardioli, a veteran of almost six years of experience working at NATO. Sadly, she died in February 2022 while holidaying back home[106]; she was succeeded by Paolo Crudele who continues to foster closer bilateral ties.

Things seemed to be improving between Italy and Australia in the 2020s. A treaty-level Agreement on Scientific, Technological and Innovation Cooperation was ratified by Australia in 2019, and then by Italy in 2021. A second woman, Margaret Twomey was appointed Australian Ambassador to Italy in July 2020. An Italo-Australian woman, Chiara Porro, was appointed Australian Ambassador to the Holy See in September 2020. Among recent developments, in October 2021 then PM Scott Morrison visited Rome for the G20 summit; in December of the same year Qantas announced it would resume direct flights to Rome after an 18-year hiatus (the only European country along with the UK to have such an option); in 2022 then Italian PM Mario Draghi and Australian PM Anthony Albanese held a number of meetings, while in 2023 Italian Undersecretary of State Giorgio Silli made an official visit to Australia.[107]

In this long history of waxing and waning relationships, at last some upward signs were there in the 2020s. Italy and Australia have a rich and often productive connection that has managed to survive world wars

---

[105] See Gabriele Abbondanza, 'Time for a strategic partnership: The scope for international cooperation between Italy and Australia, in Gabriele Abbondanza and Simone Battiston, eds, *Italy and Australia: Redefining Bilateral Relations for the Twenty-first Century* (London: Palgrave Macmillan, 2024), pp. 155–187.

[106] Lorenzo Tondo, 'Italy's ambassador to Australia dies in fall from balcony in home town', *The Guardian*, 21 February 2022.

[107] Robyn Ironside, 'Qantas launches direct flights to Rome', *The Australian*, 16 December 2021, 15.

and economic downturns. In the 2020s decade, with global crises accelerated by the pandemic and the Ukraine War, Italy and Australia have common international interests, the capacity for shared defence, opportunities for stronger trade, a proven record of scientific cooperation, and strong networks of personal friendships. The election in May 2022 of Anthony Albanese, Australia's 31st prime minister, the first with an Italian background,[108] might prove a symbolic moment in relations between the two countries.

BIBLIOGRAPHY

PRIMARY SOURCES

Australia. Department of External Affairs. 'Agreement between the Government of Australia and the Government of Italy for Assisted Migration, Melbourne, 29 March 1951', *Australian Treaty Series* No. 1951 No. 12. [http://www.austlii.edu.au/au/other/dfat/treaties/1951/12.html] [1951].

Australia. Department of the Prime Minister and Cabinet. Press release, 23 July 1967 (https://pmtranscripts.pmc.gov.au/release/transcript-1630, accessed 3 January 2022).

Booker, Malcolm, *The Last Domino: Aspects of Australia's Foreign Relations* (Collins, 1976).

Candida-Gonzaga, Berardo, *Memorie delle famiglie nobili delle province meridionali d'Italia* (Bologna: Forni Editore, 1875).

Capra, Giuseppe, *L'Italiano in Australia e Nuova Zelanda: guida practica* (Ivrea: Ditta Francesco Viassone, 1914).

Crocker, Walter, *Australian Ambassador: International Relations at First Hand* (Melbourne: Melbourne University Press, 1971).

Giorgio Mangiamele, dir., *Il Contratto*, 92 mins, b/w, Ronin Films and National Film and Sound Archive, 2011 [1953].

Hazzard, Shirley, *Collected Stories* (London: Virago Press, 2020).

Jones, Philip M., *La Bora* (Sydney: Angus & Robertson, 1961).

McGuire, Paul, *There's Freedom for the Brave: An Approach to World Order* (Melbourne: W. Heinemann, 1949).

Stirling, Alfred Thorp, *The Italian Diplomat: And, Italy and Scotland* (Melbourne: Hawthorn Press, 1971).

Stirling, Alfred Thorp, *A Distant View of the Vatican* (Melbourne: Hawthorn Press, 1975).

---

[108] James Massola, 'Albanese says heritage sends positive message', *The Age*, 13 May 2022, 15.

Zampa, Luigi, dir. *Bello, onesto, emigrato Australia sposerebbe compaesana illibata*, 1 hr 53m, 1971.

SECONDARY SOURCES

Abbondanza, Gabriele, 'Italy's migration policies combating irregular immigration: From the early days to the present times', *The International Spectator*, vol. 52, issue 4, 2017, 76–92.

Abbondanza, Gabriele, 'Time for a strategic partnership: The scope for international cooperation between Italy and Australia', in Gabriele Abbondanza and Simone Battiston, eds, *Italy and Australia: Redefining Bilateral Relations for the Twenty-first Century* (London: Palgrave Macmillan, 2024), pp. 155–187.

Abbondanza, Gabriele and Simone Battiston, 'Italy and Australia in the twenty-first century: Distant connections or close partners?', in Gabriele Abbondanza and Simone Battiston, eds, *Italy and Australia: Redefining Bilateral Relations for the Twenty-first Century* (London: Palgrave Macmillan, 2024), pp. 1–23.

Baldassar, Loretta and Giulia Marchetti, 'Australians in Italy in the twenty-first century', in Gabriele Abbondanza and Simone Battiston, eds, *Italy and Australia: Redefining Bilateral Relations for the Twenty-first Century* (London: Palgrave Macmillan, 2024), pp. 81–111.

Battiston, Simone, 'Italians in Australia in the twenty-first century', in Gabriele Abbondanza and Simone Battiston, eds, Italy and Australia: redefining bilateral relations for the twenty-first century (London: Palgrave Macmillan, 2024), pp. 49–80.

Battiston, Simone, '*Salemi v MacKellar* revisited: Drawing together the threads of a controversial deportation case', *Journal of Australian Studies*, vol. 28, issue 84, 2005, 1–10.

Battiston, Simone, *Immigrants turned Activists: Italians in 1970s Melbourne* (Kibworth Beauchamp, UK: Troubador Italian Studies, 2012).

Behrman, Greg, *The Most Noble Adventure: The Marshall Plan and the Time When America Helped Save Europe* (New York: Free Press, 2007).

Bettoni, Camilla and Joseph Lo Bianco, eds, *Understanding Italy: Language, Culture, Commerce: An Australian Perspective* (Sydney: Frederick May Foundation for Italian Studies, 1989).

Bosworth, Richard, 'Conspiracy of the consuls? Official Italy and the Bonegilla riot of 1952', *Historical Studies*, vol. 22, issue 89, 1987, 547–67.

Bosworth, Richard, 'Post-War Italian immigration', in James Jupp, ed., *The Australian People: An Encyclopedia of the Nation, its People and Their Origins* (Cambridge, UK: Cambridge University Press, 2001 [1988]).

Bosworth, Richard and Romano Ugolini, eds, *War, Internment and Mass Migration: The Italo-Australian Experience, 1940–1990* (Rome: Gruppo Editoriale Internazionale, 1992).

Cresciani, Gianfranco and Bruno Mascitelli, eds, *Italy and Australia: An Asymmetrical Relationship* (Ballarat, VIC: Connor Court Publishing, 2014).

Davine, Annamaria, *Italo-Australians in the Vietnam War: A Migrant Perspective* (Melbourne: Italian Australian Institute, 2021).

Dolce, Maria Renata and Antonella Riem Natale, eds, *Bernard Hickey, A Roving Cultural Ambassador: Essays in His Memory* (Udine: Forum, University of Udine, 2009).

Easdown, Geoff, *Gualtiero Vaccari: A Man of Quality* (Melbourne: Wilkinson Publishing, 2006).

Kent, Bill, Ros Pesman and Cynthia Troup, eds, *Australians in Italy: Contemporary Lives and Impressions* (Melbourne: Monash University ePress, 2008).

Mascitelli, Bruno and Simone Battiston, *The Italian Expatriate Vote in Australia: Democratic Right, Democratic Wrong, or Political Opportunism?* (Ballan, VIC: Connor Court Publishing, 2008).

Mascitelli, Bruno and Simone Battiston, eds, Il Globo: *Fifty Years of an Italian Newspaper in Australia* (Ballan, VIC: Connor Court Publishing, 2009).

Mascitelli, Bruno, Rory Steele and Simone Battiston, *Diaspora Parliaments: How Australia Faced the Italian Challenge* (Ballan, VIC: Connor Court Publishing, 2010).

Mascitelli, Bruno Mascitelli and Riccardo Armillei, eds, *Australia's New Wave of Italian Migration: Paradise or Illusion?* (Melbourne: Australian Scholarly Publishing, 2017).

Newell, Jenny, 'Kellway, Cedric Vernon (1892–1963)', *Australian Dictionary of Biography* (https://adb.anu.edu.au/biography/kellway-cedric-ver non-10673/text1891, published in first in hardcopy 1966, accessed 31 January 2022).

Papalia, Gerardo, 'The Italian "Fifth Column" in Australia: Fascist propaganda, Italian-Australians and internment', *Australian Journal of Politics & History*, vol. 66, issue 2, 2020, 214–31.

Pascoe, Robert, *Buongiorno Australia: Our Italian Heritage* (Melbourne: Greenhouse Publications, in association with the Vaccari Italian Historical Trust, 1987).

Randazzo, Nino and Michael Cigler, *The Italians in Australia* (Melbourne: AE Press, 1987).

Venturini, V. G., *Never Give In: Three Italian Antifascist Exiles in Australia, 1924–1956* (Sydney: Search Foundation, 2007).

Italians in Australia in the Twenty-First Century

Simone Battiston

INTRODUCTION

The presence of Italians in Australia, whose origin can be traced back to the colonial period, has long been the subject of academic investigations.[1] Historians have periodised such presence in major phases, which may typically end with either the post-mass emigration period (after the

[1] For an annotated bibliography, see Matteo Pretelli, "Gli italiani in Australia: lo stato dei lavori", *Studi Emigrazione* 46, no. 176 (2009): 779–792. For a broad overview of Italians in Australia, see, among others, Robert Pascoe, *Buongiorno Australia: Our Italian heritage* (Richmond, VIC: Greenhouse Publication, 1987); Stephen Castles, Caroline Alcorso, Gaetano Rando, and Ellie Vasta, *Australia's Italians: Culture and community in a changing society* (St. Leonards, NSW: Allen & Unwin, 1992); Gianfranco Cresciani, *The Italians in Australia* (Cambridge, UK: Cambridge University Press, 2003); Fabio Baggio and Matteo Sanfilippo, "L'emigrazione italiana in Australia", *Studi Emigrazione* 48, no. 183 (2011): 477–499; Francesco Ricatti, *Italians in Australia: History, memory, identity* (Cham, Switzerland: Palgrave Macmillan, 2018).

S. Battiston (✉)
Department of Humanities and Social Sciences, Swinburne University of Technology, Melbourne, VIC, Australia
e-mail: sbattiston@swin.edu.au

© The Author(s), under exclusive license to Springer Nature Singapore Pte Ltd. 2023
G. Abbondanza and S. Battiston (eds.), *Italy and Australia*,
https://doi.org/10.1007/978-981-99-3216-0_3

49

1970s) or, for recent publications, the post-2000 period. The growing literature on recent newcomers from Italy, whose presence has sparked a debate over a new emigration wave, suggests paying a closer look to the early decades of this century, and perhaps advancing a new periodisation that may take into consideration, on the one end, the growing popularity of temporary visas such as the Working Holiday Maker (WHM) visa since 2004 and, on the other hand, the pandemic hiatus.

The aim of this chapter is to provide an overall, up-to-date picture of the Italian presence in twenty-first-century Australia by focusing on some key findings from different demographic and immigration data sets, as well as by engaging with recent scholarship. By collecting and analysing relevant domestic and international sources, this chapter chiefly employs a literature review methodology. It is divided into three sections, introduction and conclusion excluded. The first explores the complexity of the Italian-background community, and the demographic trends of some of its different components, in the first two decades or so of the third millennium. In mapping the Italian presence in Australia, a particular emphasis is placed on identifying recent signs of growth and decline. The second pays attention to the latest wave of Italian arrivals in Australia against a mobility context that is characterised chiefly by its non-permanent and transnational nature. The third and last section focuses on the pandemic break, which has characterised the early 2020s, and its impact on temporary visa holders.

Exploring Recent Demographic Trends of an Established Community

According to the 2021 Census, Australia is home to about 1.1 million residents of Italian ancestry.[2] Put differently, approximately one out of twenty-three Australian residents claim an Italian heritage, or at

---

[2] The ancestry question seeks to capture the overall cultural diversity present in the country (one's association with ancestries, ethnic origins and cultures). From 2001 to 2021, Italian ancestry responses have increased by 38,5%, from 800.256 to 1.108.364 respectively. See, Australian Bureau of Statistics (henceforth ABS), "Understanding and using ancestry data", 28 June 2022, https://www.abs.gov.au/statistics/detailed-methodology-information/information-papers/understanding-and-using-ancestry-data; ABS, "Cultural diversity of Australia", 20 September 2022, https://www.abs.gov.au/articles/cultural-diversity-australia.

least partly, as respondents can report up to two different ancestries. The Italian ancestry group is among the largest in the country, currently holding the seventh position overall. Among second-generation Australians, that is Australian-born residents with one or both parents born overseas, it is ranked even higher, third (7.9%), after English (32,5%) and Australian (30.9%) ancestries. This variable provides useful insights into the size of the Italian heritage extant in the Australian population, but it tells us little about the constituent parts or the heterogeneity of this ethnic group.[3] To understand the multifaceted character of the Italian-background community, and its recent demographic trends, we may need to look at other Census variables such as country of birth, country of birth of parent/s, and language used at home, which are conventionally employed as surrogate measures of one's ethnicity or ethnic origin.[4] These variables shed a light on the different cohorts comprising the Italian Australian diaspora,[5] including but not limited to, first-generation migrants (the Italian-born, who can be further divided up in "post-war" labour migrants, "post-1970s" skilled and professional migrants, and "new migrants"), their offspring born in Australia (the second generation), and those who speak Italian at home.[6]

[3] Loretta Baldassar, Joanne Pyke and Danny Ben-Moshe, *The Italian diaspora in Australia: Current and potential links to the homeland* (Burwood: Deakin University, 2012), 6.

[4] Robert V. Horn, "Ethnic origin in the Australian census", *Journal of the Australian Population Association* 4, no. 1 (1987): 1–12; Robert V. Horn, "The validity of Australian ancestry statistics", *Journal of the Australian Population Association* 10, no. 2 (1993): 119–126, cited in Liz Allen, "Understanding ethnicity in contemporary Australia using the census", *Australian Population Studies* 5, no. 1 (2021): 56–64.

[5] There is no generally accepted term that refers to Italian migrants and their descendants in Australia, due to different theoretical frameworks and (multi)disciplinary approaches. For a critical review of the applicability of the paradigms of diaspora and transnationalism to the Italian-Australian history and migration contexts see, for example, Stefano Luconi, "I paradigmi recenti dell'emigrazione italiana e il caso australiano", *Studi Emigrazione* 46, no. 176 (2009): 793–816.

[6] Loretta Baldassar and Joanne Pyke, "Intra-diaspora knowledge transfer and 'new' Italian migration", *International Migration* 52, no. 4 (2014): 128–129. Note that a subgroup of the Italian-born is the so-called 1.5 generation migrants, namely those born overseas who moved to Australia before or during their early teens, somewhat placed between the first and the second generation.

Most Italian migrants came to Australia from 1947 to 1976.[7] Rightly, these post-war migrants are regarded the "statistical backbone" of the Italian-Australian community.[8] Census data of the 1990s portrayed a community of Italian-born that largely reflected previous migration programmes, which allowed a few hundred thousand Italians, chiefly unskilled or semi-skilled, to settle in Australia: the majority of the Italian-born (two-thirds) resided in the states of Victoria and New South Wales, just over 40% were part of the labour force with the sectors of trade (wholesale and retail) and manufacturing attracting the highest number of the Italian-born, and for those employed the main occupation was to be found in the trades and related fields. As a whole, this group was reasonably well-off, but still lagging in terms of earning power compared to the wider population. Besides, only one quarter of the Italian-born had obtained some form of qualification, two-thirds did not continue schooling past the age of 16, and gender imbalances and gaps were still prevalent across many different fields, from labour force participation to occupation to education levels.[9]

Since reaching its peak in 1971, when the Census recorded the presence of 289,476 Italian-born residents, first-generation Italians have been reducing in numbers progressively (see Fig. 3.1). Due to improved economic conditions in Italy, which favoured return migration, and an Australian immigration programme prioritising skilled labour, the number of arrivals from Italy in the last quarter of the twentieth century slowed to a trickle contributing indirectly to a gradual ageing of the Italian-born.[10] Fifty years on, the Italian-born group has almost halved, numbering a total of 163,326 in 2021. In the five-year period 2016–2021, this group of residents recorded "the biggest decrease of all countries of birth",

---

[7] The net migration from Italy between 1947 and 1976 was of about 270,000; of the over 360,000 Italians that came during this period, about a quarter (90,000) returned to Italy. See Stephen Castles, "Italians in Australia: The impact of recent migration on the culture and society of a postcolonial nation", *Center for Migration Studies special issues* 11. no. 3 (1994): 346.

[8] Francesco Cavallaro, "Italians in Australia: Migration and profile", *Altreitalie* 26 (2003): 67.

[9] Cavallaro, "Italians in Australia", 70–81.

[10] Donatella Strangio and Alessandra De Rose, "A new Italian migration toward Australia? Evidences from the last decades and associations with the recent economic crisis", in *The History of Migration in Europe: Perspectives from Economics, Politics and Sociology*, ed. Francesca Fauri (London: Rutledge, 2014), 203.

dropping by almost 11,000 people.[11] The ageing process of this group can be observed in at least two ways, from the median age that rose from 50 years in 1986 to 73 years in 2021, and the changes in the age distribution over time. In 1976, for example, the under 45s represented well over half (59.5%) of the Italian-born population. Four decades later, this percentage has dropped 48.1 percentage points. Contrarywise, those aged 45 and above have more than doubled during the same period, from 40.5 percentage points (1976) to 88.7 percentage points (2016). Of all the age groups taken into consideration, those aged 65+ have recorded the largest (tenfold) increase in percentage points, from 8.3 (1976) to 81.2 (2016). In absolute numbers, the 65+ cohort have increased from 23,284 (1976) to 114.075 (2016).[12]

Two decades into the third millennium, the latest Census has recorded two predictable trends for the Italian-born population: a significant drop in absolute numbers and the predominant position of the group aged 65+ above all others, despite the negligible decrease of this age group from 81.2 percentage points (2016) to 81.1 percentage points (2021). Yet, the same Census recorded a noteworthy change in the age distribution of the Italian-born, which can be observed in the prime working-age group of the 25–44s.[13] The Italian-born males of this age group, in particular, have increased their share from 10.4 percentage points to 13.5 percentage points during the five-year Census interval. In absolute numbers, this group, males and females combined, has increased by 3,623 persons, from 15.104 (2016) to 18.727 (2021). Since 2016, it has made the largest increase after the group of those aged 85+ (+5,790). As a result, the under 45s have expanded in the inter-census period by 2,767 persons, namely from 19,712 (2016) to 22,479 (2021)—in spite of the number of the Italian-born under the age of 25 decreasing by one-fifth during the same period. On the other hand, the over 45s have dropped by 13,518 persons,

[11] ABS, "Cultural diversity of Australia".

[12] Helen Ware, *A profile of the Italian community in Australia* (Melbourne: Australian Institute of Multicultural Affairs & Co.As.It Italian Assistance Association, 1981).

[13] On the impact of recent Italian arrivals in prime working-age group of the Italian-born, see also Luna Fumagalli, Michele Grigoletti, and Silvia Pianelli, "Dalle spiagge di Sydney alla campagna di Griffith. I quartieri della nuova migrazione italiana", in *Rapporto Italiani nel Mondo 2016*, ed., D. Licata (Todi: Tau Editrice/Fondazione Migrantes, 2016), 400.

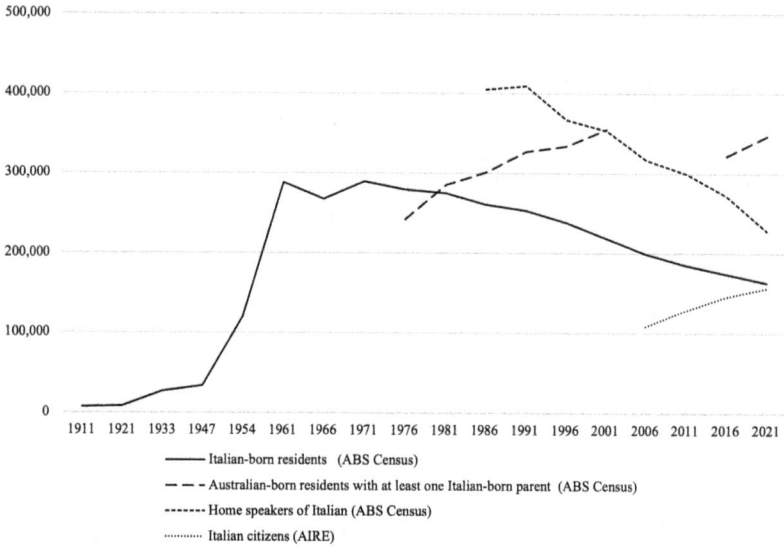

500,000

400,000

300,000

200,000

100,000

0

1911 1921 1933 1947 1954 1961 1966 1971 1976 1981 1986 1991 1996 2001 2006 2011 2016 2021

————— Italian-born residents (ABS Census)

— — - Australian-born residents with at least one Italian-born parent (ABS Census)

------- Home speakers of Italian (ABS Census)

·········· Italian citizens (AIRE)

Fig. 3.1 The Italian presence in Australia, selected data (*Note* In the 2006 and 2011 Australian censi, responses of individual countries of birth of parents were not collected; the only options for birthplace of parent [mother or father] were either "Australia" or "Overseas". *Source* Australian Bureau of Statistics [ABS] Census; Registry of Italians Living Abroad [AIRE])

from 154,352 (2016) to 140,834 (2021). What changes in the age distribution of the last two censi may show is the demographic contribution of recent arrivals from Italy. Net Overseas Migration (NOM) figures reveal that between 2004 and 2015 alone, 20,188 Italian newcomers settled in Australia.[14] This modest contingent of settlers may have contributed nonetheless to the softening of the overall decline of the Italian-group, while simultaneously increasing the share of the working age groups.

Another critical component of the Italian-background community in Australia is that of the second generation, the offspring of at least

---

[14] Riccardo Armillei, "A statistical analysis of the 'new Italian migration' to Australia: Redressing recent overstatements", in *Australia's New Wave of Italian Migration: Paradise or Illusion?* eds. B. Mascitelli and R. Armillei (North Melbourne: Australian Scholarly Publishing, 2017), 56–57. Please note that cited NOM figures include all long-term temporary and permanent migration.

one Italian-born parent. Census data indicate that the Australian-born (second generation) overtook the Italian-born (first generation) in absolute numbers at the start of the 1980s. By 1991, the offspring of Italian parentage totalled 327,101, surpassing the first generation (254,776) by over 70,000 persons. For the next decade, the size of the second generation has increased further reaching well over one third of a million at the beginning of this century. By 2016, this figure had dropped below the 1991 level. Responses of individual countries of birth of parents were not collected in the 2006 and 2011 censi, but it is possible to infer that this decrease in numbers might have also been a response to both the ageing and shrinking size of the first generation. Yet, the 2021 Census measured a notable increase by about 25,000 persons, when compared with the previous Census, bringing the total number of this group to 347,000 (2021) from 322,000 (2016).[15] This growth could be read in conjunction with the increase of Italian settlers in Australia and the recent rise of the Italian-born in the prime working-age (and reproductive age) group.

Second-generation Italian-Australians have proved to be considerably more upwardly mobile and better qualified than the first generation, but overall less inclined to maintain the parents' language at home.[16] With the number of native proficient speakers declining and ageing, the active home use of Italian as immigrant language has experienced a characteristic intergenerational loss and diminishing social usage, with the result that this language has been driven further into the "...domains of intimacy within the original migrating generation".[17] On the other hand, Italian has been flourishing within the Australian education sector, showing a particular vitality in primary schools, and above all in the state of Victoria. This suggests that Italian at the formal education level has been enjoying

[15] ABS, "Cultural diversity of Australia".

[16] Cavallaro, "Italians in Australia: Migration and Profile", 81–86; Siew-Ean Khoo, Peter McDonald, Dimi Giorgas and Bob Birrell, *Second generation Australians* (Canberra: Department of Immigration and Multicultural and Indigenous Affairs, 2002); ABS, "Cultural diversity of Australia".

[17] Joseph Lo Bianco, "Italian in Australia: Society, education and future Planning", in *L'italiano in Australia. Prospettive e tendenze nell'insegnamento della lingua e della cultura / Italian in Australia: Perspectives and Trends in the Teaching of Language and Culture*, eds. A. Rubino, A. R. Tamponi and J. Hajek (Firenze: Franco Cesati Editore, 2021), 28.

acceptance well beyond the core of proficient speakers, although the erosion of its use at home might be detrimental in the long run.[18]

In addition to the variables so far described, we wish to add a fourth one: foreign citizenship. In a country, Australia, where just over half of the population is either born overseas or has at least one parent born overseas, according to the latest Census, and where several million people hold dual citizenship, this variable allows us to measure the effects in Australia of Italian citizenship law changes, which since 1992 have allowed dual citizenship, but also favoured the reinstallation of Italian citizenship if previously lost due to naturalisation, or its reclaiming among Australians of Italian ancestry via *jus sanguinis* provisions. Changes to the Italian nationality law, along with ongoing emigration and births abroad of citizens by descent, have boosted the number of Italian nationals worldwide dramatically.[19] In Australia, almost 35.000 residents (re)claimed Italian citizenship from 1998 to 2007.[20]

One way to measure the effects and legacy of such changes is to look at *Anagrafe degli Italiani Residenti all'Estero* (Registry of Italians Living Abroad, AIRE) statistics of Italy's Ministry of the Interior. Notwithstanding its limitations (e.g. the issue of underestimating the number of

[18] John Hajek, Renata Aliani and Yvette Slaughter, "From the periphery to center stage: The mainstreaming of Italian in the Australian education system (1960s to 1990s)", *History of Education Quarterly* 62, no. 4 (2022): 475–497; Lo Bianco, "Italian in Australia", 41.

[19] According to *Anagrafe degli Italiani Residenti all'Estero* (Registry of Italians Living Abroad, AIRE) statistics, from 2006 to 2020, the number of Italians living abroad has increased by 76.6%, from 3,1 million to 5,5 million respectively. See Delfina Licata, "Da tradizione storica a fatto strutturale: la presenza italiana all'estero dal 2006 al 2020", in *Rapporto Italiani nel Mondo 2020*, ed. D. Licata (Todi: Tau Editrice/Fondazione Migrantes, 2020), 4. See, also, Greg Brown, "Political bigamy? Dual citizenship in Australia's migrant communities", *People and Place* 10, no. 1 (2002): 71–77; Tanja Brøndsted Sejersen, "'I vow to thee my countries' – The expansion of dual citizenship in the 21st Century", *International Migration Review* 42, no. 3 (2008): 523–549; Guido Tintori, "More than one million individuals got Italian citizenship abroad in twelve years (1998–2010)", *EUDO Citizenship News*, 21 November 2012; David Cook-Martín, *The scramble for citizens: Dual nationality and state competition for immigrants* (Standford: Standford University Press, 2013), 104.

[20] Guido Tintori, *Fardelli d'Italia? Conseguenze nazionali e transnazionali delle politiche di cittadinanza italiane* (Roma: Carocci, 2009), 39.

Italian citizens abroad),[21] the AIRE offers a snapshot of size and composition of the community of Italian nationals residing outside of Italy on a long-term or permanent basis. In Australia, from 2006 (108.309) to 2022 (156.777), the community of Italian citizens grew by 44.7%, according to the AIRE.[22] This growth is ascribable in part to past citizenship policy changes, which have swollen the cohort of citizens by descent born outside of Italy. If "expatriation" (51,7%) is still the main reason for enrolment in the registry in Australia, as of 2022, "birth" (38,7%) stands out as the second motive of AIRE membership.[23]

Consistent with an ethno-nationalist view of community, the AIRE population is a central component of Italy's politics of inclusion of the emigrants and their descendants in the Italian *demos*.[24] As such, Italian citizens abroad are the primary recipients of a complex "diaspora infrastructure",[25] which includes a network of consular, cultural, and educational institutions, as well as locally elected consultation bodies,[26]

[21] Guido Tintori and Valentina Romei, "Emigration from Italy after the crisis: The shortcomings of the brain drain narrative", in *South-North migration of EU citizens in times of crisis*, eds. J.-M. Lafleur and M. Stanek (Cham: Springer, 2017), 53–54.

[22] Bearing in mind that the key criterion for enrolment in the registry is citizenship, not place of birth, this figure includes Italian nationals born in Italy and elsewhere, as well as dual citizens. It is worth noting the growing presence in AIRE population of Italian citizens born in South America, some of whom opt to apply for Australian visas and/or permanent residency as Italian passport holders. See Michele Grigoletti, *Dal Rio Grande do Sul (Brasile) al Nuovo Galles del Sud (Australia): movimento migratorio, presenza e caratteristiche dei giovani italo-brasiliani in Australia*, in *Rapporto Italiani nel Mondo 2019*, ed. D. Licata (Todi: Tau Editrice/Fondazione Migrantes, 2019), 130–139.

[23] Delfina Licata, "Gli italiani nel mondo. Una comunità sempre più interculturale e transnazionale", in *Rapporto Italiani nel Mondo 2022*, ed. D. Licata (Todi: Tau Editrice/Fondazione Migrantes, 2022), 13.

[24] Guido Tintori, "Italian mobilities and the *demos*" in *Italian Mobilities*, eds. R. Ben-Ghiat and S. M. Hom (London: Routledge, 2015), 111–132.

[25] On the concept of diaspora infrastructure and its application in the European Union (EU) context, see Jean-Michel Lafleur and Daniela Vintila, "Do EU member states care about their diasporas' access to social protection? A comparison of consular and diaspora policies across EU27", in *Migration and social protection in Europe and beyond (Volume 2): Comparing consular services and diaspora policies*, eds. J.-M. Lafleur and D. Vintila (Cham: IMISCOE Research Series/Springer, 2020), 10–26.

[26] For a summary of the different activities carried out by each of the six *Comitati degli Italiani all'Estero* (Italian Abroad Committees, COMITES) in Australia, the primary advocacy group for Italians abroad and their descendants before the Italian authorities, see Rodrigo Praino and Vinicius Guedes Gonçalves de Oliveira, "La rappresentanza degli

regional emigration councils, a parliamentary representation,[27] special Italian government actions, and a network of *Patronati*, welfare agencies funded by the Italian Social Security Authority (INPS).[28]

New Arrivals and Departures

In the last two decades or so, Australia has seen the arrival (and departure) of tens of thousands of Italians on a temporary or long-stay visa. Pushed by the economic reasons and in search of new employment and lifestyle opportunities,[29] the bulk of Italians coming to Australia in recent times, visitors excluded, have been working-holiday makers, students, and skilled workers. Italy's inclusion in the Working Holiday Maker (WHM) programme, allowing young adults aged 18–30 to holiday, study and seek short-term employment in Australia for a period of a year (extendable an certain conditions), has encouraged temporary migration as never before

italiani in Australia: l'efficacia della rappresentanza su un territorio vasto e poliforme", in *Rapporto Italiani nel Mondo 2022*, ed. D. Licata (Todi: Tau Editrice/Fondazione Migrantes, 2021), 231–239.

[27] Since 2006, one Deputy and one Senator, coincidentally both from Australia, have represented the Africa-Asia-Oceania-Antarctica electoral subdivision in Rome's Parliament. See, Simone Battiston, "Il voto degli italiani in Australia fra continuità e segnali di cambiamento", in *Autopsia di un diritto politico. Il voto degli italiani all'estero nelle elezioni del 2018*, eds. S. Battiston and S. Luconi (Turin: Accademia University Press, 2018), 145–161. For an overview of the Italian foreign constituency and the activity of the abroad-elected MPs, see Rossana Sampugnaro, "The Italian foreign constituency and its MPs", *Contemporary Italian Politics* 9, no. 2 (2017): 162–184; Rossana Sampugnaro, "La rappresentanza parlamentare degli italiani all'estero tra vecchie e nuove *issues*. Due legislature a confronto", in *Cittadini oltre confine. Storia, opinioni e rappresentanza degli italiani all'estero*, eds. S. Battiston, S. Luconi and M. Valbruzzi (Bologna: Il Mulino, 2022), 225–256.

[28] Italian citizens abroad are the recipients of Italian social protection legislation, including pensions; Australia is home to the second-highest number of Italian pensioners outside of Italy (47,529 for a total annual expenditure of over 90 million euros, 2016 data). By 2019, this figure has dropped by about 23%, placing Australia in third position after Germany and Canada. See, Caldarini, "Diaspora policies, consular services and social protection for Italian citizens broad", in *Migration and social protection in Europe and beyond (Volume 2): Comparing consular services and diaspora policies*, eds. J.-M. Lafleur and D. Vintila (Cham: IMISCOE Research Series/Springer, 2020), 275, 283; Daniele Russo and Susanna Thomas, "Le pensioni pagate all'estero e dall'estero come effetto delle migrazioni", in *Rapporto Italiani nel Mondo 2020*, ed. D. Licata (Todi: Tau Editrice/ Fondazione Migrantes, 2020), 66.

[29] Strangio and De Rose, "A new Italian migration toward Australia?", 194–213.

(see Fig. 3.2).[30] This larger than usual movement of Italian nationals has spawned a growing presence of *temporanei*, which has been detected by the quarterly snapshots of temporary visa holders. Between 2012 and 2015, the number of Italian temporary visa holders present in Australia (annual average) has risen sharply, from 15,660 to 24,543 respectively. For the reminder of the decade, this presence has stayed around or above the 24.000 mark. Working holiday makers have been the most represented category in this group, with a share of around 40% during the 2004–2015 period.[31] On the other hand, students and skilled workers have constituted a minor yet growing share of Italian temporary entrants; the former has grown from 11,5% (2012) to 19,8% (2019), and the latter from 10,7% (2012) to 15,1% (2019).[32] Despite the relatively large numbers, recent Italian arrivals have generated a modest net gain for Australia in terms of settlers. As aforementioned, some 20.000 Italians settled in Australia between 2004 and 2015. This number was slightly above that of French nationals who settled in Australia during the same period, but approximately one-tenth of those who came from the UK. The difference is even greater if a comparison is made with Indian or Chinese cohorts.

To contextualise the growing presence of Italian newcomers in Australia, we need to consider the broader migration context. It has been argued that Italy has entered a new emigration phase since the

---

[30] The WHM programme between Italy and Australia came into force in 2004. See Graeme Hugo, "From permanent settlement to transnationalism – Contemporary population movement between Italy and Australia: Trends and implications", *International Migration* 52, no. 4 (2014): 102.

[31] Riccardo Armillei and Bruno Mascitelli, *From 2004 to 2016: A new Italian 'exodus' to Australia?* Melbourne: Comites Victoria & Tasmania, 2016, 21.

[32] Author's own calculations based on data from Department of Home Affairs, BP0019 Number of Temporary visa holders in Australia, https://data.gov.au/. See also, Michele Grigoletti, Silvia Pianelli and Giordano Dalla Bernardina, "L'emigrazione di giovani italiani in Australia", in *Rapporto Italiani nel Mondo 2014*, ed. D. Licata (Todi: Tau Editrice/Fondazione Migrantes, 2014): 216; Alessandro Bilotta, Michele Grigoletti and Silvia Pianelli, "Nuovi emigrati italiani e nuovi cittadini australiani", in *Rapporto Italiani nel Mondo 2015*, ed. D. Licata (Todi: Tau Editrice/Fondazione Migrantes, 2015), 135; Michele Grigoletti and Veronica Olivetto, "Giovani italiani in Australia: moderni percorsi di emigrazione, di formazione e selezione professionale", in *Rapporto Italiani nel Mondo 2018*, ed. D. Licata (Todi: Tau Editrice/Fondazione Migrantes, 2018), 249.

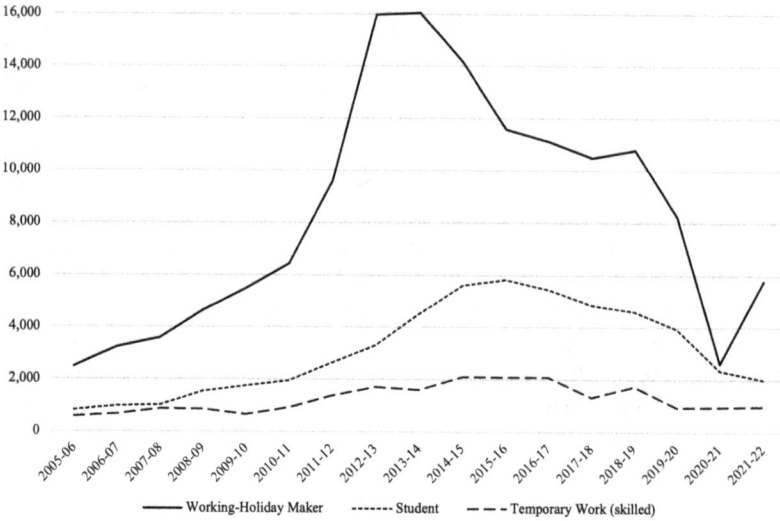

Fig. 3.2 Number of Australian visas granted to Italian citizens, selected categories (*Note* Visa grant data by country of citizenship, not country of birth; Working-Holiday [subclass 417] includes offshore, first and subsequent visas; Student, primary and secondary applicants included; Temporary Work [skilled], primary and secondary applicants included. *Source* Author's own calculations based on data from Department of Home Affairs, BP0017 Working Holiday Maker visas granted pivot table; BP0015 Student visas granted pivot table; BP0014 Temporary Work [skilled] visas granted pivot table, https://data. gov.au/)

Global Financial Crisis (GFC).[33] In the 2008–2016 period alone, Italy has recorded a net population loss of about 400.000 people as a direct impact of emigration.[34] A sharp increase in both outward and inward

---

[33] Enrico Pugliese, *Quelli che se ne vanno. La nuova emigrazione italiana* (Bologna: Il Mulino, 2018), 9–14.

[34] Official Italian statistical figures are in all likelihood underestimating the magnitude of the new emigration phenomenon; see Pugliese's considerations in 26–31. On the chronic delay of Italian emigrants self-reporting to the AIRE once settled abroad, which may contribute to the issue of emigration data underreporting, see Tintori, "Italian mobilities and the *demos*", 126–127 (note 17); Maria Chiara Prodi, "AIRE e nuova mobilità: il dover dare notizia di sé", in *Rapporto Italiani nel Mondo 2018*, ed. D. Licata (Todi: Tau Editrice/Fondazione Migrantes, 2018), 170–179.

mobility has indeed marked the 2010s, with key indicators such as permanent departures and returns trebling (from about 40.000 in 2010 to over
120.000 in 2019) and doubling respectively (from about 30.000 in 2010
to just under 60.000 in 2019). Data show that emigration flows have
continued unabated, although not as intensely, throughout the pandemic
years too.[35] European countries—Germany, the UK (Brexit notwithstanding), Switzerland, France, and Spain, especially—have attracted the
majority of newcomers from Italy.[36] Freedom of movement and residence
within the European Union, better job and career opportunities, and
close geographical proximity have certainly played a role in continuing
to make the European continent, and above all EU member states, a pole
of attraction for modern-day Italian emigrants as they did in the post-war
period. Non-European destinations have also attracted and retained thousands of Italians since the early 2000s, although not as successful as some
European countries. For example, according to the Italian National Institute of Statistics (ISTAT), net migration figures indicate that some 14,300
Italians have moved to the United States in the 2004–2014 period, as did
5,800 to Australia, and 3,700 to Canada. This latest emigration phase has
exhibited new features that set it apart from previous ones, such as the
preeminence among emigrants of those originating from the wealthier
regions of Northern Italy and the widespread job security of the post-
Fordist era. It has also prompted a critical review of the brain drain and
export of talents rhetoric as the majority of the post-GFC Italian migrants
have been not university-educated.[37]

[35] Silvia Bruzzone and Francesca Licari, "Le iscrizioni e cancellazioni anagrafiche degli
italiani da e per l'estero: aspetti demografici e caratteristiche della mobilità", in *Rapporto
Italiani nel Mondo 2021*, ed. D. Licata (Todi: Tau Editrice/Fondazione Migrantes, 2021),
24–40. As travel restrictions have been progressively eased, emigration trends are said to
return to pre-pandemic levels during the 2020s.

[36] Pugliese, *Quelli che se ne vanno*, 38–43; Licata, "Da tradizione storica a fatto
strutturale"; Berti and Alberio, "Italiani che lasciano l'Italia", 15–18.

[37] See, for example, Elena Caneva, "La nuova emigrazione italiana: cosa ne sappiamo,
come ne parliamo", *Cambio* 6, no. 11 (2016): 195–207; Tintori and Romei, "Emigration
from Italy after the crisis"; Fabio Berti and Marco Alberio, "Italiani che lasciano l'Italia.
Le nuove emigrazioni tra continuità e cambiamenti", in *Italiani che lasciano l'Italia. Le
nuove emigrazioni al tempo della crisi*, eds. M. Alberio and F. Berti (Milano: Mimesis,
2020), 7–29.

The relatively high volume of Italians coming to Australia during the global age of perpetual crisis,[38] which has drawn parallels with the number of arrivals from Italy experienced in the 1950s and 1960s,[39] points to a complex mobility model where conventional net migration figures may be ill-suited to comprehend the gamut of movements. New models tend to consider permanent settlement of Italians in Australia, as well as the transnational nature of contemporary movements (the involvement of third countries), the circulatory patterns of migration trajectories (return migration and circular migration), along with short and long stays.[40] Australia's temporary migration paradigm, characterised by being "open-ended and demand driven", has tolerated, even encouraged, "high level of temporariness".[41] Consequently, permanent residency is often proceeded by multiple temporary visas, while migration has become a multi-step process, as underscored by the Productivity Commission.[42]

---

[38] See the definition of the Tens (2010s) offered by Andy Beckett, "The age of perpetual crisis: How the 2010s disrupted everything but resolved nothing", *The Guardian*, 17 December 2019.

[39] Michele Grigoletti and Silvia Pianelli, eds. *Giovani italiani in Australia. Un "viaggio" da temporaneo a permanente* (Todi: Tau Editrice/Fondazione Migrantes, 2016). See also, Riccardo Armillei, "A statistical analysis of the 'new Italian migration' to Australia: Redressing recent overstatements", in *Australia's new wave of Italian migration: Paradise or illusion?* eds. B. Mascitelli and R. Armillei (North Melbourne: Australia Scholarly Publishing, 2017): 53–78.

[40] See the 'Model of the Italy/Australia Migration System' in Graeme Hugo, "From Permanent Settlement to Transnationalism", 95–96. On the phenomenon of Italian return migration and on the presence of Australians of Italian background in Italy, see Giulia Marchetti and Loretta Baldassar, "Australians in Italy in the twenty-first century", in *Italy and Australia: Redefining bilateral relations for the twenty-first century*, eds. Gabriele Abbondanza and Simone Battiston (London: Palgrave Macmillan, 2024), pp. 81–111. On the circular migration model, Loretta Baldassar, "Italian migrants in Australia and their relationship to Italy: Return visits, transnational caregiving and the second generation", *Journal of Mediterranean Studies* 20, no. 2 (2011): 255–282.

[41] Peter Mares, "Putting the new wave of Italian migration to Australia in context", *Studi Emigrazione* 54, no. 207 (2017): 478–479; see also, Peter Mares, "Australia's permanent shift to temporary migration", in *Australia's new wave of Italian migration: Paradise or illusion?* eds. B. Mascitelli and R. Armillei (North Melbourne: Australia Scholarly Publishing, 2017): 110–135.

[42] Productivity Commission, *Migrant Intake into Australia*, Inquiry Report No. 77 (Canberra: Commonwealth of Australia, 2016), 415–420. Different studies have painstaking reconstructed and researched the multi-step visa process faced by Italian applicants. See, for instance, Grigoletti and Pianelli, *Giovani italiani in Australia*; Emanuela Canini, "Recent Italian immigration to Australia: The view of the migration agent", in

There is a growing literature on recent newcomers from Italy, which has so far offered valuable insights into broad issues, including modern transnational mobilities, patterns of belonging, but also experience and reproduction of inequities, precarious work, and detention and removal of illegal migrants, among others.[43] Moving beyond statistics and policy considerations, the latest wave of Italian migration should not be defined however by their "quantitative significance" or "its temporary/permanent character", but by its "qualitative traits".[44] For Robert Pascoe and Caterina Cafarella, the more recent Italian arrivals, coined *"globalisti* (globe-trotters)", brought with them to Australia "a set of skills, competencies and values formed in the hometowns" which helped them cope with the migration process and the complexities of today's world.[45] Similarly to the group of the post-1970 Italian migrants, the *globalisti* arrived in Australia hardly ever with a kin, but rather with peers and friends,

---

Australia's new wave of Italian migration: Paradise or illusion? eds. B. Mascitelli and R. Armillei (North Melbourne: Australia Scholarly Publishing, 2017), 218–248; Emanuela Canini, "Long-term temporary migration: Evolution of a new reality in modern Australian society", *Altreitalie* 59 (2019): 118–130.

[43] Hernán Cuervo, Mauro Giardiello, Babak Dadvand and Rosa Capobianco, *Mobility and belonging: A study of Italian youth diaspora in Australia* (Melbourne: Youth Research Centre, University of Melbourne); Iain Campbell, Maria Azzurra Tranfaglia, Joo-Cheong Tham and Martina Boese, "Precarious work and the reluctance to complain: Italian temporary migrant workers in Australia", *Labour and Industry: A Journal of the Social and Economic Relations of Work* 29, no. 1 (2019): 98–117; Mauro Giardiello, Hernan Cuervo and Rosa Capobianco, "A study of Italian young adults' transnational mobility to Australia: The reproduction of unequal trajectories in the host society", *International Migration* 61, no. 2 (2023): 283–296, https://doi.org/10.1111/imig.13009; Giulia Marchetti, Loretta Baldassar, Anita Harris and Shanthi Robertson, "Sideways moves to adult life: The transnational mobility and transitions of young Italians to Australia", *Journal of Ethnic and Migration Studies* (2022), https://doi.org/10.1080/1369183X. 2022.2145275; Giulia Marchetti, *Becoming adults elsewhere: The recent migration of young Italians to Australia*, unpublished PhD thesis (Perth: The University of Western Australia, 2022); Michele Grigoletti, "Detenzione ed espulsione di cittadini italiani illegalmente in Australia", in *Rapporto Italiani nel Mondo 2018*, ed. D. Licata (Todi: Tau Editrice/ Fondazione Migrantes, 2018), 117–125.

[44] John J. Kinder, Alessia Dipalma and Marinella Caruso, "Migration old and new: Perceptions of/in Italian communities in Australia", *Studi Emigrazione* 54, no. 207 (2017): 471–472.

[45] Robert Pascoe and Caterina Cafarella, "The latest wave of Italians in Australia", *Altreitalie* 59 (2019): 116.

and regarded themselves more as global citizens than migrants.[46] Unlike their predecessors, though, they relied heavily on internet technologies for migratory, communication, and socialising purposes.[47] Yet, they ought not to be viewed as a uniform group. Borrowing Deleuzo-Guattarian terminology, Pascoe and Cafarella identified in their study of the *globalisti*, for example, a division "between *striated* and *smooth*", that is between "those who see a continuation of their academic and professional careers in Australia, and those who see in the new country an uncomfortable reminder of the divisions in Italy which they grew up".[48]

The Pandemic Intermezzo

When first emerged, the Covid-19 health emergency impacted international travel and migration flows in a swift and dramatic fashion. In the first half of 2020, Italian authorities, as elsewhere in Europe and beyond, enacted strict border closure policies to contain the spread of the novel strain of coronavirus, which significantly disrupted or halted, albeit temporarily, both international and inter-regional travel. Mobility data show that immigration to Italy almost halved in the initial months of the pandemic, when compared with the average of the previous five years. Similarly, border closures had altered emigration mobility from Italy as well. In the first six months of 2020, less Italians moved abroad, when compared with the average of the 2015–19 period. Additionally, at the start of the pandemic, Italy's Ministry of Foreign Affairs and International Cooperation (MAECI) repatriated Italians in the excess of 110.000, chiefly tourists who found themselves stranded abroad. However, tourists were not the only ones caught up in the international mobility commotion. The General Committee of Italians Abroad (CGIE) estimated that as many as 100.000 Italian expatriates moved back to Italy by the end of 2020 alone because of the pandemic. It is speculated that Italian students

---

[46] Pascoe and Cafarella, "The latest wave of Italians in Australia", 102; Baldassar, Pyke and Ben-Moshe, *The Italian Diaspora in Australia*, 7.

[47] Pascoe and Cafarella, "The latest wave of Italians in Australia", 104–106; Catherine Davis, "The role of social media: 'New Italian migrants' on Facebook groups", in *Australia's new wave of Italian migration: Paradise or illusion?*, eds. B. Mascitelli and R. Armillei (North Melbourne: Australia Scholarly Publishing, 2017): 136–161.

[48] Robert Pascoe and Caterina Cafarella, "The Latest Wave of Italians in Australia", *Altreitalie* 59 (2019): 106.

abroad, along with Italian workers not covered locally by wage subsidies or welfare assistance, and those with no adequate health insurance, were more likely to return to Italy, on a temporary or permanent basis, due to the pandemic emergency.[49]

In Australia, state and federal government authorities alike adopted travel restriction policies that severely limited mobility. Not only did they impede travel between, and in some instances within, States and Territories, but also internationally. By late March 2020, air passenger traffic to and from Australia was brought to a virtual halt. Border closures impacted residents and travellers in different ways. Some Italian travellers scrambled to return to Italy at the start of the pandemic, while others postponed their departure to a later date. Italian Embassy in Canberra data reveal that in the March–April 2020 period, 3,450 Italian nationals received consular assistance, while 2,561 were repatriated.[50] By the year's end, the overall number of those repatriated grew to several thousands. Overseas arrivals and departures data indicate in over 5.800 the number of Italians repatriated from 1 April to 31 December 2020, the majority of whom (95%) were holders of a temporary visa; permanent and dual citizens constituting the remaining 5%.[51]

The prolonged travel restrictions, which lasted almost two years, affected one category of residents above all others: temporary visa holders. Among them, Working Holiday Makers (WHMs) represented a significant share. A decade after Italy formally joined Australia's WHM Program, the number of working-holiday visas granted to Italian citizens peaked in the financial year of 2013/2014, with just over 16,000 permits issued to young Italians, one-fifth of which had applied for a second WHM visa, having undertaken three months of work in regional Australia during their stay, in the agriculture, mining or construction

---

[49] Corrado Bonifazi, Cinzia Conti, Antonio Sanguinetti and Salvatore Strozza, "La pandemia di Covid-19 e le migrazioni internazionali in Italia", *Studi Emigrazione* 58, no. 221 (2021): 46; Rodolfo Ricci, "Pandemia e riflessività dei movimenti migratori. Italiani all'estero e immigrati in Italia", *Studi Emigrazione* 58, no. 221 (2021): 58.

[50] Marco Fedi, "Gli italiani e il welfare australiano durante la crisi", in *Il mondo si allontana? Il COVID-19 e le nuove migrazioni italiane*, eds. M. Tirabassi and A. Del Pra' (Torino: Accademia University Press, 2020), 129.

[51] Michele Grigoletti and Silvia Pianelli, "Sidney. Creatività pandemica nella 'prigione più bella del mondo'", in *Rapporto Italiani nel Mondo 2021*, ed. D. Licata (Todi: Tau Editrice/Fondazione Migrantes, 2021), 487.

industries—the notorious "88 days".[52] Since then, the annual number of visa applications (and accordingly visa granted) has been steadily declined in line with the overall downward trend for this visa category.[53] In 2017/ 2018, the number of WHM visas granted to Italians was about one-third less than the number recorded four years before. This downward trajectory was temporarily reversed the following year, which recorded a marginal increase; an upward trend shared by the cohort of Italian temporary (skilled) visa holders whose numbers moved sensibly up from the previous year. Such modest increases were short-lived. Data show the number of Italian working holiday makers, skilled workers, and students nosedived between 2019/2020 and 2020/2021 due to the pandemic disruption. As border restrictions were lifted and international travel resumed, 2021/22 figures indicate a growing presence of Italian WHM visa holders, followed by a gradual increase of Italian students and temporary (skilled) workers and their dependants (see Fig. 3.3).

Temporary visa holders who willy-nilly remained in Australia during the pandemic intermezzo faced the daunting prospect of being unable to travel interstate and enduring lengthy lockdowns. Crucially, they faced limited or no access to health services, wage subsidies, and welfare assistance in a fast-deteriorating employment situation. Support programmes sponsored by state and territory governments notwithstanding, the Australian federal government categorically "excluded international students and other temporary migrants from the JobKeeper and JobSeeker support packages", which were designed to support permanent residents and citizens who had lost work because of pandemic restrictions.[54] To Australian federal authorities, temporary residents, who were to experience increased social isolation and exclusion from vital

---

[52] Michele Grigoletti and Silvia Pianelli, eds., *Giovani italiani in Australia. Un "viaggio" da temporaneo a permanente* (Todi: Tau editrice/Fondazione Migrantes, 2016), 48–95.

[53] Possible causes for the declining popularity of this type of visa include extended media coverage in Italy of instances of working-holiday makers' exploitation and visa abuses, a growing difficulty in obtaining permanent residency, and an increased cost of living. See Canini, "Recent Italian immigration to Australia", 224–226; Armillei and Mascitelli, "From 2004 to 2016: A new Italian 'exodus/ to Australia?", 24.

[54] Laurie Berg and Bassina Farbenblum, *As if we weren't humans: The abandonment of temporary migrants in Australia during COVID-19* (MWJI, 2020), 11; Andy Symington, "Migrant workers and the COVID-19 crisis in Australia: An overview of governmental responses", *Australian Journal of Human Rights* 26, no. 3 (2021): 507–519.

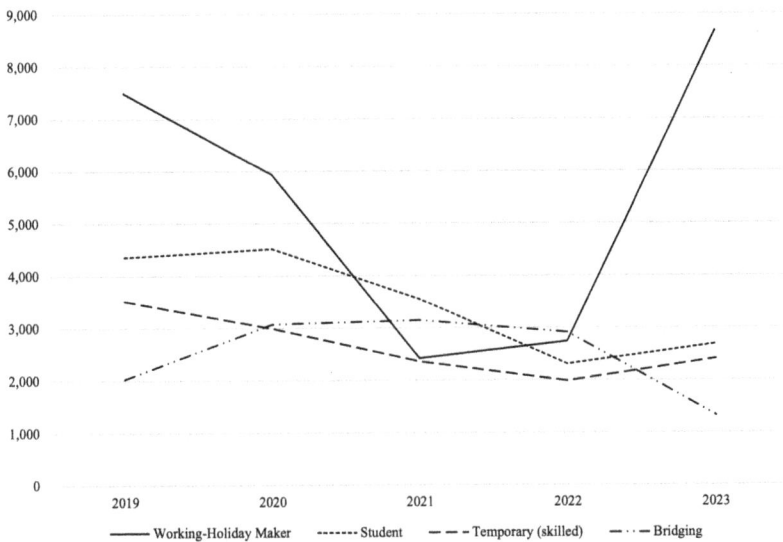

Fig. 3.3 Number of Italian visa holders present in Australia, selected categories (*Note* Annual figures from 2019 to 2022 refer to 30 June; for 2023, figures refer to 31 January. Primary and secondary applicants included; visa holders by country of citizenship, not country of birth. *Source* Author's own calculations based on data from Department of Home Affairs, BP0019 Number of Temporary visa holders in Australia, https://data.gov.au/)

supporting networks and services, remained purposely "invisible".[55] Paradoxically, temporary migrants concentrated in the very industries the economic shutdown had impacted heavily, and their exclusion from policies such as JobKeeper intensified the migrants' insecurities, making ever more evident the effect of "the Australian state's neoliberal immigration policy" and its long-standing "exclusionary approach".[56] JobKeeper, in

---

[55] NOMIT, "Gli invisibili in Australia", in *Il mondo si allontana? Il COVID-19 e le nuove migrazioni italiane*, eds. M. Tirabassi and A. Del Pra' (Torino: Accademia University Press, 2020), 139; Olivera Simic, "Locked in and locked out: A migrant woman's reflection on life in Australia during the COVID-19 pandemic", *Journal of International Women's Studies* 22, no. 9 (2021): 400–426.

[56] Chris F. Wright and Stephen Clibborn, "COVID-19 and the policy-induced vulnerability of temporary migrant workers in Australia", *Journal of Australian Political Economy* 85 (2020): 64, 68.

particular, increased "the dualization of the Australian labour market" between eligible and non-eligible workers and institutionalised "lay-offs inequities for workers holding a temporary visa".[57] As the Covid-19 containment policies isolated Australia even further from the rest of the world, not only were structural inequalities strengthened, but xenophobic and anti-immigrant sentiments, especially towards the Asian background population, also flared up.[58]

Many Italian newcomers faced the thorny dilemma of whether to stay or return to Italy, possibly for good. The Melbourne-based collective NOMIT well captured such dilemma as follows:

> [...] little was said of the many who have chosen not to [return to Italy], perhaps because they did not feel up to it, to abandon loved ones without knowing if they would have had the opportunity to return [to Australia]. Others [did not return to Italy] because they have fought for years to find their own place in the new adopted society and have tried to resist, often without any kind of help. Many have suffered, torn between the need to return to stay close to loved ones in Italy, or stay alongside a newly built family abroad. There are so many stories like these.[59]

Without a suitable supporting network, or a solid occupational situation, temporary visa holders found themselves among the most vulnerable during the pandemic. This extraordinarily challenging situation translated into an increase of calls for mental health support. For instance, the Italian Consulate General of Sydney, which activated for about three months a helpdesk and a dedicated phone line for Italian nationals in need, pointed out that psychological support, especially for young nationals, was one of

---

[57] Emmanuelle Walkowiak, "JobKeeper: The Australian short-time work program", *Australian Journal of Public Administration* 80, no. 4 (2021): 1046–1053.

[58] Antonella Biscaro and Vivian Gerrand, "La 'Fortezza Australia' e la crisi di Covid-19'", in *Dossier Statistico Immigrazione 2021*, ed. Centro di Studi e Ricerche IDOS (Roma: IDOS, 2021), 86; Francesco Ricatti, "Migrazione e pandemia in Australia", *Studi Emigrazione* 58, no. 221 (2021): 107–113; Francesco Ricatti, "Migrazione, lavoro e pandemia: alcune riflessioni dall'Australia", in *Migranti, Covid, Mercato del Lavoro 2020–2021: tra paura e speranza*, eds. L. Prencipe and M. Sanfilippo (Roma: CSER), 111–118; Sylvia Ang and Fethi Mansouri, "Racialized (im)mobilities: The pandemic and sinophobia in Australia", *Journal of Intercultural Studies* 44, no. 2 (2023): 160179.

[59] NOMIT, "Quello che gli emigranti non dicono. Riflessioni per cambiare il racconto della diaspora italiani negli anni 2000", *Altreitalie* 62 (2021): 102. Note: Author's own translation from Italian to English.

the most requested services at the time. In the Sydney area again, but possibly elsewhere too, Italian-speaking psychologists were particularly sought after. The emotional and psychological toll of forced separation from loved ones did not only affect Italian nationals on temporary visas. It also impacted Italians with permanent residency permits or dual citizens too, some of whom contemplated or actively prepared a return to Italy, not to mention the wider population.[60]

The situation could have been direr, for some at least, if community-led or corporate-led initiatives that aimed to offset the lack of government assistance were not quick to respond. This has been the case, among others, of the Italo-Australian Welfare and Cultural Centre and Bendigo Bank in the Perth area, which offered temporary accommodation, food stamps, and emergency relief, or the case of the CO.AS.IT agency of Sydney, which offered psychological services online for Australians of Italian background as well as Italians with a permanent or temporary visa, or still the "Lampo" initiative (lit. flash) by NOMIT. Albeit localised and relatively small in scale, Lampo offered as much a financial lifeline as an emotional one. It provided an emergency payment of $100 to those directly affected by the pandemic and deemed most in need amid the loose group of *temporanei* (temporary visa holders). Funds were generously supplied by the Italian-Australian community through a Radiothon initiative that took place on Easter Monday 2020, in collaboration with *Rete Italia* and the Padre Anastasio Gonelli Charitable Foundation, which collected over $100,000 in cash, plus a grant-in-aid of $20,000 by the CO.AS.IT agency of Melbourne.[61]

Along with the $100 payment relief, NOMIT provided a telephone line for information and support, with the goal of breaking social isolation created by the pandemic and the Covid-19 containment policies. "Lampo" was followed by "Mano" (lit. hand), a mutual aid and micro-credit initiative, again by NOMIT. Mano provided individuals with a one-off payment of $500. Recipients were not charged interests. Recipients were not even obliged to refund the collective. Instead, they were encouraged to return the funds back if and when their financial situation

---

[60] Grigoletti and Pianelli, "Sidney", 493, 496.

[61] Loretta Baldassar and Giulia Marchetti, "Perth. L'impatto del Covid-19 sui giovani italiani immigrati", in *Rapporto Italiani nel Mondo 2021*, ed., D. Licata (Todi: Tau Editrice/Fondazione Migrantes, 2021), 470–478; NOMIT, "Gli invisibili in Australia", 140; Grigoletti and Pianelli, "Sidney", 492–493.

improved. In doing so, they allowed others in need to tap into the funds, according to the principle of sharing resources, or *di mano in mano* (from one to another) as NOMIT put it. By mid-June 2020, over 200 people were assisted, and 165 Lampo and 42 Mano payments were disbursed.[62]

The health emergency had somewhat galvanised different components of the Italian-background community to act together or in solidarity with other organisations[63] stimulating intracommunal cohesion and renewed grassroots activism. The pandemic experience resonated well beyond those on non-permanent visas. One example is offered by the collective Ascolta Women; a group of women "of creative, multigenerational, Italian Australian, and Italian affiliated" background that had formed at the start of the pandemic period and found ways to break the forced isolation by meeting periodically online from such diverse places as Melbourne, Mildura, Wollongong, Adelaide, and London. The collective chronicled the lived experience of its members, some of which later populated the *Stories from the inside* collection, acknowledging that for many of its members the pandemic reminded them of "the legacy inherited from a period in world history when people's lives were in upheaval, mobility alternatively forced and constrained, enforced seclusion and separation of families, and the longing and desiring of *home*".[64]

Others went through a deep introspective and reflective phase, and used different devices to express confusion, insecurity and stress, triggered by the pandemic and prolonged lockdowns. Examples can be found in Claudia Diamante and Alice Simonetti-Morrison, who conveyed their emotions on artistic expressions and diary entries, which in turn helped them regaining self-esteem and a feeling of happiness. For Michele Grigoletti and Silvia Pianelli, the forced isolation situations experienced during the pandemic strikingly resembled the liminal experience faced by many young Italian backpackers during the "88 days" period of

---

[62] See the case of the "digital union" Hospo Voice in the hospitality sector in NOMIT, "Gli invisibili in Australia", 139–140.

[63] Luca M. Esposito, Enrico Moscon, and Fabrizio Venturini, "Melbourne. Tutti nella stessa tempesta ma non sulla stessa barca", in *Rapporto Italiani nel Mondo*, ed. D. Licata (Todi: Tau Editrice/Fondazione Migrantes, 2021), 400–401; Silvana D'Intino, "Mi sposto come posso tra due emisferi", in *Il mondo si allontana? Il COVID-19 e le nuove migrazioni italiane*, eds. M. Tirabassi and A. Del Pra' (Torino: Accademia University Press, 2020), 147, 149.

[64] Ascolta Women, ed., *Stories from the inside* (Melbourne: Minuteman Press, 2021), 1, 3, emphasis in the original.

work in regional or remote Australia, a "rite of passage" from which some emerged stronger and better aware of their own abilities and potential—the pandemic may have acted in a similar fashion.[65]

CONCLUSION

Recent population statistics regarding the Italian presence in Australia offer useful insights into the demographic trends of different components of this established community, including the Italian-born (first generation), the Australian-born with at least one Italian-born parent (second generation), the home speakers of Italian, and the Italian citizens. They point to signs of both decline and growth. If the overall cohort of the Italian-born is projected to diminish and age further in the incoming decades, the impact of recent arrivals from Italy has generated a modest yet noteworthy contribution in terms of settlers, especially among the under 45s. Newcomers may have softened the ongoing decline of the Italian-born, while increasing the share of residents in the prime working age groups. The second-generation cohort, which has arguably plateaued around one third of a million in this century, has recently shown signs of vitality, which may also be attributed, in part, to recent arrivals from Italy. Conversely, the number of home speakers of Italian continues to drop, reflecting the ongoing declining trend of the original migrant population. Yet, Italian is flourishing in the education sector suggesting a vitality that goes beyond the core of native speakers.[66] One variable that captures further the Italian presence in Australia, besides place of birth (or place of birth of parent/s) and language spoken at home, is foreign citizenship. Thanks to Italy's politics of inclusion of emigrants and their descendants, the community of Italian citizens in Australia has grown rapidly since the start of the century. By being the recipient of a complex diaspora infrastructure, this community plays a critical intermediary role between the broad Italian-background community and Italian authorities and institutions.

---

[65] Grigoletti and Pianelli, "Sidney", 497–498.

[66] Cristiana Palmieri, "Connecting Australia and Italy through language", in *Italy and Australia: redefining bilateral relations for the twenty-first century*, eds. Gabriele Abbondanza and Simone Battiston (London: Palgrave Macmillan, 2024), pp. 137–154.

The Italian presence in Australia in the twenty-first century cannot be comprehensively understood, however, if temporary migration statistics are not considered. The relatively high volume of Italians coming to Australia since the early 2000 has initially suggested a revival of post-war emigration flows. Unlike the arrivals from Italy experienced in the 1950s and 1960s, the latest wave has been made up overwhelmingly by *temporanei* (holders of a temporary or long-term visa) that has generated a limited gain for Australia in terms of settlers. The inclusion of Italy in the Working Holiday Maker programme has certainly played a leading role in expanding the cohort of temporary visa holders throughout the 2010s. Yet, the growing presence of Italian working-holiday makers, as well as students and skilled workers, needs to be viewed against the broader contemporary migration context and the post-Fordist era, which has encouraged greater levels of mobility but equally of temporariness and job insecurity. In addition, recent expressions of mobility should not be viewed as separate from the historic settlement of post-war migrants from Italy, but as the latest manifestation of the long-standing relationship between Italy and Australia.[67] Linkages largely forged by the historic migration waves of the post-war period have created a "... corridor which has been activated several generations later by temporary skilled migrants" from Italy.[68] Moving beyond statistical considerations and the temporary/permanent character, the growing literature on the latest wave of Italian migration is focused on the qualitative, rather than quantitative, traits of Italian newcomers, uncovering similarities and differences within this cohort and with past generations of migrants.

The pandemic has halted one defining feature of the *globalisti* generation, as Pascoe and Cafarella defined the latest wave of Italian migration: mobility. Due to prolonged travel restriction policies and lockdown measures, temporary visa holders found themselves unable to travel or work as before. If thousands of *globalisti* left Australia in the first year of the pandemic, those who remained faced the daunting prospect of living throughout the pandemic years with limited or no access to health

---

[67] Gabriele Abbondanza and Simone Battiston, "Italy and Australia in the twenty-first century: distant connections or close partners?", in *Italy and Australia: redefining bilateral relations for the twenty-first century*, eds. Gabriele Abbondanza and Simone Battiston (London: Palgrave Macmillan, 2024), pp. 1–23.

[68] Graeme Hugo, "From permanent settlement to transnationalism", 108.

services, wage subsidies, and welfare assistance. Unlike Australian permanent residents or citizens, temporary visa holders remained excluded from vital supporting services, enhancing their vulnerable position in the host society. This extraordinarily challenging situation translated into an increase of calls for assistance, including mental health support. It also impacted Italians with permanent residency permits or dual citizens, some of whom contemplated or actively prepared a return to Italy. Yet, the pandemic had somewhat galvanised different components of the Italian-background community to act together or in solidarity with other organisations stimulating intracommunal cohesion and renewed grassroots activism. Several community or corporate-led initiatives, along with aid provided by local consular authorities, sought to compensate the lack of government assistance and support temporary visa holders in dire straits. As Australia's borders reopened to fully vaccinated international travellers in February 2022, after almost two years of forced closure, the latest migration data suggest that the number of Italian temporary visa holders is once again increasing, potentially in a manner not dissimilar to what occurred around the mid-2000s.

References

Abbondanza, Gabriele and Simone Battiston. "Italy and Australia in the twenty-first century: Distant connections or close partners?" In *Italy and Australia: Redefining bilateral relations for the twenty-first century*, edited by Gabriele Abbondanza and Simone Battiston, pp. 1–23. London: Palgrave Macmillan, 2024.

Allen, Liz. "Understanding ethnicity in contemporary Australia using the census". *Australian Population Studies* 5, no. 1 (2021): 56–64.

Ang, Sylvia and Fethi Mansouri. "Racialized (im)mobilities: The pandemic and sinophobia in Australia". *Journal of Intercultural Studies* 44, no. 2 (2023): 160–179.

Armillei, Riccardo. "A statistical analysis of the 'new Italian migration' to Australia: Redressing recent overstatements". In *Australia's new wave of Italian migration: Paradise or illusion?* edited by B. Mascitelli and R. Armillei, 53–78. North Melbourne: Australian Scholarly Publishing, 2017.

Armillei, Riccardo and Bruno Mascitelli. *From 2004 to 2016: A new Italian 'exodus' to Australia?* Melbourne: Comites Victoria & Tasmania, 2016.

Ascolta Women, ed. *Stories from the inside*. Melbourne: Minuteman Press, 2021.

Australian Bureau of Statistics, "Understanding and using ancestry data", 28 June 2022, https://www.abs.gov.au/statistics/detailed-methodology-inform ation/information-papers/understanding-and-using-ancestry-data.

Australian Bureau of Statistics, "Cultural diversity of Australia", 20 September 2022, https://www.abs.gov.au/articles/cultural-diversity-australia.

Baggio, Fabio and Matteo Sanfilippo. "L'emigrazione italiana in Australia". *Studi Emigrazione* 48, no. 183 (2011): 477–499.

Baldassar, Loretta. "Italian migrants in Australia and their relationship to Italy: Return visits, transnational caregiving and the second generation". *Journal of Mediterranean Studies* 20, no. 2 (2011): 255–282.

Baldassar, Loretta. "Transnational families and aged care: The mobility of care and the migrancy of ageing". *Journal of Ethnic and Migration Studies* 33, no. 2 (2007): 275–297.

Baldassar, Loretta and Giulia Marchetti. "Perth. L'impatto del Covid-19 sui giovani italiani immigrati." In *Rapporto Italiani nel Mondo 2021*, edited by D. Licata, 470–478. Todi: Tau Editrice/Fondazione Migrantes, 2021.

Baldassar, Loretta, Joanne Pyke, and Danny Ben-Moshe, *The Italian diaspora in Australia: Current and potential links to the homeland*. Burwood: Deakin University, 2012.

Baldassar, Loretta and Joanne Pyke. "Intra-diaspora knowledge transfer and 'new' Italian migration". *International Migration* 52, no. 4 (2014): 128–143.

Battiston, Simone. "Il voto degli italiani in Australia fra continuità e segnali di cambiamento". In *Autopsia di un diritto politico. Il voto degli italiani all'estero nelle elezioni del 2018*, edited by S. Battiston and S. Luconi, 145–161. Turin: Accademia University Press, 2018.

Beckett, Andy. "The age of perpetual crisis: How the 2010s disrupted everything but resolved nothing". *The Guardian*, 17 December 2019.

Berg, Laurie and Bassina Farbenblum. *As if we weren't humans: The abandonment of temporary migrants in Australia during COVID-19*. MWJI, 2020.

Berti, Fabio and Marco Alberio. "Italiani che lasciano l'Italia. Le nuove emigrazioni tra continuità e cambiamenti". In *Italiani che lasciano l'Italia. Le nuove emigrazioni al tempo della crisi*, edited by M. Alberio and F. Berti, 7–29. Milano: Mimesis, 2020.

Bilotta, Alessandro, Michele Grigoletti, and Silvia Pianelli. "Nuovi emigrati italiani e nuovi cittadini australiani". In *Rapporto Italiani nel Mondo 2015*, edited by D. Licata, 135–145. Todi: Tau Editrice/Fondazione Migrantes, 2015.

Biscaro, Antonella and Vivian Gerrand. "La 'Fortezza Australia' e la crisi di Covid-19'". In *Dossier Statistico Immigrazione 2021*, edited by Centro di Studi e Ricerche IDOS, 84–89. Roma: IDOS, 2021.

Bonifazi, Corrado, Cinzia Conti, Antonio Sanguinetti, and Salvatore Strozza. "La pandemia di Covid-19 e le migrazioni internazionali in Italia". *Studi Emigrazione* 58, no. 221 (2021): 41–55.

Brown, Greg. "Political bigamy? Dual citizenship in Australia's migrant communities". *People and Place* 10, no. 1 (2002): 71–77.

Bruzzone, Silvia and Francesca Licari. "Le iscrizioni e cancellazioni anagrafiche degli italiani da e per l'estero: aspetti demografici e caratteristiche della mobilità". In *Rapporto Italiani nel Mondo 2021*, edited by D. Licata, 24–40. Todi: Tau Editrice/Fondazione Migrantes, 2021.

Caldarini, Carlo. "Diaspora policies, consular services and social protection for Italian citizens abroad". In *Migration and social protection in Europe and beyond (Volume 2): Comparing consular services and diaspora policies*, edited by J.-M. Lafleur and D. Vintila, 273–288. Cham: IMISCOE Research Series/Springer, 2020).

Campbell, Iain, Maria Azzurra Tranfaglia, Joo-Cheong Tham and Martina Boese. "Precarious work and the reluctance to complain: Italian temporary migrant workers in Australia". *Labour and Industry: A Journal of the Social and Economic Relations of Work* 29, no. 1 (2019): 98–117.

Caneva, Elena. "La nuova emigrazione italiana: cosa ne sappiamo, come ne parliamo". *Cambio* 6, no. 11 (2016): 195–207.

Canini, Emanuela. "Recent Italian immigration to Australia: The view of the migration agent". In *Australia's new wave of Italian migration: Paradise or illusion?* edited by B. Mascitelli and R. Armillei, 218–248. North Melbourne: Australia Scholarly Publishing, 2017.

Canini, Emanuela. "Long-term temporary migration: Evolution of a new reality in modern Australian society". *Altreitalie* 59 (2019): 118–130.

Castles, Stephen, Caroline Alcorso, Gaetano Rando, and Ellie Vasta. *Australia's Italians: Culture and community in a changing society*. St. Leonards, NSW: Allen & Unwin, 1992.

Castles, Stephen. "Italians in Australia: The impact of recent migration on the culture and society of a postcolonial nation". *Center for Migration Studies special issues* 11, no. 3 (1994): 342–367.

Cavallaro, Francesco. "Italians in Australia: Migration and profile". *Altreitalie* 26 (2003): 65–90.

Cook-Martín, David. *The scramble for citizens: Dual nationality and state competition for immigrants*. Standford: Standford University Press, 2013.

Cresciani, Gianfranco. *The Italians in Australia*. Cambridge, UK: Cambridge University Press, 2003.

Cuervo, Hernán, Mauro Giardiello, Babak Dadvand and Rosa Capobianco, *Mobility and belonging: A study of Italian youth diaspora in Australia*. Melbourne: Youth Research Centre, University of Melbourne, 2019.

Davis, Catherine. "The role of social media: 'New Italian migrants' on Facebook groups". In *Australia's new wave of Italian migration: Paradise or illusion?* edited by B. Mascitelli and R. Armillei, 136–161. North Melbourne: Australia Scholarly Publishing, 2017.

D'Intino, Silvana. "Mi sposto come posso tra due emisferi". In *Il mondo si allon-tana? Il COVID-19 e le nuove migrazioni italiane*, edited by M. Tirabassi and A. Del Pra', 145–150. Torino: Accademia University Press, 2020.

Esposito, Luca M., Enrico Moscon and Fabrizio Venturini. "Melbourne. Tutti nella stessa tempesta ma non sulla stessa barca". In *Rapporto Italiani nel Mondo 2021*, edited by D. Licata, 396–405. Todi: Tau Editrice/Fondazione Migrantes, 2021.

Fedi, Marco. "Gli italiani e il welfare australiano durante la crisi". In *Il mondo si allontana? Il COVID-19 e le nuove migrazioni italiane*, edited by M. Tirabassi and A. Del Pra', 127–135. Torino: Accademia University Press, 2020.

Fumagalli, Luna, Michele Grigoletti, and Silvia Pianelli. "Dalle spiagge di Sydney alla campagna di Griffith. I quartieri della nuova migrazione italiana". In *Rapporto Italiani nel Mondo 2016*, edited by D. Licata (Todi: Tau Editrice/Fondazione Migrantes, 2016), 399–407.

Giardiello, Mauro, Hernan Cuervo and Rosa Capobianco. "A study of Italian young adults' transnational mobility to Australia: The reproduction of unequal trajectories in the host society". *International Migration* 61, no. 2 (2023): 283–296.

Grigoletti, Michele. *Dal Rio Grande do Sul (Brasile) al Nuovo Galles del Sud (Australia): movimento migratorio, presenza e caratteristiche dei giovani italo-brasiliani in Australia.* In *Rapporto Italiani nel Mondo 2019*, edited by D. Licata, 130–139. Todi: Tau Editrice/Fondazione Migrantes, 2019.

Grigoletti, Michele. "Detenzione ed espulsione di cittadini italiani illegalmente in Australia". In *Rapporto Italiani nel Mondo 2018*, edited by D. Licata, 117–125. Todi: Tau Editrice/Fondazione Migrantes, 2018.

Grigoletti, Michele, Silvia Pianelli and Giordano Dalla Bernardina. "L'emi-grazione di giovani italiani in Australia". In *Rapporto Italiani nel Mondo 2014*, edited by D. Licata, 215–226. Todi: Tau Editrice/Fondazione Migrantes, 2014.

Grigoletti, Michele and Silvia Pianelli. "Sidney. Creatività pandemica nella 'pri-gione più bella del mondo'". In *Rapporto Italiani nel Mondo 2021*, edited by D. Licata, 487–498. Todi: Tau Editrice/Fondazione Migrantes, 2021.

Grigoletti, Michele and Silvia Pianelli, eds. *Giovani italiani in Australia. Un "viaggio" da temporaneo a permanente.* Todi: Tau Editrice/Fondazione Migrantes, 2016.

Grigoletti, Michele and Veronica Olivetto. "Giovani italiani in Australia: moderni percorsi di emigrazione, di formazione e selezione professionale". In *Rapporto Italiani nel Mondo 2018*, edited by D. Licata, 249–259. Todi: Tau Editrice/Fondazione Migrantes, 2018.

Hajek, John, Renata Aliani and Yvette Slaughter. "From the periphery to center stage: The mainstreaming of Italian in the Australian education system (1960s to 1990s)". *History of Education Quarterly* 62, no. 4 (2022): 475–497.

Horn, Robert V. "The validity of Australian ancestry statistics". *Journal of the Australian Population Association* 10, no. 2 (1993): 119–126.

Horn, Robert V. "Ethnic origin in the Australian census". *Journal of the Australian Population Association* 4, no. 1 (1987): 1–12.

Hugo, Graeme. "From permanent settlement to transnationalism—Contemporary population movement between Italy and Australia: Trends and implications". *International Migration* 52, no. 4 (2014): 92–111.

Khoo, Siew-Ean, Peter Mcdonald, Dimi Giorgas and Bob Birrell, *Second Generation Australians* (Canberra: Department of Immigration and Multicultural and Indigenous Affairs, 2002).

Kinder, John J., Alessia Dipalma and Marinella Caruso. "Migration old and new: Perceptions of/in Italian communities in Australia". *Studi Emigrazione* 54, no. 207 (2017): 467–476.

Lafleur, Jean-Michel and Daniela Vintila. "Do EU member states care about their diasporas' access to social protection? A comparison of consular and diaspora policies across EU27". In *Migration and social protection in Europe and beyond (Volume 2): Comparing consular services and diaspora policies*, edited by J.-M. Lafleur and D. Vintila, 1–31. Cham: IMISCOE Research Series/Springer, 2020.

Licata, Delfina. "Gli italiani nel mondo. Una comunità sempre più interculturale e transnazionale". In *Rapporto Italiani nel Mondo 2022*, edited by D. Licata, 3–14. Todi: Tau Editrice/Fondazione Migrantes, 2022.

Licata, Delfina. "Da tradizione storica a fatto strutturale: la presenza italiana all'estero dal 2006 al 2020". In *Rapporto Italiani nel Mondo 2020*, edited by D. Licata, 3–17. Todi: Tau/Fondazione Migrantes, 2020.

Lo Bianco, Joseph. "Italian in Australia: Society, education and future planning". In *L'italiano in Australia. Prospettive e tendenze nell'insegnamento della lingua e della cultura / Italian in Australia: Perspectives and trends in the teaching of language and Culture*, edited by A. Rubino, A. R. Tamponi and J. Hajek, 27–45. Firenze: Franco Cesati Editore, 2021.

Luconi, Stefano. "I paradigmi recenti dell'emigrazione italiana e il caso australiano". *Studi Emigrazione* 46, no. 176 (2009): 793–816.

Marchetti, Giulia and Loretta Baldassar. "Australians in Italy in the twenty-first century". In *Italy and Australia: Redefining bilateral relations for the twenty-first century*, edited by Gabriele Abbondanza and Simone Battiston, pp. 81–111. London: Palgrave Macmillan, 2024.

Marchetti, Giulia, Loretta Baldassar, Anita Harris and Shanthi Robertson. "Sideways moves to adult life: The transnational mobility and transitions of young Italians to Australia". *Journal of Ethnic and Migration Studies* (2022), https://doi.org/10.1080/1369183X.2022.2145275.

Marchetti, Giulia. *Becoming adults elsewhere: The recent migration of young Italians to Australia*, unpublished PhD thesis. Perth: The University of Western Australia, 2022.

Mares, Peter. "Putting the new wave of Italian migration to Australia in context". *Studi Emigrazione* 54, no. 207 (2017): 477–484.

Mares, Peter. "Australia's permanent shift to temporary migration". In *Australia's new wave of Italian migration: Paradise or illusion?* edited by B. Mascitelli and R. Armillei, 110–135. North Melbourne: Australia Scholarly Publishing, 2017.

NOMIT. "Quello che gli emigranti non dicono. Riflessioni per cambiare il racconto della diaspora italiani negli anni 2000". *Altreitalie* 62 (2021): 85–112.

NOMIT. "Gli invisibili in Australia". In *Il mondo si allontana? Il COVID-19 e le nuove migrazioni italiane*, edited by M. Tirabassi and A. Del Pra', 137–143. Torino: Accademia University Press, 2020.

Palmieri, Cristiana. "Connecting Australia and Italy through language". In *Italy and Australia: redefining bilateral relations for the twenty-first century*, edited by Gabriele Abbondanza and Simone Battiston, pp. 137–154. London: Palgrave Macmillan, 2024.

Pascoe, Robert. *Buongiorno Australia: Our Italian heritage*. Richmond, VIC: Greenhouse Publication, 1987.

Pascoe, Robert and Caterina Cafarella. "The latest wave of Italians in Australia". *Altreitalie* 59 (2019): 101–117.

Pretelli, Matteo. "Gli italiani in Australia: lo stato dei lavori". *Studi Emigrazione* 46, no. 176 (2009): 779–792.

Praino, Rodrigo and Vinicius Guedes Gonçalves de Oliveira. "La rappresentanza degli italiani in Australia: l'efficacia della rappresentanza su un territorio vasto e poliforme", in *Rapporto Italiani nel Mondo 2022*, edited by D. Licata, 231–239. Todi: Tau Editrice/Fondazione Migrantes, 2022.

Prodi, Maria Chiara. "AIRE e nuova mobilità: il dover dare notizia di sé". In *Rapporto Italiani nel Mondo 2018*, edited D. Licata, 170–179. Todi: Tau Editrice/Fondazione Migrantes, 2018.

Productivity Commission. *Migrant Intake into Australia*, Inquiry Report No. 77. Canberra: Commonwealth of Australia, 2016.

Pugliese, Enrico. *Quelli che se ne vanno. La nuova emigrazione italiana*. Bologna: Il Mulino, 2018.

Ricatti, Francesco. *Italians in Australia: History, memory, identity*. Cham, Switzerland: Palgrave Macmillan, 2018.

Ricatti, Francesco. "Migrazione e pandemia in Australia". *Studi Emigrazione* 58, no. 221 (2021): 107–113.

Ricatti, Francesco. "Migrazione, lavoro e pandemia: alcune riflessioni dall'Australia". In *Migranti, Covid, Mercato del Lavoro 2020–2021: tra paura e speranza*, edited by L. Prencipe and M. Sanfilippo, 111–118. Roma: CSER, 2022.

Ricci, Rodolfo. "Pandemia e riflessività dei movimenti migratori. Italiani all'estero e immigrati in Italia". *Studi Emigrazione* 58, no. 221 (2021): 57–68.

Russo, Daniele and Susanna Thomas. "Le pensioni pagate all'estero e dall'estero come effetto delle migrazioni". In *Rapporto Italiani nel Mondo 2020*, edited by D. Licata, 62–73. Todi: Tau Editrice/Fondazione Migrantes, 2020.

Sampugnaro, Rossana. "La rappresentanza parlamentare degli italiani all'estero tra vecchie e nuove *issues*. Due legislature a confronto". In *Cittadini oltre confine. Storia, opinioni e rappresentanza degli italiani all'estero*, edited by S. Battiston, S. Luconi, and M. Valbruzzi, 225–256. Bologna: Il Mulino, 2022.

Sampugnaro, Rossana. "The Italian foreign constituency and its MPs". *Contemporary Italian Politics* 9, no. 2 (2017): 162–184.

Sejersen, Tanja B. "'I vow to thee my countries'—The expansion of dual citizenship in the 21st Century". *International Migration Review* 42, no. 3 (2008): 523–549.

Simic, Olivera. "Locked in and locked out: A migrant woman's reflection on life in Australia during the COVID-19 pandemic". *Journal of International Women's Studies* 22, no. 9 (2021): 400–426.

Strangio, Donatella and Alessandra De Rose. "A new Italian migration toward Australia? Evidences from the last decades and associations with the recent economic crisis". In *The history of migration in Europe: Perspectives from economics, politics and sociology*, edited by F. Fauri, 194–213. London: Routledge, 2014.

Symington, Andy. "Migrant workers and the COVID-19 crisis in Australia: An overview of governmental responses". *Australian Journal of Human Rights* 26, no. 3 (2020): 507–519.

Tintori, Guido. "Italian mobilities and the *demos*". In *Italian Mobilities*, edited by R. Ben-Ghiat and S. M. Hom, 111–132. London: Routledge, 2015.

Tintori, Guido. "More than one million individuals got Italian citizenship abroad in twelve years (1998–2010)". *EUDO Citizenship News*, 21 November 2012.

Tintori, Guido. *Fardelli d'Italia? Conseguenze nazionali e transnazionali delle politiche di cittadinanza italiane*. Roma: Carocci, 2009.

Tintori, Guido and Valentina Romei. "Emigration from Italy after the crisis: The shortcomings of the brain drain narrative". In *South-North Migration of EU Citizens in Times of Crisis*, edited by J.-M. Lafleur and M. Stanek, 49–64. Cham: IMISCOE Research Series/Springer, 2017.

Walkowiak, Emmanuelle. "JobKeeper: The Australian short-time work program". *Australian Journal of Public Administration* 80, no. 4 (2021): 1046–1053.

Ware, Helen. *A profile of the Italian community in Australia*. Melbourne: Australian Institute of Multicultural Affairs & Co.As.It Italian Assistance Association, 1981.

Wright, Chris F. and Stephen Clibborn. "COVID-19 and the policy-induced vulnerability of temporary migrant workers in Australia". *Journal of Australian Political Economy* 85 (2020): 62–70.

Australians in Italy in the Twenty-First Century

Giulia Marchetti and Loretta Baldassar

INTRODUCTION

Australia is best known as a country of immigration, where the majority of the population were either born overseas themselves, making up approximately 7 million people (28%), or have at least one overseas-born parent (48%).[1] However, around 1 million Australians (out of a total population of 25 million) are estimated to be currently living outside of their homeland on a permanent or long-term basis.[2] In 2019, over 200,000 Australian citizens left the country with the intention of remaining

---

[1] "Cultural Diversity: Census 2021," Australian Bureau of Statistics, Media release, released June 28, 2022, https://www.abs.gov.au/tags/census-2021-media-releases.

[2] Department of Foreign Affairs and Trade, Assisting Australians Overseas: Consular State of Play 2019–2020. https://www.dfat.gov.au/sites/default/files/consular-state-of-play-2019-20.pdf.

G. Marchetti (✉) · L. Baldassar
School of Arts and Humanities, Edith Cowan University, Mount Lawley, WA, Australia
e-mail: g.marchetti@ecu.edu.au

© The Author(s), under exclusive license to Springer Nature
Singapore Pte Ltd. 2023
G. Abbondanza and S. Battiston (eds.), *Italy and Australia*,
https://Doi.org/10.1007/978-981-99-3216-0_4

81

abroad for at least a year.[3] According to Hugo,[4] the Australian expatriate community fulfils the first three of Butler's four defining criteria of contemporary diasporas: two or more destinations, a relationship with an actual or imagined homeland, common group identity shared among communities abroad, and existence over at least two generations of migrants.[5] The Australian 'diaspora' has been described as comprising relatively well-educated, prosperous and successful individuals.[6] And yet, despite significant and growing numbers, research on the Australian diaspora remains relatively thin. However, the COVID-19 pandemic and the closure of the Australian borders have recently led to some interest in the life and experiences of Australians stranded abroad.[7]

The main destinations of mobile Australians are high-income, English-speaking countries including the UK, USA and New Zealand as well as Asian countries such as Japan, Singapore and Hong Kong.[8] As regards the Australian presence in Italy, the most comprehensive account is Kent, Pesman and Troup's pioneering volume, *Australians in Italy*,[9] which explores both historical and contemporary encounters between the two countries, including artistic, institutional, academic, as well as imaginative endeavours. In this chapter we focus in particular on Italian-Australian mobilities. This topic immediately brings to mind the many Italians who, especially in the post-second world war period, migrated to Australia;

---

[3] Department of Home Affairs, datasets, accessed July 1, 2022, https://data.gov.au/data/organization/immi.

[4] Graeme Hugo, "An Australian Diaspora?," *IOM International Migration* 44, no. 1 (2006): 106–133.

[5] Kim D. Butler, "Defining Diaspora, Refining a Discourse," *Diaspora* 10, no. 2 (2001): 189–219.

[6] Michael Fullilove and Chloë Flutter, "Diaspora: The World Wide Web of Australians," Lowy Institute for Institutional Policy, no. 4 (2004): 1–120.

[7] Anna Larson, "'You Should Have Come Back Earlier': The Divisive Effect of Australia's COVID-19 Response on Diaspora Relations," *Australian Geographer* 53, no. 2 (2022): 131–148.

[8] Hugo, "An Australian Diaspora?" 106–133; Bryan Mercurio and George Williams, "The Australian Diaspora and the Right to Vote," *University of Western Australia Law Review* 32, no. 1 (2004): 1–29; Kelly L. Parker, "Transnational Networks and Identifications of Australia's Diaspora in the USA," *Journal of Intercultural Studies* 33, no. 1 (2012): 39–52.

[9] Bill Kent, Ros Pesman, and Cynthia Troup (eds.), *Australians in Italy: Contemporary Lives and Impressions* (Clayton, VIC: Monash University Publishing, 2008).

a slice of history that is expertly reconstructed by Abbondanza and Battiston in Chapter 1 of this volume.[10] Escaping a country brought to its knees by wartime defeat, these mostly peasant-worker migrants were searching for better opportunities in Australia, writ large in their imagination as 'an America'. Many received an ambivalent welcome as their presence pushed the boundaries of perceived 'whiteness' amid the racialised hierarchies of migrant preference at the time.[11]

In many ways, this Italian-Australian post-war migration history, characterised by family reunion and chain migration, was a precursor and foundation for the smaller migration wave of more middling (aspiring to the middle-class) migrants that followed in the 1970s. These were Italians for whom Australia represented a 'final frontier' of adventure and opportunity, and many migrated after falling in love with an Australian.[12] With the possible exception of migration 'for love', it is difficult to argue a connection between the migration flows from Italy to Australia and the beginnings of Australian overseas tourism in the latter half of the twentieth century, when Australians began to travel to Italy for cultural sustenance.[13] After all, the 'high culture' Italy of Dante and Michelangelo was not easily reconciled with the subaltern Italy of patron saints and migrant clubs.[14]

Beginning in the 1970s with the initiation of a skilled migration stream, followed by the introduction of a points-based system in the 1990s, Australian migration policy has become increasingly selective.

---

[10] Gabriele Abbondanza and Simone Battiston, "Italy and Australia in the Twenty-First Century: Distant Connections or Close Partners?" in *Italy and Australia: Redefining Bilateral Relations for the Twenty-First Century*, eds. Gabriele Abbondanza and Simone Battiston (London: Palgrave Macmillan, 2024), pp. 1–23.

[11] Francesco Ricatti, *Italians in Australia: History, Memory, Identity* (Cham: Palgrave, 2018).

[12] Loretta Baldassar and Joanne Pyke, "Intra-Diaspora Knowledge Transfer and 'New' Italian Migration," *International Migration* 52, no. 4 (2013): 128–143.

[13] Ros Pesman, "Australians in Italy: The Long View," in *Australians in Italy: Contemporary Lives and Impressions*, eds. Bill Kent, Ros Pesman, and Cynthia Troup (Clayton, VIC: Monash University Publishing, 2008), 1–19.

[14] Stephen Castles, Caroline Alcorso, Gaetano Rando, and Ellie Vasta (eds.), *Australia's Italians: Culture and Community in a Changing Society* (Sydney: Allen & Unwin, 1992).

Most recently, as Battiston discusses in Chapter 3 of this volume,[15] migration policies in Australia have shifted to an increasing focus on temporary migration streams. In this context, Italians are migrating in the form of skilled, temporary and predominantly young, mostly well-educated migrants, for whom Australia represents freedom from clientelism and an opportunity to experience a meritocracy.[16] Their general acceptance by Australians is in no small part attributable to the financial success of the post-war Italian migrants and the upward social mobility of the second and subsequent generations, which has arguably made all Australians feel 'a little bit Italian'.[17] Not surprisingly, Italy remains one of the preferred destinations of Australian tourists in the twenty-first century. Most Australians have some familiarity with Italian language and culture from the Italian migrant presence at home, as well as Italian language classes in primary school, the ubiquity of which was a direct result of policy supporting community languages.[18] As Cristiana Palmieri argues in her chapter in this volume, Australians in general are fascinated by Italy in the fields of language, fashion, creativity, design and engineering.[19]

Despite this long and substantial history of Italian migration to Australia, the experiences of Australians moving to and living in Italy in

[15] Simone Battiston, "Italians in Australia in the Twenty-First Century," in *Italy and Australia: Redefining Bilateral Relations for the Twenty-First Century*, eds. Gabriele Abbondanza and Simone Battiston (London: Palgrave Macmillan, 2024), pp. 49–80.

[16] Giulia Marchetti, Loretta Baldassar, Anita Harris, and Shanthi Robertson, "Italian Youth Mobility: The Case for a Mediterranean Model of 'Family-Centred' Mobile Transitions," *Ethnicities* 22, no. 1 (2022): 108–127.

[17] Jock Collins, "Cappuccino Capitalism: Italian Immigrants and Australian Business," in *Australia's Italians: Culture and Community in a Changing Society*, eds. Stephen Castles, Caroline Alcorso, Gaetano Rando, and Ellie Vasta (Sydney: Allen & Unwin, 1992), 73–84. This embracing of Italian culture in Australia was no doubt aided by the arrival of less preferable (and less white) migrants from Asia, the Middle East and Africa, see Laksiri Jayasuriya, David R. Walker, and Jan Gothard (eds.), *Legacies of White Australia* (Crawley: University of Western Australia Press, 2003).

[18] Joseph Lo Bianco and Renata Aliani (eds.), *Language Planning and Student Experiences* (Bristol: Multilingual Matters, 2013); Antonia Rubino, Anna Rita Tamponi, and John Hajek (eds.), *L'italiano in Australia. Prospettive e tendenze nell'insegnamento della lingua e della cultura/Italian in Australia. Perspectives and trends in the teaching of language and culture* (Firenze: Franco Cesati Editore, 2021).

[19] Cristiana Palmieri, "Connecting Australia and Italy Through Language," in *Italy and Australia: Redefining Bilateral Relations for the Twenty-First Century*, eds. Gabriele Abbondanza and Simone Battiston (London: Palgrave Macmillan, 2024), pp. 137–154.

the twenty-first century seem like an almost entirely unrelated topic. A far cry from the grainy images of *Australia, Oceania* and *Neptunia*, the three ships that carried Italians to Australia numerous times in the 1950s and 60s, the movement we reflect on in this chapter occurs several decades later, flows in the opposite direction, and its protagonists are Australians. There have been significant social changes in this period. Mobility has become a ubiquitous experience and Internet communication technologies connect people world-wide. Thus, when we talk about Australians deciding to live in Italy today, the first question to ponder is: are we talking about migration or something else?

This question forms the focus of the next background section that explores changes in the way migration has been conceptualised, and is followed by a discussion of migration statistics, illustrating several types of Australian migration to Italy. Following this, we present an ethnographic case study featuring the small Australian community in Florence (Tuscany) to develop some preliminary reflections on a wider understanding of 'love migration'. While various types of migration can coincide and overlap in a person's biographical and migratory history, Australians in Italy, whatever the main reason that brought them there, enjoy a certain privileged status as migrants. However, as emerged from our interviews, their integration process is not without obstacles.

BACKGROUND: FROM ONE-WAY MIGRATION TO THE 'TRANSNATIONAL TURN'

Is the movement of Australians to Italy a form of migration? This question is at the heart of recent changes in the approach to migration studies, represented by the 'transnational mobility turn'.[20] In this literature, migration is no longer seen as a permanent unidirectional event, motivated by economic necessity and finalised by settlement in the host country. With 281 million persons living outside of their country of

---

[20] Nina G. Schiller, Linda Basch, and Cristina S. Blanc, "From Immigrant to Transmigrant: Theorizing Transnational Migration," *Anthropological Quarterly* 68, no. 1 (1995): 48–63.

origin,[21] all the world is on the move today (at least it was so pre-COVID-19, and certainly most people are eager to be on the move again) and even so-called non-migrants cannot escape the experience of transnational lives when most people are engaged in support networks where at least some members are not proximate.[22] Rather than a one-way movement from home to host setting, resulting in truncated ties with the sending area, migration is now conceived of as a transnational social field that connects people both here and there, often characterised by back-and-forth travel for visits.

This new 'mobilities paradigm'[23] offers new ways to conceptualise the transnational movement of Australians to Italy and raises a set of terminological issues. Migration is a term that has begun to be reserved to define people who move for economic betterment and originate from less privileged areas of the world, with a reduced capacity for agency and freedom within these movements. It implies forced constraints and subaltern positions in the arrival country's society and labour market. In contrast, the term mobility tends to be used to refer to people who move, generally from privileged areas of the world, thanks to their own transnational jobs or for other non-economic and lifestyle reasons. As Oommen puts it, "mobility and associated privileged positionality go side by side".[24]

The privileged nature of contemporary migration from Australia to Italy is even clearer when we consider the immigration landscape of Italy as a destination country which, due to its similarities with other southern European countries, is called the Mediterranean model of immigration.[25] Since the 1970s, Italy has become a country of immigration for people, often women, including countries from the Global South

[21] United Nations Department of Economic and Social Affairs, Population Division. (2020). International Migration 2020 Highlights (ST/ESA/SER.A/452). www.unpopulation.org.

[22] Loretta Baldassar, Cora V. Baldock, and Raelene Wilding, *Families Caring Across Borders: Migration, Ageing and Transnational Caregiving* (New York: Palgrave MacMillan, 2007).

[23] Mimi Sheller and John Urry, "The New Mobilities Paradigm," *Environment and Planning* 38 (2006): 207–226.

[24] Elsa T. Oommen, "Privilege and Youth Migration: Polarised Employment Patterns of Youth Mobility Workers in London," *Journal of Ethnic and Migration Studies* 42, no. 9 (2019): 1554–1573.

[25] Enrico Pugliese, "The Mediterranean Model of immigration," *Academicus* 3, no. 3 (2011): 96–107.

and more recently from post-Soviet countries, employed in the subaltern sectors of the economy, mainly family services (care of the elderly) and seasonal agricultural work.[26] With the construction of Fortress Europe, people have continued to arrive in the form of asylum and humanitarian protection seekers. The environment that these migrants encounter in Italy and the rest of Europe is increasingly less benevolent towards them. For example, even the Italy-born children of immigrants struggle to obtain citizenship in Italy where racism and xenophobia are an integral part of public, cultural and political discourse and therefore, to a certain extent, are socially legitimised.[27] "These migrants", as Dal Lago observes,[28] "are the new lower class, the symbolic and political enemy on whom to project all the ills of Italian society".

Against this backdrop, it is clear that Australians in Italy, as well as all the other non-nationals originating from rich countries, are "invisible migrants",[29] meaning that migrants who move within the Global North are not "othered" by the host society.[30] The scarce attention to this type of privileged migration relates to the unthreatening character of this mobile population: highly educated, professional migrants are not seen as economic or social burdens for the host society.[31] Often, they are also invisible in terms of ethnicity and race. In fact, "elite migrants do not often consider themselves to be 'immigrants' and many in the origin and destination countries also do not consider them as such - hence they

---

[26] Gabriele Abbondanza, "Italy's Migration Policies Combating Irregular Immigration: From the Early Days to the Present Times," *The International Spectator* 52, no. 4 (2017): 76–92.

[27] Alessandro Dal Lago, "Note sul razzismo culturale in Italia," in *Il discorso ambiguo sulle migrazioni*, ed. Salvatore Palidda (Messina: Mesogea, 2010), 11–21. Loretta Baldassar and Roberta Raffaetà, "It's Complicated, Isn't It: Citizenship and Ethnic Identity in a Mobile World," *Ethnicities* 18, no. 5 (2018): 735–760.

[28] Dal Lago, "Note sul razzismo," 11.

[29] Allan M. Findlay, "Skilled Transients: The Invisible Phenomenon?" in *The Cambridge Survey of World Migration*, ed. Robin Cohen (New York: Cambridge University Press, 1995), 515–522.

[30] Carol Reid and Jock Collins, "'No-One Ever Asked Me': The Invisible Experiences and Contribution of Australian Emigrant Teachers," *Race Ethnicity and Education* 16, no. 2 (2013): 268–290.

[31] Allan M. Findlay, "Skilled Transients: The Invisible Phenomenon?" in *The Cambridge Survey of World Migration*, ed. Robin Cohen (New York: Cambridge University Press, 1995), 515–522.

are absent from the current discourses on immigration".[32] In Italy, where the aftermath of the global financial crisis has resulted in a retrogression of the middle class much like the rest of the Global North,[33] Australians and other elite migrants contribute to the country's middle and upper classes and are perceived as a symbolic and political friend.

AUSTRALIA TO ITALY MOBILITY: DEMOGRAPHIC CHARACTERISTICS

Despite the fragmentation of statistical information, a preliminary look at Eurostat data[34] is useful to understand Australian mobility to Italy in the wider European context.[35] The majority of Australian mobility to Europe is directed to the UK (in 2019, the most recent year available for this country, 81,059 Australian citizens were counted as part of the UK's resident population). In 2020, a total of about 33,000 Australian citizens resided in the countries of the European Union. While this information is partial as not all countries provide reports, it is interesting to note that Italy ranks 6th, with 1749 individuals holding Australian citizenship. The first three countries (Germany, the Netherlands and Ireland) represent 68% of the Australian presence in the EU countries (Fig. 4.1).

If we look instead at the resident population that was born in Australia (Fig. 4.2), Italy ranks first, with 19,588 individuals, proving that much of the Australian presence in Italy is due to the return of Italian migrants and ensuing generations as a consequence of the significant history of Italian migration to Australia. By way of comparison, in 2019 the Australian-born residents in the UK were 141,833.

From 2000 to 2020, the number of Australians in Europe increased by almost 55%, with Germany doubling its Australian population over time.

---

[32] Johanna Leinonen, "'Money Is Not Everything and That's the Bottom Line': Family Ties in Transatlantic Elite Migrations," *Social Science History* 36, no. 2 (2012): 246.

[33] Vincenzo Nicoletta, "Crisi e stratificazione sociale. Come cambiano le disuguaglianze sociali in Italia." *Sociologia del Lavoro* 131 (2013): 171–189.

[34] Eurostat, accessed July 1, 2022, https://ec.europa.eu/eurostat.

[35] We draw on three main Istat migration-related sources: residence permits, resident population by citizenship, and annual registrations at the municipal office of Australian citizens. These sources do not consider dual citizenship (Italian and Australian) because they enter Italy as Italians. However, we provide an estimate in Fig. 4.2 (resident population born in Australia).

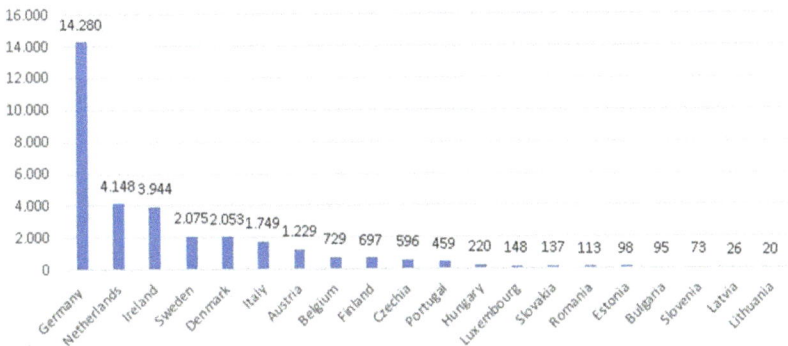

Fig. 4.1 EU27*. Resident population. Australian citizens. 2020 (*Source* Eurostat. *No data available for Spain, Greece, France, Croatia, Cyprus, Malta and Poland)

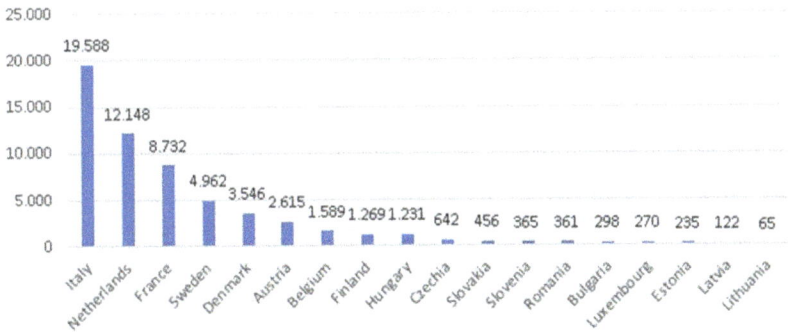

Fig. 4.2 EU27*. Resident population born in Australia. 2020 (*Source* Eurostat. *No data available for Germany, Ireland, Greece, Spain, Croatia, Cyprus, Malta, Poland and Portugal)

In Italy, instead, the number of Australian citizens decreased by 38.5% (they were **2842** in 2000) (Table 4.1).

What is interesting about the Australian presence in Italy is that it is predominantly female (60%) (Fig. 4.3).

Table 4.1 EU27*. Resident population. Australian citizens. 2000 and 2020

UE Countries	2000	2020	2020–2000	% variation
Belgium	648	729	81	12.5
Denmark	850	2053	1203	141.5
Estonia	6	98	92	1533.4
Finland	444	697	253	57.0
Germany	7481	14,280	6799	90.9
Hungary	269	220	−49	−18.2
Italy	2842	1749	−1093	−38.5
Latvia	21	26	5	23.8
Netherlands	2522	4148	1626	64.5
Portugal	463	459	−4	−0.9
Slovenia	19	73	54	284.2
Sweden	1646	2075	429	26.0
Total	17,211	26,607	9396	54.6

Source Eurostat. *No data available for Spain, Greece, France, Croatia, Cyprus, Malta, Poland, Bulgaria, Czechia, Ireland, Lithuania, Luxembourg, Austria, Romania and Slovakia

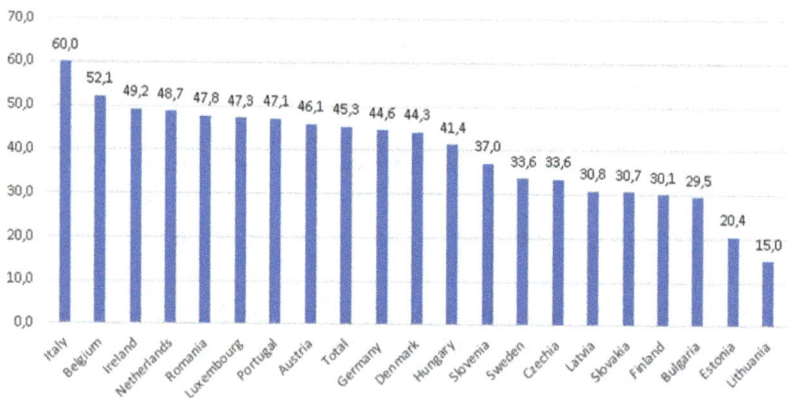

Fig. 4.3 EU27*. Resident population. Australian citizens. Female %. 2020 (*Source* Eurostat. *No data available for Spain, Greece, France, Croatia, Cyprus, Malta and Poland)

According to Istat,[36] in 2020 Italy counted about 5 million foreign citizens, 8.4% of the total population, which is in line with the average percentage in EU-27 (8.2%). This is mainly an immigration originating from developing countries[37] (92.6%). While the North of Italy attracts more migrants in general (58.3%), Australian citizens living in Italy are distributed across Northern (42.5%), Central (34.4%) and Southern Italy and islands (23%), suggesting that their mobility is not solely motivated by economic factors (Fig. 4.4).

The regional distribution of Australians in Italy indicates that 5 out of the 20 Italian regions are home to the majority (59.4%), comprising Lombardy (17.8%), Lazio (16.3%), Tuscany (12.6%), Sicily (6.6%) and Veneto (6.0%) (Table 4.2). Out of 100 Australians living in an Italian region, on average, 29 live in its capital city. However, this number varies according to the region. Those living in Lombardy and Lazio are concentrated in the respective capital regional cities (44.9% of the Australians in Lombardy live in Milan and 67.0% of those in Lazio live in Rome),

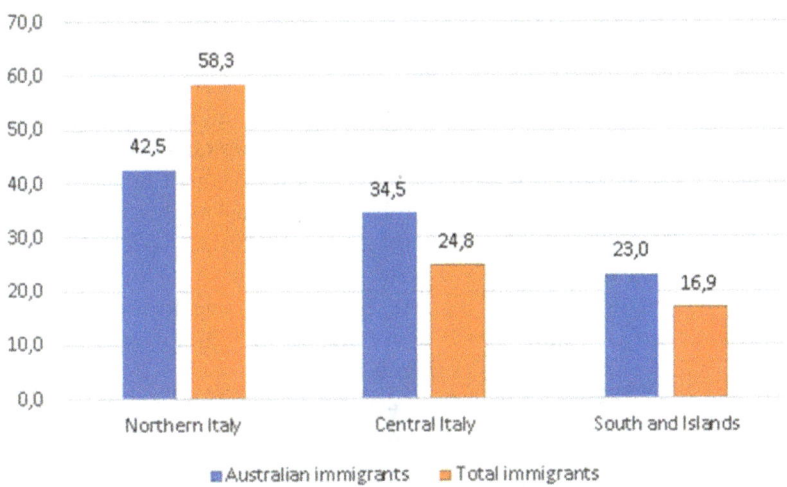

Fig. 4.4 Australian and total foreign population residing in Italy by great area of residence 2020 (*Source* Istat)

---

[36] Istat, accessed July 1, 2022, http://dati.istat.it/, www.demoistat.it.

[37] Here defined as all the countries that are not OCSE member states.

Table 4.2   Australian citizens resident in Italy by main region of residence. 2020

Italian regions	Australians		Residing in the regional capital		
	N	%		N	%
Lombardy	312	17.8	Milan	140	44.9
Lazio	285	16.3	Rome	191	67.0
Tuscany	220	12.6	Florence	56	25.5
Sicily	116	6.6	Palermo	5	4.3
Veneto	105	6.0	Venice	18	17.1
Others	711	40.6	Other city capitals	99	13.9
Total	1749	100.0	Total city capitals	509	29.1

Source Istat

likely attracted by these major centres of financial and cultural interest. The Australians in Tuscany, Sicily and Veneto are instead more dispersed across the regional territory.

In 2019, the residence permits, divided by types, granted to 'Oceania'[38] and total migrants indicated the main reason for residence was study (32.7%). Ranking 10th globally by number of international students, Italy is a steady destination for overseas students, Australians included. Family reasons (30.6%) ranked second, and include reunification with family members who have already migrated to Italy and marriage to an Italian citizen or a foreigner legally resident in Italy. Work reasons (21.8%) are also relevant, indicating a much higher proportion than is calculated for total immigration. In fact, after the closing of Italian borders to extra-EU workers as a result of the cessation of amnesties for undocumented non-national workers employed in the informal labour market, extra-EU migrants still arrive mostly for family reunification (56.9%) and for asylum (15.6%) (Fig. 4.5).

In Fig. 4.6, we can see that Australian women are over-represented in all types of residence permits except work and elective residence.

To conclude this section, we report on the number of movements of registered residents. In 2019, 226 Australians transferred their residence from Australia to an Italian municipality and 2275 Italians cancelled their

---

[38] In 'Oceania' Istat includes Australia, New Zealand and the Pacific Ocean Islands such as: Fiji, Kiribati, Marshall Islands, Federated States of Micronesia, Nauru, Palau, Papua New Guinea, Solomon Islands, Samoa, Tonga, Tuvalu, Vanuatu, New Caledonia.

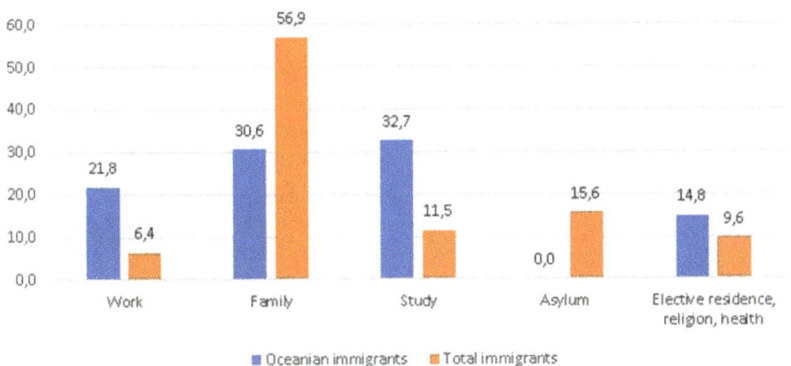

Fig. 4.5   Residence permits granted to Oceanians and total immigration. Percentage. 2019 (*Source* Istat)

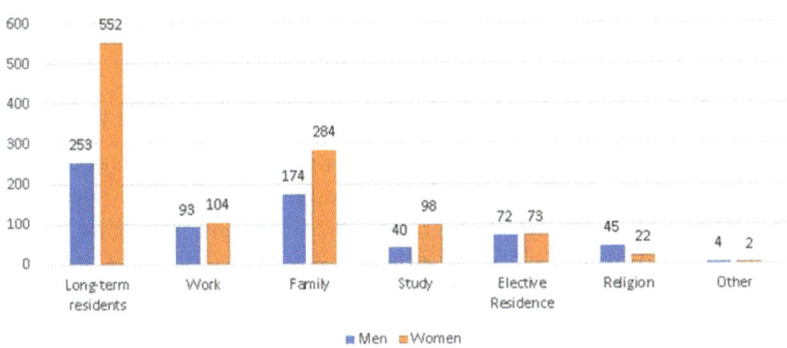

Fig. 4.6   Types of residence permits granted to Australians by sex. 2019. (*Source* Istat)

residence to migrate to Australia. These two groups not only differ in number but also, and above all, in age. Australians migrating to Italy belong to more mature age groups (36.3% are 18–39, 35.0% are 40–64 and 18.6% are over 65) while Italian migration to Australia is mainly youthful (74.8% are 18–39) (Fig. 4.7).

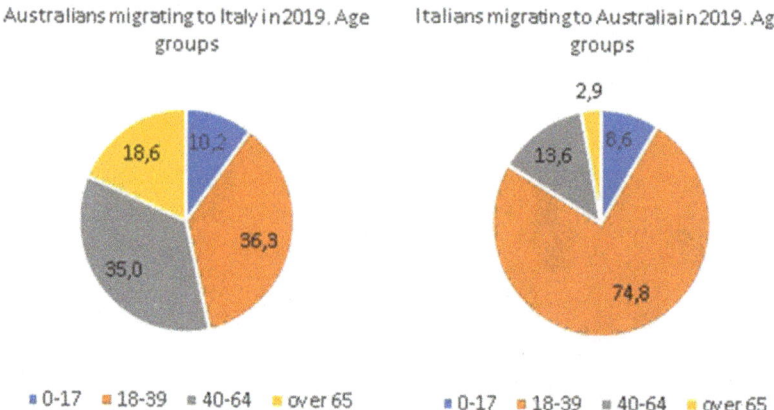

Fig. 4.7   Registrations of Australians in the municipal registry offices and cancellations from the registry offices of Italians who have emigrated to Australia. Age groups. 2019 (*Source* Istat)

Types of Australian Migrations to Italy

In this section we discuss the different types of Australian migrations to Italy, which can be overlapping. Return migration and roots migration are supported by an extensive literature given the long history of Italian migration to Australia, while the other types of Australian migration to Italy—elite, lifestyle, retirement and love—are less researched because they are newer, are not traditionally defined as migrants (as discussed above) or are directed to other countries.

Return migration (repatriation) is the return to the homeland of former Italian migrants who settled in Australia, many of whom became Australian citizens.[39] Despite building a successful life in Australia, working and raising their children and grandchildren, these migrants never lost their sense of belonging to Italy. Some return to Italy alone or with their spouse, while their children, now adults and economically independent, remain in Australia. If the return is carried out after retirement, it may be motivated by a desire to spend the final years of life in the country of birth, and to die and be buried there. This

[39] Loretta Baldassar, *Visits Home* (Carlton South, VIC: Melbourne University Press, 2001).

scenario bears similarities with retirement migration, although the latter usually involves movement to a new country (different from country of birth). The current Italian migration to Australia, very well described by Battiston in Chapter 3,[40] may lead in future years to new returns. Interestingly, citizenship rights can pose a challenge to the repatriation of post-war Italian migrants, most of whom lost their Italian citizenship on becoming Australians before dual citizenship was permitted (in 1992), and for whom the process of regaining citizenship is not simple, requiring a 12-month stay in Italy.[41]

Roots migration refers to the migration of Australians with Italian heritage who are motivated to move to Italy to discover their family origins.[42] It often involves young people from the subsequent migrant generations in the midst of their transition to adulthood who are eager to discover more about their family history. In this sense, the journey may represent a symbolic rite of passage, involving the 'identity work' commonly experienced by second and third generation Italians who often feel not fully Italian and not fully Australian.[43] Such roots migrations can involve building meaningful relationships with family members they hardly knew, as well as confronting realities about people and places that do not match their idealised expectations.[44] This migration may take many forms, including long-term settlement, a gap year to spend time travelling and working in Italy, or even study migration to attend a university course, most commonly to improve their Italian language skills. Roots migration is often facilitated by the fact that these migrants can access

[40] Simone Battiston, "Italians in Australia in the Twenty-First Century," in *Italy and Australia: Redefining Bilateral Relations for the Twenty-First Century*, eds. Gabriele Abbondanza and Simone Battiston (London: Palgrave Macmillan, 2023), pp. 49–80.

[41] Loretta Baldassar and Roberta Raffaetà, "It's Complicated, Isn't It: Citizenship and Ethnic Identity in a Mobile World," *Ethnicities* 18, no. 5 (2018): 735–760.

[42] Susanne Wessendorf, "'Roots Migrants': Transnationalism and 'Return' Among Second-Generation Italians in Switzerland," *Journal of Ethnic and Migration Studies* 33, no. 7 (2007): 1083–1102; Emanuela Sala and Loretta Baldassar, "Leaving Family to Return to Family: Roots Migration Among Second-Generation Italian-Australians," *Ethos* 45, no. 3 (2017): 386–408.

[43] Loretta Baldassar, "Italian Migrants in Australia and Their Relationship to Italy: Return Visits, Transnational Caregiving and the Second Generation," *Journal of Mediterranean Studies* 20, no. 2 (2011): 255–282.

[44] Loretta Baldassar, *Visits Home* (Carlton South, VIC: Melbourne University Press, 2001).

Italian citizenship by descent, including through their grandparents. It may be an opportunity to stay in Italy for the time required to apply for the country's sought-after citizenship, which, in the context of the EU Schengen Agreement, is a pass for other future stays in Europe.

Elite migration features the mobility of highly educated, skilled and often polyglot professionals who are used to very mobile careers. It is facilitated by advances in information and communication technologies and the construction of a global space with multinational institutions having branches world-wide.[45] Australian elite migration to Italy features the scientific/academic sector, the creative arts sector and the financial/business sector.[46]

Life-style migration refers to an increasing number of relatively affluent individuals who decide to migrate based on their belief that there is a more fulfilling way of life available to them elsewhere.[47] For example, Australian life-style migration has been studied in terms of London's attraction as a cosmopolitan capital and its appeal to younger generations.[48] Australian life-style migrants to Italy vary in age, from young adults to advanced older age and, as Cristiana Palmieri explains in Chapter 6, they are increasingly attracted to Italy and to its language for culture, fashion, events and so on.[49] The nature of this new trend appears to be a historical continuation of the Grand Tour, now combined with the ideology of escape. Benson and O'Reilly present three types of lifestyle migrants: the 'residential tourist', the 'seeker of idyllic rural life' and the 'bourgeois bohemian'.[50] Cohen et al. argue that such lifestyle

---

[45] Johanna Leinonen, "'Money Is Not Everything and That's the Bottom Line': Family Ties in Transatlantic Elite Migrations," *Social Science History* 36, no. 2 (2012): 246.

[46] Bill Kent, Ros Pesman, and Cynthia Troup (eds.), *Australians in Italy: Contemporary Lives and Impressions* (Clayton, VIC: Monash University Publishing, 2008).

[47] Michaela Benson and Karen O'Reilly, "Migration and the Search for a Better Way of Life," *The Sociological Review* 57, no. 4 (2009): 608–625.

[48] Graeme Hugo, "An Australian Diaspora?" *IOM International Migration* 44, no. 1 (2006): 106–133.

[49] Cristiana Palmieri, "Connecting Australia and Italy Through Language," in *Italy and Australia: Redefining Bilateral Relations for the Twenty-First Century*, eds. Gabriele Abbondanza and Simone Battiston (London: Palgrave Macmillan, 2023), pp. 137–154.

[50] Michaela Benson and Karen O'Reilly, "Migration and the Search for a Better Way of Life," *The Sociological Review* 57, no. 4 (2009): 608–625.

practices are connected to the shifts in late modernity, where aesthetic consumption practices define people's identities.[51]

If migration studies focus predominantly on work and economic factors, research on lifestyle mobilities features life outside of work. In the case of Australians moving to Italy, they are likely more interested in the quality of life that they can enjoy there, rather than career opportunities, including accepting a demotion or deviation in their career pathways and lower incomes in order to embrace the life-style they seek. They may aspire to a stereotyped idea of what life is like in Italy: 'la bella vita', a simple life, beautiful architecture and al fresco restaurants. Such stereotypes are nourished by popular TV series such as *House Hunters International Italy* (Imdb), *My Big Italian Adventure* (Imdb), *Italy's One Euro Homes* (SBS) and novels/movies like *Eat, Pray, Love*. Lifestyle migration is both growing and diversifying and involves an increasing number of younger (working-age) migrants.

Retirement migration is the mobility of older people after they are freed from work and family responsibilities: they are no longer active in the job market and migrate as singles or as couples without their adult children. They may know the country as a past holiday destination. If we consider that the long-studied labour migrations of the post-World War II era were young adults with family responsibilities motivated to migrate for a better future for their children, we can appreciate how retirement migration is a relative novelty in contemporary migration/mobility studies. It depends not only on changing cultural values but also on the increased life expectancy in good health—for the elderly of the privileged world. These mobile retirees are wellbeing-driven and relocate to more comfortable climates for leisure and health reasons.[52] Usually, the country of their choice has lower living costs and an efficient public health sector and reciprocal health and pension arrangements between the sending and receiving countries. More recently the return of these migrants to their home country has also been investigated by Hall, Betty and Giner,[53] who

---

[51] Scott A. Cohen, Tara Duncan, and Maria Thulemark, "Lifestyle Mobilities: The Crossroads of Travel, Leisure and Migration," *Mobilities* 10, no. 1 (2015): 155–172.

[52] Anthony M. Warnes and Allan Williams, "Older Migrants in Europe," *Journal of Ethnic and Migration Studies* 32, no. 8 (2006): 1257–1281.

[53] Kelly Hall, Charles Betty, and Jordy Giner, "To Stay or to Go? The Motivations and Experiences of Older British Returnees from Spain," in *Return Migration and Psychosocial Wellbeing*, eds. Zana Vathi and Russell King (London: Routledge, 2017), 221–239.

argue that continued ageing—from active 'young-old' to frail 'old-old'—brings with it increased vulnerability and changing social and emotional needs, and hence the desire or need to return to the home country and be close to family support.

Love migration refers to migrations to a partner's country in order for a couple to be together. Finding a partner in a country when one is temporarily present often transforms the mobility project into a quest for permanent settlement for sentimental reasons. In a global society which is more and more interconnected, the growing number of people traveling abroad for tourism, education and work along with the increasing diffusion of online dating websites and apps is resulting in the increased formation of couples with partners of different national and cultural background. 'Love migration' and the 'transnationalism of intimacy'[54] are part of an 'emotional turn' in migration and mobility studies "which explicitly places emotions, especially love and affection, at the heart of migration decision making and behaviour".[55] Today, Australian-Italian couples in Italy "are bringing up a dynamic generation of young people often equally at ease with Australian English and Italian".[56] In the recent past, the formation of Australian-Italian couples living in Italy depended mostly on tourism, study abroad and business exchange. In the new millennium, it is reinforced by the consistent presence of young Italians moving to Australia on a temporary basis (Working Holiday or Student visa), which can result in the formation of sentimental relationships and the couple's decision to relocate to Italy.

In her analysis of post-Erasmus mobility of young Italians in the European space, Cucchiarato[57] expands on the concept of love migration: "young Italians move to another country not only out of love for the person they met during the Erasmus period abroad (a sort of 'family

---

[54] Russell King, "Towards a New Map of European Migration," *International Journal of Population Geography* 8 (2002): 89–106.

[55] Nicola Mai and Russell King, "Love, Sexuality and Migration: Mapping the Issue(s)," *Mobilities* 4, no. 3 (2009): 296. Paolo Boccagni, and Loretta Baldassar, "Emotions on the Move: Mapping the Emergent Field of Emotion and Migration," *Emotion, Space and Society* 16 (2015): 73–80.

[56] Bill Kent, Ros Pesman and Cynthia Troup, "Introduction," in *Australians in Italy. Contemporary Lives and Impressions*, eds. Bill Kent, Ros Pesman, and Cynthia Troup (Clayton, VIC: Monash University Publishing, 2008), xvi.

[57] Claudia Cucchiarato, "Guerra di cifre: perché è così difficile capire: chi e quanti sono gli italiani all'estero?" *Altre Italie* 43 (2011): 67.

reunification') but also out of love for the country and city where they lived and studied for a certain time during their studies (a sort of 'cultural reunification')". In her assessment, Italy seems to be excluded from these dynamics as these young transnational couples rarely choose to live in Italy and international students who have spent an Erasmus period of study in Italy rarely choose to stay there because of the Italian economic situation, which offers few opportunities for young people.

To this list of common types of migrants, there is arguably a case to be made for an additional migration type: the *virtual migrant*. More than ever, today's migrants gather in the virtual space of Facebook groups and WhatsApp chats, where they join together based on nationality and the country or the city of new residence. With 2404 members (December 2021), the 'Australians in Italy/Australiani in Italia' is a private Facebook group that began in 2011. It is a forum where participants share information, including tips on how to overcome Italian bureaucracy, solve visa-related problems, interpret Italian cultural habits, suggest places to visit, post wonderful pics of the views from their Italian homes' as well as online videos of their Australian native cities, share Australian recipes and commemorate Australian national holidays. In the comment section, they joke, make friends, commiserate, argue and get offended. While it is likely that not all the Australians in Italy are members of this groups, other groups of people also participate including Australians who are thinking about moving to Italy in the future; Australians who have returned to Australia and remain Facebook page members as an emotional link to Italy; Italians in Australia and Italians in Italy. This last category comprises repatriated Italians who returned from Australia as well as Italians who have never travelled to Australia but hope to find students for their Italian classes or tenants for their apartments.

The next and final section of this chapter presents our case study, which offers some qualitative insights on the small but significant Australian community of Florence. We examine who they are, what they do and why they chose Florence, as well as their experiences of everyday life as Australian "migrants" in Italy. The motivation to migrate to a non-English speaking, low-income country such as Italy for many Australians is out of love: love for their roots, love for their Italian partner, and in some cases love for a particular city in Italy.

THE AUSTRALIANS IN FLORENCE: A CASE STUDY

Life is too darn short not to wake each morning to be met by views from your window of ancient rivers, of inland seas and of long dormant volcanoes; it's too short not to feel the gentle curves of cobblestoned street under your feet as you make your way to the local store, past castles and moat and noble palaces that seem to have been there forever. From a Facebook post, dated 22 March 2022, by an Australian woman in Italy.

Between November 2021 and January 2022, we conducted in-depth qualitative interviews with 7 Australians living in Florence, four women and three men between the ages of 30 and 82, from Perth, Brisbane, Melbourne, Sydney and Canberra. They were recruited through ads on the 'Australians in Italy' Facebook group.[58] We chose to explore Florence because it remains one of the most popular destinations, as it was for the 1700s Grand Tour, the educational journey for descendants of aristocratic families in Europe, artists and men of culture.[59] Choosing to live in Florence today still reflects the privileged nature of this type of mobility which, however, is no longer, as in the past, a male prerogative only.

An informal association, by the name 'Australians in Florence', has been active in Florence since 2008, with about 50 members and a leadership that has changed four times. It does not have a Facebook presence but functions through emails coordinated by the organiser, including recruiting new contacts based on information from existing members. The aim of this association is to facilitate a friendship network among Australians in Florence through events such as potluck dinners at private

---

[58] The participants gave their signed consent to be interviewed and pseudonyms are used to illustrate quotes. The one-hour interviews were audio-recorded, transcribed verbatim and analysed thematically using qualitative software tool, MAXQDA. In two cases, the interviewees preferred to conduct the interview in Italian. Following the participants' preference, three interviews were conducted online and four face-to-face as this research was conducted at a time when wearing face masks was compulsory in Italy. The small sample size is explained by the purely exploratory nature of this study. However, it is well established that qualitative studies of 7–10 cases are the optimal number to achieve substantial theme representation. Diane S. Young and Erin A. Casey, "An Examination of the Sufficiency of Small Qualitative Samples," *Social Work & Criminal Justice Publications* 500 (2018): 1–17.

[59] Pierluca Birindelli, "Cultural Experiences in Florence and Italy: The Grand Tour Narrative in the 21st Century," *Società Mutamento Politica* 10, no. 20 (2019): 191–205.

homes once a month and on special occasions such as Christmas and Australia Day. Its members, mostly women in their 50s and 60s, have been living in Florence for a long time or in a few cases have a second home in the city and visit frequently. They have a sentimental bond with Florence and most of them live in the historical city centre. They work as lawyers, artists, tour guides, writers and real estate agents.[60]

In 2019 an Australian bistro—Melaleuca Restaurant and Bakery— was opened on the Lungarno which, despite the lockdowns during the COVID-19 pandemic, has become a meeting point for the Australian community and beyond. Owned by a couple who met in Australia, she is an Australian and he is an Italian-American, they did what many Italians did when they migrated in the past; open a restaurant. Thanks to the 'Ozzie' menu, the laid-back attitude of the staff, the simple decor and the proximity to the river, in this bistro Australians find a home away from home.

In what follows we include representative excerpts from the interviews to explore key themes in the data, including reasons for choosing Florence, work and social integration and (self) perceptions. Three participants (Marie, Olivia and Mark) moved to Florence because that was the hometown of their Italian partner. Their mobility is a mix of love and roots migration, which we refer to as *nonni's call*. In fact, these are couples with young children who have relocated to Florence in order for the Italian grandparents and grandchildren to develop more solid and lasting relationships. This reflects the intergenerational solidarity that characterizes the Italian family: the grandparents, in fact, provide help in managing the children and in the future may themselves need to receive support from the children returned from abroad.[61] After meeting her future husband in Melbourne, Marie lived with him in the UK as a couple and finally they relocated to Italy as a couple with children.

---

[60] From our personal email communication with the current Coordinator on April 1, 2022.

[61] Vern L. Bengtson and Robert E. L. Roberts, "Intergenerational Solidarity in Aging Families," *Journal of Marriage and the Family* 53, no. 4 (1991): 856–870. For an analysis of transnational mobility and family solidarity see Loretta Baldassar, "Transnational Families and Aged Care: The Mobility of Care and the Migrancy of Ageing," *Journal of Ethnic and Migration Studies* 33, no. 2 (2007): 275–297.

> *We decided to leave the UK and return to Italy 'cause we had a baby and it was kind of nicer to have some family around and also because I had lived in Italy before, and I knew the language a bit and had some familiarity with it and so we made the decision to come here, back to where his parents are. [...] They're really helpful.* Marie, 40, 4 years in Italy.

The Australian partner is inevitably catapulted into the Italian family system. Mark moved to Florence to follow his Italian partner who obtained a postdoc position in Italy after completing her PhD in Australia. He reflects on the positive and negative sides of being part of an Italian family:

> *Before we lived in the centre of Florence, and they were just like really close. Now they live in the same place but we moved like 40 minutes away. Which is good and bad. It used to be a bit annoying for me because then out of nowhere there's the- my mother-in-law in the morning without any notice. You know I didn't like this but it was useful for the kids.* Mark, 40, 3 years in Italy.

In this type of mobility, the Australian partners are supported by access to visas (partner visa or Italian citizenship through marriage) and the help they receive from their Italian partners, which is particularly important in the early stages, when they are not familiar with the Italian language. However, living in the partner's country can also imply a diminished level of autonomy, independence and agency, as suggested by Olivia, who met her Italian husband in Germany in her early 20s and lived with him for many years in London, where their two children were born.

> *And the other thing is that when we lived in London, I controlled everything in the house, so I paid all the bills, and I did all the mortgage reviews, and all of that. And now that is on my husband, so he has to do all these things because I just don't feel comfortable given my* [knowledge of] *Italian.* Olivia, 40, 3 years in Italy.

The other participants, instead, deliberately chose Florence. For John, a retired Australian man with previous and prolonged experience of work and life both in the UK and in Italy, living today in Florence is the fulfilment of a lifestyle. He first discovered Florence when he was a young man, camping at 19 in the Piazzale Michelangelo, and fell in love with the city and its pink rooves. On a student visa, today he shares a flat with an opera singer and poses for painters, living a sort of bohemian and privileged life (dinners, concerts, parties). He plans to live in Italy until his health forces him to move back to Australia. In his 10 years in Florence, he has built a tight-knight, English-speaking circle of friends, which includes Australian, American and British people and also upper-class Italians.

> *Rome is too big to live in. I have a three-wheel bike here, I ride my bike, cycling around, and you can walk, or get busses. In Florence you can go anywhere. In Australia some people invite you for dinner, I live on one side of Melbourne and they might live on the other side, that's 50 kilometres. Here, you just cross the road.* John, 82, 10 years in Italy.

Lucrezia and Diego are both of Italian descent. They moved to Italy independently with a desire to discover their roots as well as due to decisions and events surrounding their transition to adulthood in Australia. Diego decided to leave Australia after the end of his marriage, putting on standby his already established career as a creative. Lucrezia moved to Florence at 24 as a way to enjoy her youth and interrupt a fulltime job that was proving to be too overwhelming. Interestingly, they chose Florence even though their Italian relatives live in other parts of Italy. In Lucrezia's case, Florence had been recommended as the best place to learn "real Italian". Diego instead, who at the time could not speak Italian, was attracted by the offer of English-speaking art classes provided by several American universities in Florence. For both Diego and Lucrezia, a trip that was at first meant to be temporary has become long-term over time due to the formation of romantic relationships in Italy.

All participants are highly educated with professions already started before arriving in Italy. Two of them work remotely and avoid the constraints ingrained in the Italian labour market, have an English-speaking work environment and show more satisfaction towards their level of earnings.

> *My profession is dead here. It doesn't exist. My colleagues in Italy work for free. That's why all my projects are in Australia. For 10 years I've been working like everybody does now* [online because of COVID-19] *and it's very easy to do it.* Diego, 45, 11 years in Italy.

For Olivia, finding a remote- and home-based position was a precondition to her moving to Florence, also proving that the role of the non-national partner is a major factor in the decision-making process around the move back to Italy.

> *I specifically found a job that was remote-based and I talked to them in the interview back in 2018 about that I would have eventually liked to move to Italy and I wanted to find a company that would potentially support me to do that. [...] So, my job essentially has allowed us to then move to Italy.* Olivia, 40, 3 years in Italy.

However, for those participants without such job conditions, moving to Italy has meant that they had to start afresh or invent a new career. Teaching English is a common and utilitarian option, especially in the early stages. However, over time it can become a trap that is difficult to escape. Marie, for example, was a speech therapist both in Australia and in London, while in Italy she is a freelance English teacher. She is currently a stay-at-home mother after the birth of their second child and is organising documentation needed to have her degree recognised so that she can go back to her profession in the future.

> *If I had stayed in London, my life would have been easier because I would have my job, I would have my qualification recognized, I would have gone on maternity leave, and back to the same job. And it would have been so much easier. The UK recognized my qualification. In Italy the process is not as clear and here is so much documentation and all needs to be translated. It's going to be like a book.* Marie, 40, 4 years in Italy.

Mark reinvented himself as a Tuscan cooking teacher for a school in Florence whose main students are American and European tourists. The Italian language is still a barrier to him and adds to his frustration with the Italian job market. These factors contribute to his lack of social integration in the local society, and is one of the reasons he would like to return to Australia.

> [Back in Australia] *I would have a better job, getting paid more, and I would have lots of hours. No question. And I could choose from different industries as well because I worked in lots of different fields, so I think, if I went back, I would find an ok job very quickly.* Mark, 40, 3 years in Italy.

An Italian job market characterised by low wages is also an issue for Lucrezia, despite the fact that she has managed to leave her initial English teaching jobs, is currently perfectly fluent in Italian and has found a job in line with her qualifications and degree.

The salary in Italy doesn't satisfy me, I have to be honest, because we earn very little for what we do and also for the hours we work, because in Australia I used to work from 8.30 to 4.30, so I could still see the sun at the end of the day. Now that the days are shorter, I arrive in the dark and I leave in the dark. Lucrezia, 30, 5 years in Italy.

One aspect that emerged from these interviews—and is consistent with our broader research findings—concerns gender relations. Indeed, both Olivia and Lucrezia reported incidents that had to do with normative constructions of Italian masculinity and gender roles, both in ordinary life and at work.

Actually, when I first moved here, I had lot of troubles with men following me, it was really awful. And I used to wear a fake wedding ring even before we got married because I would try and kind of being like: "Oh no, look, sono sposata, lasciami in pace [I'm married, leave me alone]". *[…] In Australia men are not that style. You can basically walk down a main street in your bikini or whatever and they wouldn't even turn their head. Here I changed the style of dress as well.* Olivia, 40, 3 years in Italy.

At work I saw that some clients initially questioned my skills just because I was a woman, and I had to prove my skills. Now it's less but, in the beginning, I felt so much this difference between male and female because in parts of Italy there is still the old idea that women do the housework, and in fact this is something I had to overcome even with my boyfriend. I am very feminist. So even sharing the housework was not easy. Because Italian mothers don't prepare, or at least they didn't prepare before, their children for life outside the home. I had to teach my boyfriend how to clean a toilet, how to clean a shower, how to do a washing machine, because he didn't know. Lucrezia, 30, 5 years in Italy.

The Australians in Florence find friends among the larger group of American and British people living in Florence, reinforcing their identity as English-speaking Anglo-Saxons. However, Italians in Florence react differently to these diverse groups: they are a bit annoyed by the Americans (due to the presence of many exchange students in the city where central apartments have also become luxury holiday apartments for American tourists), they are not impressed by the British as the UK is more familiar, they are generally more enthusiastic about the Australians, as Olivia explains;

> *Because I look very English as well, I quite often have people that think that I'm English and then I say actually I'm Australian and they: "Oh Australia!" And, you know, their whole persona and their voice change and they are like: "Yay!!!" And then they say: "I've got a cousin that lives in Australia!"* Olivia, 40, 3 years in Italy.

Typically, the initial amazement leaves room for disbelief:

> *Another classic thing is: "Ah, but why are you here? Australia is so beautiful!"* Diego, 45, 11 years in Italy.

This disbelief originates from the familiarity of Italians with the local economic situation that, especially after the 2008 global financial crisis, is leading a growing number of Italians to leave the country. The Australians in Florence also experience day-to-day problems ingrained in the Italian culture. They may not experience prejudice and racism when they are in line at the Questura (Police headquarters) to renew their visa as other immigrants do, but they are disappointed by the bureaucracy, services and civic practices.[62]

> *Lots of bureaucracy, even though I have dual citizenship. I had to redo my license from scratch. I redid everything from scratch, theory, driving. The theory test was difficult. The first driving lesson I got in the car and put the gearshift on and he said: "Hey, you can drive," and I said, "Yes, I have been driving for 12 years". It's pure bureaucracy.* Lucrezia, 30, 5 years in Italy.

They all agree that their compatriots regard Australians living in Tuscany with a mixture of curiosity, admiration, jealousy and romanticising stereotypes.

> *I think it is a lot of stereotypes but part of it is real. The stereotypes are almost annoying though. Do you know that book Under the Tuscan Sun? It's nice but it's annoying. They're all living in Italy doing up a mansion, eating fresh pressed olive oil, yes it can be over-romanticised. But the reality is really*

---

[62] Loretta Baldassar, and Roberta Raffaetà, "It's Complicated, Isn't It: Citizenship and Ethnic Identity in a Mobile World," *Ethnicities* 18, no. 5 (2018): 735–760.

nice too, because you do get restored houses and eat fresh pressed olive oil, so it's really a privileged place to live, it's really beautiful. Marie, 40, 4 years in Italy.

CONCLUSION

Among the Australians we talked to, only Mark categorically refuses the term expat as a way to describe his mobility because he does not like the social class implication of this term. In general, though, Australians are perceived—and perceive themselves—as expatriates or 'expats'.[63] They are the neighbours that Italians like to have in their streets and apartment buildings, the classmates sought after for their children, the new additions in their friendship network, the customers and clients for their businesses. They speak a language that Italians are always eager to learn and practice. They come from a country which many young Italians would like to visit. As Leinonen points out,[64] these migrants' high social status does not necessarily guarantee them privileged treatment by the formal nation state. However, it generally assures them a privileged place in the *comunità nazionale leggera* ["light national community"] of Italy.[65] In some respects, in fact, the cultural closure towards immigrants from poor countries is counterbalanced in Italy by a tradition of cultural openness towards the Anglo-Saxon world. As Galli Della Loggia argues,[66] in Italy "the entire acculturation to modernity and in the end all acculturation in general from a certain point onwards took place according to languages, mythologies, historical and social perspectives adopted directly from beyond the Ocean [Oltreoceano]".

The invisibility of Australians as migrants however leads to an underestimation of the problems that even these people, despite being white

---

[63] The colloquial form, expat, first appeared in a 1962 poem by the British author D. J. Enright. For an exhaustive historical explanation and change of meanings over time of the term expatriate see Nancy L. Green, "Expatriation, Expatriates and Expats: The American Transformation of a Concept," *The American Historical Review* 114, no. 2 (2009): 307–328.

[64] Johanna Leinonen, "'Money Is Not Everything and That's the Bottom Line': Family Ties in Transatlantic Elite Migrations," *Social Science History* 36, no. 2 (2012): 243–268.

[65] Walter Barberis, *Il bisogno di patria* (Torino: Giulio Einaudi editore, 2004).

[66] Ernesto Galli della Loggia, *La morte della patria. La crisi dell'idea di nazione tra Resistenza, antifascismo e Repubblica* (Roma-Bari: Laterza, 1996), 132.

and privileged, face every day in the new society and on which it is worth reflecting: the lack of their primary support networks of family and friends, the complicated process for the formation of transnational families, linguistic and cultural barriers, identity work and psychological wellbeing, a downward mobility, in some cases, in their career pathway and income level, a sense of loneliness and nostalgia for Australia that the Australian COVID travel ban has recently exacerbated.

This chapter explored the movement of Australians to Italy in the twenty-first century and contributes to a surprisingly small literature on the Australian 'diaspora'. The demographic characteristics and 'lived experiences' reported here raise a question central to contemporary migration studies: is this movement best defined as migration or mobility? Interestingly, it is on this point that the phenomenon of Australia to Italy mobilities resembles the contemporary experience of movement in the reverse direction, of young Italians moving to Australia. Both reflect the increasing economic and cultural interconnections at a global level.

BIBLIOGRAPHY

Abbondanza, Gabriele. "Italy's Migration Policies Combating Irregular Immigration: From the Early Days to the Present Times." *The International Spectator* 52, no. 4 (2017): 76–92.

Abbondanza, Gabriele, and Simone Battiston. "Italy and Australia in the Twenty-First Century: Distant Connections or Close Partners?" In *Italy and Australia: Redefining Bilateral Relations for the Twenty-First Century*, edited by Gabriele Abbondanza and Simone Battiston, pp. 1–23. London: Palgrave Macmillan, 2024.

Baldassar, Loretta. *Visits Home.* Carlton South, VIC: Melbourne University Press, 2001.

Baldassar, Loretta. "Transnational Families and Aged Care: The Mobility of Care and the Migrancy of Ageing." *Journal of Ethnic and Migration Studies* 33, no. 2 (2007): 275–297.

Baldassar, Loretta. "Italian Migrants in Australia and Their Relationship to Italy: Return Visits, Transnational Caregiving and the Second Generation." *Journal of Mediterranean Studies* 20, no. 2 (2011): 255–282.

Baldassar, Loretta, and Joanne Pyke. "Intra-Diaspora Knowledge Transfer and 'New' Italian Migration." *International Migration* 52, no. 4 (2013): 128–143.

Baldassar, Loretta, and Roberta Raffaetà. "It's Complicated, Isn't It: Citizenship and Ethnic Identity in a Mobile World." *Ethnicities* 18, no. 5 (2018): 735–760.

Baldassar, Loretta, Cora V. Baldock, and Raelene Wilding. *Families Caring Across Borders: Migration, Ageing and Transnational Caregiving*. New York: Palgrave MacMillan, 2007.

Barberis, Walter. *Il bisogno di patria*. Torino: Giulio Einaudi editore, 2004.

Battiston, Simone. "Italians in Australia in the Twenty-First Century." In *Italy and Australia: Redefining Bilateral Relations for the Twenty-First Century*, edited by Gabriele Abbondanza and Simone Battiston, pp. 49–80. London: Palgrave Macmillan, 2024.

Bengtson, Vern L., and Robert E. L. Roberts. "Intergenerational Solidarity in Aging Families." *Journal of Marriage and the Family* 53, no. 4 (1991): 856–870.

Benson, Michaela, and Karen O'Reilly. "Migration and the Search for a Better Way of Life." *The Sociological Review* 57, no. 4 (2009): 608–625.

Birindelli, Pierluca. "Cultural Experiences in Florence and Italy: The Grand Tour Narrative in the 21st Century." *Società Mutamento Politica* 10, no. 20 (2019): 191–205.

Boccagni, Paolo, and Baldassar, Loretta. "Emotions on the Move: Mapping the Emergent Field of Emotion and Migration." *Emotion, Space and Society* 16 (2015): 73–80.

Butler, Kim D. "Defining Diaspora, Refining a Discourse." *Diaspora* 10, no. 2 (2001): 189–219.

Castles, Stephen, Caroline Alcorso, Gaetano Rando, and Ellie Vasta (eds.). *Australia's Italians: Culture and Community in a Changing Society*. Sydney: Allen & Unwin, 1992.

Cohen, Scott A., Tara Duncan, and Maria Thulemark. "Lifestyle Mobilities: The Crossroads of Travel, Leisure and Migration." *Mobilities* 10, no. 1 (2015): 155–172.

Collins, Jock. "Cappuccino Capitalism: Italian Immigrants and Australian Business." In *Australia's Italians: Culture and Community in a Changing Society*, edited by Stephen Castles, Caroline Alcorso, Gaetano Rando, and Ellie Vasta, 73–84. Sydney: Allen & Unwin, 1992.

Cucchiarato, Claudia. "Guerra di cifre: perché è così difficile capire: chi e quanti sono gli italiani all'estero?" *Altre Italie* 43 (2011): 64–74.

Dal Lago, Alessandro. "Note sul razzismo culturale in Italia." In *Il «discorso» ambiguo sulle migrazioni*, edited by Salvatore Palidda, 11–21. Messina: Mesogea, 2010.

Findlay, Allan M. "Skilled Transients: The Invisible Phenomenon?" In *The Cambridge Survey of World Migration*, edited by Robin Cohen, 515–522. New York: Cambridge University Press, 1995.

Fullilove, Michael, and Chloë Flutter. "Diaspora: The World Wide Web of Australians." *Lowy Institute for Institutional Policy*, no. 4 (2004): 1–120.

Galli della Loggia, Ernesto. *La morte della patria. La crisi dell'idea di nazione tra Resistenza, antifascismo e Repubblica.* Roma-Bari: Laterza, 1996.

Green, Nancy L. "Expatriation, Expatriates and Expats: The American Transformation of a Concept." *The American Historical Review* 114, no. 2 (2009): 307–328.

Hall, Kelly, Charles Betty, and Jordy Giner. "To Stay or to Go? The Motivations and Experiences of Older British Returnees from Spain." In *Return Migration and Psychosocial Wellbeing*, edited by Zana Vathi and Russell King, 221–239. London: Routledge, 2017.

Hugo, Graeme. "An Australian Diaspora?" *IOM International Migration* 44, no. 1 (2006): 106–133.

Jayasuriya, Laksiri, David R. Walker, and Jan Gothard (eds.). *Legacies of White Australia*. Crawley, WA: University of Western Australia Press, 2003.

Kent, Bill, Ros Pesman, and Cynthia Troup (eds.). *Australians in Italy: Contemporary Lives and Impressions.* Clayton, VIC: Monash University Publishing, 2008.

King, Russell. "Towards a New Map of European Migration." *International Journal of Population Geography* 8 (2002): 89–106.

Larson, Anna. "'You Should Have Come Back Earlier': The Divisive Effect of Australia's COVID-19 Response on Diaspora Relations." *Australian Geographer* 53, no. 2 (2022): 131–148.

Leinonen, Johanna. "'Money Is Not Everything and That's the Bottom Line': Family Ties in Transatlantic Elite Migrations." *Social Science History* 36, no. 2 (2012): 243–268.

Lo Bianco, Joseph, and Renata Aliani (eds.). *Language Planning and Student Experiences*. Bristol: Multilingual Matters, 2013.

Mai, Nicola, and Russell King. "Love, Sexuality and Migration: Mapping the Issue(s)." *Mobilities* 4, no. 3 (2009): 295–307.

Marchetti, Giulia, Loretta Baldassar, Anita Harris, and Shanthi Robertson. "Italian Youth Mobility: The Case for a Mediterranean Model of 'Family-Centred' Mobile Transitions." *Ethnicities* 22, no. 1 (2022): 108–127.

Mercurio, Bryan, and George Williams. "The Australian Diaspora and the Right to Vote." *University of Western Australia Law Review* 32, no. 1 (2004): 1–29.

Nicoletta, Vincenzo. "Crisi e stratificazione sociale. Come cambiano le disuguaglianze sociali in Italia." *Sociologia del Lavoro* 131 (2013): 171–189.

Oommen, Elsa T. "Privilege and Youth Migration. Polarised Employment Patterns of Youth Mobility Workers in London." *Journal of Ethnic and Migration Studies* 42, no. 9 (2019): 1554–1573.

Palmieri, Cristiana. "Connecting Australia and Italy Through Language." In *Italy and Australia: Redefining Bilateral Relations for the Twenty-First Century,* edited by Gabriele Abbondanza and Simone Battiston, pp. 137–154. London: Palgrave Macmillan, 2024.

Parker, Kelly L. "Transnational Networks and Identifications of Australia's Diaspora in the USA." *Journal of Intercultural Studies* 33, no. 1 (2012): 39–52.

Pesman, Ros. "Australians in Italy: The Long View." In *Australians in Italy: Contemporary Lives and Impressions*, edited by Bill Kent, Ros Pesman, and Cynthia Troup, 1–19. Clayton, VIC: Monash University Publishing, 2008.

Pugliese, Enrico. "The Mediterranean Model of Immigration." *Academicus* 3, no. 3 (2011): 96–107.

Reid, Carol, and Jock Collins "'No-One Ever Asked Me': The Invisible Experiences and Contribution of Australian Emigrant Teachers." *Race Ethnicity and Education* 16, no. 2 (2013): 268–290.

Ricatti, Francesco. *Italians in Australia: History, Memory, Identity*. Cham: Palgrave, 2018.

Rubino, Antonia, Anna Rita Tamponi, and John Hajek (eds.). *L'italiano in Australia. Prospettive e tendenze nell'insegnamento della lingua e della cultura/ Italian in Australia. Perspectives and trends in the teaching of language and culture*. Firenze: Franco Cesati Editore, 2021.

Sala, Emanuela, and Loretta Baldassar. "Leaving Family to Return to Family: Roots Migration Among Second-Generation Italian-Australians." *Ethos* 45, no. 3 (2017): 386–408.

Schiller, Nina G., Linda Basch, and Cristina S. Blanc. "From Immigrant to Transmigrant: Theorizing Transnational Migration." *Anthropological Quarterly* 68, no. 1 (1995): 48–63.

Sheller, Mimi, and John Urry. "The New Mobilities Paradigm." *Environment and Planning* 38 (2006): 207–226.

Warnes, Anthony M., and Allan Williams. "Older Migrants in Europe." *Journal of Ethnic and Migration Studies* 32, no. 8 (2006): 1257–1281.

Wessendorf, Susanne. "Roots Migrants: Transnationalism and 'Return' Among Second-Generation Italians in Switzerland." *Journal of Ethnic and Migration Studies* 33, no. 7 (2007): 1083–1102.

Young, Diane S., and Erin A. Casey. "An Examination of the Sufficiency of Small Qualitative Samples." *Social Work & Criminal Justice Publications* 500 (2018): 1–17.

CHAPTER 5

First Nations Sovereignty: Towards a Decolonial Approach to Italy–Australia Relations

Francesco Ricatti and Matteo Dutto

INTRODUCTION

As the editors of this volume emphasise in the introduction, there is still limited research on Italy-Australia relations.[1] It is thus perhaps not surprising that even less attention has been devoted to Italy's relations with First Nations. Despite some significant exceptions, especially in the area of migration history and transcultural studies, the study of relations

---

[1] See Gabriele Abbondanza and Simone Battiston, "Italy and Australia in the Twenty-First Century: Distant Connections or Close Partners?" in *Italy and Australia: Redefining Bilateral Relations for the Twenty-First Century*, ed. Gabriele Abbondanza and Simone Battiston (London: Palgrave Macmillan, 2024), pp. 1–23.

F. Ricatti (✉)
Italian Studies, Australian National University, Canberra, ACT, Australia
e-mail: francesco.ricatti@anu.edu.au

M. Dutto
European Research Foundation, Monash University, Prato, Italy

113

between Italy and Australia has, to date, largely ignored First Nations people and their sovereignty.[2] Decolonial approaches to the study of International Relations have insisted on the importance of developing broad multidisciplinary methods that are centred around Indigenous ontologies and epistemologies.[3] There is an urgent and crucial need to question the linear and Nation-focused approach to relations between Italy and Australia that, to date, has rendered largely invisible the existence and centrality of Indigenous sovereignty. This chapter aims to foster further dialogue, theorisation and research in this area, through a decolonial and multidisciplinary methodological perspective. Too often rigid disciplinary approaches limit difficult yet necessary dialogues. A more open disciplinary approach may help identify the areas in which potential decolonial methodologies can be more effectively employed, and is consistent with the multidisciplinary approach employed in this volume.[4]

The most respectful and productive Italian engagements with Indigenous people, lands and cultures, to date, have not come from the Italian Nation State and its political institutions (such as diplomacy), but rather from Italian individuals, associations, and, in some instances, cultural institutions. Australia is a settler-colonial nation, and its economic success and geopolitical power have been founded on racist ideologies, institutions, laws and practices. The genocide of Indigenous people, cultures and languages has, in fact, been functional to the continuing appropriation and exploitation of unceded Indigenous Countries. As argued by Patrick Wolfe, and many other scholars since, Australian settler colonialism is not an event concluded in the past, but rather an ever-evolving

---

[2] Key literature on the topic includes Dutto, "A Migrant Filmaker"; Dutto, "Reframing Encounters"; Indelicato, "Beyond Whiteness"; Pascoe et al. "First Nations Australians"; Pugliese, "Migrant Heritage"; Pugliese, "De-Anthropocentrising Migrant Historiography"; Ricatti et al. "Forum"; Ricatti, "The Emotion of Truth"; Ricatti, "Indigenous Sovereignty."

[3] See for instance Blaney and Tickner, "Wordling, Ontological Politics"; Capan, "Decolonising International Relations"; Chipato and Chandler, "Another Decolonial Approach"; Taylor, "Decolonizing International Relations"; Tucker, "Unraveling Coloniality"; Capan (2017) in Tucker (2018); Blaney and Tickner (2017); Zondi, "Decolonising International Relations."

[4] See Gabriele Abbondanza and Simone Battiston, "Italy and Australia in the Twenty-First Century: Distant Connections or Close Partners?" in *Italy and Australia: Redefining Bilateral Relations for the Twenty-First Century*, ed. Gabriele Abbondanza and Simone Battiston (London: Palgrave Macmillan, 2024), pp. 1–23.

structure of power that continues to shape Australian society, culture, politics, economy and international relations.[5] At the same time, Italy has its own colonial history, and racist ideologies still play an important role in the political life of the nation, and in its international relations, while neocolonial and neoliberal practices continue to play a central role in Italian economic and industrial development.[6] Such a situation makes it particularly difficult to imagine how these two Nation States could promote Indigenous sovereignty and decolonising practices as core elements of their reciprocal interactions. Instead, the potentiality for decolonial processes is mostly to be found in the initiatives of individuals, associations, and at times publicly funded institutions that have centred the relations between Italy and Australia around Indigenous rights and sovereignty, rather than economic and geopolitical concerns. It is, in fact, in the dialogues and shared activism with Indigenous people that a new way of imagining Italy's relations with Australia can start to take shape and gain visibility.

In the first part of this chapter, we will therefore consider the concept of Indigenous sovereignty and its implications, as providing the fundamental methodological frame. In the second section, we will then argue that the complex and ambiguous positioning of Italian migrants within the Australian settler-colonial context provides some important points of reference and orientation in rethinking the relations between Italy and First Nations. The third section will illustrate how past and present relations between Italian and First Nations artists, activists and curators have provided fertile ground for the development of more active and productive interactions between Italy and First Nations, and for the fundamental recognition of Indigenous sovereignty.

INDIGENOUS SOVEREIGNTY AND ITS IMPLICATIONS

In developing the study of Italy-Australia relations we acknowledge that Australia is a settler-colonial nation built on, and prospering from, genocide and the expropriation of Indigenous land. This also requires an understanding of how contemporary Indigenous conceptions of

---

[5] Wolfe, "Settler Colonialism." See also Kauanui, "A Structure, Not an Event."

[6] Mezzadra, "La condizione postcoloniale"; Mezzadra and Rahola, "The Postcolonial Condition."

sovereignty are founded on deep and complex ontologies and relations to Country, and how they have further developed since colonisation, through anticolonial struggles and activism. While it is not possible to provide a comprehensive and detailed history here, we think it is pivotal to recall some of the key moments and aspects of this struggle for sovereignty. And furthermore, we acknowledge that sovereignty in this context is to be understood in relation to Indigenous ontologies, epistemologies, lives and forms of resistance. That is, in imagining how international relations between Italy and First Nations could develop in the future, Indigenous conceptions of sovereignty should prevail over established Italian, Australian and international understandings of the term. To give priority to Indigenous perspectives, and to acknowledge the centrality of their anticolonial resistance, is, in fact, the first and most important step in any decolonial process.

The settler-colonial project that shapes contemporary Australia has its roots in British settlers' attempt at forming a new permanent society predicated on what Australian historian Patrick Wolfe famously defines as a "logic of elimination" of Indigenous sovereignties and Indigenous people.[7] Unlike in other settler colonies, such as New Zealand, Canada and the United States, the British colonisation of Australia did not recognise Indigenous people's occupation and connection to their land, claiming that the newly acquired lands were instead *terra nullius*, that is "land belonging to no-one", and could thus be invaded and placed under Crown Sovereignty without treaties or payments.[8] Settler domination was established and maintained to this day through strategies that range from physical and cultural elimination, forced dispossession, relocation and exclusions to assimilation and recognition policies.[9]

Since the early days of the British invasion of Eora Country in 1788, in the place that we know today as Sydney, Indigenous Australians have resisted the invasion of their sovereign Countries in a variety of different ways. Armed resistance and guerrilla warfare campaigns lasted until the 1930s across all of Australia, and are remembered today as the "frontier

---

[7] Wolfe, "Settler Colonialism and the Elimination of the Native," 388.

[8] See Fitzmaurice, "The Genealogy of Terra Nullius"; Borch, "Rethinking the Origins of Terra Nullius"; Watson, "Re-Centring First Nations Knowledge and Places in a Terra Nullius Space."

[9] See Wolfe, *Settler Colonialism and Transformation*.

wars".[10] Political activism and efforts to build support for Indigenous human and land rights among non-Indigenous Australians had emerged already in the 1920s, with the foundation of the Australian Aboriginal Progress Association (AAPA) in Sydney by Worimi activist Fred Maynard. Indigenous communities and organisations across Australia led numerous protests in the following decades, including the 1938 Day of Mourning, the Yirrkala Bark Petitions in 1963, the 1965 Freedom Ride and the Wave Hill walk-off in 1966, demanding full citizen status and equal rights. The 1960s and 1970s then saw a new generation of young Indigenous activists and intellectuals placing self-determination, land rights and culture at the centre of the political discourse. Indigenous-controlled and community-driven organisations, such as the Aboriginal Legal Services and the Aboriginal Health Service, that emerged in the 1970s in the Sydney suburb of Redfern, provided the blueprint for numerous other Indigenous organisations across Australia.[11] High-profile and radical protests, like the 1972 Aboriginal Tent Embassy, established communication and performance strategies that were first able to bring the fight for land rights to the world stage and continue to be used by groups of Indigenous activists such as the Warriors of Aboriginal Resistance to this day.[12]

Indigenous resistance and the ongoing fight for sovereignty, self-determination and land rights should not only be understood through Indigenous political activism. As Goenpul scholar Aileen Moreton-Robinson argues, Indigenous resistance practices are varied and layered, working across personal, cultural, historical and political dimensions.[13] This crucial point is also connected to the form that sovereignty takes in Indigenous ways of knowing, the differences this form has to Western understandings of sovereignty and to the profound implications this has for land rights demands. When the 1992 *Mabo v. Queensland (No. 2)* High Court judgement first recognised the persistence of traditional

[10] For a detailed historical account of the frontier wars see Reynolds, *The Other Side of the Frontier: Aboriginal Resistance to the European Invasion of Australia*; Reynolds, *Forgotten War*.

[11] Burgmann, *The Aboriginal Movement in Power, Profit and Protest: Australian Social Movements and Globalisation*, 55.

[12] Foley, Howell, and Schaap, *The Aboriginal Tent Embassy: Sovereignty, Black Power, Land Rights and the State*.

[13] Moreton-Robinson, "I Still Call Australia Home: Indigenous Belonging and Place in a White Postcolonising Society," 128.

Indigenous law over specific parts of Australia, it did not challenge the validity of Crown sovereignty over Indigenous Countries, reserving the right to extinguish native title rights through compensation. As Tanganekald and Meintangk lawyer and scholar Irene Watson explains, by formulating colonisation as an "Act of State" that cannot be disputed in an Australian Court, the judgement effectively ruled out the issue of Indigenous sovereignty as non-justiciable.[14]

Native title rights must thus be negotiated through the Australian law system, imposing a burden of proof on Indigenous people, and not accounting for the modern dimension of Indigenous experiences and the impact of the colonial domain.[15] Following the Mabo judgement, numerous Indigenous and non-Indigenous scholars have argued that definitions of sovereignty that privilege issues of property and territoriality do not account for what Indigenous people mean by sovereignty.[16] Indigenous scholar and writer Tony Birch has proposed that Indigenous sovereignty is better understood as a "multifaceted concept", one that is not defined only through European law but "is maintained through pre-existing, pre-European models of governance. Such models continue to be culturally and politically sustainable, regardless of the lack of legal recognition by Australian governments".[17] For Birch and other scholars, sovereignty is at the same time embodied, psychological and political, a concept that exists both in the now and in the sacred, and is better understood as an expression of identity, and as an act of self-determination that predates colonial sovereignty, while at the same time questioning its authority.

When taking into consideration these complex and nuanced understandings of Indigenous sovereignty, we must then also consider the role that foreign nations and their people may have played in processes of colonisations, as well as in supporting anticolonial resistance and struggle. In the case of Italy, three aspects seem particularly relevant. The first, which we will consider in the next section, is that millions of Italians

---

[14] Watson, "Nungas in the Nineties," 11.

[15] Nicoll, "De-Facing Terra Nullius and Facing the Secret of Indigenous Sovereignty in Australia."

[16] Behrendt, *Achieving Social Justice*; Langton et al., *Honour Among Nations? Treaties and Agreements with Indigenous People*; Moreton-Robinson, *Sovereign Subjects*.

[17] Birch, "The Invisible Fire," 107.

migrated to settler-colonial nations, including Australia, since the nine-teenth century. From the perspective of Indigenous sovereignty, they migrated to First Nations' Country. The complicity and essential role that migrants have played in settler colonialism must therefore be recognised and researched, and new relevance must be given to their encounters, clashes, negotiations and complex relationships with Indigenous people. The second, which we will discuss in the following section, is that *artivists* and activists whose work has been shaped by a deep and genuine respect for Indigenous sovereignty may provide a model for the further develop-ment of decolonial relations between Italy and First Nations. The third, which we will argue in our concluding remarks, is that the Italian Nation itself, including its diplomatic representations abroad, should start to take Indigenous sovereignty seriously. While we remain sceptical of the possibility of seeing this final point implemented in the near future, we also believe that political and constitutional change within Australia may encourage Italy and its diplomats in Australia to start considering this matter more closely.

MIGRATION, DIASPORA COLONIALISM AND DECOLONISATION

As for many other countries that have experienced a large influx of Italian migrants, the development of political, economic and cultural relations between Italy and Australia has been influenced by the large presence of Italians in Australia, their processes of settlement, and their transna-tional relations and networks. This is true for the first generation, as well as for the second and subsequent generations. In different, complex and ever-evolving forms, they have maintained substantial linguistic, cultural, political and economic bridges between the two countries.[18] Currently, more than one million people in Australia claim Italian ancestry—approximately 4.4% of the population—and they have had a significant impact on Australian society and culture.[19] Given Australia's history as a racist, settler-colonial nation, and Italy's own history as a colonial and racist power, it is not surprising that in the process of settlement, and in the development and maintenance of transnational connections,

[18] Ricatti, *Italians in Australia*.
[19] Australian Bureau of Statistics.

Italian migrants and their descendants have also become complicit in the establishment, development and strengthening of Australia's settler colonialism. At the same time, within an ideologically and politically variegated Italian community, and through complex processes of transculturation and exchange, many Italian migrants, whom often experienced racism and discrimination themselves, have also become partners, friends and comrades of First Nations people, and have supported their struggles for life, knowledge, justice, respect, sovereignty and Country.

The study of existing and potential relations between Italy and First Nations needs to develop first and foremost from a critical analysis of Italian migrants' complicity with and resistance to racism and settler colonialism. Dominant settler-colonial narratives have long separated migrant and Indigenous histories in Australia, positioning non-Anglo migrants as perpetual outsiders and Indigenous people as non-Australians within the White nation-space.[20] To recognise the entangled histories of "migrant-cum-settlers" and Indigenous people is a potentially powerful way of challenging dominant narratives and rethinking Australian history and society, including its international and transnational relations.[21] In multicultural, settler-colonial countries a strong tension exists between the need for promoting migrants' rights and social inclusion, and the need to recognise the key role that migration and multiculturalism have played in the occupation and exploitation of Indigenous land. There are two essential steps in resolving such tension, decolonisation based on Indigenous sovereignty, and transculturation.

First and foremost, Indigenous sovereignty has to be acknowledged as foundational to any form of antiracist activism. Effective antiracist strategies in a settler-colonial country must start from, and be shaped by, resistance to the racial discrimination of Indigenous people. Without that, any expectation or request that Italian migrants should not be subjected to racism, becomes not just hypocritical and ineffective, but violent. This becomes apparent in Italian migrants' recurring narratives according to

---

[20] See Hage, *White Nation: Fantasies of White Supremacy in a Multicultural Nation*; Nicolacopoulos and Vassilacopoulos, "Racism, Foreigner Communities and the Onto-Pathology of White Australian Subjectivity"; Sonn et al., "Negotiating Belonging in Australia Through Storytelling and Encounter."

[21] Curthoys, "An Uneasy Conversation: The Multicultural and the Indigenous"; Persian and Agutter, "European Post-War Migrants"; Piperoglou, "Migrant-cum-Settler"; Balint and Simic, "Histories of Migrants"; Teo, "Multiculturalism."

which, while they certainly experienced racism in Australia, they worked hard and through sacrifice and conformity to the law demonstrated their value to the Australian nation, which now treats them well. In this narrative, racism does not constitute the structural foundation of Australian society itself. Instead, it is naturalised and normalised as a form of understandable mistrust of others, which can be overcome when these others, for instance Italian migrants, prove their worth and their gratitude to the hosting Nation. Implied here, and at times actually made explicit in migrant discourse and narratives, is the idea that those migrant and Indigenous communities that continue to experience racism, deserve such treatment.[22] This is why any form of antiracism that is aimed exclusively at the protection and recognition of a particular migrant community, rather than the contestation of structural racism, is itself fundamentally racist and violent.

The second key step, which is subordinate to the recognition of Indigenous sovereignty, but is nevertheless essential, is a new understanding of Australian history and society through the prism of transculturation. Starting from the work of Ortiz on Cuba, and other scholars since, the transcultural approach aims to recognise how cultural influences in colonial contexts are never unidirectional (the acculturation of minorities into the dominant group).[23] Instead, colonial and racist processes of deculturation, in which Indigenous people and slaves or indentured labourers are forced to lose language and culture, are resisted through complex and rich processes of cultural and linguistic resilience, and through reciprocal cultural interactions and collaboration between Indigenous people and other subaltern groups. In turn, the creative and political potential of such relations also impacts and transforms the cultures and languages of the dominant settlers, as evidenced by the profound transformation of Australian society since colonisation.

With regard to the specific case of Italian migrants, this approach requires that we reconsider their history of migration to, and settlement in Australia by centring Indigenous sovereignty, and acknowledging migrants' relations with Indigenous people. Many aspects of this complex history have only recently begun to be explored.[24] Among the many

[22] Balla, "Blak Female."
[23] Ortiz, "Cuban Counterpoint."
[24] See Ricatti et al. "Forum."

themes that are still to be carefully studied, we would like to note those that seem potentially more productive for the establishment of decolonial relations.

Firstly, a growing body of work has considered the racial ambiguity of Italian (and other Mediterranean) migrants in Australia and elsewhere.[25] Yet much remains to be researched on the specific functions that such racial ambiguity has played in fundamental historical shifts, such as the transformation of imperial settler colonies into settler-colonial nations, the end of slavery and indentured labour and the emergence of racialised capitalism. Many of these political, social and economic transformations have benefited from the flexibility provided by migrants who were racially ambiguous, including Southern Italians. Such ambiguity has in fact allowed the dominant white class to identify these migrant groups as white, almost white, or almost black, depending on the different roles these migrants came to have within shifting political and economic contexts. At the same time, such racial ambiguity and flexibility have encouraged many Italian migrants to reinstate their whiteness to the detriment of Indigenous people and darker or more recent migrants.

We still know relatively little about the role that Italian geographers, ethnographers, missionaries and journalists have played in the imaginary construction of the Indigenous other. Preliminary studies on this suggest these "explorers" and "pioneers" have often replicated and spread the dominant stereotypes they learnt in Australia. Nevertheless, we should not underestimate the influence of Hispanic and Latin American representations, especially through the influence of the Catholic Church—for instance, see the study of Vatican collections, and the case of the New Norcia monastery in Western Australia.[26]

A third, crucial aspect is the study of mixed Indigenous Italian families. The limited research developed to date suggests that even though we are probably talking about a few thousand people, these family histories, memories and current experiences can provide transcultural and intersectional models for decolonial and antiracist social processes, including the importance of promoting the co-existence of both migrant and Indigenous local identities as an alternative to the national identities that shape

[25] See Andreoni, "Olive or White?"; Caiazza, "Are Italians White?"; Guglielmo and Salerno, "Are Italians White?"; Indelicato, "Beyond Whiteness"; Luconi, "Whiteness and Ethnicity"; Vitale, "The Chinese of Europe."

[26] Aigner, "Australia"; Verdina and Kinder, "Selvaggi o nativi?"

the dominant multicultural model.[27] These stories also highlight that such transcultural and multilingual processes often develop within intimate and familial contexts in which different ontologies, epistemologies and ideologies can be negotiated through affect; or conversely hindered by racism, domestic violence and essentialised understandings of ethnic identities.

A final essential aspect, to which we devote part of the next section in this chapter, is the role that Italian migrants have played in sustaining the development of Indigenous activism and art. This short section could not provide an accurate and comprehensive analysis of the relations between Indigenous people and Italian migrants in Australia. Rather, the aim was to emphasise the potential of this still underdeveloped field of research in informing the positive roles that migrants can play in future relations between Italy and First Nations, while also acknowledging the limitations of an almost exclusive focus on Italian migrants' contribution to the economic and social development of Australia.[28]

RELATIONS BETWEEN ITALIAN AND FIRST NATIONS ARTISTS AND ACTIVISTS

As discussed earlier in this chapter, Indigenous resistance to settler colonialism takes many forms. Since the early years of invasion, storytelling has been a crucial strategy for reassertions of sovereignty by showcasing the dynamic and diverse sense of Indigenous agency and survival in the present.[29] As Sium and Ritskes explain, telling stories is one of the most effective strategies of Indigenous resistance in the ongoing struggle for land rights and sovereignty:

Indigenous stories are a reclamation of Indigenous voice, Indigenous land, and Indigenous sovereignty. They are vital to decolonization. Indigenous storytelling works to both deconstruct colonial ways of coming to know, as well as construct alternatives - recognizing that these two processes do

---

[27] Pallotta-Chiarolli and Ricatti, "Migrant Lives."

[28] See Gabriele Abbondanza and Simone Battiston, "Italy and Australia in the Twenty-First Century: Distant Connections or Close Partners?" in *Italy and Australia: Redefining Bilateral Relations for the Twenty-First Century*, ed. Gabriele Abbondanza and Simone Battiston (London: Palgrave Macmillan, 2024), pp. 1–23.

[29] Vizenor, *Manifest Manners: Narratives on Postindian Survivance.*

not happen in a linear trajectory; if we are waiting for the dismantling of colonial structures before we focus on rebuilding Indigenous and decolonial alternatives, we will always be too late. Indigenous stories are a creative force, grounded in rootedness and relationality.[30]

Storytelling reinscribes Indigenous presence over *terra nullius*. It makes visible the existence of other ways of understanding sovereignty and of relating to the land that cannot be framed solely through non-Indigenous notions of belonging and identity.[31] Focusing on the act of telling stories, on how they are told and on who tells them, can thus prove extremely fruitful when exploring the relations between Italian migrants and Indigenous Australians from a different epistemological lens. A critical exploration of what Indigenous scholar Shino Konishi identifies as the "long histories of entanglement between Indigenous people and non-Anglo migrants" and of how these stories have been told by Indigenous and migrant cultural producers, has the potential of breaking down these long-standing separations, complicating our understandings of these relationships and of the complex processes of transculturation that they generated. Doing so requires us to shift our focus from understandings of migrant storytelling that place emphasis on the lived experience of individuals and their communities and on their relations with the host country, to a wider definition that also includes collaborations between migrants and Indigenous artists on projects that focus instead on Indigenous histories and cultures. It is in these stories of collaboration that, as we argue, more productive methodologies for active and critical interactions between Italy and First Nations have emerged, in many instances providing different models of belonging and storytelling that have at their heart the recognition of Indigenous sovereignty and a deep engagement with Indigenous epistemologies and ways of knowing.

A brief overview of how these histories of entanglement have unfolded and been represented through film, documentary and media productions by Italian and Indigenous activists can provide a better understanding of the untapped potential in this area of research, and of the richness and

[30] Sium and Ritskes, "Speaking Truth to Power: Indigenous Storytelling as an Act of Living Resistance," viii.

[31] Dutto, *Legacies of Indigenous Resistance: Pemulwuy, Jandamarra and Yagan in Australian Indigenous Film, Theatre and Literature*.

complexity that could emerge through further studies. Films and documentaries by Italian and Australian filmmakers detailing the lives of Italian
migrants to Australia have very rarely engaged with the entanglements
and relations between Indigenous Australians and Italian communities, choosing to focus instead on the relations and clashes between
migrants and Anglo-Celtic settlers.[32] In the few instances where Indigenous characters were indeed featured, such as in Luigi Zampa's 1971
film *Bello, onesto, emigrato Australia sposerebbe compaesana illibata,* they
were portrayed as exotic, innocent and mostly voiceless "noble-savages",
thus contributing to further popularising settler-colonial ideologies and
stereotypes among the Italian audience.[33] Yet, since the 1970s, Italian
producers and filmmakers have established prolific "behind the camera"
collaborations with Indigenous artists and communities in films and documentaries that attempt to break settler-colonial ideologies to showcase
Indigenous sovereignty through the lens of indigenous aesthetics and
epistemologies.[34] These relations can be traced back to the documentaries
of Alessandro Cavadini, an Italian filmmaker and activist who migrated to
Australia in 1969, and between 1972 and 1982 realised numerous documentaries in collaboration with his brother Fabio, Australian filmmaker
Carolyn Strachan and numerous Indigenous activists and communities
across Australia.

His first effort *Ningla A-Na* (1972) saw him work with Indigenous
activists and the Redfern Indigenous community of Sydney to realise
a documentary on the history of the Aboriginal Tent Embassy and
the 1972 Indigenous land rights movement.[35] As the first film shot
from the perspective of the Indigenous activists, this work proved to
be a powerful tool for international advocacy and transcultural engagement. To this day it remains one of the first instances in which what

[32] Dutto, "Reframing Encounters Between Italian Migrants and Indigenous Australians
in Far Away Is Home. La Storia Di Clely (Diego Cenetiempo, Australia/Italy, 2012)."

[33] For more details on the cinematic representations of the "noble savage" trope in
Australian cinema see Peters-Little, "Nobles and Savages."

[34] Dutto, "Unsettling Migrant Frames: Reflections on the Cinematic Encounters
between Italian Migrants and Indigenous Australians"; see also Rando, "Migrant Images
in Italian Australian Movies and Documentaries"; Rando, *Emigrazione e Letteratura: Il
Caso Italoaustraliano,* 179–226.

[35] For a detailed account of the production and distribution history of the film see
Dutto, "A Migrant Filmmaker at the Aboriginal Tent Embassy."

Seneca scholar Michelle Raheja has termed "visual sovereignty" was enacted in Australia. As she explains, visual sovereignty is best understood as a strategy to screen and make tangible and accessible to a larger audience the sacred, historical, embodied and psychological aspects of Indigenous sovereignty that are often excluded from settler-colonial understandings of sovereignty and therefore from legal discourse and native title negotiations.[36] Film and other visual media thus offer the possibility of intervening in these larger discussions, "locating and advocating for Indigenous cultural and political power both within and outside of Western legal jurisprudence".[37] The films that Cavadini directed in the following years all speak to this desire to collaborate with Indigenous activists and communities to contribute to the ongoing fight for Indigenous land rights and sovereignty by facilitating the emergence of Indigenous perspectives and opening lines of communication between Indigenous activists and non-Anglo migrants. As visual anthropologist Faye Ginsburg explains, the documentaries that Cavadini realised in collaboration with his brother Fabio, Australian filmmaker Carolyn Strachan and Indigenous communities across Australia constitute a radical "paradigm shift" in the transnational history of ethnographic filmmaking that forever changed the approach to cross-cultural filmmaking and deeply influenced the development of Indigenous media in Australia.[38]

Nowhere is this more visible than in his most famous work *Two Laws* (1982), commissioned by the Mara, Yanula, Garrawa and Gurdandji people of the Borroloola community of the Gulf Region in the Northern Territory to Alessandro Cavadini and Carolyn Strachan in 1981. The two-hour, ground-breaking documentary was created with the objective of supporting their land claim during native title negotiations and keeping Borroloola Law and history alive. Refusing to replicate the colonial gaze of previous non-Indigenous ethnographic productions and following a two-year process of consultation and participation, Cavadini and Strachan decided to, as Davis and Plate argue, "surrender control" of the camera and of the production of the film to the community itself,

[36] Raheja, *Reservation Reelism: Redfacing, Visual Sovereignty, and Representations Of Native Americans in Film.*

[37] Raheja, "Reading Nanook's Smile: Visual Sovereignty, Indigenous Revisions of Ethnography, and Atanarjuat (The Fast Runner)," 1151.

[38] Ginsburg, "Breaking the Law with Two Laws: Reflections on a Paradigm Shift."

foregrounding Borroloola perspectives and aesthetics.[39] The result is a collectively authored reflexive documentary where oral testimonies and dramatic community re-enactments blend together to create an active and legitimate enactment and record of Booroloola law and history that was of pivotal importance for the final 2006 deliberation that saw some of the land originally requested returned to the community.

The work of Alessandro Cavadini and the ongoing collaborations of his brother Fabio with Indigenous producers and directors such as Gadrian Jarwijalmar Hoosan, Larissa Behrendt and Jason De Santolo are but one of the numerous instances in which Italian and Italian Australian directors collaborated with Indigenous communities on projects that sought to decolonise settler-colonial historiographies and understandings of sovereignty. While a full historical analysis of these relations is yet to be produced, it is worth remembering the work of Italo-Australian director Fred Schepisi with Murrungun actor Tom E. Lewis on *The Chant of Jimmie Blacksmith* (1978), as well as the role of producer/director Rosa Colosimo on the TV documentary series *Women of the Sun* (1981). Jan Cattoni's 2001 short film *Hey Sista* is another example of how these collaborations can inform better understandings of the history of Italian migration to Australia and of migrants' understandings of belonging that refuse settler-colonial narratives and engage instead with the richness and complexity of First Nations ways of knowing. In this short drama set in 1975, the teenage Italian Australian protagonist is rejected by her Italian community and establishes an unexpected friendship with the local female Indigenous basketball team, in a story that showcases the racism of Italian migrants towards Indigenous Australians and the different sense of identity and acceptance that the young protagonist is able to build through her relations with Indigenous teenagers. A similar story of dissent and of engagement with Indigenous understandings of identity and belonging is told by Diego Cenetiempo in his 2012 documentary *Far Away is Home: la Storia di Clely*. Here, the Italian director tells the story of Clely Quaiat Yumbulul, a Triestine Italian migrant who after moving to Galiwin'ku on Elcho Island married Warramiri leader and artist Terry Yumbulul and identifies herself as part Triestine and part Indigenous, rejecting modes of

---

[39] Davis and Plate, "Surrendering Control: Two Laws as Collaborative Community Film-Making: An Interview with Carolyn Strachan and Alessandro Cavadini."

belonging that would see her as either divided between Italy and Australia or assimilated into Warramiri culture.[40]

Digital storytelling projects such as *Black Post White* (2013) are also bringing to light further stories of entanglements between Italian migrants and Indigenous Australians. In this project, realised by filmmaker Vincent Lamberti in collaboration with Culture Victoria and the Gippsland & East Gippsland Aboriginal Co-operative, Indigenous elders bring to life the story of Gunai/Kurnai Country through a collection of life stories that include reflections on their encounters, exchanges and alliances with Italian migrant farmers, thus reframing migration narratives from within an Indigenous perspective. Recent transnational film and media productions about current Italian migration, such as the web series *Italian Dreamtime* (Denis Strickner and Emiliano Bechi Gabrielli, 2015) have framed the experience of highly mobile and skilled youth in nationalistic narratives of rootedness and expatriation that portray Australia as the multicultural land of the "fair-go" and Italy as a source of reminiscence and nostalgia.[41] Yet, they have also introduced elements of dissent that shift our perspective on Italian youth mobility and sense of belonging. In its depiction of the cross-generational and transcultural encounters of their protagonists, *Italian Dreamtime* ultimately challenges some of the stereotypes about the Italian community in Australia, offering new insights into the role of migrants in a settler-colonial society, the transnational network of connections that they establish with other migrant and Indigenous communities and the transcultural experiences that shape their imagination and sense of self. In the web series, this is best seen in the episode dedicated to the story of Fiorino Fiorini, an Italian musician who has travelled extensively throughout Arnhem Land to learn and play the yidaki with musicians such as Djalu Gurruwiwi and Alan Dargin, and organises every year the Forlimpopoli Didjin'OZ festival. Now in its twentieth year, the festival constitutes one of the largest celebrations of Indigenous cultures in Italy, featuring a rich program of events across music, film, dance, literature, photography and visual arts.

---

[40] Dutto, "Reframing Encounters."

[41] For more on current Italian migration to Australia see Simone Battiston, "Italians in Australia in the Twenty-First Century," in *Italy and Australia: Redefining Bilateral Relations for the Twenty-First Century*, ed. Gabriele Abbondanza and Simone Battiston (London: Palgrave Macmillan, 2024), pp. 49–80.

While this section has focused on documentary films, it is also important to note that interesting developments in similar directions can be
noted within the broader field of visual and performing art. For instance,
the presence and relevance of Indigenous art in Italy, including at prestigious events such as the Venice Biennale, and through private galleries,
suggest the potential for fruitful cultural and commercial exchanges
between Italian and Indigenous artists and curators.[42] Artist residencies
have also brought a number of Indigenous artists to Italy. In 2009 a
cultural exchange project led by Italian Australian cultural promoter Maria
Sanciolo-Bell through the Institute of Culture Sicily-Australia (ICSA)
brought Indigenous artist Billy Doolan to Sicily for an art residency. Interviewed by the ABC about his experience, the north-Queensland artist
recalls how the voice of the land and the stories Sicilians shared with him
resonated with him and his own Country. As he puts it: "There were
stories that I was told there that were very similar to Aboriginal culture.
There were stories about seasons. And being Indigenous people themselves, I had this - I just felt comfortable with them".[43] The result of this
cultural exchange was eight paintings where Doolan's impressions of the
Sicilian landscape, folklore and history engage in dialogue with his own
visual language and with the style and iconography of Northern Queensland Indigenous cultures. As Maria Sanciolo-Bell argues in the same
interview, these "are not traditionally Indigenous paintings. They're not
Italian, they're not European-style paintings. They have created almost –
they live in a genre of their own".[44] Doolan's impressions of Sicily were
exhibited in 2010 in Melbourne at the Italian Institute of Culture, and
were in 2011 part of *Dreamtime*, a collective large-scale exhibition on
Australian Indigenous art at the MAN museum in Nuoro (Italy). The
exhibition was curated by Maree Clarke e Amanda Reynolds and was
organised by ICSA and MAN in collaboration with the Koorie Heritage
Trust, with funding from the Sardinia region and the Italian Ministry
of Foreign Affairs and the support of the Italian Embassy in Canberra,
the Australian Embassy in Rome, and the Italian Institute of Culture and
Consulate in Melbourne.

---

[42] Kerry Gardner (2021), Australia at the Venice Biennale.

[43] Billy Doolan in *Italy through Australian Eyes*.

[44] Maria Sanciolo-Bell in *Italy through Australian Eyes*.

Dreamtime was at the time the largest public showing of Indigenous art outside of Australia. It featured over 300 items from over 90 different Indigenous artists, including Clifford Possum, John e Luke Cummins, Trevor Turbo Brown and Craig Charles.[45] Conceived to showcase the richness and diversity of contemporary Australian Indigenous art, the exhibition also drew parallels with local Sardinian culture and art and attracted over 25,000 participants.[46] Despite its success, *Dreamtime* also speaks to the numerous difficulties that processes of transculturation and exchange encounter at an institutional level. While the Italian Government funded a large part of the exhibition's budget, the Australian Government refused to finance a travel grant that would have allowed eight Indigenous artists to present their work.[47] Billy Doolan's experience in Sicily and the Dreamtime exhibition in Nuoro thus speak to how many of these artistic exchanges and transcultural encounters have been spearheaded and promoted by single institutions and associations, or even individuals, and largely outside of wider cultural diplomacy and international relationships agreements between Italy and Australia.[48]

In recent years, we have also witnessed the emergence of *artivists* of mixed Indigenous and Italian background, who have demonstrated not just political integrity and artistic talent, but also the capacity to explore the complex transcultural intersections between Indigenous and Italian cultures; among them, Paola Balla (Wemba-Wemba, Gunditjmara, Italian, and Chinese), Lisa Waup (Gunditjmara, Torres Strait Islander, and Italian) and the emerging Moorina Bonini (Yorta Yorta, Wurundjeri Woi Wurrung, and Italian).[49]

[45] "Dreamtime."

[46] "Billy Doolan—Aboriginal Artist | Dreamtime Lo Spirito Dell'Arte Aborigena."

[47] "Billy Doolan—Aboriginal Artist | Dreamtime Lo Spirito Dell'Arte Aborigena"; *Italy through Australian Eyes.*

[48] For other examples see the exchange between Sicilian and Indigenous artists organised by Miriam La Rosa (https://www.segmento.com.au/post/an-exchange-art-residency-between-sicily-and-australia); and the inclusion of Indigenous artists like Maree Clarke and Hayley Millar Baker in the "artist in residency" program at the Monash University Prato Centre (see https://www.monash.edu/prato/research/visual-residency).

[49] See https://www.paolaballa.art/; https://artjewelryforum.org/interviews/contin uity/; https://www.moorinabonini.com/about.

Concluding Remarks

While we write the concluding remarks for this chapter, a new Australian Government, led by the Labor Prime Minister Anthony Albanese, has just been elected to replace a conservative Government. Albanese's first statement after the victory was to acknowledge Indigenous people and to promise the implementation of the Uluru Statement from the Heart, including the establishment of an Indigenous voice to Parliament, a *Makarata* (Yolngu word for treaty), and truth telling. While it was rightly noted that Albanese failed to make reference to the specific Country and people on which he was, thus failing to properly acknowledge Indigenous sovereignty, the intention to implement the Uluru Statement is a sign of the Australian Government finally moving towards a higher level of formal recognition of Indigenous sovereignty, with significant legal, political and cultural implications. Some of these changes may require the support of the conservative opposition as well, as constitutional changes in Australia require a referendum, and referenda almost never succeed without bipartisan support.[50] It is thus not surprising that, at the moment, the focus of activists and politicians who support the Uluru Statement is mostly on the political debate within the Australian nation and among First Nations. Yet we would like to suggest that these changes also have deep implications with regard to international laws and international relations. How should, for instance, a country like Italy acknowledge, support and eventually embrace such changes, before and after they will hopefully be implemented?

In this chapter, we have emphasised three essential responses to this challenge: firstly, the recognition of Indigenous sovereignty, if not at a formal diplomatic level, at least as a crucial ethical imperative that may shape institutional relations, cultural exchanges and economic developments; secondly, the acknowledgement of the complex and contradictory role that Italian migrants have played and will continue to play on these matters, as one of the largest and most established ethnic communities in Australia; and thirdly, the consideration of existing positive and productive relationships between Italians and Indigenous people, within

---

[50] Gabriele Abbondanza, "The Republic of Murrawarri and the Debate on Aboriginal Sovereignty in Australia," *Indigenous Policy Journal* 28, no. 3 (2018): 1–16.

families of mixed background, and even more so within the arts and political activism—these relations may provide potential models and points of orientation for further and broader interactions and collaborations between Italians and Indigenous people.

REFERENCES

Abbondanza, Gabriele. "The Republic of Murrawarri and the Debate on Aboriginal Sovereignty in Australia." *Indigenous Policy Journal* 28, no. 3 (2018): 1–16.

Abbondanza, Gabriele, and Simone Battiston. "Italy and Australia in the Twenty-First Century: Distant Connections or Close Partners?" In *Italy and Australia: Redefining Bilateral Relations for the Twenty-First Century*, edited by Gabriele Abbondanza and Simone Battiston, pp. 1–23. London: Palgrave Macmillan, 2024.

Aigner, Katherine. *Australia: The Vatican Museum's Indigenous Collection.* Canberra: Aboriginal Studies Press and Musei Vaticani, 2017.

Andreoni, Helen. "Olive or White? The Colour of Italians in Australia." *Journal of Australian Studies* 27, no. 77 (2003): 81–92.

Australian Bureau of Statistics. *Cultural Diversity: Census*, 2021. https://www.abs.gov.au/statistics/people/people-and-communities/cultural-diversity-census/latest-release.

Balint, Ruth, and Zora Simic. "Histories of Migrants and Refugees in Australia." *Australian Historical Studies* 49, no. 3 (2018): 378–409.

Balla, Paola. "Blak Female Acts of Disruption (Continued)." In Ricatti, Francesco, Paola Balla, John Kinder, Matteo Dutto, Maria Pallotta-Chiarolli, Joseph Pugliese, and Federica Verdina. "Forum: Towards a Decolonial History of Italian Migration." *Altreitalie*, no. 59 (2019): 16–26.

Battiston, Simone. "Italians in Australia in the Twenty-First Century". In *Italy and Australia: Redefining Bilateral Relations for the Twenty-First Century*, edited by Gabriele Abbondanza and Simone Battiston, pp. 49–80. London: Palgrave Macmillan, 2024.

Behrendt, Larissa. *Achieving Social Justice: Indigenous Rights and Australia's Future.* Annandale, NSW: Federation Press, 2003.

"Billy Doolan—Aboriginal Artist | Dreamtime Lo Spirito Dell'Arte Aborigena." Accessed September 11, 2022. http://billydoolan.com.au/__artworks3.php.

Birch, Tony. "The Invisible Fire: Indigenous Sovereignty, History and Responsibility." In *Sovereign Subjects: Indigenous Sovereignty Matters*, edited by Aileen Moreton-Robinson, 105–17. Crows Nest: Allen & Unwin, 2007.

Blaney, David L., and Arlene B. Tickner. "Worlding, Ontological Politics and the Possibility of a Decolonial IR." *Millennium: Journal of International Studies* 45, no. 3 (2017): 293–311.

Borch, Merete. "Rethinking the Origins of Terra Nullius." *Australian Historical Studies* 32, no. 117 (2001): 222–39.

Burgmann, Verity. *The Aboriginal Movement in Power, Profit and Protest: Australian Social Movements and Globalisation*. Crows Nest, NSW: Allen & Unwin, 2003.

Caiazza, Tommaso. "Are Italians White? The Perspective from the Pacific." *California Italian Studies* 8, no. 2 (2018): 1–15

Capan, Zeynep Gulsah. "Decolonising International Relations?" *Third World Quarterly* 38, no. 1 (2017): 1–15.

Chipato, Farai, and David Chandler. "Another Decolonial Approach Is Possible: International Studies in an Antiblack World." *Third World Quarterly* 43, no. 7 (2022): 1783–97.

Curthoys, Ann. "An Uneasy Conversation: The Multicultural and the Indigenous." In *Race, Colour and Identity in Australia and New Zealand*, edited by John Docker and Gerhard Fischer, 21–36. Sydney: New South Wales University Press, 2000.

Davis, Therese, and Cassi Plate. "Surrendering Control: Two Laws as Collaborative Community Film-Making: An Interview with Carolyn Strachan and Alessandro Cavadini." *Studies in Documentary Film* 2, no. 2 (2008): 149–68.

Dutto, Matteo. "A Migrant Filmmaker at the Aboriginal Tent Embassy: Alessandro Cavadini's Ningla A-Na (1972) as a Transcultural Space of Encounter." *Australian Historical Studies* (2021): 1–17.

———. *Legacies of Indigenous Resistance: Pemulwuy, Jandamarra and Yagan in Australian Indigenous Film, Theatre and Literature*. Bern, Switzerland: Peter Lang UK, 2019.

———. "Reframing Encounters between Italian Migrants and Indigenous Australians in Far Away Is Home. La Storia Di Clely (Diego Cenetiempo, Australia/Italy, 2012)." *FULGOR: Flinders University Languages Group Online Review* 5, no. 1 (2016).

———. "Unsettling Migrant Frames: Reflections on the Cinematic Encounters between Italian Migrants and Indigenous Australians." *Altreitalie* 59 (2019).

Fitzmaurice, Andrew. "The Genealogy of Terra Nullius." *Australian Historical Studies* 38, no. 129 (2007): 1–15.

Foley, Gary, Edwina Howell, and Andrew Schaap, eds. *The Aboriginal Tent Embassy: Sovereignty, Black Power, Land Rights and the State*. London, UK: Taylor & Francis Group, 2013. http://ebookcentral.proquest.com/lib/monash/detail.action?docID=1323346.

Ginsburg, Faye. "Breaking the Law with Two Laws: Reflections on a Paradigm Shift." *Studies in Documentary Film* 2, no. 2 (2008): 169–74.

Guglielmo, Jennifer, and Salvatore Salerno, eds. *Are Italians White? How Race Is Made in America*. New York: Routledge, 2003.

Hage, Ghassan. *White Nation: Fantasies of White Supremacy in a Multicultural Nation*. Sydney: Pluto Press, 1998.

Indelicato, Maria Elena. "Beyond Whiteness: Violence and Belonging in the Borderlands of North Queensland." *Postcolonial Studies* 23, no. 1 (2020): 99–115.

Italy through Australian Eyes. Australian Broadcasting Corporation, 2011. https://www.abc.net.au/7.30/italy-through-australian-eyes/2670318.

Kauanui, J. Kēhaulani. "A Structure, Not an Event": Settler Colonialism and Enduring Indigeneity." *Lateral* 5, no. 1 (2016): n.p.

Langton, Marcia, Lisa Palmer, Maureen Tehan, and Kathryn Shain. *Honour Among Nations? Treaties and Agreements with Indigenous People*. Carlton, VIC: Melbourne University Press, 2004.

Luconi, Stefano. "Whiteness and Ethnicity in Italian American Historiography." In *The Status of Interpretation in Italian American Studies*, edited by Jerome Krase, 146–63. Stony Brook, NY: Forum Italicum Publishing, 2011.

MAN_Museo d'Arte Provincia di Nuoro. "Dreamtime." Accessed September 11, 2022. http://www.museoman.it/it/mostre/mostra/LA-MAGNIFICA-OSSESSIONE-00001/.

Mezzadra, Sandro. *La condizione postcoloniale: storia e politica nel presente globale*. Verona: Ombre Corte, 2008.

Mezzadra, Sandro, and Federico Rahola. "The Postcolonial Condition: A Few Notes on the Quality of Historical Time in the Global Present". In *Reworking Postcolonialism*, edited by Pvan Kumar Malreddy, Birte Heidemann, Ole Birk Laursen, and Janet Wilson, 36–54. London: Palgrave Macmillan, 2015.

Monture-Angus, Patricia. *Journeying Forward: Dreaming Aboriginal People's Independence*. Sydney: Pluto Press, 2000.

Moreton-Robinson, Aileen. "I Still Call Australia Home: Indigenous Belonging and Place in a White Postcolonising Society." In *Uprootings/Regroundings: Questions of Home and Migration*, edited by Sara Ahmed, Claudia Castada, and Anne-Marie Fortier, 23–40. Oxford; New York: Berg, 2003.

———. *Sovereign Subjects: Indigenous Sovereignty Matters*. Crows Nest, NSW: Allen & Unwin, 2007.

Nicolacopoulos, Toula, and George Vassilacopoulos. "Racism, Foreigner Communities and the onto-Pathology of White Australian Subjectivity." In *Whitening Race: Essays in Social and Cultural Criticism*, edited by Aileen Moreton-Robinson, 32–47. Canberra, ACT: Aboriginal Studies Press, 2004.

Nicoll, Fiona. "De-Facing Terra Nullius and Facing the Secret of Indigenous Sovereignty in Australia." *Borderlands* 1, no. 2 (2002).

Ortiz, Fernando. *Cuban Counterpoint: Tobacco and Sugar*. New York: Alfred A. Knopf, 1947.

Pallotta-Chiarolli, Maria, and Francesco Ricatti. "Migrant Lives on First Nation Land: Greek-Australian Memories of Titjikala in the 1960s." *Journal of Intercultural Studies* 43, no. 5 (2022): 535–57.

Pascoe, Robert, Roy Mcpherson, and Barry Golding. "First Nations Australians in the Nineteenth-Century Italian Imaginary." *Australian Historical Studies* 53, no. 4 (2022): 531–43.

Persian, Jayne, and Karen Agutter. "European Post-War Migrants and Indigenous Australians: A History in Fragments." *History Australia* 18, no. 1 (2021): 112–29.

Peters-Little, Frances. "'Nobles and Savages' on the Television." *Aboriginal History* 27 (2003): 16–38.

Piperoglou, Andonis. "Migrant-Cum-Settler: Greek Settler Colonialism in Australia." *Journal of Modern Greek Studies* 38 no. 2 (2020): 447–71.

Pugliese, Joseph. "De-Anthropocentrising Migrant Historiography: More-Than-Human Nodes of Empire, Diaspora and Settler Colonialism." *Altreitalie*, no. 59 (2019): 67–98.

———. "Migrant Heritage in an Indigenous Context: For a Decolonising Migrant Historiography." *Journal of Intercultural Studies* 23, no. 1 (2002): 5–8.

Raheja, Michelle H. "Reading Nanook's Smile: Visual Sovereignty, Indigenous Revisions of Ethnography, and Atanarjuat (The Fast Runner)." *American Quarterly* 59, no. 4 (2007): 1159–85.

———. *Reservation Reelism: Redfacing, Visual Sovereignty, and Representations of Native Americans in Film.* Lincoln: University of Nebraska Press, 2011.

Rando, Gaetano. *Emigrazione e Letteratura: Il Caso Italoaustraliano.* Cosenza, Italy: Pellegrini, 2004.

———. "Migrant Images in Italian Australian Movies and Documentaries." *Altreitalie* 16 (1997).

Reynolds, Henry. *Forgotten War.* Sydney: Sydney : NewSouth Publishing, 2013.

———. *The Other Side of the Frontier: Aboriginal Resistance to the European Invasion of Australia.* Sydney, NSW: University of New South Wales Press, 2006.

Ricatti, Francesco. "The Emotion of Truth and the Racial Uncanny: Aborigines and Sicilians in Australia." *Cultural Studies Review* 19, no. 2 (2013): 125–49.

———. *Italians in Australia: History, Memory, Identity.* London: Palgrave, 2018.

———. "Indigenous Sovereignty and Italian Trunscultural Studies." *Italian Studies in Southern Africa* 35, no. 1 (2022): 87–91.

Ricatti, Francesco, Paola Balla, John Kinder, Matteo Dutto, Maria Pallotta-Chiarolli, Joseph Pugliese, and Federica Verdina. "Forum: Towards a Decolonial History of Italian Migration." *Altreitalie*, no. 59 (2019): 8–66.

Sium, Aman, and Eric Ritskes. "Speaking Truth to Power: Indigenous Story-telling as an Act of Living Resistance." *Decolonization: Indigeneity, Education & Society* 2, no. 1 (2013): I–X.

Sonn, Christopher C., Amy F. Quayle, Cynthia Mackenzie, and Siew Fang Law. "Negotiating Belonging in Australia Through Storytelling and Encounter." *Identities* 21, no. 5 (2014): 551–69.

Taylor, Lucy. "Decolonizing International Relations: Perspectives from Latin America." *International Studies Review* 14, no. 3 (2012): 386–400.

Teo, Hsu-Ming. "Multiculturalism and the Problem of Multicultural Histories: An Overview of Ethnic Historiography." In *Cultural History in Australia*, edited by Hsu-Ming Teo and Richard White, 142–55. Sydney: University of New South Wales Press, 2003.

Tucker, Karen. "Unraveling Coloniality in International Relations: Knowledge, Relationality, and Strategies for Engagement." *International Political Sociology* 12, no. 3 (2018): 215–32.

Verdina, Federica, and John Kinder. "Selvaggi or Nativi? European and Colonial Perspectives on the Encounter with the Other in the Experience of a Missionary in Nineteenth Century Western Australia." In Ricatti, Francesco, Paola Balla, John Kinder, Matteo Dutto, Maria Pallotta-Chiarolli, Joseph Pugliese, and Federica Verdina. "Forum: Towards a Decolonial History of Italian Migration." *Altreitalie*, no. 59 (2019): 27–34.

Vitale, Luke. "The Chinese of Europe and Pioneer Legends: Race, labour and Italians in White Australia, 1888 to 1940." PhD Thesis, University of New South Wales, 2021.

Vizenor, Gerald Robert. *Manifest Manners: Narratives on Postindian Survivance.* Lincoln, NE: University of Nebraska Press, 1999.

Watson, Irene. "Nungas in the Nineties." In *Majah–Indigenous Peoples and the Law*, edited by Greta Bird, Gary Martin, and Jennifer Nielsen, 1–12. Sydney: The Federation Press, 1996.

———. "Re-Centring First Nations Knowledge and Places in a Terra Nullius Space." *AlterNative: An International Journal of Indigenous Peoples* 10, no. 5 (2014): 508–20.

Wolfe, Patrick. *Settler Colonialism and the Transformation of Anthropology: The Politics and Poetics of an Ethnographic Event.* London: Cassell, 1999.

———. "Nation and Miscegenation: Discursive Continuity in the Post-Mabo Era." *Social Analysis: The International Journal of Social and Cultural Practice*, no. 36 (1994): 93–152.

———. "Settler Colonialism and the Elimination of the Native." *Journal of Genocide Research* 8, no. 4 (2006): 387–409.

Zondi, Siphamandla. "Decolonising International Relations and Its Theory: A Critical Conceptual Meditation." *Politikon* 45, no. 1 (2018): 16–31.

Connecting Australia and Italy Through Language

Cristiana Palmieri

INTRODUCTION

This chapter explores the role language has been playing in connecting Australia and Italy and how English and Italian languages have contributed to shape the relationship between the two countries. I firstly examine the status of the Italian culture and language in Australia, exploring the role Italian has played as a foreign and second language[1] in this country and the specific Australian social context in which the learning of Italian occurs. Gilardoni (2014) argues that the appeal of a language is inherently interwoven with the cultural values that represent the context in which the language originated. Thus, exploring the dynamics through which languages are learnt allows us to consider their

---

[1] The foreign language context refers to contexts in which the target language is accessible in language learning settings only, while the second language context refers to environments where the target language is spoken outside the classroom setting.

C. Palmieri (✉)
School of Languages and Cultures, University of Sydney, Sydney, NSW, Australia
e-mail: cristiana.palmieri@sydney.edu.au

appealing features and their capacity to expand beyond their geographical boundaries. As I will argue, while the main reasons to learn Italian are cultural, and are linked mainly to Italy's historical and artistic heritage, other context-specific factors contribute to the appeal of Italian in Australia. In particular, the presence of a large and well-established Italian migrant community plays a pivotal role in attracting learners to various aspects of the culture of Italy. Secondly, I provide an overview of the spread of the English language in Italy and elaborate on its perceived value as an international language passport. I also explore the current job market conditions in Italy and how these conditions have contributed to an increased number of young Italians temporarily leaving Italy to relocate in Australia, and how in this context the English language is considered as a tool to access better job opportunities and better salaries.

The chapter also references a case study on learners of Italian that was conducted in Sydney to investigate the attitudes of Australians towards the Italian language and the role played by the Italian migrant community in promoting and disseminating Italian culture and language in Australia (Palmieri, 2019). The study comprised the administration of a questionnaire and a qualitative investigation aimed at examining in more depth socio-culturally situated aspects of second language learning motivation.

THE ITALIAN LANGUAGE IN THE AUSTRALIAN CONTEXT

According to Australian Census data, in 2006 Italian was used by a large number of the population (316,894 people), making it the most spoken language at home after English (ABS, 2006). The most recent census conducted in 2021 showed a marked decrease, to 228,000 speakers (1.2% of total population), so that Italian is now the seventh—rather than the first—most spoken immigrant language (ABS, 2021). This outline included in the Australia Census data 2021, reported below, provides a succinct but pertinent overview of Italian migration trends that helps to contextualise the role played by the Italian language in Australia.

Change in Italian-born migrants – Fifty years ago, Italy was the second highest country of birth after England. In 2021 it had the biggest decrease of all countries of birth since 2016, dropping by almost 11,000 people. Between 1947 and 1976, over 360,000 Italian migrants came to Australia to work in agriculture and major infrastructure projects. About one-fifth of these arrived under the 1951 Italian Assisted Migration scheme. By the early 1970s, as economic conditions in Italy improved, more Italian-born people were leaving Australia than entering. In 1971, the number of the Italian-born population peaked at 290,000 but had declined to 163,000 in 2021. As most migrants from Italy arrived in the post-war migration wave, in 2021 the median age of the Italian-born population was 72 years and more than two thirds (69.4%) arrived in Australia more than 50 years ago. Despite the decrease in the number of overseas-born Italians, the number of second generation Australians with one or both parents born in Italy increased from 322,000 in 2016 to 347,000 in 2021. The number of Australians reporting an Italian ancestry also increased from 1 million in 2016 to over 1.1 million in 2021, making Italian the seventh largest ancestry in Australia. Italian was also the seventh largest non-English language used at home in Australia with 228,000 speakers. (ABS, 2021)

This overview establishes the Italian migration to Australia has a long history. The first Italian to settle in Australia was a convict transported on the First Fleet (Iuliano, 2001, p. 33). In those early years of the British colony, there were also numerous Italian adventurers, naturalists, and missionaries you left Italy to come to Australia (Abbondanza & Battiston, 2023). However, the incidence of the Italian language in the Australian society is largely a consequence of the migration programme that Australia introduced in the late 1940s (Castles, 1992). Between 1945 and 1976 approximately 300,000 Italians relocated permanently in Australia, adding on average 18,000 Italian migrants annually (Iuliano, 2001, pp. 80–81). This migration flow significantly decreased after the 1970s, with only an average of about 400 Italian migrants settling permanently in Australia each year, even if there has been a moderate increase of arrivals in the last few years (DIBP, 2022). In 2011, almost one million, out of a national population of about twenty-two million, reported an Italian heritage, representing the third-largest community of non-English speaking background (Rubino, 2014b). Italians have managed to integrate well into the social fabric of Australian society, becoming entrepreneurs, professionals, restaurateurs, retail traders in the clothing, textiles, shoes, and food industries (among others) (Bettoni & Mauceri, 2008).

This historical background contributes to explain why Italian (by and large a by-product of post-Second World War migration patterns) is now one of the most popular languages in Australia, at all levels of the education system. On the one hand, Italian is the language spoken by one of the largest non-English-speaking migrant communities. On the other, a long tradition of 'Italophilia' has positioned Italian as a language of high culture, with well-established literary and cultural studies at the university level. The longstanding appreciation for Italian culture in Australia commenced in the second half of the nineteenth century (Bettoni & Mauceri, 2008). Following the British tradition of the *Grand Tour*[2] and the opening of the Suez Canal, the Australian upper class commenced to include Italy in their European travelling, to visit the places where the Renaissance originated. This contributed to spreading the interest in Italian amid the affluent and well-educated Australians who had become fascinated with Italy, but also its culture and language. The expansion of air travels from the late 1960s and the increase of mass tourism contributed to raise significantly the number of Australians visiting Italy and to consolidate their appreciation for both Italian language and culture (Bettoni & Mauceri, 2008).

The prestige of the Italian language in Australia was subsequently confirmed by the fact that since the 1970s it has been a subject taught in Australian secondary schools. The dissemination of the Italian language in Australia owes much to the Italian migrant community that influenced the establishment of a network of Italian language courses held on Saturdays. The so-called 'Saturday schools' were run by independent migrant organisations to provide opportunities to learn Italian and to ensure language maintenance for migrants' children (Ozolins, 1993). In the late 1960s, Italian started to be taught as a community language in government primary schools, in various States including New South Wales. This period was followed by a wide campaign promoted by the Italian community advocating for teaching Italian not merely as a language for the benefit of Italian migrant children, but as a language taught as part of the curriculum in Australian schools for all children (Baker, 2001; Clyne, 1988; Di Biase & Paltridge, 1985; Dixon, 1980; Lo Bianco & Aliani, 2013). In the early 1980s this advocacy campaign, aimed at making Italian part of the mainstream curriculum, changed the position of Italian from a language learned either by migrant children in 'Saturday schools' or by a few 'Italophiles', to a language offered by the Australian school system to all students. As Slaughter and Hajek (2015, p. 184) point out, "the

[2] This was a custom spread among wealthy European young men in the seventeenth century, who travelled to Italy to admire first-hand the beauties of classical antiquity and the Renaissance and to complete their education before taking up their roles as members of the ruling classes Towner, J. (1985). The Grand Tour: a key phase in the history of tourism. *Annals of tourism research, 12*(3), 297–333.

purpose of such a stance was to encourage greater social acceptance of Italians and their language and culture, and to facilitate social cohesion and understanding through contact and exposure in Australian schools". Thus, among the many migrant groups of non-English-speaking background, the Italian community was among the first to have its language included in the Australian primary schools' curriculum. "One reason for this success has undoubtedly been the sheer demographic weight of Italian migration to Australia. [...] and Italians formed the largest non-English-speaking community in Australia for many decades" (Slaughter & Hajek, 2015, p. 182). The advocacy process promoted by the Italian community was facilitated by the implementation of multicultural policies on the part of the Australian government in the late 1970s and by various independent activist groups advocating for multilingualism in Australia, such as the Ethnic Communities Councils of Australia (Nicholas, 2015; Ozolins, 1993; Rubino et al., 2021).

Another aspect that contributed to the spread of the Italian language in Australia was the attitude of the Italian migrant community, eager to share their language with the wider Australian society. As Clyne (1994, p. 125) argues they were keen to see "their language to be part of the shared heritage of multicultural Australia rather than to claim special proprietary rights over it". In 1987, the Australian government formally adopted The National Policy on Languages (NPL), a national framework for teaching languages, with a strong focus on language maintenance and the opportunity of learning a second language offered to all students (Clyne, 1994; Nicholas et al., 1993). The introduction of the NLP significantly supported the maintenance and learning of community languages "as a valuable asset to all Australians which would not only enrich the cultural and intellectual life in the community, but would also serve external needs in business, trade and foreign relations" (Pauwels, 2007, p. 112). In 2012, Italian was included as one of the first two languages, alongside Mandarin, to be considered in the project of a national curriculum on languages (ACARA, 2015). Even though not all States and Territories have adopted the national framework, this testifies to the importance held by the Italian language within the Australian context and it demonstrates how the history of the Italian migration to this country has shaped, and is still shaping, strategic government decisions on education matters (Lo Bianco, 2021).

As a consequence of these historical conditions, in today's Australian society, Italian attracts students because of its social prestige and sophisticated culture that bestow the language a prominent position (Hajek, 2000; Lo Bianco & Aliani, 2013; Macaro, 2010). Italian is "the 'classic', the one most successfully included in public education, becoming the second most widely taught language in the country, exceeding French and German in the European languages category" (Lo Bianco & Aliani, 2013, p. 38). A revitalised interest among Australians in learning Italian may be due to new interpretations of what Italy represents internationally, not only as expressions of a celebrated artistic and cultural heritage, but also as a sought-after lifestyle (Rubino, 2002). All these elements of contemporary Italian culture exert a certain appeal in the Australian socio-cultural context, sustaining a strong and increasing interest in learning, not only a language, but a lifestyle (Caruso & Brown, 2021; Rubino, 2014a; Vedovelli, 2002).

AUSTRALIANS LEARNING ITALIAN IN SYDNEY: A CASE STUDY

To investigate the attitudes of Australians towards the Italian language and the role played by the Italian migrant community in shaping their interest towards the language, a recent study on learners of Italian was conducted in continuing education settings in Sydney (Palmieri, 2019). Data was collected in two institutions specialised in teaching languages. The target population comprised three cohorts of adult students enrolled at beginner, intermediate, and advanced levels. The study comprised the administration of a questionnaire and a qualitative investigation aimed at examining in more depth socio-culturally situated aspects of second language learning motivation. This part of the study relied on 68 semi-structured interviews with survey respondents who expressed their interest in participating in the qualitative investigation.

The study reveals that attraction for Italian people, positive attitudes towards them, and the desire to belong to a community of Italian speakers are among the strongest motivating factors influencing Australians to learn Italian. These findings indicate their appreciation for Italians and their propensity to become part of the Italian cultural context. Most learners have been to Italy and travelling there also contributes to nurturing their desire to become closer to Italian people by exposing themselves to positive experiences of Italian culture which, in turn, triggers their positive attitudes towards Italians. These combined factors ignite learners' interest in Italian culture and people, promoting their investment to learn the language (Norton Peirce, 1995). The study's results clearly indicate participants' willingness to embrace Italian culture at various degrees of engagement, using the language as the key to access an Italian community of Italian speakers. This attraction towards Italian culture has its roots in the longstanding tradition of Italophilia in Australia, which is strongly anchored in the artistic heritage of Italy, and in the profound appeal that the Italian artistic heritage exerts on many Australians who desire to learn Italian to better appreciate the cultural context in which the Italian artistic production originated (Palmieri, 2019).

In addition to the artistic past, the findings clearly indicate that Italy's contemporary socio-cultural context also influences participants' motivations: the food and wine tradition, combined with the Italian appreciation for conviviality and the pleasures of the table, make Italian society a cherished and appreciated lifestyle. The positive experiences in interacting with Italian people in Italy are a strong motivational drive to learn the language. Travelling in Italy, and being exposed to the Italian language and culture triggers learners' willingness to be part of a community of Italian speakers. Through these positive experiences learners developed a strong emotional sentiment of connectedness with Italy and Italians that motivated them to continue with the study of the language. Speaking Italian represents a means to connect with a community of Italian speakers and to become an integral part of it, developing an emotional attachment and sentiments of belonging, to the point that Italy becomes a 'home' for some of them (Palmieri, 2019).

The study also reveals the significant role played by the Sydney-based Italian migrant community in shaping the learners' interest in studying Italian. The legacy of Italian migration to Australia, where just over one million people now claimed Italian heritage in one way or another, can explain the influence of the local Italian community on attitudes and motivations of Australians to learn Italian. The presence of a well-integrated Italian community, one that is perceived as an asset in contemporary multicultural Australian society, contributes to creating an appealing image of Italy and Italians. The large Italian community exposed the participants to contact with Italian people at different stages in their lives, through growing up and living in suburbs with a high concentration of Italian families, attending school with children of Italian migrants and frequenting their homes, and being in daily contact with Italians and hearing Italian spoken in the streets. This exposure to various aspects of the culture of Italy stimulated learners' interest in Italians and their culture and, as a consequence, triggered their motivation to learn the language. Contacts that occurred through the patronage of Italian businesses, such as restaurants, fashion boutiques, and shops, also prompted their desire to communicate and interact with the community of Italian migrants, thus impacting on their motivation to learn the language. Importantly, too, the disposition of Italian migrants to share their language and their culture contributed to sustain the interest of Australians to learn Italian, endowing a fertile environment for the success of Italian as a second language in Australia (Palmieri, 2019).

Overall, the findings indicate a strong intrinsic motivation to learn Italian. Speaking Italian is perceived as a pure reward, unrelated to any potential professional benefits or material gain to improve work opportunities. Becoming a fluent speaker of Italian is regarded as a highly valued personal accomplishment, enhancing their sense of worth, and enriching their identity. The appeal of learning Italian derived from the reward gained through the immaterial gratification of sentiments of refinement and sophistication related to a projected ideal Italian identity associated with the ability to speak a language that is considered, among other languages, the epitome of European refinement (Palmieri, 2019).

ITALIANS AND THE ENGLISH LANGUAGE

According to the Education First English Proficiency Index (EF EPI), ranking 112 Countries and Regions by English Skills (Education First, 2021), Italy currently ranks 35th, with a moderate level of proficiency. The data of the EF EPI are based on test data from more than 2,000,000 test takers around the world who took the EF Standard English Test (EF SET) or one of the EF English placement tests in 2020.

In most European Union countries students learn a foreign language as a compulsory subject in primary schools. Italy is among this group since a new bill was approved in 2003, making English a compulsory subject from the first year of primary school (Baggiani, 2017).

Notwithstanding the implementation of the new legislation, Italy still needs to improve the level of proficiency to align with other countries in the European Union (Italy only ranks 26th in Europe in relation to the EF EPI) to be able to compete on the international market. Among the largest four economies of the Eurozone (Germany, France, Italy, and Spain) Italy is the country that scores the lowest when it comes to the language of international trading. According to the EF EPI data previously mentioned, only 30% of secondary and high school students in the public system reach the B2[3] level that is the minimum level required by the job market to access many universities. The situation looks better in the private school system, where 40% of the students reach the B2 level and 20% C1 and C2 levels (in contrast with just 10% in the public system). Italian public schools are below average and only the private school system is keeping up with other European countries. In Europe more than 60% of students reach B1 level, 50% B2 level, and 20% of grammar school students settle on C1 level (Bitetto, 2019).

Despite this erratic scenario, Italy is now among those European countries where students start learning English earliest in schools. Following a series of government reforms, the age dropped from 11 years old in 1984 to 6 years old by 2007. English is compulsory in primary schools, and general exposure to English starts earlier in various pre-school settings (British Council, 2018). Young children attend language schools to reach a proficiency level that allows them to study at a tertiary level in another language, mainly English, to invest in their future as global citizens, thus improving their employability and professional mobility worldwide. An increasing number of universities offer English-taught programmes to attract foreign students and at the same time respond to the need to become tertiary institutions that can provide domestic students with the required level of English proficiency. Specifically, in Italy there are over 185 English-taught Bachelors, over 700 English-taught Masters, over 70 English-taught PhDs, and over 150 English-taught distance-learning (online) courses (StudyPortals, 2022). These data suggest that the comparatively low level of English proficiency in the Italian population is likely connected to the relatively low level of tertiary education attainment: Italy ranks second to last among European countries in terms

---

[3] The Common European Framework of Reference for Languages (CEFR) describes foreign language proficiency at six levels: A1 and A2, B1 and B2, C1 and C2. It also defines three 'plus' levels (A2+, B1+, B2+).

(Council of Europe. Common European Framework of Reference for Languages (CEFR).   https://www.coe.int/en/web/common-european-framework-reference-lan guages).

of percentage of the population who has completed a tertiary education cycle (Eurostat, 2022). Therefore, the problem does not appear to be a lack of interest in learning English, but rather a more structural educational deficit.

This flourishing of English-taught programmes is also driven by the fact that economic uncertainty and scarcity of job opportunities, especially for young people, have prompted a new wave of migration (De Lazzari, 2017). When the Global Financial Crisis hit in 2008–2009, the youth unemployment rate reached 25.3% (the country's overall unemployment rate is currently 8.8%) (ISTAT, 2022). It has fluctuated ever since, reaching its peak (42.7%) in 2014. The latest available statistics put the youth unemployment rate back at 25.3% (ISTAT, 2022). Because of this high youth unemployment rate in the last decade, proficiency in written and spoken English has become a pathway to employability outside Italy, providing young Italians who can speak good English the opportunity to seek work in a global job market. In this scenario, Australia has been a sought-after destination for many educated young Italians who, finding increasingly difficult to enter the Italian job market in the post-Global Financial Crisis context, decide to move overseas, often temporarily but also in search of long-term resettlement opportunities (Armillei & Mascitelli, 2016; Armillei, 2017; De Lazzari, 2017).

This new cohort of migrants primarily consists of young Italians who enter the country as Working Holiday Makers, students, or temporary resident (skilled) visa holders to work mainly in the hospitality industry, study English, and enjoy a new life experience. In 2019, 17,923 Italian citizens arrived in Australia to stay for more than six months, of which 5895 were Working Holiday Makers and 630 student visa (Government, 2022). Many of these new arrivals are highly educated (Armillei, 2017; Marchetti & Baldassar, 2023; Battiston, 2023) and have previously worked in Italy as white-collar employees or professionals in a variety of industries, including hospitality, education and training, arts, design, entertainment, architecture, and engineering (Armillei & Mascitelli, 2016). This new group is not quantitatively substantial, but it is steadily increasing (Pascoe & Cafarella, 2013), especially after 2011 (Armillei & Mascitelli, 2016) and it is becoming relevant in terms of cultural impact as it offers the opportunity to the third and fourth generation of Italian Australians to engage with Italian people who have elected Australia as their country of choice (Kinder, 2009). The border closures that followed the Covid-19 pandemic have completely stopped the flow of short-term visitors in 2020 and 2021. It remains to be seen whether in the next few years the pre-pandemic trends will be reversed.

Once arrived in Australia, a large proportion of these temporary visa holders find occupation in the well-established hospitality industry. While Italian restaurants are a central feature of the Australian catering industry since the 1960s, in recent years the arrival of a cohort of food and wine professionals from Italy has boosted the offering and the reputation of Italian cuisine in Australia (McNeilage, 2015). Consequently, Australians who appreciate the diversity of the Italian gastronomic tradition can enjoy an increased opportunity to meet and interact with Italians, whose educational background and language skills facilitate communication, reinforcing the image of contemporary Italian lifestyle and culture. These 'newcomers' bring along a current and refreshed image of Italy and Italians, but also help to disseminate a more contemporary Italian language. But how do they place themselves in relation to the English language? Which sentiment do they develop towards English? The findings of the case study presented in the section above indicate Australians display a strong intrinsic motivation to learn Italian, unrelated to any potential professional benefits or material gain to improve work opportunities. Does the same apply to the above-mentioned new cohort of migrants primarily made of young Italians who enter the country with various temporary visas?

To explore this further, I refer to the body of work conducted in the field of second language acquisition. The phenomenon of globalisation, the increasing mobility of people, and the rise of migration flows are major contributors "to the inexorable spread of 'global English'" (Dörnyei & Ushioda, 2009, p. 1). The emerging status of English as a *lingua franca* and the consequent proliferation of 'English varieties' (Jenkins, 2007), impacts significantly on motivation to learn World English for people who want to identify with the globalised community of English speakers. These major global changes have created what Warschauer (2000, p. 512) defines as "a new society, in which English is shared among many groups of non-native speakers". Learners of global English as a second language may not associate the language with a specific cultural background they feel attracted to and want to join, but with a more generic "international English-speaking community, disassociated from any particular culture" (Kaylani, 1996, p. 87). These circumstances can be a conduit towards employment opportunities and the possibility to live and work in a globalised society where English represents an international language passport.

As Pavlenko (2002) argues, global English is learned for a variety of different reasons, including work and family-related necessities, political stances, and economic motives.

This inclination to join an English-speaking community is corroborated by a study carried out on Japanese students of English at the tertiary level, in which Yashima (2002) developed the concept of international posture. International posture refers to the propensity of individuals to identify themselves with the global English-speaking community, rather than with a specific target cultural group. As Yashima (2002, p. 57) argues, "Included in the concept are interest in oreignn or international affairs, willingness to go overseas to stay or work, readiness to interact with intercultural partners...". The elements incorporated in the definition of international posture bring with them the idea that learners of global English wish to join not a precisely identifiable foreign community, but the international global community of English speakers.

These considerations can apply to the new cohort of young Italians who are moving to Australia. A study conducted in 2016 to investigate the cohort of Italians that arrived in Australia after 2004 shows that 72% of this cohort falls into the age group between 25 and 40 (Armillei, 2017). When the survey was conducted, 39% of the interviewees had been living in Australia for more than a year and 34% for over 4 years. The most common visa to enter the country was the Working Holiday Visa (49%). The study respondents are highly educated, holding either a bachelor's degree (24%), a master's degree (27%), or even a Ph.D. (9%) (Armillei, 2017, p. 86). The study shows that 57% of the respondents indicated that their level of English was good or very good before moving to Australia and 48% of the respondents indicated that the reason to move to Australia was related to better job opportunities. This could suggest that the possession of a degree of proficiency in English is instrumental in determining this cohort intention to moving to Australia.

Differently from previous generations of Italian migrants, who arrived in Australia with little or no English, attracted by the opportunity for non-specialised labour, these contemporary migrants understand that being able to speak the language is essential for entering the Australian job market and being able to enjoy the lifestyle. In both cases, however, the relationship with the language is purely transactional, in that the learning of the language is driven by its function as an entry key in a desirable lifeworld. The in-depth interviews conducted as part of this study corroborate the survey data, showing that participants rated their experience in Australia according to the work opportunities they were offered, implying that job and wage were the main reasons for moving to Australia and possibly, learning English (Armillei, 2017). This contrasts with the finding of Palmieri (2019), in which Australian learners indicated a strong intrinsic motivation to learn Italian and described the experience as a personal development journey, unrelated to any potential professional benefits or material gain to improve work opportunities.

CONCLUSIONS

In this chapter, I examined the status of the Italian culture and language in Australia and described the main reasons that motivate Australians to learn Italian. I explored how Italy's historical and artistic heritage, alongside the presence of a large and well-established Italian migrant community, play a pivotal role in attracting learners to various aspects of the culture of Italy and contribute to the appeal of the Italian language in Australia. The attraction towards Italian language and culture has its roots in the longstanding tradition of "Italophilia" in Australia, which is strongly anchored in the artistic heritage of Italy. The profound appeal that the Italian culture exerts on many Australians explains the widespread desire to learn Italian, to better appreciate the cultural context in which the Italian artistic production originated. In addition to the artistic past, Italy's contemporary socio-cultural context and its sought-after lifestyle also influence the attraction towards learning Italian. Through the process of learning Italian, Australian learners develop a strong emotional sentiment of connectedness with Italy and Italians. Speaking Italian represents a means to connect with a community of Italian speakers and to become an integral part of it, developing an emotional attachment and sentiments of belonging, to the point that Italy becomes a 'home' for some of these learners.

The chapter also explored the reasons that motivate Italians to learn English, with a specific focus on those who come to Australia, describing the characteristics of a recent cohort of Italian migrants that arrived in Australia in the last two decades. The unsteadiness of the Italian economy, especially in the wake of the Global Financial Crisis, has determined a significant youth unemployment rate, which has prompted many young Italians to consider moving abroad in search for job opportunities. In turn, this has stimulated them to study English, which is viewed as a tool to access a job market that offers better opportunities and better salaries.

A similar phenomenon has also interested many of the young Italians who took advantage of the possibility to spend time in Australia on a Working Holiday Visa. The opportunity to access the job market, allowing them to fund their travel to Australia, together with the attractiveness of the Australian lifestyle, have motivated them to learn English. Therefore, in the case of Italian learners of English, the relationship with the English language appears to be a transactional one, that is, a view of the language as a necessary access key to job and travel opportunities.

Together with this trend, my survey of the literature has revealed a considerable research gap on the motivation of Italians who learn English. It is possible that, in time, the purely instrumental use of the language will evolve into a more complex relationship, also involving identity trajectories, as it is the case of Australian learners of Italian. Therefore, it would be valuable to explore learning dynamics that drive the phenomenon of an increased number of Italians studying and learning English, both in Italy and abroad, to unpack their motivational drives, reasons, and expectations, beyond the notion of English language learnt as an international passport. Moreover, this chapter has shown that language is a powerful tool to foster closer ties between the two countries. It is suggested that an ongoing investment to support language learning promotion through national policies and the dissemination of language schools and language-focused initiatives could improve the already fruitful cooperation between Italy and Australia, as well as their "cordial bilateral relations since the 1970s" (Abbondanza & Battiston, 2023, p. 2).

REFERENCES

Abbondanza, G., & Battiston, S. (2024). Italy and Australia in the twenty-first century: distant connections or close partners? In G. Abbondanza & S. Battiston (Eds.), *Italy and Australia: redefining bilateral relations for the twenty-first century* (pp. 1–23). Palgrave Macmillan.

ABS. (2006). *Census data*. Australian Bureau of Statistics. Retrieved 16/10/2014 from http://goo.gl/Pvdk8l.

ABS. (2021). *Cultural diversity of Australia*. Australian Bureau of Statistics. Retrieved 21/09/22 from https://www.abs.gov.au/articles/cultural-diversity-australia#language.

ACARA. (2015). *Languages*. Retrieved 20/8/2015 from http://goo.gl/KJnYTu.

Armillei, R., & Mascitelli, B. (2016). *From 2004 to 2016: a new Italian 'exodus' to Australia?* https://goo.gl/RF2zhe.

Armillei, R. A. (2017). Statistical analysis of the "New Italian Migration" to Australia: redressing recent overstatements. In B. Mascitelli & R. Armillei (Eds.), *Australia's new wave of Italian migration. Paradise or illusion.* Australian Scholarly.

Baggiani, S. (2017). L'insegnamento delle lingue straniere a scuola in Europa. https://eurydice.indire.it/linsegnamento-delle-lingue-straniere-a-scu ola-in-europa/.

Baker, C. (2001). *Foundations of bilingual education and bilingualism.* Multilingual Matters.

Battiston, S. (2024). Italians in Australia in the twenty-first century. In G. Abbondanza & S. Battiston (Eds.), *Italy and Australia: redefining bilateral relations for the twenty-first century* (pp. 49–80). Palgrave Macmillan.

Bettoni, C., & Mauceri, M. C. (2008). *Gli italiani nel mondo. Il caso dell'inglese d'Australia.* Unpublished manuscript.

Bitetto, G. (2019). L'italia e' l'ultima in Europa. E' il fallimento della scuola. *The Vision.* https://thevision.com/cultura/italia-conoscenza-inglese.

British Council. (2018). *The future demand for English in Europe: 2025 and beyond.* https://www.britishcouncil.it/sites/default/files/future_dem and_for_english_in_europe_2025_and_beyond_british_council_2018_0.pdf.

Caruso, M., & Brown, J. (2021). L'italiano all'università tra aspirazioni di cittadinanza globale e il magnetismo dell'Italia contemporanea. In A. Rubino, A. R. Tamponi, & J. Hajek (Eds.), *L'italiano in Australia. Prospettive e tendenze nell'insegnamento della lingua e della cultura/Italian in Australia. Perspectives and trends in the teaching of language and culture* (pp. 115–132). Franco Cesati Editore.

Castles, S. (1992). Italian migration and settlement since 1945. In S. Castles, C. Alcorso, G. Rando, & E. Vasta (Eds.), *Australia's Italians: culture and community in a changing society.* Allen & Unwin.

Clyne, M. (1988). Bilingual education—What can we learn from the past? *Australian Journal of Education, 32*(1), 95–114.

Clyne, M. (1994). *The future of Italian in multicultural Australia.* Proceedings of the Conference: "Italian towards 2000", Melbourne.

De Lazzari, C. (2017). New Italian emigration globally: who they are and where they go. In B. Mascitelli & R. Armillei (Eds.), *Australia's new wave of Italian migration. Paradise or illusion.* Australian Scholarly.

Di Biase, B., & Paltridge, B. (Eds.). (1985). *Italian in Australia: language or dialect in schools? Sull'italiano in Australia: Lingua o dialetto nelle scuole?.* FILEF Italo-Australian Publications.

DIBP. (2022). *Historical migration statistics.* Department of Immigration and Border Protection, Australian Government. Retrieved 18/3/2022 from https://data.gov.au/data/dataset/historical-migration-statistics/resource/ b59a15df-86ea-4c4c-95be-4dd9fc9f8ac4?view_id=7b284560-fe98-4a8a-86a9-c1225aeeaea5.

Dixon, R. M. (1980). *The languages of Australia*. Cambridge University Press.
Dörnyei, Z., & Ushioda, E. (Eds.). (2009). *Motivation, language identity and the L2 self*. Multilingual Matters. http://usyd.summon.serialssolutions.com/2.0.0/link/0/eLvHCXMwY2BQSDYxszBOM0wyBjbFLQ1SU80s0lISzU2NzC3M0pJTLNNQhrGRSnM3IQam1DxRBlk31xBnD13QhvN46CBGf JKxmTGorjM0FGNgAXaMU8UZWEqKSoEUsMwUB-oXZ-CIsAwPtYj09o NwhWBcvWLw_iW9whJxYBENjl5dYz0DAMUdJ9g.
Education First. (2021). *English proficiency index*. https://www.ef.com/ass etscdn/WIBIwq6RdJvcD9bc8RMd/cefcom-epi-site/reports/2021/ef-epi-2021-english.pdf.
Eurostat. (2022). *Educational attainment statistics*. Retrieved 7/6/22 from https://ec.europa.eu/eurostat/statistics-explained/index.php?title=Edu cational_attainment_statistics.
Gilardoni, S. (2014). *La Didattica dll'Italiano L2. Approcci teorici e orientamenti applicativi*. EDUCatt.
Government, A. (2022). *Overseas arrivals and departures*. Retrieved 7/6/22 from https://data.gov.au/dataset/ds-dga-5a0ab398-c897-4ae3-986d-f94452 a165d7/details?q=arrivals.
Hajek, J. (2000). Whither Italian? Italian in Australia's Universities. Why it is important and how to save it. Proceedings of the Conference: "In search of the Italian Australian into the new millennium", Melbourne.
ISTAT. (2022). *Occupati e disoccupati (dati provvisori)*. Retrieved 7/6/22 from https://www.istat.it/it/archivio/266914.
Iuliano, S. (2001). *Sebben Che SiamoDonne (although we are women): a comparative study of Italian immigrant women in post-war Canada and Australia*. [PhD, McGill University, Montreal].
Jenkins, J. (2007). *English as a lingua franca: attitude and identity*. Oxford University Press.
Kaylani, C. (1996). The influence of gender and motivation on EFL learning strategy use in Jordan. In R. Oxford (Ed.), *Language learning strategies around the world: cross-cultural perspectives*. Second Language Teaching & Curriculum Center, University of Hawaii at Mānoa.
Kinder, J. (2009). Come insegnare italiano agli oriundi italiani? Il caso dell'Australia. In P. Diadori (Ed.), *La Ditals risponde: certificazione di competenza in didattica dell'italiano a stranieri, 6*. Guerra.
Lo Bianco, J. (2021). Italian in Australia: society, education and future planning. In A. Rubino, A. R. Tamponi, & J. Hajek (Eds.), *L'italiano in Australia. Prospettive e tendenze nell'insegnamento della lingua e della cultura/Italian in Australia. Perspectives and trends in the teaching of language and culture* (pp. 27–45). Franco Cesati Editore.
Lo Bianco, J., & Aliani, R. (2013). *Language planning and student experiences intention, rhetoric and implementation*. Channel View Publications.

Macaro, E. (2010). Review of recent research (2000–2008) on applied linguistics and language teaching with specific reference to L2 Italian. *Language Teaching*, *43*(2), 127–153. https://doi.org/10.1017/s0261444809990358.

Marchetti, G., & Baldassar, L. (2024). Australians in Italy in the twenty-first century. In G. Abbondanza & S. Battiston (Eds.), *Italy and Australia: redefining bilateral relations for the twenty-first century* (pp. 81–111). Palgrave Macmillan.

McNeilage, A. (2015). A new wave of Italian food washes over Sydney. *Good Food.* http://www.goodfood.com.au/eat-out/news/a-new-wave-of-italian-food-washes-over-sydney-20150112-12m777.

Nicholas, H. (2015). Losing bilingualism while promoting second language acquisition in Australian language policy. In J. Hajek, Y. Slaughter, & F. Cavallaro (Eds.), *Challenging the monolingual mindset* (Vol. 56). Multilingual Matters. http://usyd.summon.serialssolutions.com/2.0.0/link/0/eLvHCXMwdV07b8IwED7xWLoVWigFJEuVqjKAEudc7BmBGBjZUVy fJ5pKhP7_XhKThraM1kmWZflen---A4jkIpj_sglk0So0Dk0cpigTQseBMlIaW m1dOVShgWzXxReXYo76h_enB_0va2IlbJZW36K5ZZXnLAR1G9oqChra XAIzEdvrZTH_IUxYqiU7OM8NdVnrK9K-0hNt7qFLRXtCD1qU9WG48 3BjLl7FrmZIzvswqvpuhdfdXLx5gunZA7ys_AQVdluCA0DBT7GY3cM7Hc UHJ-k5nR9hulnvV9t5cYKDB3kOBrXk7Al1NIBO9pnREwi1VDaxSNa8S4zJ KcUuy-jApXHKcYkeweD_PZ5vCcZwxwFDXEEQE-icT180re7iG8ELjr4.

Nicholas, H. R., Moore, H., Clyne, M., & Pauwels, A. (1993). *Languages at the crossroads. The report of the national enquiry into the employment and supply of teachers of languages other than English.* The National Languages and Literacy Institute of Australia.

Norton Peirce, B. (1995). Social identity, investment, and language learning. *TESOL Quarterly*, *29*(1), 9–31.

Ozolins, U. (1993). *The politics of language in Australia.* Cambridge University Press. http://usyd.summon.serialssolutions.com/2.0.0/link/0/eLvHCX MwdV1NC8IwDA1OL978Gn4NehH0MNnWdt3OovgDva9mU_Ayhf1_M HWdqMxjCLSENn3No3kF4Mk-Cn_OBH6lBEduci0zLI2KDSaCwC9CTL mWP8x2V9341YDeMhiEvlYR3QOPiryPrKTNRNd8wlaRu_5U-9GWkK0 hVJY6wadP59u2fvWlzPeCm9MI-rYFYQw9rCawaDpomcvCmm2dVPRuCht aZfZonrDV7G5YSz-yW8XeNMYMgtPxcjiHdqLCETZF6cKKEx_61b3COb BE5xqxVFJFWmRWUUalkitC-9gmrVyA3z3G8p9jBcPm8Z6lE9YwMLT dMWhifgLv73Ti.

Palmieri, C. (2019). *Identity trajectories of adult language learners. Learning Italian in Australia.* Multilingual Matters.

Pascoe, R., & Cafarella, C. (2013, 4–6 December). *I Globalisti—The Fourth Wave.* ACIS 7th Biennial Conference. Re-imagining Italian Studies Adelaide.

Pauwels, A. (2007). Maintaining a language other than English through higher education in Australia. In A. Pauwels, J. Winter, & J. Lo Bianco (Eds.), *Maintaining minority languages in transnational contexts*. Palgrave Macmillan.

Pavlenko, A. (2002). Poststructuralist approaches to the study of social factors in second language learning and use. In V. Cook (Ed.), *Portraits of the L2 user*. Multilingual Matters.

Rubino, A. (2002). Italian in Australia: past and new trends. Proceedings of the Conference: "Innovations in Italian Teaching Workshop", Brisbane.

Rubino, A. (2014a). L'italiano in Australia tra lingua immigrata e lingua seconda. In A. De Meo, M. D'Agostino, G. Iannaccaro, & L. Spreafico (Eds.), *Varieta' dei contesti di apprendimento linguistico*. Associazione Italiana di Linguistica Applicata.

Rubino, A. (2014b). *Trilingual talk in Sicilian-Australian migrant families: playing out identities through language alternation*. Palgrave Macmillan.

Rubino, A., Tamponi, A. R., & Hajek, J. (2021). Prospettiva generale: l'insegnamento dell'italiano in Australia. In A. Rubino, A. R. Tamponi, & J. Hajek (Eds.), *L'italiano in Australia. Prospettive e tendenze nell'insegnamento della lingua e della cultura/Italian in Australia. Perspectives and trends in the teaching of language and culture* (pp. 11–21). Franco Cesati Editore.

Slaughter, Y., & Hajek, J. (2015). Mainstreaming of Italian in Australian schools: the paradox of success? In J. Hajek & Y. Slaughter (Eds.), *Challenging the monolingual mindset*. Multilingual Matters.

StudyPortals. (2022). *Best English-taught universities in Italy in 2022*. Retrieved 7/6/22 from https://www.mastersportal.com/articles/2992/best-english-taught-universities-in-italy-in-2022.html.

Towner, J. (1985). The Grand Tour: a key phase in the history of tourism. *Annals of tourism research*, *12*(3), 297–333.

Vedovelli, M. (2002). *L'italiano degli stranieri: storia, attualità e prospettive*. Carocci.

Warschauer, M. (2000). The changing global economy and the future of English teaching. *TESOL Quarterly*, *34*(3), 511–535.

Yashima, T. (2002). Willingness to communicate in a second language: the Japanese EFL context. *The Modern Language Journal*, *86*(1), 54–66. http://www.jstor.org/stable/1192769.

CHAPTER 7

Time for a Strategic Partnership: The Scope for International Cooperation Between Italy and Australia

Gabriele Abbondanza

INTRODUCTION

Relations between Italy and Australia are undoubtedly cordial, yet complex and somewhat undervalued.[1] Historical accounts reveal that they trace back to even before Italy and Australia reached statehood in 1861 and 1901, respectively, although they developed meaningfully only in

---

[1] An earlier version of this research was presented at the 2021 Australian Political Science Association (APSA) conference, for the panel titled "Rethinking Australian-Italian Relations in the 21st Century".

G. Abbondanza (✉)
Complutense University of Madrid, Madrid, Spain
e-mail: gabriabb@ucm.es

School of Social and Political Sciences, University of Sydney, Sydney, NSW, Australia

Istituto Affari Internazionali (IAI), Rome, Italy

155

the course of the twentieth century.[2] As outlined in the introductory
chapter to this volume,[3] they were sustained by both official diplomatic activities and remarkably varied people-to-people links, consisting
of wealthy adventurers, missionaries, politically active migrants, and large
numbers of skilled and unskilled labourers. The human dimension of
Italian-Australian relations was promoted by what was, for the most
part, a one-sided flow of migrants from Second World War-torn Italy
to Australia, and in time the literature exploring bilateral relations came
to concentrate on this noticeable and significant phenomenon.[4] Such a
scholarly focus was justified by the multifarious implications of Italian
migration to Australia, which are widely considered to be a constitu-
tive element of modern-day Australia.[5] However, this well-established
approach arguably ended up defining what Italian-Australian relations
were seemingly all about, supported by the lack of "ballast" in governmental activities between the two countries.[6] In other words, the scholarly
sub-field of Italian-Australian relations has come to be almost equated to
Italian migration to Australia. However important,[7] this viewpoint is not
sufficient to comprehensively portray current bilateral relations, a rationale that prompted the idea behind this book in general, and this chapter
more specifically.

[2] Gianfranco Cresciani, *The Italians in Australia* (Cambridge: Cambridge University Press, 2003), 26–50.

[3] Gabriele Abbondanza and Simone Battiston, "Italy and Australia in the Twenty-First Century: Distant Connections or Close Partners?", in *Italy and Australia: Redefining Bilateral Relations for the Twenty-First Century*, eds. Gabriele Abbondanza and Simone Battiston (London: Palgrave Macmillan, 2024), pp. 1–23.

[4] See Bruno Mascitelli, "Italy and Australia: A Relationship Made and Unmade By Immigration", *Australian Journal of International Affairs* 69, no. 3 (2015): 339–355.

[5] Stephen Castles, "Italians in Australia: The Impact of a Recent Migration on the Culture and Society of a Postcolonial Nation", *Center for Migration Studies Special Issues* 11, no. 3 (1994): 342–367.

[6] Mascitelli, "Italy and Australia".

[7] For an up-to-date analysis of the importance of migration studies in Italian-Australian relations, see Simone Battiston, "Italians in Australia in the Twenty-First Century", in *Italy and Australia: Redefining Bilateral Relations for the Twenty-First Century*, eds. Gabriele Abbondanza and Simone Battiston (London: Palgrave Macmillan, 2024), pp. 49–80; and Giulia Marchetti and Loretta Baldassar, "Australians in Italy in the Twenty-First Century", in *Italy and Australia: Redefining Bilateral relations for the twenty-first century*, eds. Gabriele Abbondanza and Simone Battiston (London: Palgrave Macmillan, 2024), pp. 81–111.

Starting from these premises, this research seeks to address this clear gap in the literature by providing a novel and broad understanding of what Italian-Australian relations look like in the twenty-first century, exploring how they could be strengthened, and why this has not occurred yet. To wit, it ought to be acknowledged that many like-minded countries tend to cooperate through multilateral agreements and within international organisations they share membership of. In this respect, Italy and Australia make no exception, and their interactions often take place under such *multilateral* conditions. However, the potential deriving from closer *bilateral* ties is still largely unexpressed, since it concerns underdeveloped areas of cooperation that cannot be addressed multilaterally. Such is the case of strategic, defence, cultural, social, economic, and scientific cooperation, as this chapter attests. In essence, while recognising the importance of multilateral cooperation in Italian-Australian relations, it is here argued that the potential of stronger bilateral ties warrants a more specific and novel assessment, which is the rationale behind this research and its proposal of a strategic partnership. In consideration of the wide scope of this objective, and building upon this volume's multidisciplinary approach, this chapter adopts an international relations (IR) perspective that seeks to complement the different viewpoints advanced in other chapters. Due to the predominantly comparative nature of this research, it employs the comparative case study methodology (CCS) by simultaneously assessing the scope for future cooperation in five distinct fields, as outlined below.[8] Moreover, given that bilateral relations have been underexamined so far, it also makes use of the literature review methodology to collect and analyse relevant Italian, Australian, and international sources from the five aforementioned fields of research.[9]

To achieve these research goals, the chapter is structured as follows. First, it employs relevant theoretical and conceptual elements that help to clarify how closer bilateral relations could be obtained. This dedicated theoretical framework thus draws on great and middle power theory to

---

[8] For methodological considerations on the comparative case study (CCS), see Lesley Bartlett and Frances Vavrus, *Rethinking Case Study Research: A Comparative Approach* (London: Routledge, 2016).

[9] For a critique of the literature review method in the social sciences, see Anthony J. Onwuegbuzie, Nancy L. Leech, and Kathleen M. Collins, "Qualitative Analysis Techniques for the Review of the Literature", *Qualitative Report* 17 (2012): 1–28.

locate Rome and Canberra in the international society of states,[10] and makes use of an updated version of Miller's five conditions for cooperation.[11] Along with these conceptual tools to justify why greater bilateral cooperation is not only feasible, but desirable, a definition of what a strategic partnership entails is offered. Second, it pursues the case for greater cooperation by focusing on the unexpressed potential between Rome and Canberra. This empirical analysis investigates five distinct elements, comprising: (i) international goals; (ii) defence capabilities; (iii) trade; (iv) scientific cooperation; and (v) people-to-people links. Third, it examines why closer ties have not been developed despite the mutual advantages that both states would derive from them, and by doing so it sheds light on a range of issues that currently hinder greater levels of both official (state-level) and non-governmental cooperation.[12] Lastly, it concludes by arguing that a strategic partnership between Italy and Australia would address a significant proportion of these issues, while propelling twenty-first-century cooperation in a number of fields.

THEORETICAL FRAMEWORKS
FOR INTERNATIONAL COOPERATION

To examine whether two states can achieve greater levels of synergy—and the strategic partnership advanced in this chapter would arguably qualify as a major step forward—it is useful to draw on existing notions concerning international cooperation. This is appropriate not only since relevant theoretical frameworks lead to a greater understanding of the two countries' status and role in global affairs, but also because they shed light on how they perceive themselves, how they wish to be perceived by others, and what they seek through their international relations. Consequently, great power theory is outlined to explore Italy's international status, and middle power theory is employed to examine Australia's, with

---

[10] Gabriele Abbondanza, "Middle Powers and Great Powers Through History: The Concept from Ancient Times to the Present Day", *History of Political Thought* 41, no. 3 (2020): 397–418.

[11] John D. Bruce Miller, "The Conditions for Co-operation", in *India, Japan, Australia: Partners in Asia?*, ed. J.D.B. Miller (Canberra: Australian National University Press, 1968), 195–210.

[12] Gabriele Abbondanza, "Italy and Australia: Time for a Strategic Partnership", *IAI Commentaries* 20, no. 87 (2020): 1–5.

the goal of answering the question of whether their international standing favours or hinders closer ties from a theoretical viewpoint. This is followed by an updated iteration of Miller's five conditions for cooperation, and by a definition of the strategic partnership proposed in this chapter.

Starting with the first conceptual element, the global power hierarchy places great powers below the superpowers (the United States and China) and above secondary states.[13] Great power scholars define them through a range of parameters, which could be summarised as superior (top-10) placement across the full spectrum of states' capabilities; external recognition as such (a permanent seat at the UN Security Council and/or G7-G8 membership); as well as an assertive behaviour when pursuing their interests, often resorting to unilateral actions.[14] Accordingly, great power theory identifies slightly less than 10 states that qualify, including Italy.[15] The latter, however, represents an atypical exemplar of great power— much like Germany and Japan—due to a number of reasons, including its cooperative approach to international affairs. As a result, Italy has been defined as an "awkward great power" on account of its great power-like capabilities but deviant behaviour.[16] To wit, Rome relies on multilateralism and concerted actions for much of its foreign policy (regionally with the EU and partners in the MENA region, extra-regionally with

---

[13] Barry Buzan and Ole Wæver, *Regions and Powers: The Structure of International Security* (Cambridge: Cambridge University Press, 2003), 27–39.

[14] Great powers' inclusion criteria are the object of a lively debate, like many other concepts in international relations. For the main definitions, see Kenneth Waltz, *Theory of International Politics* (New York: McGraw-Hill, 1979), 131; Barry Buzan and Ole Wæver, *Regions and Powers: The Structure of International Security* (Cambridge: Cambridge University Press, 2003), 11; Samuel P. Huntington, "The Lonely Superpower", *Foreign Affairs* 78, no. 2 (1999): 35–49; John Mearsheimer, *The Tragedy of Great Power Politics* (New York: W. W. Norton, 2001), 37–40; Randall L. Schweller, "Realism and the Present Great Power System: Growth and Positional Conflict Over Scarce Resources", in *Unipolar Politics: Realism and State Strategies After the Cold War*, eds. E. B. Kapstein and M. Mastanduno (New York: Columbia University Press, 1999), 28–68; and Gabriele Abbondanza, "Middle Powers and Great Powers Through History: The Concept from Ancient Times to the Present Day", *History of Political Thought* 41, no. 3 (2020): 397–418.

[15] Among the many examples, see Congyan Cai, "New Great Powers and International Law in the 21st Century", *European Journal of International Law* 24, no. 3 (2013): 755–795; and Risto E. J. Penttilä, *The Role of the G8 in International Peace and Security* (London: Routledge, 2013), 17–32.

[16] Gabriele Abbondanza, "The Odd Axis: Germany, Italy, and Japan as Awkward Great Powers", in *Awkward Powers: Escaping Traditional Great and Middle Power Theory*, eds. G. Abbondanza and T. Wilkins (London: Palgrave Macmillan, 2021), 43–71.

transatlantic and NATO relations, and globally through the UN), and is therefore an atypical great power since it traditionally resorts to international cooperation in its global affairs.[17] This is of particular interest for the research goals of this chapter, since it attests that Italy's global status complements its multilateral approach to international affairs, and thus allows for greater levels of cooperation with comparable democracies like Australia.

Secondly, middle powers like Australia represent a larger group of states (around 20) that sit below great powers in the global power hierarchy. Thanks to increasingly high levels of scholarly attention, it is possible to encapsulate the main elements of middle power theory with five specific criteria.[18] They are position in the global hierarchy (top-30 states placed below the great powers); norms (constant support for—and promotion of—the international law); behaviour (multilateral and cooperative approach to global affairs); identity (self-identification as middle powers, consequently leading to a specific foreign policy); and systemic impact (tangible influence of their foreign policies).[19] Despite some concerns over recent foreign policy developments, Australia is regarded as a "traditional middle power" since it generally satisfies these criteria, and has been acknowledged as one since the end of the Second World War.[20] As with the Italian case, this shows that Australia's international status is conducive to bilateral, minilateral, and multilateral forms of cooperation

---

[17] For relevant information, see "Cooperazione Internazionale", Italian Ministry of Foreign Affairs, accessed 9 September 2022, https://www.esteri.it/it/politica-estera-e-cooperazione-allo-sviluppo/cooperaz_sviluppo.

[18] Middle power theorists are even more prolific than great power theorists, and this has created a degree of definitional confusion. See Jeffrey Robertson, "Middle-Power Definitions: Confusion Reigns Supreme", *Australian Journal of International Affairs* 71, no. 4 (2017): 355–370.

[19] Andrew F. Cooper, Richard A. Higgott, and Kim R. Nossal, *Relocating Middle Powers: Australia and Canada in a Changing World Order* (Vancouver: UBC Press, 1993), 17–19; Thomas Wilkins, "Defining Middle Powers Through IR Theory: Three Images," in *Rethinking Middle Powers in the Asian Century: New Theories, New Cases*, eds. T. Struye de Swielande, D. Vandamme, D. Walton, and T. Wilkins (London: Routledge, 2019), 45–61; Andrew Carr, "Is Australia a Middle Power? A Systemic Impact Approach", *Australian Journal of International Affairs* 68, no. 2 (2014): 70–84.

[20] Gabriele Abbondanza, "Australia the 'Good International Citizen'? The Limits of a Traditional Middle Power", *Australian Journal of International Affairs* 75, no. 2 (2021): 178–196.

with like-minded countries, and indeed Canberra's diplomatic relations attest such a posture.[21]

While great and middle power theory shows that the global status of the two countries poses no obstacles to greater levels of synergy, the literature on international cooperation provides additional and complementary insights. Miller's framework for cooperation has been an authoritative guide for scholars and practitioners for over five decades,[22] and an updated version of it is formulated and presented here with the goal of more accurately portraying a multipolar and globalised world that is remarkably different from the Cold War era in which the original framework was conceived. This article considers five distinct conditions for more effective bilateral cooperation in the twenty-first century: (i) socio-cultural similarity; (ii) economic equality and complementarity; (iii) previous forms of cooperation; (iv) shared international goals and concerns; and (v) systemic pressures. As further explicated in the sections that follow, both countries are part of the so-called "Global North" with a long history of mutual connections thanks to many forms of socio-cultural influences and significant migration phenomena. Second, they have large economies within the same order of magnitude (Italy's GDP is worth 2.1 trillion US dollars, Australia's 1.6) and a complementary economic structure. Third, there have been several high-profile initiatives that would mitigate the inevitable uncertainties surrounding discussions of an enhanced form of cooperation.[23] Fourth, they both advocate and actively uphold a rules-based understanding of the international order. Fifth, they are both concerned with recent challenges to the aforementioned international order and are both formal allies of the United States.

Starting from these theoretical and empirical considerations, which reveal much-unexpressed potential in terms of bilateral relations, this

---

[21] For relevant information, see "International Relations", Australian Department of Foreign Affairs and Trade, accessed 9 September 2022, https://www.dfat.gov.au/intern ational-relations/Pages/international-relations.

[22] Miller's fivefold framework comprised similarity of cultural background; economic equality (or lack of economic inequality); the habit of association in past international enterprises; a sense of common danger; and pressure from a greater power. See John D. Bruce Miller, "The Conditions for Co-operation", in *India, Japan, Australia: Partners in Asia?*, ed. J.D.B. Miller (Canberra: Australian National University Press, 1968), 195–210.

[23] See "Bilateral Relations", Italian Embassy in Australia, accessed 9 September 2022, https://ambcanberra.esteri.it/ambasciata_canberra/en/i_rapporti_bilaterali.

chapter proposes a strategic partnership as a viable option to address this issue and align the two countries' shared goals and means. The relevant literature defines this foreign policy tool as "a novel and versatile mechanism for diplomatic, security, and economic cooperation", which does not imply any security guarantee or defence pact and is therefore distinct from the more significant and traditional notion of the alliance.[24] Strategic partnerships thus fall under the post-Cold War trend of alignments as a flexible means with which to foster closer ties between states with common international objectives.[25] Consequently, a strategic partnership takes the form of a treaty with which enhanced levels of cooperation across select areas are established, along with preferential treatment over countries that are not included in the treaty. It is against this backdrop that a strategic partnership between Rome and Canberra is here advanced as both a feasible and a desirable new phase in the two countries' bilateral relations, in consideration of the reciprocal benefits that would follow in terms of international goals, defence capabilities, trade, scientific cooperation, and people-to-people links (see Table 7.1).

THE CASE FOR GREATER COOPERATION

International goals

Italy and Australia uphold the same international values, employ similar means when pursuing them, and both implement a multi-layered foreign policy consisting of regional, extra-regional, and global interests and concerns. An analysis of official documents is sufficient to attest as much. Italy's latest 2015 Defence White Paper states that the nation's core interests rest on an international system based on "freedom, rights, and development", adding that the Rome seeks to "actively preserve" it.[26] Similarly, Australia's 2017 Foreign Policy White Paper shows that

[24] Thomas Wilkins, "From Strategic Partnership to Strategic Alliance?: Australia-Japan Security Ties and the Asia–Pacific", *Asia Policy* 20, no. 1 (2015): 82; Sean Kay, "What Is a Strategic Partnership?", *Problems of Post-Communism* 47, no. 3 (2000): 15–24.

[25] Thomas Wilkins, "'Alignment', not Alliance'—The Shifting Paradigm of International Security.
   Cooperation: Toward a Conceptual Taxonomy of Alignment", *Review of International Studies* 38, no. 1 (2012): 53–76.

[26] *White Paper for International Security and Defence* (Rome: Italian Ministry of Defence, 2015), 35.

Canberra seeks to uphold and "protect" the rules-based order (RBO) with like-minded partners.[27] The means with which to reach these goals are equally similar. Rome emphasises the role of the UN and partners with shared goals and concerns, while openly stating that its foreign policy does not seek to protect national interests alone, but also the human and development rights of peoples in volatile regions.[28] Similarly, with the more recent 2020 Defence Strategic Update, Canberra reiterates the paramount role of the United States in the international system and adds that it engages multilaterally "with the United Nations, and through bilateral partnerships [...] to support shared interests in global rules and norms".[29] In other words, beyond the political jargon, both countries underline the inevitability of a multilateral approach when facing significant regional or global challenges, and do not eschew forceful measures with like-minded partners when diplomatic means fail. Moreover, both countries are formal allies of the United States (Italy through NATO and Australia through ANZUS), a country that is spearheading a tougher approach towards a rising and revisionist China, which plainly fulfils the 4th and 5th conditions for cooperation that have been outlined previously ("shared international goals and concerns" and "systemic pressures").

Such commitments are not limited to the assessment of *international* relations in general, but have recently started to play an increasing role in *bilateral* relations as well. On the one hand, Australia's Department of Foreign Affairs (DFAT) writes that "Australia and Italy are pursuing stronger bilateral relations, driven by shared values and interests that are increasingly aligned", and that additional cooperation is likely to result from the future EU–Australia free trade agreement and from Italy's contribution to the EU Global Gateway Initiative to the EU Indo-Pacific strategy.[30] On the other, Italy's Ministry of Foreign Affairs highlights the cordiality of bilateral relations, and the potential for increased cooperation within the G20 and other coalitions of like-minded countries on a

---

[27] *2017 Foreign Policy White Paper* (Canberra: Australian Government, 2017), 7.

[28] *White Paper for International Security and Defence* (Rome: Italian Ministry of Defence, 2015), 31.

[29] *2020 Defence Strategic Update* (Canberra: Australian Government, 2020), 24.

[30] *Italy Country Fact Sheet* (Canberra: Australian Department of Foreign Affairs and Trade, 2021), 1.

range of issues.[31] Moreover, the warm relationship between former Italian Prime Minister Mario Draghi and Australian Prime Minister Anthony Albanese has been emphasised by both on several occasions with public statements and private meetings. In essence, this brief review of official statements concerning both international and bilateral relations shows that Rome and Canberra share the same international values and interests, utilise similar means to pursue them, and openly call for greater bilateral cooperation in accordance to their respective great and middle power capabilities and visions.

Given the convergence of strategic, normative, and political interests, a greater degree of cooperation could occur in a number of ways that would be facilitated by a strategic partnership. First, following Brexit, Australia is seeking alternative access to the EU market, which remains the third-largest globally, very close to the Chinese one which currently ranks 2nd. While an EU–Australia free trade agreement is still under negotiation at the time of writing,[32] the recent tensions ensuing the AUKUS announcement have slowed down the process and might dilute some of its outcomes. In light of this, Italy could become Australia's new platform within the EU, by virtue of its founding member status, and its position as 2nd largest manufacturing country and 3rd largest economy among the 27 Union members.[33] Second, much like all large European countries, Italy is paying increasing attention to the Indo-Pacific macro-region, as also discussed by Benvenuti in Chapter 9.[34] To wit, Italy has recently concluded several deployments to the region—including freedom of navigation operations in the South China Sea—and might develop a fully-fledged Indo-Pacific strategy in the near future, based on economic, strategic, and normative pillars. Additional deployments might follow

---

[31] "Bilateral Relations", Italian Embassy in Australia, accessed 9 September 2022, https://ambcanberra.esteri.it/ambasciata_canberra/en/i_rapporti_bilaterali.

[32] "Towards an EU-Australia Trade Agreement", European Commission, accessed 9 September 2022, https://ec.europa.eu/trade/policy/in-focus/eu-australia-trade-agr eement.

[33] *Italy: Business Conditions Snapshot* (Canberra: Australian Department of Foreign Affairs and Trade, 2021).

[34] Andrea Benvenuti, "The Australian Interest in the European Union and the Italian Interest in the Asia-Pacific", in *Italy and Australia: Redefining Bilateral Relations for the Twenty-First Century*, eds. Gabriele Abbondanza and Simone Battiston (London: Palgrave Macmillan, 2024), pp. 189–212.

soon[35] and would complement the country's inclusive, multilateral, and respectful approach to the Indo-Pacific, which would work well with many of the region's institutions and nations, including Australia.[36] Australia is known for its wide network of free trade agreements in this region, and would be the ideal partner to facilitate new levels of Italian cooperation, broader engagement, and trade in this remarkably dynamic part of the world.[37]

Third, one of the many policy outcomes deriving from the challenges posed by the COVID-19 pandemic is the heightened importance of digital diplomacy[38]—also referred to as virtual diplomacy or eDiplomacy—which has been successfully employed for vaccine diplomacy and reciprocal vaccination requirements, among other issues. While they are far from being flawless and cannot fully replace traditional diplomatic means, digital negotiations are granted the same legitimacy as traditional ones.[39] Consequently, they are resulting into closer and more frequent politico-diplomatic links between the two countries, and may thus expedite the otherwise lengthy proceedings involving the establishment of a new formal partnership. Recent surveys among diplomats reveal that a majority of them wish to maintain digital diplomacy in the future, combining it with traditional diplomatic means in order to create a new model of "hybrid diplomacy".[40] The ease of communication and the increased pace of discussions and decisions would therefore support policymakers, diplomats, academics, and other experts who continue to foster

---

[35] Gabriele Carrer and Emanuele Rossi, "Italy Looks to the Indo-Pacific by Sending Carrier, Fostering Defence Ties", Decode39, accessed 17 March 2023, https://decode39.com/6143/cavour-carrier-indo-pacific-italy.

[36] Gabriele Abbondanza, "Italy's quiet pivot to the Indo-Pacific: Towards an Italian Indo-Pacific strategy", *International Political Science Review* (2023): 1–11. https://doi.org/10.1177/01925121231190093.

[37] See "Australia's Free Trade Agreements", Australian Department of Foreign Affairs and Trade, accessed 9 September 2022, https://www.dfat.gov.au/trade/agreements/trade-agreements.

[38] The author is grateful to Ambassador Margaret Twomey for her insights into digital diplomacy.

[39] Corneliu Bjola and Michaela Coplen, "Virtual Venues and International Negotiations: Lessons from the COVID-19 Pandemic", *International Negotiation* (2022): 1–25. https://doi.org/10.1163/15718069-bja10060.

[40] Corneliu Bjola and Ilan Manor, "The Rise of Hybrid Diplomacy: From Digital Adaptation to Digital Adoption", *International Affairs* 98, no. 2 (2022): 471–491.

tighter cooperation in international forums such as the G20, the UN, the WTO, and many others, a positive implication that would also affect the hypothetical strategic partnership proposed in this research. Fourth, the unexpressed potential in terms of bilateral relations involves a number of additional key areas, which are explored in the following sections.

Defence capabilities

While the two states' goals and interests are entirely compatible because of their similarity, their defence capabilities are conducive to greater cooperation due to their complementarity. On the one hand, in line with its great power credentials, Italy is a top-10 defence contractor. According to the latest data released by the Stockholm International Peace Research Institute (SIPRI), it ranks 4th by arms exports on a global level, and it ranked 7th on average over the past 10 years.[41] Importantly, Italy is one of the relatively few countries with advanced domestic capabilities across all five domains (land, air, sea, space, and cyberspace), and is expanding its presence in the Indo-Pacific thanks to large contracts with India, Indonesia, the United States, on top of defence agreements with other states.[42] On the other hand, Australia has a vast military expenditure for a middle power, and, while it does not have a significant domestic military industrial complex, it compensates for this shortcoming with steady and substantial defence procurement. According to SIPRI, the country is currently the 5th largest arms importer globally, and on average it has ranked 4th in the past 10 years.[43]

Yet, bilateral arms trade has been scarce in the same time frame, and negligible in the past three years.[44] In the light of the complementarity of the two countries' exports and imports, this might seem

---

[41] "TIV of arms exports from the top 50 largest exporters, 2021–2021", Stockholm International Peace Research Institute, accessed 9 September 2022, https://armstrade.sipri.org/armstrade/html/export_toplist.php.

[42] See "Pressroom", Italian Ministry of Foreign Affairs, accessed 9 September 2022, https://www.esteri.it/en/sala_stampa.

[43] "TIV of arms exports from the top 50 largest importers, 2021–2021", Stockholm International Peace Research Institute, accessed 9 September 2022, https://armstrade.sipri.org/armstrade/html/export_toplist.php.

[44] "TIV of arms exports to Australia, 2011–2021", Stockholm International Peace Research Institute, accessed 9 September 2022, https://armstrade.sipri.org/armstrade/html/export_values.php.

counterintuitive. To wit, Australia is undergoing a cross-domain moderni-
sation of its armed forces, spurred by a more volatile Indo-Pacific region
and recently promoted by the AUKUS enhanced strategic partnership
with the United States and the United Kingdom.[45] More specifically,
Canberra has been acquiring aircraft, ships, missiles, and sensors,[46] and,
while Italy does not export 5th generation aircraft[47] and its submarines
are designed for Mediterranean and African missions rather than oceanic
ones, its helicopters, frigates, destroyers, multi-range missiles, and sensors
are some of the most advanced globally and are widely exported to
key Australian allies and partners, including the United States.[48] Consequently, this chapter argues that the lack of a "special relationship" similar
to the one with Anglosphere partners is behind this otherwise perplexing
condition and that a strategic partnership would at least partially address
the discrepancy between what Canberra continuously acquires and what
Rome routinely exports.

Moreover, the two countries' strategic interests overlap in several
key areas beyond defence procurement. Rome's sphere of interest is
the so-called "Enlarged Mediterranean" (*Mediterraneo Allargato*) which
stretches to Central Africa to the south and the Arabian Sea to the
east,[49] while Australia's conception of the Indo-Pacific encompasses the
shores of the Arabian Peninsula and Eastern Africa.[50] The intersection of
these two macro-regions highlights the importance of the western Indian

[45] *2020 Defence Strategic Update* (Canberra: Australian Government, 2020), 34–35;
"Joint Leaders Statement on AUKUS", Australian Department of the Prime Minister
and Cabinet, accessed 9 September 2022, https://pmtranscripts.pmc.gov.au/release/tra
nscript-44109.

[46] "TIV of arms exports to Australia, 2011–2021", Stockholm International Peace
Research Institute, accessed 9 September 2022, https://armstrade.sipri.org/armstrade/
html/export_values.php.

[47] At the time of writing, Italy is jointly developing the 6th-generation "Tempest"
aircraft with the UK and Japan.

[48] "TIV of arms exports from Italy, 2011–2021", Stockholm International Peace
Research Institute, accessed 9 September 2022, https://armstrade.sipri.org/armstrade/
html/export_values.php.

[49] Valeria Di Cecco, *Mediterraneo Allargato e Grande Medio Oriente: la Politica, la
Sicurezza, l'Economia* (Rome: Forum di Relazioni Internazionali, 2005).

[50] For a discussion about the Indo-Pacific's boundaries, see Rory Medcalf, "In Defence
of the Indo-Pacific: Australia's New Strategic Map", *Australian Journal of International
Affairs* 68, no. 4 (2014): 470–483.

Ocean for both countries (see Fig. 7.1), and it should also be noted that Rome is now more intensely pivoting to the broader Indo-Pacific, as mentioned earlier. Therefore, it should not surprise that Rome has recently signed several strategic partnerships and defence agreements with key Indo-Pacific players,[51] and that Canberra is increasing its ties with major powers like India both bilaterally through a future comprehensive strategic partnership and minilaterally.[52]

Relatedly, both countries actively cooperate with ASEAN, Italy as a Development Partner and Australia as a Dialogue Partner. In the light of this, a strategic partnership between Italy and Australia would also align select components of their regional and extra-regional interests, which could be further strengthened by participating in joint military exercises with common partners as partially done so far. Additionally, both states

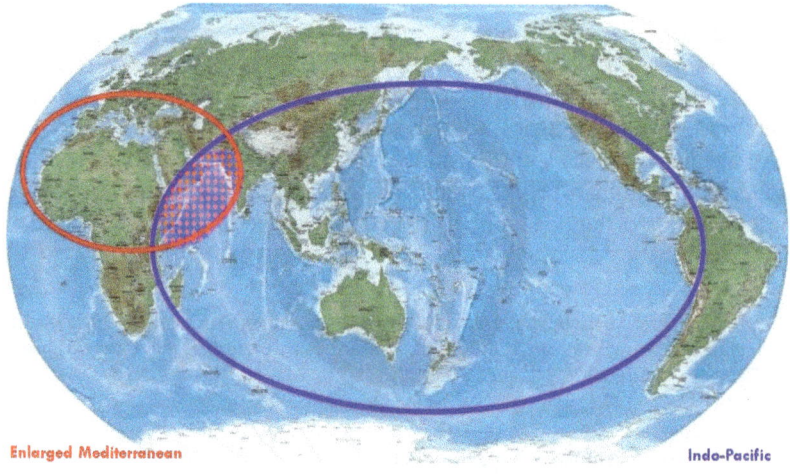

Enlarged Mediterranean   Indo-Pacific

Fig. 7.1 The overlap between the Enlarged Mediterranean ("Mediterraneo Allargato") and the Indo-Pacific (*Source: author*)

[51] Gabriele Abbondanza, "L'Italia volge lo sguardo all'Indo-Pacifico", AffarInternazionali, accessed 6 March 2023, https://www.affarinternazionali.it/italia-politica-estera-indo-pacifico.

[52] "India country brief", Australian Department of Foreign Affairs and Trade, accessed 9 September 2022, https://www.dfat.gov.au/geo/india/india-country-brief.

view irregular migration as a potential security risk,[53] and both implement strict and controversial seaborne migration policies through the offshore processing of asylum seekers.[54] Notwithstanding the entirely comparable response to a similar phenomenon, and despite the fact that the two countries are among the few with such policies in place, Italy and Australia do not engage in any form of dialogue on seaborne migration, a venue for further cooperation that could be included in the discussions concerning a strategic partnership. These common regional and global objectives, and the complementarity of the means with which to achieve them, consequently satisfy the 4th condition for cooperation ("shared international goals and concerns").

Trade

The two countries are long-standing trading partners and regularly cooperate in the major global economic forums. Rome regards the Australian economy as an excellent market for trade and investment opportunities, mainly due to its enviable economic growth, its continuous infrastructural development, the potential of the mining and energy sectors, a simpler bureaucracy, and its network of free trade agreements with Indo-Pacific countries, which could serve Italy's growing regional presence well.[55] On the other hand, the Australian Trade and Investment Commission states that:

> Italy has global expertise across all five of the Australian Government's investment priorities (infrastructure, resources and energy, tourism infrastructure, agribusiness and food, and advanced manufacturing, technology and services). Consequently, Italy holds potential as a key investment

---

[53] *White Paper for International Security and Defence* (Rome: Italian Ministry of Defence, 2015), 27; *2017 Foreign Policy White Paper* (Canberra: Australian Government, 2017), 32.

[54] Gabriele Abbondanza, "A Sea of Difference? Australian and Italian Approaches to Irregular Migration and Seaborne Asylum Seekers", *Contemporary Politics* 29, no. 1 (2023): 93–113. https://doi.org/10.1080/13569775.2022.2080959.

[55] "Perché Australia" Italian Ministry of Foreign Affairs, accessed 9 September 2022, https://www.infomercatiesteri.it/perchepaese.php?id_paesi=119.

partner and is regarded as an important market for investment into Australia.[56]

Trade in goods between Italy and Australia has come through the global financial crisis and the COVID-19 pandemic relatively unscathed, but it is stagnating in overall terms. According to the latest data provided by the UN International Trade Statistics Database (Comtrade), two-way merchandise trade was worth 6.6 billion US dollars in 2021, which is virtually equivalent to data from almost 15 years ago (6.1 billion dollars in 2008).[57] Italy currently is Australia's 31st largest export market and the 11th import market, whereas Australia is Italy's 28th export market and the 65th import market.[58] Trade in services (worth 1.6 billion dollars in total) follows a similar fashion in terms of both trend and balance, while foreign direct investment shows that Australia invests in Italy around six times what Italy invests in Australia (9.3 billion dollars in total).[59] These values and trends hold several significant implications for the future of Italian-Australian trade, as well as for the two countries' potential economic cooperation through regional and international organisations.

As with the previous section, there is a strong case for greater cooperation due to the economic profiles of the two countries, whose imports and exports are remarkably compatible. Like all great powers, Italy is a top-10 trading nation (ranking 7th by exports and 10th by imports). Its main exports of goods are machinery, pharmaceutical and chemical products, vehicles and boats, plastics, and refined oil, while its main imports are crude oil and gas, cars, electrical equipment, and minerals. In terms of services, Italy's main export is tourism-related travel and its main import item is business services.[60] On the other hand, in typical middle power

[56] "Insights into Italy", Australian Trade and Investment Commission, accessed 9 September 2022, https://www.austrade.gov.au/ArticleDocuments/4984/Italy_Market_Snapshot_December_2017.pdf.aspx.

[57] "International trade in goods and services based on UN Comtrade data", United Nations International Trade Statistics Database, accessed 9 September 2022, https://comtrade.un.org.

[58] *Ibidem.*

[59] "Italy economy fact sheet", Australian Department of Foreign Affairs and Trade, accessed 9 September 2022, https://www.dfat.gov.au/sites/default/files/ital-cef.pdf.

[60] "Italy", Observatory of Economic Complexity, accessed 9 September 2022, https://oec.world/en/profile/country/ita.

fashion, Australia is a top-25 trading nation (ranking 22nd by exports and 24th by imports). It exports predominantly minerals and gas, and it imports chiefly machinery, cars and boats, refined oil, and plastics. Trade in services is similarly structured, as Australia's main exports and imports are travel as a general category (thus comprising both tourism and temporary migration through the working holiday visa program).[61]

The complementarity of the two countries' trade profiles is evident, and the current structure of two-way trade reflects this condition, albeit to a much smaller extent than the level of trade complementarity might suggest. This is further attested by the Observatory of Economic Complexity, whose bilateral analysis highlights the comparative advantage that Rome and Canberra have in very diverse fields,[62] thus supporting calls for stronger trade relations between the two. On that note, the two diplomatic networks play a significant role in fostering closer economic ties, and both former Australian Ambassador to Italy, Margaret Twomey, and Italian Deputy Head of Mission in Australia, Roberto Rizzo, recently underlined the great potential and the positive outlook in terms of bilateral trade.[63] Current relations, led by Italian Ambassador to Australia Paolo Crudele and Australian Head of Mission to Italy Mary Ellen Miller—as of December 2023—continue to display positive and promising outcomes. While the ongoing negotiations of an EU–Australia free trade agreement will likely bring overall positive results for the economic interactions of Italy and Australia, there are some specific elements that both sides identify as obstacles towards closer trade relations. On the one hand, Rome seeks stronger laws protecting

[61] "Australia", Observatory of Economic Complexity, accessed 9 September 2022, https://oec.world/en/profile/country/aus.

[62] "Italy/Australia", Observatory of Economic Complexity, accessed 9 September 2022, https://oec.world/en/profile/bilateral-country/ita/partner/aus.

[63] "Governo australiano crede nell'importanza di un buon rapporto con l'Europa. Intervista con l'Ambasciatore Margaret Twomey", Tribuna Economica, accessed 9 September 2022, https://www.etribuna.com/aas/it/interviste/75919-governo-austra liano-crede-nell-importanza-di-un-buon-rapporto-con-l-europa-intervista-con-l-ambasciat ore-margaret-twomey.html; "Australia: tenuta dei conti pubblici, facilita' nel fare impresa, apertura al commercio internazionale. Intervista a Roberto Rizzo", Tribuna Economica, accessed 9 September 2022, https://www.etribuna.com/aas/it/interviste/75982-austra lia-tenuta-dei-conti-pubblici,-facilita%E2%80%99-nel-fare-impresa,-apertura-al-commercio-internazionale-intervista-a-roberto-rizzo.html.

its products in Australia and a steadier environment for gas and oil explorations in Australia. On the other, Canberra is worried by Italy's often stagnant economy, its cumbersome bureaucracy and reform processes, and economic imbalances that penalise Australia. These could be directly targeted during the negotiation rounds of a strategic partnership, and are therefore discussed towards the end of his chapter, along with other hindrances to stronger bilateral relations. Moreover, the two countries are effectively cooperating in international fora such as the G20, the WTO, the UN, and others, which shows the potential for multilateral cooperation involving trade and economic issues. In sum, their condition of industrialised nations with complementary economic profiles clearly meets the 2nd condition for cooperation presented in the theoretical section of this study ("economic equality and complementarity").

Scientific cooperation

Unlike the fields previously explored, scientific cooperation between Italy and Australia is substantial and is enjoying a positive trend. The two countries are significant players in the global scientific community, despite Australia's modest demographic base and Italy's use of English as a non-primary language. According to Scimago's International Science Ranking (ISR), which measures both the quality and the quantity of scientific research through a global database, Italy ranks 8th and Australia ranks 10th globally,[64] which shows that Italy's scientific profile is in line with its great power capabilities, while Australia "punches above its weight" in this field. Their comparable scientific impact is partially due to their status of highly developed countries with shared research goals, a condition that thus satisfies the 1st condition for cooperation outlined earlier in this research ("socio-cultural similarity"). Scientific cooperation as measured by joint publications has more than tripled in the last decade, and the high H Index of co-authored studies attests their quality and influence. Data from the Italian Embassy in Australia reveal that the main areas of cooperation are astronomy and astrophysics, particles and fields physics,

[64] "International Science Ranking", Scimago, accessed 9 September 2022, www.scimagojr.com/countryrank.php.

oncology, genetics, and clinical neurology.[65] This has not only resulted in joint studies, but also in practical developments. These include the Square Kilometre Array Project, experiments on the practical applications of synchrotron radiation, hypersonic scramjet engines, underground physics laboratories studying particle and gravitational waves, hadrontherapy for oncological treatments, high-altitude balloon-borne radars, substantial joint initiatives concerning space research, as well as over 200 bilateral agreements between universities and research institutes, among the many ongoing and future forms of cooperation outlined in detail by Pagani and Torresi in Chapter 12.[66]

Bilateral scientific cooperation is supported by hundreds of agreements with different levels of priority, and by two significant treaty-level agreements formally signed by the two governments, all of which attests a series of long-standing interactions that fulfil the 3rd condition for cooperation ("previous forms of cooperation"). The first one is the 1975 Agreement of Cultural Cooperation between Australia and Italy, and the second one is the 2017 Agreement on Scientific, Technological, and Innovation Cooperation, ratified by Australia in January 2019, and ratified by Italy almost two and half years later, in May 2021.[67] Italy's unhurried approach is due to a number of technical reasons pertaining to its almost unique "perfect bicameralism",[68] although this issue would have been addressed much earlier had a preferential treatment has been in place thanks to a strategic partnership. Moreover, the latter would not only

---

[65] "Bilateral scientific cooperation", Italian Embassy in Australia, accessed 9 September 2022, https://ambcanberra.esteri.it/ambasciata_canberra/en/i_rapporti_bilaterali/cooper azione%20scientifica/politica_ricerca_e_sviluppo.

[66] See Ilaria S. Pagani and Tiziana Torresi, "Italian-Australian Scientific and Research Cooperation", in *Italy and Australia: Redefining Bilateral Relations for the Twenty-First Century*, eds. Gabriele Abbondanza and Simone Battiston (London: Palgrave Macmillan, 2024), pp. 243–267.

[67] "Agreement on Scientific, Technological and Innovation Cooperation between the Government of Australia and the Government of the Italian Republic", Australian Department of Foreign Affairs and Trade, accessed 9 September 2022, https://www.info.dfat.gov.au/Info/Treaties/treaties.nsf/3328431b218f8d59ca256 ae1000029b8/eb293512381a8ac8ca2581f3007f4d49?OpenDocument.

[68] According to the Italian Constitution, both Chambers of the Italian Parliament must carry out the same functions, a post-war provision that today considerably encumbers the legislative process. See Andrea Pedrazzani and Francesco Zucchini, "'Useless Approvals'. Italian Bicameralism and its Decisional Capacity", *The Journal of Legislative Studies* 26, no. 4 (2020): 578–605.

help to accelerate lengthy parliamentary proceedings that hamper bilateral cooperation, but would also address the unexpressed scientific potential between Rome and Canberra.

For instance, the ISR shows in which research fields countries are more influential, thus also outlining where they perform less well. More specifically, Italy's research output is trailing behind Australia in the social sciences,[69] and Australia's could be strengthened with reference to physics, astronomy, and mathematics.[70] The new scientific cooperation treaty will surely be helpful in this respect, but a strategic partnership would allow for much larger funds to be allocated to joint projects. Moreover, the issue of funds is not limited to research projects alone, but is also relevant to the establishment of foundations, councils, and institutes operating jointly. Both countries have a number of such organisations established with other states,[71] but no Italy–Australia foundation exists. Additionally, Australian efforts concerning energy transition have been slowed down for years due to political reasons—despite the country's enormous potential in this field—and former Italian Ambassador to Australia Francesca Tardioli had politely prodded Australian policymakers into addressing climate change mitigation more meaningfully. Australia's new Labor government has pledged to quicken the pace, allocate 20 billion dollars to modernise the power grid, and initiate a domestic energy transition, which could further strengthen scientific and economic cooperation between the two countries. Italian technology in the field of renewable sources is already at work in Australia through its giant companies Enel, Eni, and Webuild, and the possibility of realising untapped potential is therefore within reach. These and other issues would be comprehensively dealt with by a strategic partnership—as they would be discussed during the many negotiation stages—which would further

[69] "Italy", Scimago, accessed 9 September 2022, https://www.scimagojr.com/countrysearch.php?country=IT.

[70] "Australia", Scimago, accessed 9 September 2022, https://www.scimagojr.com/countrysearch.php?country=AU.

[71] See "Elenco dei Protocolli Esecutivi scientifici e tecnologici bilaterali", Italian Ministry of Foreign Affairs, accessed 9 September 2022, https://www.esteri.it/it/diplomazia-culturale-e-diplomazia-scientifica/cooperscientificatecnologica/programmiesecutivi/accordi_programmi_culturali_tecnologici; "Foundations, councils and institutes", Australian Department of Foreign Affairs and Trade, accessed 9 September 2022, https://www.dfat.gov.au/people-to-people/foundations-councils-institutes.

elevate what already are significant levels of bilateral scientific cooperation with much scope for further expansion.

People-to-people links

The fifth field that this chapter argues would benefit from a strategic partnership is people-to-people (P2P) links, traditionally thought as an area in which cooperation is strong and continuing. In terms of tourism, data concerning 2019 are the most relevant, as the following two years experienced drastic drops in numbers due to the COVID-19 pandemic and are therefore not useful for a comparative analysis based on typical trends. Official data show that, despite the geographical distance, both Italians and Australians enjoy visiting each other's country. With just over one million tourists, Australians rank 15th among Italy's international tourists, and rank 10th by total spending during their trip (1.1 billion euros) thus surpassing the Japanese, the Brazilians, the Belgians, the Russians, and the Polish notwithstanding smaller number of arrivals.[72] Conversely, around 75,000 Italians visited Australia in 2019 (though these numbers do not comprise short-term migration of different nature), ranking 20th by number of arrivals and 19th by total spend in absolute terms. More specifically, Italians visiting Australia spend more than any other European nationality and, with the sole exception of Chinese tourists, this applies to all Asian nationalities as well (total spend was 0.5 billion Australian dollars).[73] Apart from the similarly high spending propensity, there is a noticeable imbalance in terms of tourist flows, which strongly favours Italy. This is due to a number of reasons that are not within the scope of this chapter, although Qantas' recent launch of a new direct route between Perth and Rome, in June 2022, is a positive development (the United Kingdom is the only other European country with such a link). Nevertheless, the lack of a more complete cultural and social reciprocal knowledge arguably plays a significant role in preventing larger Italian tourist flows to Australia.

---

[72] "Indagine sul turismo internazionale—2020", Bank of Italy, accessed 9 September 2022, https://www.bancaditalia.it/pubblicazioni/indagine-turismo-internazionale/2021-indagine-turismo-internazionale/statistiche_ITI_18062021.pdf.

[73] "International market performance statistics", Tourism Australia, accessed 9 September 2022, https://www.tourism.australia.com/en/markets-and-stats/tourism-statistics/international-market-performance.html.

This could be partially addressed by reinforcing the second component of P2P links discussed in this chapter, which highlights the role of culture and cultural cooperation. Italian culture—broadly understood—is well-known in Australia and is supported by a number of elements, including the large presence of Australians with Italian heritage, the influence of Italian culture in numerous aspects of the Australian society,[74] the attractiveness of the country's lifestyle, fashion, and language,[75] and a solid network of institutional and private organisations. The most prominent ones are the Italian Institutes of Culture of Sydney and Melbourne (branches of the Italian Ministry of Foreign Affairs), the 10 Dante Alighieri Societies (private not-for-profit associations that have been operating in Australia since 1896), and the four CoAsIt (language and care services) currently operating in Australia.[76] These, along with the teaching of the Italian language in numerous universities, colleges, and schools, and the presence of large cultural events including the *Biennale* and several film festivals, have contributed to a significant Italian cultural proficiency among Australians, which further supports the 1st criterion for cooperation ("socio-cultural similarity").

However, the opposite cannot be said about the Italians' knowledge of Australia and its culture. On the one hand, Australian migration to Italy—albeit present and ongoing—has been much smaller in numbers and has left a "lighter mark" on the Italian society.[77] On the other, there is no such a thing as an "Australian Institute of Culture", nor there are private entities seeking to disseminate the many layers of Australian culture, broadly defined. As with the issue of foundations operating

[74] Stephen Castles, "Italians in Australia: The Impact of a Recent Migration on the Culture and Society of a Postcolonial Nation", *Center for Migration Studies special issues* 11, no. 3 (1994): 342–367.

[75] Cristiana Palmieri, "Connecting Australia and Italy Through Language", in *Italy and Australia: Redefining Bilateral Relations for the Twenty-First Century*, eds. Gabriele Abbondanza and Simone Battiston (London: Palgrave Macmillan, 2024), pp. 137–154.

[76] See "Cultural network", Italian Ministry of Foreign Affairs, accessed 9 September 2022, https://italiana.esteri.it/italiana/en/chi-siamo/lista-sedi/?nome-sede=&tipologia-sede=iic-en; "Contact details", Dante Alighieri Society, accessed 9 September 2022, https://www.dante.global/en/contacts.

[77] Giulia Marchetti and Loretta Baldassar, "Australians in Italy in the Twenty-First Century", in *Italy and Australia: Redefining Bilateral Relations for the Twenty-First Century*, eds. Gabriele Abbondanza and Simone Battiston (London: Palgrave Macmillan, 2024), pp. 81–111.

jointly, discussed in the previous section, a strategic partnership would be able to pave the way for the establishment of such an organisation. This would be pursued with the goal of strengthening bilateral cultural cooperation and reciprocal knowledge, and could also be implemented elsewhere if this first endeavour proves to be successful.

Lastly, P2P links could be further reinforced by improving some visa-related and work-related issues. To begin with, Italy and Australia are among the select number of countries (currently 19) that enjoy reciprocal access to the Working Holiday Visa (WHV) program for people aged 18 to 30–35, and there is a reciprocal health agreement covering short-term migrants for the first six months of their stay.[78] Changes made at the end of 2018 allow Canadian, French, and Irish citizens aged up to 35 to apply for the Australian WHV. This seemingly minor difference broadens the pool of potential applicants by extending it to hundreds of thousands of people, and is due to closer ties in the form of either a strategic partnership (France) or a comprehensive set of bilateral agreements and select partnerships (with Canada and Ireland). Italians (and other nationalities) had to wait more than three-and-a-half years to benefit from this. While this issue was eventually addressed successfully, it remains one of the many examples showing what the lack of a more direct relation implies. Moreover, the lack of an appropriate mechanism for the recognition of overseas qualifications and skills between Italy and Australia additionally hampers business migration and professional cooperation, a condition that has started to exert a negative impact even on the numbers of the popular WHV program.[79] On both accounts, a strategic partnership would be able to effectively address these visa-related and work-related issues, as has occurred in the case of comparable countries that have established a strategic partnership to foster closer ties.

---

[78] "Working Holiday Visa", Italian Consulate General in Melbourne, accessed 9 September 2022, https://consmelbourne.esteri.it/consolato_melbourne/en/per-chi-si-reca-in-italia/working-holiday-visa-for-australian.html; "First Working Holiday Visa", Australian Department of Home Affairs, accessed 9 September 2022, https://immi.homeaffairs.gov.au/visas/getting-a-visa/visa-listing/work-holiday-417/first-working-holiday-417.

[79] Bruno Mascitelli and Riccardo Armillei, "Nuovi sviluppi, riflessioni e scoperte sugli italiani che migrano in Australia", in *Gli italiani in Australia Memoria storica e nuovi modelli di mobilità*, eds. B. Mascitelli and R. Armillei (Perugia Stranieri University Press, 2018), 253–281.

THE CURRENT LIMITATIONS
OF THE BILATERAL RELATIONSHIP

As the extensive comparative analysis of this chapter has demonstrated, the similarities between the two countries' values and goals and the complementarity of their international profiles present a strong case for greater bilateral cooperation. All of which begs the question of why this has not taken place yet, if—as displayed—there is much to be gained from addressing this unexpressed potential. While there are several reasons, ranging from international trends to technical issues, two elements in particular are more conspicuous than others (see Table 7.1).

Table 7.1 A framework for Italian-Australian cooperation, supporting the case for a strategic partnership

Main elements	Context
i. International goals	Shared both bilaterally and multilaterally. Significant systemic pressures, due to the two countries' role in upholding the rules-based order and as formal US allies, warrant closer cooperation. Italy's growing engagement in the Indo-Pacific represents another area of cooperation with Australia
ii. Defence capabilities	Highly complementary defence industries. Italy is a top-10 exporter and Australia a top-5 importer, yet arms trade is weak
iii. Trade	Highly complementary economic and trade profiles. The nature of trade flows reflect this, but growth is stagnant
iv. Scientific cooperation	Both are top-10 players in the global scientific community and cooperate with success. Even more could be achieved
v. People-to-people links	Australian tourism in Italy is significant, but the opposite does not apply. Smaller emigration flows and the lack of Australian Cultural Institutes hinder Australian cultural proficiency among Italians. Visa- and work-related issues hamper closer people-to-people links
Updated framework for cooperation	All five conditions are satisfied both in theory and in practice
Current limitations	Different foreign policy traditions, technical issues, geographical distance, lack of a "sense of urgency", hiatus in reciprocal Prime Ministerial visits since 2018 (not insurmountable issues)

First, Italy and Australia have different foreign policy traditions and supranational identities. Rome's international relations have traditionally pivoted around Europe (as one of the founding and largest members of the European Union), the MENA region, and the Horn of Africa (as both a former colonial power and a steady partner of countries in the region), and transatlantic/NATO relations.[80] Canberra, on the other hand, has consistently relied on "great and powerful friends" in its international relations, due to a challenging strategic environment and a subsequent "fear of abandonment".[81] Its key allies have traditionally been the United Kingdom (the British Empire previously) and the United States: in other words, the Anglosphere.[82] In more recent times, the country has opened itself to Asia–Pacific (a regional concept driven by economic connotations) and then to the Indo-Pacific (one with normative and security connotations added), which complete its "dual track" statecraft once added to its relations with the Anglosphere.[83] Put differently, these decades-long foreign policies and supranational identities have effectively traced some tangible directions and boundaries in the two countries' international relations, as per the mechanisms outlined by path dependency.[84] In turn, such boundaries have made it difficult to nuance the traditional paths (not to deviate from them, for the two countries are highly compatible in this respect, as discussed previously), and this may prevent the implementation of "creative foreign policy" that would benefit both.

Secondly, there are some specific issues that both countries highlight as obstacles to greater levels of cooperation, especially in the trade and services fields. As already discussed, Rome mentions the absence of strong measures against counterfeit luxury products, the lack of protection for

---

[80] David Felsen, "La politica estera del governo Gentiloni: i «tre cerchi» valgono ancora nel 2017?", in *Politica in Italia. I fatti dell'anno e le interpretazioni. Edizione 2018*, eds. Carolyn Forestiere and Filippo Tronconi (Bologna: Il Mulino, 2018), 113–137.

[81] Allan Gyngell, *Fear of Abandonment: Australia in the World Since 1942* (Carlton: La Trobe University Press, 2021).

[82] Jack Holland, *Selling War and Peace: Syria and the Anglosphere* (Cambridge: Cambridge University Press, 2020), 51–83.

[83] Andrew Phillips, "Australia and the Challenges of Order-Building in the Indian Ocean Region", *Australian Journal of International Affairs* 67, no. 2 (2013): 125–140.

[84] B. Guy Peters, Jon Pierre, and Desmond S. King, "The Politics of Path Dependency: Political Conflict in Historical Institutionalism", *The Journal of Politics* 67, no. 4 (2005): 1275–1300.

geographical indications and traditional specialties, the difficult process of qualifications' recognition, the uncertainty of gas and oil exploration in Australia due to political opposition, Australia's restrictive skilled visas, and its preferential mechanisms involving Anglosphere countries. On the other hand, Canberra emphasises Italy's weak economic growth, a complicated bureaucracy, an unsteady political landscape, the slow adoption of macro-economic reforms, its trade surplus with Australia, and the low levels of direct investment in Australia.[85] It is understood that this is a simplified understanding of why Italy and Australia have not pursued closer ties—there are additional issues, including geographical distance, the lack of a "sense of urgency", a temporary hiatus in reciprocal Prime Ministerial visits following the 2018 frigate tender—but these impediments are hardly insurmountable obstacles to address, especially in consideration of the two countries' common international goals and values. In essence, the conclusion drawn by this research is that a strategic partnership like the one Australia has with France or Germany would be an effective tool to address such issues, since it could systematically consider them during the many negotiation rounds that are required to reach a mutually satisfactory agreement. Additionally, the benefits deriving from digital diplomacy practices are already favouring closer ties and would be able to do so to a greater extent if intensified, extended to political, academic, and relevant professional circles, and protracted through time. The year 2024 marks the 65th anniversary of the establishment of diplomatic relations between the two countries, and could serve well to elevate bilateral ties accordingly.

CONCLUSION: A STRATEGIC PARTNERSHIP FOR THE FUTURE

This chapter has sought to provide an innovative framework for greater Italian-Australian cooperation in the twenty-first century. Against the backdrop of long-standing relations that have been thought to revolve predominantly around migration, it has unveiled the many ongoing avenues of bilateral cooperation, arguing that a more institutional approach—in the form of a strategic partnership—would be able to propel

---

[85] Gabriele Abbondanza, "Italy and Australia: Time for a Strategic Partnership", *IAI Commentaries* 20, no. 87 (2020): 1–5.

Italian-Australian relations in several fields, including non-governmental ones. Drawing on great and middle power theory, this chapter has shown that the two countries' position and role in the international system have the potential for greater synergy, while Miller's updated conditions for cooperation have provided a conceptual compass to that end. Moreover, the comparative analysis of the Italian and the Australian profiles in the five fields of international goals, defence capabilities, trade, scientific cooperation, and people-to-people links—carried out with a range of Italian, Australian, and international sources—reveals the sheer extent of this unexpressed potential. The chapter has also provided some explanations relating to why this has not resulted in closer ties yet, arguing that these impediments could be addressed successfully with joint negotiations. Lastly, recent developments such as the election of a Labor government led by Anthony Albanese set the scene for a broader and more inclusive Australian foreign policy, a condition which could indeed boost Italian-Australian relations for the twenty-first century, supported by Italy's more pronounced interest in the Indo-Pacific. To that end, the visit of Assistant Minister Tim Ayres to Italy, in January 2023, and the visit of Italian Undersecretary of State Giorgio Silli to Australia, in November 2023, are a promising first step.

While this research has adopted an international relations perspective—thus focusing on states and the international system—there are several other perspectives that are complementary to this one. They nuance both the nature and the extent of the strengthened bilateral cooperation argued for by this chapter specifically and by this whole book more in general. To this end, the volume's numerous and impressive contributions show that the synergy produced by Italian and Australian historical ties, reciprocal migration, indigenous relations, linguistic and cultural influences, political insights, geopolitical and geoeconomic interests, trade flows, and scientific collaboration is not only significant, but holds promise for even greater endeavours, should it be supported by a formal agreement such as that of a strategic partnership.[86] In conclusion, the unexpressed potential that this chapter has sought to shed light upon bears crucial implications for two like-minded and often complementary states such

---

[86] Simone Battiston and Gabriele Abbondanza, "Where to from here? The need for a long-term strategy in Italian-Australian relations", in *Italy and Australia: Redefining Bilateral Relations for the Twenty-First Century*, eds. Gabriele Abbondanza and Simone Battiston (London: Palgrave Macmillan, 2024), pp. 269–280.

as Italy and Australia, and the nuanced and multidisciplinary rationale presented by this volume is hopefully going to serve as a sufficient incentive for a renewed awareness of this in both the institutional and the non-governmental sphere.

BIBLIOGRAPHY

Abbondanza, Gabriele and Simone Battiston. "Italy and Australia in the Twenty-First Century: Distant Connections or Close Partners?". In *Italy and Australia: Redefining Bilateral Relations for the Twenty-First Century*, edited by G. Abbondanza and S. Battiston, pp. 1–23. London: Palgrave Macmillan, 2024.

Abbondanza, Gabriele. "A Sea of Difference? Australian and Italian Approaches to Irregular Migration and Seaborne Asylum Seekers". *Contemporary Politics* 29, no. 1 (2023): 93–113. https://doi.org/10.1080/13569775.2022.2080959.

Abbondanza, Gabriele. "Italy's quiet pivot to the Indo-Pacific: Towards an Italian Indo-Pacific strategy". *International Political Science Review* (2023): 1–11. https://doi.org/10.1177/01925121231190093.

Abbondanza, Gabriele. "Australia the 'Good International Citizen'? The Limits of a Traditional Middle Power". *Australian Journal of International Affairs* 75, no. 2 (2021): 178–196.

Abbondanza, Gabriele. "The Odd Axis: Germany, Italy, and Japan as Awkward Great Powers". In *Awkward Powers: Escaping Traditional Great and Middle Power Theory*, edited by G. Abbondanza and T. Wilkins, 43–71. London: Palgrave Macmillan, 2021.

Abbondanza, Gabriele. "Italy and Australia: Time for a Strategic Partnership". *IAI Commentaries* 20, no. 87 (2020): 1–5.

Abbondanza, Gabriele. "Middle Powers and Great Powers Through History: The Concept from Ancient Times to the Present Day". *History of Political Thought* 41, no. 3 (2020): 397–418.

Australian Department of Foreign Affairs and Trade. *Italy Country Fact Sheet*. Canberra: Australian Department of Foreign Affairs and Trade, 2021.

Australian Department of Foreign Affairs and Trade. *Italy: Business Conditions Snapshot*. Canberra: Australian Department of Foreign Affairs and Trade, 2021.

Australian Department of Foreign Affairs and Trade. "Agreement on Scientific, Technological and Innovation Cooperation Between the Government of Australia and the Government of the Italian Republic". Accessed 9 September 2022. https://www.info.dfat.gov.au/Info/Treaties/treaties.nsf/3328431b218f8d59ca256ae1000029b8/eb293512381a8ac8ca2581f3007f4d49?OpenDocument.

Australian Department of Foreign Affairs and Trade. "Australia's Free Trade Agreements". Accessed 9 September 2022. https://www.dfat.gov.au/trade/agreements/trade-agreements.

Australian Department of Foreign Affairs and Trade. "Foundations, Councils and Institutes". Accessed 9 September 2022. https://www.dfat.gov.au/people-to-people/foundations-councils-institutes.

Australian Department of Foreign Affairs and Trade. "India Country Brief". Accessed 9 September 2022. https://www.dfat.gov.au/geo/india/india-cou ntry-brief.

Australian Department of Foreign Affairs and Trade. "International Relations". Accessed 9 September 2022. https://www.dfat.gov.au/international-relati ons/Pages/international-relations.

Australian Department of Foreign Affairs and Trade. "Italy Economy Fact Sheet". Accessed 9 September 2022. https://www.dfat.gov.au/sites/default/files/ital-cef.pdf.

Australian Department of Home Affairs. "First Working Holiday Visa". Accessed 9 September 2022. https://immi.homeaffairs.gov.au/visas/getting-a-visa/visa-listing/work-holiday-417/first-working-holiday-417.

Australian Department of the Prime Minister and Cabinet. "Joint Leaders Statement on AUKUS". Accessed 9 September 2022. https://pmtranscripts.pmc.gov.au/release/transcript-44109.

Australian Government. *2020 Defence Strategic Update*. Canberra: Australian Government, 2020.

Australian Government. *2017 Foreign Policy White Paper*. Canberra: Australian Government, 2017.

Australian Trade and Investment Commission. "Insights into Italy". Accessed 9 September 2022. https://www.austrade.gov.au/ArticleDocuments/4984/Italy_Market_Snapshot_December_2017.pdf.aspx.

Bank of Italy. "Indagine sul turismo internazionale – 2020". Accessed 9 September 2022. https://www.bancaditalia.it/pubblicazioni/indagine-tur ismo-internazionale/2021-indagine-turismo-internazionale/statistiche_ITI_18062021.pdf.

Bartlett, Lesley, and Frances Vavrus. *Rethinking Case Study Research: A Comparative Approach*. London: Routledge, 2016.

Battiston, Simone. "Italians in Australia in the Twenty-First Century". In *Italy and Australia: Redefining Bilateral Relations for the Twenty-First Century*, edited by G. Abbondanza and S. Battiston, pp. 49–80. London: Palgrave Macmillan, 2024.

Battiston, Simone, and Gabriele Abbondanza. "Where to From Here? The Need for a Long-Term Strategy in Italian-Australian Relations". In *Italy and Australia: Redefining Bilateral Relations for the Twenty-First Century*, edited by G. Abbondanza and S. Battiston, pp. 269–280. London: Palgrave Macmillan, 2024.

Benvenuti, Andrea. "The Australian Interest in the European Union and the Italian Interest in the Asia-Pacific". In *Italy and Australia: Redefining Bilateral Relations for the Twenty-First Century*, edited by G. Abbondanza and S. Battiston, pp. 189–212. London: Palgrave Macmillan, 2024.

Bjola, Corneliu and Ilan Manor. "The Rise of Hybrid Diplomacy: From Digital Adaptation to Digital Adoption". *International Affairs* 98, no. 2 (2022): 471–491.

Bjola, Corneliu and Michaela Coplen. "Virtual Venues and International Negotiations: Lessons from the COVID-19 Pandemic". *International Negotiation* (2022): 1–25. https://doi.org/10.1163/15718069-bja10060.

Buzan, Barry and Ole Wæver. *Regions and Powers: The Structure of International Security*. Cambridge: Cambridge University Press, 2003.

Cai, Congyan. "New Great Powers and International Law in the 21st Century". *European Journal of International Law* 24, no. 3 (2013): 755–795.

Carr, Andrew. "Is Australia a Middle Power? A Systemic Impact Approach". *Australian Journal of International Affairs* 68, no. 2 (2014): 70–84.

Carrer, Gabriele and Emanuele Rossi. "Italy Looks to the Indo-Pacific by Sending Carrier, Fostering Defence Ties". Decode39. Accessed 17 March 2023. https://decode39.com/6143/cavour-carrier-indo-pacific-italy.

Castles, Stephen. "Italians in Australia: The Impact of a Recent Migration on the Culture and Society of a Postcolonial Nation". *Center for Migration Studies Special Issues* 11, no. 3 (1994): 342–367.

Cooper, Andrew F., Richard A. Higgott, and Kim R. Nossal. *Relocating Middle Powers: Australia and Canada in a Changing World Order*. Vancouver: UBC Press, 1993.

Cresciani, Gianfranco. *The Italians in Australia*. Cambridge: Cambridge University Press, 2003.

Dante Alighieri Society. "Contact Details". Accessed 9 September 2022. https://www.dante.global/en/contacts.

Di Cecco, Valeria. *Mediterraneo Allargato e Grande Medio Oriente: la Politica, la Sicurezza, l'Economia*. Rome: Forum di Relazioni Internazionali, 2005.

European Commission. "Towards an EU-Australia Trade Agreement". Accessed 9 September 2022. https://ec.europa.eu/trade/policy/in-focus/eu-australia-trade-agreement/.

Felsen, David. "La politica estera del governo Gentiloni: i «tre cerchi» valgono ancora nel 2017?". In *Politica in Italia. I fatti dell'anno e le interpretazioni. Edizione 2018*, edited by C. Forestiere and F. Tronconi, 113–137. Bologna: Il Mulino, 2018.

Gyngell, Allan. *Fear of Abandonment: Australia in the World Since 1942*. Carlton: La Trobe University Press, 2021.

Holland, Jack. *Selling War and Peace: Syria and the Anglosphere.* Cambridge: Cambridge University Press, 2020.

Huntington, Samuel P. "The Lonely Superpower", *Foreign Affairs* 78, no. 2 (1999): 35–49.

Italian Consulate General in Melbourne. "Working Holiday Visa". Accessed 9 September 2022. https://consmelbourne.esteri.it/consolato_melbourne/en/per-chi-si-reca-in-italia/working-holiday-visa-for-australian.html.

Italian Embassy in Australia. "Bilateral Relations". Accessed 9 September 2022. https://ambcanberra.esteri.it/ambasciata_canberra/en/i_rapporti_bila terali/.

Italian Embassy in Australia. "Bilateral Scientific Cooperation". Accessed 9 September 2022. https://ambcanberra.esteri.it/ambasciata_canberra/en/i_r apporti_bilaterali/cooperazione%20scientifica/politica_ricerca_e_sviluppo.

Italian Ministry of Defence. *White Paper for International Security and Defence.* Rome: Italian Ministry of Defence, 2015.

Italian Ministry of Foreign Affairs. "Cultural Network". Accessed 9 September 2022. https://italiana.esteri.it/italiana/en/chi-siamo/lista-sedi/?nome-sede=&tipologia-sede=iic-en.

Italian Ministry of Foreign Affairs. "Cooperazione Internazionale". Accessed 9 September 2022. https://www.esteri.it/it/politica-estera-e-cooperazione-allo-sviluppo/cooperaz_sviluppo.

Italian Ministry of Foreign Affairs. "Perché Australia". Accessed 9 September 2022. https://www.infomercatiesteri.it/perchepaese.php?id_paesi=119.

Italian Ministry of Foreign Affairs. "Pressroom". Accessed 9 September 2022. https://www.esteri.it/en/sala_stampa.

Italian Ministry of Foreign Affairs and Trade. "Elenco dei Protocolli Esecutivi scientifici e tecnologici bilaterali". Accessed 9 September 2022. https://www.esteri.it/it/diplomazia-culturale-e-diplomazia-scientifica/cooperscientificatecn ologica/programmiesecutivi/accordi_programmi_culturali_tecnologica.

Kay, Sean. "What Is a Strategic Partnership?". *Problems of Post-Communism* 47, no. 3 (2000): 15–24.

Marchetti, Giulia, and Loretta Baldassar. "Australians in Italy in the Twenty-First Century". In *Italy and Australia: Redefining Bilateral Relations for the Twenty-First Century,* edited by G. Abbondanza and S. Battiston, pp. 81–111. London: Palgrave Macmillan, 2024.

Mascitelli, Bruno and Riccardo Armillei. "Nuovi sviluppi, riflessioni e scoperte sugli italiani che migrano in Australia". In *Gli italiani in Australia Memoria storica e nuovi modelli di mobilità,* edited by B. Mascitelli and R. Armillei, 253–281. Perugia Stranieri University Press, 2018.

Mascitelli, Bruno. "Italy and Australia: A Relationship Made and Unmade by Immigration". *Australian Journal of International Affairs* 69, no. 3 (2015): 339–355.

Mearsheimer, John. *The Tragedy of Great Power Politics*. New York: W. W. Norton, 2001.

Medcalf, Rory. "In Defence of the Indo-Pacific: Australia's New Strategic Map". *Australian Journal of International Affairs* 68, no. 4 (2014): 470–483.

Miller, John D. Bruce. "The Conditions for Co-operation". In *India, Japan, Australia: Partners in Asia*, edited by J.D.B. Miller, 105–210. Canberra: Australian National University Press, 1968.

Observatory of Economic Complexity. "Australia". Accessed 9 September 2022. https://oec.world/en/profile/country/aus.

Observatory of Economic Complexity. "Italy". Accessed 9 September 2022. https://oec.world/en/profile/country/ita.

Observatory of Economic Complexity. "Italy/Australia". Accessed 9 September 2022. https://oec.world/en/profile/bilateral-country/ita/partner/aus.

Onwuegbuzie, Anthony J, Nancy L. Leech, and Kathleen M. Collins. "Qualitative Analysis Techniques for the Review of the Literature". *Qualitative Report* 17 (2012): 1–28.

Pagani, Ilaria S. and Tiziana Torresi. "Italian-Australian Scientific and Research Cooperation". In *Italy and Australia: Redefining Bilateral Relations for the Twenty-First Century*, edited by G. Abbondanza and S. Battiston, pp. 243–267. London: Palgrave Macmillan, 2024.

Palmieri, Cristiana. "Connecting Australia and Italy Through Language". In *Italy and Australia: Redefining Bilateral Relations for the Twenty-First Century*, edited by G. Abbondanza and S. Battiston, pp. 137–154. London: Palgrave Macmillan, 2024.

Pedrazzani, Andrea, and Francesco Zucchini. "'Useless Approvals'. Italian Bicameralism and its Decisional Capacity". *The Journal of Legislative Studies* 26, no. 4 (2020): 578–605.

Penttilä, Risto E. J. *The Role of the G8 in International Peace and Security*. London: Routledge, 2013.

Peters, B. Guy, Jon Pierre, and Desmond S. King. "The Politics of Path Dependency: Political Conflict in Historical Institutionalism". *The Journal of Politics* 67, no. 4 (2005): 1275–1300.

Phillips, Andrew. "Australia and the Challenges of Order-building in the Indian Ocean Region". *Australian Journal of International Affairs* 67, no. 2 (2013): 125–140.

Robertson, Jeffrey. "Middle-Power Definitions: Confusion Reigns Supreme". *Australian Journal of International Affairs* 71, no. 4 (2017): 355–370.

Schweller, Randall L. "Realism and the Present Great Power System: Growth and Positional Conflict Over Scarce Resources". In *Unipolar Politics: Realism and State Strategies After the Cold War*, edited by E. B. Kapstein and M. Mastanduno, 28–68. New York: Columbia University Press, 1999.

Scimago. "Australia". Accessed 9 September 2022. https://www.scimagojr.com/countrysearch.php?country=AU.

Scimago. "International Science Ranking". Accessed 9 September 2022. www.scimagojr.com/countryrank.php.

Scimago. "Italy". Accessed 9 September 2022. https://www.scimagojr.com/countrysearch.php?country=IT.

Stockholm International Peace Research Institute. "TIV of Arms Exports from the Top 50 Largest Exporters, 2020–2020". Accessed 9 September 2022. https://armstrade.sipri.org/armstrade/html/export_toplist.php.

Stockholm International Peace Research Institute. "TIV of Arms Exports from the Top 50 Largest Importers, 2020–2020". Accessed 9 September 2022, https://armstrade.sipri.org/armstrade/html/export_toplist.php.

Stockholm International Peace Research Institute. "TIV of Arms Exports to Australia, 2010–2020". Accessed 9 September 2022, https://armstrade.sipri.org/armstrade/html/export_values.php.

Stockholm International Peace Research Institute. "TIV of Arms Exports from Italy, 2010–2020". Accessed 9 September 2022. https://armstrade.sipri.org/armstrade/html/export_values.php.

Tourism Australia. "International Market Performance Statistics". Tourism Australia. Accessed 9 September 2022. https://www.tourism.australia.com/en/markets-and-stats/tourism-statistics/international-market-performance.html.

United Nations International Trade Statistics Database. "International Trade in Goods and Services Based on UN Comtrade Data". Accessed 9 September 2022. https://comtrade.un.org.

Waltz, Kenneth. *Theory of International Politics*. New York: McGraw-Hill, 1979.

Wilkins, Thomas. "Defining Middle Powers Through IR Theory: Three Images". In *Rethinking Middle Powers in the Asian Century: New Theories, New Cases*, edited by T. Struye de Swielande, D. Vandamme, D. Walton, and T. Wilkins, 45–61. London: Routledge, 2019.

Wilkins, Thomas. "From Strategic Partnership to Strategic Alliance?: Australia-Japan Security Ties and the Asia-Pacific". *Asia Policy* 20, no. 1 (2015): 81–112.

Wilkins, Thomas. "'Alignment', not 'Alliance'—The Shifting Paradigm of International Security Cooperation: Toward a Conceptual Taxonomy of Alignment". *Review of International Studies* 38, no. 1 (2012): 53–76.

CHAPTER 8

The Australian Interest in the European Union and the Italian Interest in the Asia–Pacific

Andrea Benvenuti

INTRODUCTION

Two of the most developed nations in the world and prominent members of regional politico-military alliances and economic groupings, Italy and Australia play a significant role in their respective regions. Italy is the 8th largest economy in the world and a founding member of the European Union (EU) and the North Atlantic Treaty Organisation (NATO). Australia is the world's 14th largest economy, a member of APEC and an important "spoke" in the "hub" of American alliances in the Asia–Pacific region.[1] Despite their regional focus, both share growing worldwide

---

[1] Gabriele Abbondanza, "Italy and Australia: Time for a Strategic Partnership," *IAI Commentaries* 20, no. 87 (2020), 1, https://www.iai.it/en/pubblicazioni/italy-and-aus tralia-time-strategic-partnership.

A. Benvenuti (✉)
School of Social Sciences, University of New South Wales, Sydney, NSW, Australia
e-mail: Andrea.Benvenuti@unsw.edu.au

189

interests and are committed to upholding international stability through multilateral cooperation. In this context, it is no surprise that, over the years, they have manifested a growing interest in each other's regional spheres of action and sought greater engagement with them. In doing so, however, they have followed different trajectories of engagement, as the following pages will reveal. With this in mind, this chapter will examine Italy's and Australia's political, economic and strategic interests in each other's regions. Accordingly, it will briefly explain Australia's post-war stake in European integration and security (NATO) and its rationale. Similarly, it will examine Italy's post-1945 involvement in the Asia–Pacific and chart its slow efforts to rebuild a presence in this region following Italy's defeat in the Second World War. Secondly, by looking at the last two decades, the chapter will discuss how these two countries have envisaged their role in each other's areas of primary interest and what policies they have pursued in their quest for engagement. Finally, it will focus on how Italy could promote Australian interests in the EU and how Australia could support Italian interests in the Asia–Pacific. Drawing from the existing historical literature on these two countries' external relations and relying on recently declassified archival sources, this chapter is a historical study that aims to shed new light on some of the less well-known aspects of their political, economic and strategic engagement with each other's primary sphere of action. In doing so, it makes a historical contribution to the existing literature on Italian and Australian foreign relations.

ITALY IN THE ASIA–PACIFIC (1945–2000)

Italy's interest in the Asia–Pacific developed slowly after the war. Several were the reasons for this state of affairs—some historical and some linked to Italy's situation at the time. Except for the interwar years when Benito Mussolini's regime sought to play a more active role in this vast region, Italy's presence and interest had been historically limited.[2] Apart from the Tianjin Concession in China, Liberal Italy (1861–1922) had no territorial presence in Asia. Having achieved nationhood late and with relatively limited economic and military capabilities, Liberal Italy had been a late-comer to the nineteenth-century scramble for colonies. Italy's defeat in

---

[2] On Fascist Italy see Giuseppe Spagnulo, *Il Risorgimento dell'Asia: India e Pakistan nella Politica Estera dell'Italia Repubblicana, 1946–1980* (Firenze: Le Monnier, 2020), Kindle edition.

the Second World War put paid for its role as a great power. It lost its colonies, and its status of defeated power limited its freedom of manoeuvre. Only after the revision of the Italian Peace Treaty of 1947 and its entry into the United Nations (UN) in 1955 did Italy regain full international status. Its parlous economic situation at the war's end and its internal ideological divisions militated against an assertive foreign policy. At the same time, raising Cold War tensions forced Rome to focus on continental security. In 1948–1949, Alcide De Gasperi's Centrist government sought, not without difficulty, to join the Atlantic Pact and capitalise on the military umbrella it provided.

In the early 1950s, in an attempt to create a bulwark against the Soviet Union, regain international status and boost its economy, Rome invested significant political capital in European supranational schemes. It successfully pursued membership of the European Coal and Steel Community (ECSC), the ill-fated European Defence Community (EDC) and the European Economic Community (EEC). In these challenging international and domestic environments, Italy's interest in the Asia–Pacific region remained low-key. Italian diplomacy focused principally on establishing initial political contacts with the region's new post-colonial nations, seeking economic opportunities and enhancing cultural links. As Pietro Quaroni, one of Italy's top diplomats at the time, painfully reminded De Gasperi in September 1945, Italy had never been a first-rate great power and would never be one. With its "provincial" attitude fixated on Europe, Rome had never taken much interest in the world outside Europe. Nor was Italy's defeat in the war likely to improve the country's fortunes in Asia. Italy had neither the means, credibility or necessary knowledge to play a major role in this area. In these circumstances, the only sensible thing to do was, according to Quaroni, to patiently foster economic and cultural cooperation with the emerging nations of Asia in the hope that this would help Italy enhance its presence and profile in the region.[3] Unbeknownst to Quaroni, his remarks to De Gasperi turned out to be remarkably prescient, for they were to fully capture the essence of Italian diplomacy in the Asia–Pacific during the Cold War.

Despite these shortcomings, De Gasperi's Italy wasted no time establishing political links with the emerging post-colonial states of South and Southeast Asia. In 1947 and 1948, Rome established formal diplomatic

[3] *Documenti Diplomatici Italiani* (henceforth *DDI*), 10th series, vol. 2, doc. 589, Quaroni to De Gasperi, September 30, 1945.

relations with India and Pakistan, respectively.[4] It saw friendly ties with them as an opportunity to secure their support for the revision of Italy's peace treaty and its entry into the UN.[5] Alas, the Indian and Pakistani attitude to the question of Italy's former colonies was to disappoint Rome.[6] Furthermore, India's rejection of Cold War alignments made it difficult for Rome to deepen its political cooperation with New Delhi.[7] Beyond India and Pakistan, relations were also established with the Philippines (1947), Burma (1950), Ceylon (1951) and Indonesia (1951).[8] Diplomatic contacts were also re-established with Thailand and Japan.[9] In the Pacific, recognition was also extended to Australia. In 1949, an Australian legation opened in Rome, later upgraded to an embassy in 1959.[10] More complex was the question of China. Given the latter's permanent membership in the UN Security Council, Italy re-established relations with it soon after the war. However, the collapse of Chiang Kai-Shek's regime resulted in the closure of the Italian embassy in Nanking.[11] Despite Rome's interest in establishing formal diplomatic relations with Mao Zedong's People's Republic of China (PRC), the Korean War and Beijing's participation in it precluded a diplomatic rapprochement. Like many other Western capitals, Rome followed Washington's lead on non-recognition.[12]

[4] *DDI*, 10th series, vol. 6, doc. 386, Mingone to Sforza, August 27, 1947; doc. 802, Fransoni to Orsini Ratto, December 13, 1947; *DDI*, 10th series, vol. 7, doc. 264, Gallarati Scotti to Sforza, February 13, 1948; doc. 497, Gallarati Scotti to Sforza, March 31, 1948.

[5] Spagnulo, *Risorgimento*, chap. 1.

[6] Spagnulo, *Risorgimento*, chap. 1; Luigi Vittorio Ferraris, *Manuale della Politica Estera Italiana, 1947–1993* (Bari: Laterza, 1998), 84.

[7] Spagnulo, *Risorgimento*, chap. 1; Ferraris, *Politica Estera*, 84.

[8] Ferraris, *Politica Estera*, 83–84; "Treaty of Friendship and General Relations between the Republic of the Philippines and the Italian Republic", 9 July 1947, https://web.arc hive.org/web/20150904011729/http://61.28.185.135/treaty/scanneddocs/571.pdf.

[9] Ferraris, *Politica Estera*, 83–84.

[10] Bruno Mascitelli, "Italy and Australia: A Relationship Made and Unmade by Immigration", *Australian Journal of International Affairs* 69, no. 3 (2015): 346.

[11] Ferraris, *Politica Estera*, 85–86.

[12] Valter Coralluzzo, "Italy's Foreign Policy toward China: Missed Opportunities and New Chances," *Journal of Modern Italian Studies* 13, no. 1 (2008): 6–7.

As it established diplomatic ties with Asia–Pacific nations, Italy also showed significant interest in boosting economic and trade ties with this region and, in particular, with the Indian Subcontinent, seen in Rome as a promising market for economic expansion. The first Italian economic mission to the Subcontinent occurred in February–April 1949 and included Ceylon, Burma and Afghanistan. India and Pakistan had primary resources that would meet the demand of Italian industries and needed Italian assistance for their economic development.[13] Apart from India and Pakistan, in the early 1950s, Italy negotiated trade agreements with Indonesia and Vietnam.[14] Under De Gasperi, Rome also considered fostering cultural links with the region by re-establishing the Institute for the Middle and the Far East.[15] In any case, the 1950s gradually witnessed a series of visits of Asian leaders to Italy. The prime ministers of India, Japan and Ceylon visited Rome in the early 1950s.[16] In 1956 and 1959, it was the turn of the president of Indonesia to visit Italy.[17]

With the onset of peaceful coexistence between blocs in the mid-1950s, Italy displayed a more pronounced interest in the Asia–Pacific. It viewed reduced Cold War tensions as an opportunity to raise its prestige and gain greater freedom of manoeuvre in the Afro-Asian world.[18] As its economy grew rapidly between 1950 and 1963, Rome used development assistance to increase its visibility in Asia and Africa.[19] At the same time, the trip undertaken by foreign minister Gaetano Martino to Asia between November 1955 and January 1956 signalled Italy's growing interest in

---

[13] Spagnulo, *Risorgimento,* Introduction and chap. 1.

[14] Spagnulo, *Risorgimento,* Introduction; Ferraris, *Politica Estera,* 83.

[15] Spagnulo, *Risorgimento,* Introduction.

[16] Ferraris, *Politica Estera,* 83–84.

[17] Eros Vicari, "Il Problema Afro-Asiatico e la Visita di Sukarno in Italia," *Africa: Rivista Trimestrale Di Studi e Documentazione dell'Istituto Italiano per l'Africa e l'Oriente* 11, no. 6/7 (1956): 147–149.

[18] G. Mammarella and P. Cacace, *La Politica Estera dell'Italia* (Bari: Laterza, 2006), 206; Leopoldo Nuti, "Italian Foreign Policy in the Cold War: A Constant Search for Status", in *Italy in the Post-Cold War Order. Adaptation, Bipartisanship, Visibility,* ed. M. Carbone (Lanham: Lexington Books, 2011), 35.

[19] For Italy and the Western Alliance, see Alessandro Brogi, "Ike and Italy: The Eisenhower Administration and Italy's 'Neo-Atlanticist' Agenda," *Journal of Cold War Studies* 4, no. 3 (2002): 32; Spagnulo, *Risorgimento,* chap. 1.

this region.[20] Furthermore, Italy's accession to the UN in December 1955 provided the necessary impetus for extending and deepening Italy's political and diplomatic ties with the nations of this area, except for the PRC, which had yet to join the UN.[21] However, even in this respect, some progress was made. In 1955, Italy and the PRC established bilateral commercial links.[22]

Italy's growing interest in the Asia–Pacific region notwithstanding, its role remained low-key compared to that of other European powers such as the United Kingdom (UK) and France.[23] Italy, for instance, shied away from major regional controversies such as the 1962 Sino-Indian war despite cautiously supporting India and providing some aid.[24] In the 1960s, Rome's desire to see a solution to the conflict in Vietnam produced no appreciable result.[25] The 1970s began with Italy's recognition of the PRC (November 1970) and its growing interest in that country.[26] The 1970s, however, witnessed Italy's adoption of a low profile in foreign policy. The twin problems of domestic terrorism and economic crisis temporarily turned Italy into the sick man of Europe, thus "hampering its foreign policy ambitions".[27] Overall, therefore, its engagement with the region turned out to be weaker than Rome would have hoped for. For all the interest in China, Italy's commercial ties with the Middle Kingdom gained little traction until the mid-1980s, when political and economic contacts became "more frequent and intense" in the aftermath of Prime Minister Bettino Craxi's visit to China (the first by an

---

[20] Ferraris, *Politica Estera*, 185–186.

[21] Ferraris, *Politica Estera*, 196.

[22] Ferraris, *Politica Estera*, 187.

[23] That said, Rome maintained a strong interest in the Middle East, an area of strategic importance for post-war Italy. See Gabriele Abbondanza, "Time for a Strategic Partnership: The Scope for International Cooperation between Italy and Australia" in *Italy and Australia: Redefining Bilateral Relations for the Twenty-First Century*, eds. Gabriele Abbondanza and Simone Battiston (London: Palgrave Macmillan, 2024), pp. 155–187.

[24] Spagnulo, *Risorgimento*, chap. 1.

[25] Ferraris, *Politica Estera*, 190–196.

[26] Coralluzzo, "Policy toward China", 7–9.

[27] Nuti, "Search for Status", 38.

Italian head of government).[28] Relations with India also failed to gather momentum in the 1970s, partly due to political instability in Delhi. Only with the return of Indira Gandhi to power in the early 1980s, did relations between the two countries pick up.[29] Gandhi visited Italy in 1981 and Prime Minister Giovanni Goria travelled to India in 1988, the first ever made by an Italian head of state or government.[30] Perhaps even more importantly, Italy also "lagged behind other European countries in terms of studies, cultural initiatives and overall willingness to analyse the phenomenon [i.e. the "Asian miracle"], as other regions attracted much more interest".[31]

Italy's improved domestic political and economic conditions led to renewed foreign policy activism in the late 1980s. This was short-lived. The "Clean Hands" judicial investigation into political corruption, which rocked the Italian political establishment in the early 1990s, reduced Italy's capacity to play a more active role in international affairs, at least for a while. Even then, however, Italy took some notable steps. It supported initiatives to foster European cooperation with Asian countries, such as the Asia–Europe Meeting (ASEM) and the EU–China and EU–ASEAN partnerships.[32] These efforts notwithstanding, Italy continued to be perceived in Asia as a quintessential "trading state"—in other words, a nation intent on enhancing its regional influence through trade.[33] With no direct security interests at stake, Italy's role in the region was, almost perforce, still very much centred on trade and economics.[34] This is not to say that Italy overlooked regional political and security issues.

---

[28] Coralluzzo, "Policy toward China", 9; Ministry of External Affairs (henceforth IMEA), "India-Italy Relations", https://www.mea.gov.in/Portal/ForeignRelation/Italy_09-02_2016.pdf.

[29] Bela Butalia, "Indo-Italian Relations since 1947," *International Studies* 23, no. 2 (1986): 112–115 and 134–135.

[30] IMEA, "India-Italy Relations."

[31] Marta Dassù, "In Search of an Italian Policy towards Pacific Asia," *International Spectator* 31, no. 3 (1996): 25.

[32] Coralluzzo, "Policy toward China", 9.

[33] Nuti, "Search for Status", 39–41; Dassù, "Italian Policy," 23.

[34] Dassù, "Italian Policy," 35.

But, in general, Italy tended to see these issues as an eminently "European" responsibility and its role as supporting "the emergence of a single European strategy".[35]

AUSTRALIA IN EUROPE (1945–2000)

Although the onset of the Cold War and decolonisation in Asia pushed them to focus on regional developments, early post-war Australian governments maintained a lively interest in European affairs. Australia still relied on a close Anglo-Australian partnership to safeguard its security interests in Asia in the absence of a significant American regional footprint. In this context, Australian policymakers held stability in Europe essential to enabling the UK to continue playing what they saw as a stabilising role in Australia's neighbourhood. They knew British power would be adversely affected if Europe were to be at war again.[36] The fall of Singapore in 1942 was still a powerful reminder of how the conflict in Europe could easily hamper British defence efforts east of Suez. Australian policymakers had no illusion that London would prioritise the defence of its home front over Commonwealth interests in Asia in the event of a European war. They also appreciated the economic benefits that a flourishing Western Europe could bring to Australian exporters in terms of greater trading opportunities and higher earnings. Lastly, they understood the importance of building a strong Western Europe against perceived Soviet expansionism. Canberra, therefore, broadly welcomed early steps towards closer continental cooperation and supported American efforts to strengthen Western Europe economically and militarily through the Marshall Plan and the Atlantic Pact.[37]

At the same time, Australia also began to look to Western Europe as a source of migrants to promote its economic development. As the

---

[35] Dassù, "Italian Policy," 24 and 35.

[36] Andrea Benvenuti, "Opportunity or Challenge? Australia and European Integration, 1950–57," *Australian Economic History Review* 51, no. 3 (2011): 297.

[37] Benvenuti, "Opportunity", 320. That said, the Marshall Plan and the Atlantic Pact also generated concerns in Canberra. For concerns regarding the Marshall Plan see David Lee, "Protecting the Sterling Area: The Chifley Government's Response to Multilateralism 1945–9," *Australian Journal of Political Science* 25, no. 2 (1990): 184–188. For concerns regarding the Atlantic Pact see below.

country welcomed hundreds of European migrants, it developed diplomatic contacts with their countries of origin, namely Germany, Italy, the Netherlands and Greece.[38] However, despite its continuing interest in European affairs, Canberra was slow to develop a diplomatic network at the embassy level.[39] Such a delay was due to various reasons, including the limited resources of the new Department of External Affairs (DEA) and the priority given to the establishment of new diplomatic posts in Asia.[40]

However, closer Western European political, economic and defence cooperation was not without potential drawbacks. Australians soon showed growing reservations about efforts to create supranational continental institutions. More precisely, their anxieties centred on the prospect that London might join the EEC. In June 1961, the DEA warned Cabinet that such a step would transform the UK into a European power, hasten its military disengagement from East of Suez and make the Commonwealth a "looser group".[41] A further concern was, in the words of the Australian Department of Trade, the "widespread adverse effects" that British membership of the EEC would have on Australian trade.[42] British entry would end the imperial preferential system that had governed Commonwealth economic relations since 1932 and raise new impediments to Australian exports to the UK.[43] In this respect, Australian apprehensions concentrated on the EEC's progressive implementation of its protectionist farm regime—the Common Agricultural Policy. Should the UK join the EEC, the CAP was expected to be

[38] T.B. Millar, *Australia in Peace and War: External Relations since 1788* (Canberra: ANU Press 1991), 320.

[39] Outside the UK, Australian embassies were established in Paris (1948), The Hague (1950), Bonn (1952), Rome (1959) and Brussels (1962). See "History of the Department of External Affairs: A Study Group," *Australian Outlook* 3, no. 3 (1949): 212 and 204.

[40] For some of these reasons see the file National Archives of Australia (henceforth NAA), A1838, 80/1/3/1 part 1, "Europe—General Relations with Australia—Australia Representatives".

[41] NAA, A4940, C3368, part 1, Cabinet Submission 1183, June 26, 1961.

[42] NAA, A3917, vol. 9, Cabinet Submission 1188, July 1, 1961.

[43] Benvenuti, "Opportunity", 297.

highly detrimental to Australian exports to Europe.[44] Throughout the 1960s, Australia watched with some concern British attempts to join the EEC—attempts that ultimately crashed against unrelenting French hostility towards British entry.[45]

In the defence field, too, Australians viewed closer Western European politico-military cooperation under the aegis of NATO with mixed feelings. Although Prime Minister Ben Chifley declared in March 1949 that Australia "welcome[d] the Atlantic Pact", his government had some concerns about American and West European plans to create a European defence alliance. It worried that such an alliance would force the US and the UK to prioritise European security issues over Asian ones (such as the future of Japan and the role of communist China in Asia). It also disliked the prospect of Australia being excluded from the inner sanctum of Western strategic decision-making.[46] Robert Menzies's return to power in December 1949 hardly elicited a more enthusiastic response. For sure, Menzies's minister of external affairs, Percy Spender, expressed Australian support for NATO.[47] But even then, Australian misgivings lingered. In February 1951, Spender told Cabinet that with the creation of NATO, the Americans and West Europeans would become increasingly preoccupied "with security arrangements to resist the spread of Communism in Europe and with the provision of troops and equipment for the protection of Western Europe". Australia, he added, recognised that Europe was "of the first importance in the world-wide fight against the spread of Communist imperialism". However, the problem for Australia was that "it may come to be regarded, from the point of view of global

---

[44] Andrea Benvenuti, "Australia's Relations with the European Community in a Historical Perspective: An Elusive Partnership," *Australian Journal of International Affairs* 72, no. 3 (2018): 195; Benvenuti, "Opportunity", 309–313.

[45] Andrea Benvenuti, *Anglo-Australian Relations and the "Turn to Europe", 1961–1972* (Rochester, NY: Boydell & Brewer, 2008), 112–149 and 163–183.

[46] For Chifley's statement see NAA, A3318, L1948/3/34, Atlantic Pact—Australian Attitude: Statement by the Prime Minister, March 19, 1949. For his government's concerns see T.R. Reese, *Australia, New Zealand and the United States: A Survey of International Relations, 1941–1968* (London: Oxford University Press, 1969), 109–110.

[47] Percy Spender, "NATO and Pacific Security," *The Annals of the American Academy of Political and Social Science* 282 (1952): 114–118.

planning, as of exclusive importance, to the neglect of the security problems of the Far East and the Pacific".[48] In the early 1950s, Australian hopes to establish a formal link with NATO and participate in global allied planning came to nought.[49] The Truman Administration opposed Australia getting "a foot in the door of NATO's strategic planning".[50]

As political and defence cooperation with the US gradually deepened due to its growing involvement in Indochina, Australian fears that Washington would prioritise European commitments over Asian ones lessened. So did, to some extent, Australian anxieties over trade with Western Europe. Not long after the UK joined the European Communities (EC) in 1973, the Whitlam government sought to put the Australia-European relationship on a more even keel by calling for closer political and economic engagement with the EC.[51] Edward Gough Whitlam was confident that British membership would give Australia a better chance to influence the EC and felt that Canberra should work closely with Britain to achieve this. At the same time, he believed Australia should strengthen its ties with other large EC members, such as France, West Germany and Italy.[52] Unlike his predecessors, who had never warmed to the EC, Gough Whitlam sought to "convey openness and friendliness" and maintained a very "complimentary" attitude towards the EC, regarding it as a "great historical forward" movement and a "pillar of world-wide

[48] *Documents on Australian Foreign Policy* (henceforth *DAFP*), vol. 21, doc. 47, Submission to Cabinet by Spender, February 15, 1951, https://www.dfat.gov.au/about-us/publications/historical-documents/Pages/volume-21/47-submission-to-cabinet-by-spender.

[49] David Lowe, "Percy Spender's Quest." *Australian Journal of International Affairs* 55, no. 2 (2001): 193–194.

[50] David Lowe, "Mr Spender Goes to Washington: An Ambassador's Vision of Australian-American Relations, 1951–58," *Journal of Imperial and Commonwealth History* 24, no. 2 (1996): 284; Lowe, "Spender's Quest", 194–195.

[51] Benvenuti, "Australia's Relations", 197–198.

[52] *DAFP*, vol. 27, doc. 444, Whitlam to Armstrong, undated (March 1973), https://www.dfat.gov.au/about-us/publications/historical-documents/volume-27/Pages/444-letter-whitlam-to-armstrong. On Italy see Gabriele Abbondanza and Simone Battiston, "Italy and Australia in the Twenty-First Century: Distant Connections or Close Partners?", in *Italy and Australia: Redefining Bilateral Relations for the Twenty-First Century*, eds. Gabriele Abbondanza and Simone Battiston (London: Palgrave Macmillan, 2024), pp.1–23.

stability".⁵³ He also sought greater trade opportunities for Australia in Europe.⁵⁴ Although he and his successor, Malcolm Fraser, recognised that "there was more to the EC than the CAP", relations between Canberra and the EC never took off.⁵⁵

With the CAP perceived in Australia as an economic threat and with the EC complaining about Australian industrial protectionism, broader political considerations remained in the background.⁵⁶ Inevitably, relations worsened under Fraser.⁵⁷ Symptomatic of Australia's frustration with the EC agricultural protectionism was the "sharp warning", issued by minister for trade negotiations John Howard in 1977 to the European Commission, to solve the "acute problems" affecting the Australia–EC trading relationship.⁵⁸ In 1978 the European Commission euphemistically described relations with Australia "as passing through a delicate phase".⁵⁹ Such a delicate phase was to last nearly twenty years until the EU committed to overhauling its CAP. Under pressure from the US and the Australia-led Cairns group to make concessions to secure a favourable deal in the Uruguay Round of GATT Trade Negotiations (1985–1993), the EU agreed to reduce the protection accorded to its farmers.⁶⁰ With

⁵³ National Archives of the United Kingdom, PREM 16/300, Brussels to FCO, telegram 6051, December 17, 1974; National Archive Records Administration (henceforth NARA), RG 59, Central Policy Files, Electronic Files 1974, Brussels to Washington, telegram 10,050, December 20, 1974; Department of the Prime Minister and Cabinet, "Speech by the Prime Minister of Australia at the International Press Centre in Brussels", December 18, 1974, http://pmtranscripts.dpmc.gov.au/.

⁵⁴ Benvenuti, "Australia's Relations", 197–198.

⁵⁵ Benvenuti, "Australia's Relations", 203.

⁵⁶ Historical Archives of the European Commission (henceforth HAEC), vol. 1978/9021, COM(78)205 final, "Communication from the Commission to the Council on Relations between the Community and Australia" May 24, 1978. See also annex 1 to COM(78)205 final.

⁵⁷ Benvenuti, "Australia's Relations", 203.

⁵⁸ NARA, RG 59, Central Policy Files, Electronic Files 1977, The Hague to Washington, telegram 5306, October 18, 1977.

⁵⁹ HAEC, Vol. 1978/9021, COM(78)205 final, "Communication from the Commission to the Council on Relations between the Community and Australia", May 24, 1978.

⁶⁰ Philomena Murray and Andrea Benvenuti, "EU-Australia Relations at Fifty: Reassessing a Troubled Relationship," *Australian Journal of Politics & History* 60, no. 3 (2014): 439–441.

the agricultural question largely neutralised, Australia and the EU gradually broadened and deepened their relations.[61] The only blot on an
otherwise strengthening relationship was the failure, in 1997, to conclude
a treaty-level Framework Agreement due to the EU's insistence on, and
Australian resistance to, the inclusion of a human rights clause in the
document.[62] Albeit replaced by a non-treaty status Joint Declaration,[63]
such an agreement would have added further depth to the bilateral relationship and placed it on a firmer footing. It would take the EU and
Australia another twenty years to accomplish this.

ITALY IN THE ASIA–PACIFIC AND AUSTRALIA
IN EUROPE: THE LAST TWO DECADES

The first two decades of the twenty-first century have witnessed a renewed
Italian interest in the Asia–Pacific region.[64] Its significance for global
stability and prosperity and Europe's increasing economic interdependence with it have pushed successive Italian governments to expand and
strengthen political and economic links with it. This has occurred on three
levels—bilateral, multilateral and European. At a bilateral level, Italy has
promoted close political and economic relations with key regional actors
such as China, India and Japan. This has translated into more frequent
high-level government-to-government contacts and reinforced partnerships. Since the mid-2000s, in particular, Italy has sought to enhance
its political and economic cooperation with China despite some ups
and downs.[65] In March 2019, relations with China appeared to gather

---

[61] Murray and Benvenuti, "EU-Australia Relations", 442.

[62] Philomena Murray, *Australia and the European Superpower: Engaging with the
European Union* (Melbourne: Melbourne University Press, 2005), 136–160.

[63] Philomena Murray, "EU-Australia Relations: A Strategic Partnership in all but
Name", *Cambridge Review of International Affairs* 29, no. 1 (2016): 177.

[64] For consistency's sake, this chapter uses the term "Asia–Pacific" even though, in
recent years, "Indo-Pacific" has gained greater currency.

[65] Coralluzzo, "Policy toward China", 13–20; Giovanni Andornino, "I Rapporti con la
Cina", in *Rapporto sulla Politica Estera Italiana: Il Governo Renzi*, ed. Ettore Greco
and Natalino Ronzitti (Roma: Edizioni Nuova Cultura, 2016): 113–116, Giovanni
Andornino, "Gli Orizzonti della Politica Estera Italiana", *Torino World Affairs Institute*, undated, https://www.twai.it/articles/facciaafaccia-gli-orizzonti-della-politica-estera-
italiana-in-asia-orientale/.

further momentum following the signing of a memorandum of under-standing in support of China's Belt and Road Initiative (BRI).[66] Two years later, however, the Draghi government adopted a more critical stance towards Beijing, which supported the ever-firmer attitude of Italy's Western partners towards China's increasingly assertive foreign policy.

Despite the significant recalibration of Italian policy towards the Asian giant, the two-way trade between Italy and China rose to $5.1 billion in 2020–2021, with Italian exports showing significant growth.[67] In any case, Italy also established strategic partnerships with South Korea (2018) and Vietnam (2013) to expand and deepen bilateral collaboration beyond economic and trade issues.[68] Similarly, in 2020, India and Italy adopted an "Action Plan" to develop a closer political and economic partnership and institutionalise annual consultations at the foreign ministers' level.[69] Moreover, due to the increasingly interconnected nature of global poli-tics, greater political coordination between Italy and some of its Asian partners (China, India, Japan, Indonesia and Australia) has also taken place within groupings like the G7 (Japan) and G-20 (China, India, Japan, Indonesia and Australia). In general, Italy has prioritised efforts to expand its economic presence in the region and tap into its rapid economic growth. As the world's 8th largest economy in terms of GDP at US current prices (2022) and the 7th most industrialised country as a

---

[66] Paolo Zucconi, "The Italy-China MoU: Opportunity or Risk for Rome?", *Foreign Brief*, May 21, 2019, https://www.foreignbrief.com/asia-pacific/china/the-italy-china-mou-opportunity-or-risk-for-rome/.

[67] Lorenzo Mariani, "Il Pragmatismo di Draghi nei Rapporti con la Cina," in *Il Governo Draghi e il Nuovo Protagonismo Internazionale dell'Italia: Rapporto sulla Politica Estera Italiana*, ed. Andrea Dessì and Ferdinando Nelli Feroci (Roma: Instituto Affari Internazionali, 2022): 57–61.

[68] Ministero degli Affari Esteri e della Cooperazione Internazionale (henceforth MAECI), "Rapporti con l'Asia Nord-orientale", https://www.esteri.it/it/politica-estera-e-cooperazione-allo-sviluppo/aree_geografiche/asia/rapporti-con-lasia-nord-orientale/; "Roma e Hanoi Celebrano 45 Anni di Relazioni Diplomatiche", *AsiaNews*, March 23, 2018, https://www.asianews.it/notizie-it/Roma-e-Hanoi-celebrano-45-anni-di-relazioni-diplomatiche-43434.html.

[69] MAECI, "Rapporti con l'Asia Meridionale", https://www.esteri.it/it/politica-est era-e-cooperazione-allo-sviluppo/aree_geografiche/asia/rapporti-con-lasia-meridionale/. In 2021, Rome and New Delhi agreed to launch a bilateral strategic partnership in energy transition. See "Joint Statement on Italy-India Strategic Partnership in Energy Transition", https://www.mea.gov.in/bilateral-documents.htm?dtl/34447/Joint_Statem ent_on_ItalyIndia_Strategic_Partnership_in_Energy_Transition.

share of global manufacturing (2022), Italy has viewed the Asia–Pacific region as an area of increasing economic expansion.[70] Over the past two decades, its exports to the region (excluding the Middle East and Central Asia) have jumped from approximately US$18 billion in 2000 to nearly US$57 billion in 2019.[71] At the same time, engagement has also been driven by Rome's awareness that in an increasingly globalised and competitive world economy, economic penetration must go hand in hand with a more pronounced political presence in the area. In a sense, Ambassador Quaroni's six-decade-old exhortation to prioritise economic and cultural cooperation over political engagement as a prerequisite for achieving a more visible regional presence, has, in recent years, been over-taken by events. In other words, greater economic engagement cannot occur or be sustained without deeper political engagement.

At a multilateral level, Italy has also sought to deepen its politico-economic ties with regional countries through its UN membership and, more importantly, the Asia–Europe Meeting (ASEM). Established in 1996, ASEM, whose membership consists of the 27 members of the EU (plus the Commission), the ten nations of ASEAN (plus the ASEAN Secretary), China, South Korea, Japan, India, Pakistan and Mongolia, has been the main multilateral forum through which to encourage greater political and economic interaction between the EU and the Asian region.[72] It is also worth noting that Italy, as one of the most significant contributors to peace-support operations worldwide, has not overlooked the importance of maintaining regional stability within a multilateral context.[73] In 2002, for instance, it committed troops to the US-led (and UN-sanctioned) Enduring Freedom operation in Afghanistan.[74] As

---

[70] See https://www.imf.org/external/datamapper/NGDPD@WEO/OEMDC/ADVEC/WEOWORLD and https://www.statista.com/chart/20858/top-10-countries-by-share-of-global-manufacturing-output/.

[71] The share of Italian exports going to this area increased from approximately 7.47 to 10.53% between 2000 and 2019. See https://wits.worldbank.org/CountryProfile/en/Country/ITA/Year/2000/TradeFlow/Export.

[72] MAECI, "L'Italia e le Organizzazioni Regionali e Multilaterali Asiatiche", https://www.esteri.it/it/politica-estera-e-cooperazione-allo-sviluppo/aree_geografiche/asia/organizzazioni/.

[73] Gabriele Abbondanza, "The West's Policeman? Assessing Italy's Status in Global Peacekeeping," *The International Spectator* 55, no. 2 (2020): 127–141.

[74] Marco Clementi, "Domestic Constraints, Governmental Instability and Italian Foreign Policy" and Donatello Osti, "Italy and Japan as Security Actors: Still Free Riding

of 2019, Rome also contributes military and police personnel to peace-support operations in Lebanon, Iraq and India–Pakistan.[75] Finally, at the European level, Italy has supported the EU's increasing visibility and presence in the area.[76] Over the past two decades, for instance, the EU has established closer ties with ASEAN, China, India, Japan and South Korea through special partnerships.[77] In this context, Italy places significant importance on acting in concert with its EU partners as this allows European nations to leverage their influence. Italy, for instance, has supported the EU Commission's recent strategy paper on the Indo-Pacific.[78]

Australia, too, has sought to foster greater political and economic cooperation with Europe.[79] It has done so in recognition of the EU's large, prosperous and increasingly integrated internal market and its growing interest in the stability and prosperity of the Asia–Pacific region. In addition, Australia and the EU have increasingly perceived each other as strong supporters of a rules-based international system with a significant stake in global stability and security.[80] Against this background, it is no surprise that relations between Australia and the EU have further

on the US?", in *Italy and Japan: How Similar Are They? A Comparative Analysis of Politics, Economics, and International Relations*, ed. Silvio Beretta, Axel Berkofsky and Fabio Rugge (Milan: Springer-Verlag Italia, 2014), 269–272 and 343, respectively.

[75] Abbondanza, "The West's Policeman?", 130–131 and 133.

[76] MAECI, "L'Italia e le Organizzazioni Asiatiche."

[77] Thomas Renard, "Partnerships for Effective Multilateralism? Assessing the Compatibility Between EU Bilateralism, (inter-)regionalism and Multilateralism," *Cambridge Review of International Affairs* 29, no. 1 (2016): 24–25.

[78] European Council, "Indo-Pacific: Council Adopts Conclusions on EU Strategy for Cooperation", April 19, 2021, https://www.consilium.europa.eu/en/press/press-releases/2021/04/19/indo-pacific-council-adopts-conclusions-on-eu-strategy-for-cooperation/; Beda Romano, "La Ue Risponde alla Via della Seta Cinese e Va alla Conquista dell'Area Indo-Pacifico", *Il Sole 24 Ore*, September 17, 2021, https://www.ilsole24ore.com/art/la-ue-risponde-via-seta-cinese-e-va-conquista-dell-area-indo-pacifico-AE84lNj.

[79] Philomena Murray, Laura Allison-Reumann and Margherita Matera, "Brexit seen from Australia: Pragmatism Should Trump Nostalgia", *Friends of Europe*, April 25, 2017, https://www.friendsofeurope.org/insights/brexit-seen-from-australia-pragmatism-should-trump-nostalgia/.

[80] Philomena Murray, "Australia's Engagement with the European Union: Partnership Choices and Critical Friends," *Australian Journal of International Affairs* 72, no. 3 (2018): 216–217.

developed over the past two decades.[81] In 2003, they signed an Agenda for Cooperation identifying their mutual priorities for the following five years and the specific measures needed to advance them.[82] In 2017, after some years of negotiations, they successfully negotiated a Framework Agreement intended to foster bilateral cooperation in areas as diverse as trade, research, counterterrorism, economic development, non-proliferation, human rights, democracy promotion, climate change and justice. Currently, the Framework Agreement is awaiting ratification by all 27 EU members. In the meantime, in 2018, they went a step further by launching negotiations for a free trade agreement. In 2020, the EU represented Australia's second-largest trading partner and second-largest source of foreign investments. The EU was also the third market for outward Australian investment.[83]

Following the 9/11 terrorist attacks on the US, Australia and NATO agreed to collaborate more closely.[84] In 2012, in particular, they signed a joint political declaration, "signall[ing] their commitment to strengthening cooperation".[85] The same year, Australia appointed Brendan Nelson as its first ambassador to NATO.[86] Since 2013, such closer cooperation has materialised through a number of initiatives such as the "Individual Partnership and Cooperation Programme" and "the Partnership Interoperability Initiative", which brings together 24 NATO partners contributing to NATO's operations (in the case of Australia, to NATO

---

[81] Laura Allison-Reumann, "After Brexit: Australia's Relations with the EU and the UK", *Global Affairs* 5, no. 4–5 (2019): 567–568; Murray, "A Strategic Partnership", 177–189.

[82] Murray, "EU-Australia Relations: Partnership", 177.

[83] Department of Foreign Affairs and Trade, "European Union Brief", https://www.dfat.gov.au/geo/europe/european-union/european-union-brief.

[84] *Stephan Frühling and Benjamin Schreer*, "Australia and NATO: A Deeper Relationship?", October 10, 2010, https://archive.lowyinstitute.org/the-interpreter/australia-and-nato-deeper-relationship; Nina Markovic, "NATOs New Strategic Concept and Issues for Australia", December 17, 2010, https://www.aph.gov.au/About_Parliament/Parliamentary_Departments/Parliamentary_Library/pubs/BN/1011/NATO#_Toc280360894.

[85] NATO, "Relations with Australia", August 25, 2021 https://www.nato.int/cps/en/natohq/topics_48899.htm; "Australia-NATO Relations", undated, https://belgium.embassy.gov.au/bsls/relnato.html.

[86] "Australia Deepens Engagement with NATO, Appoints First Ambassador to the Alliance", January 20, 2012, https://www.atlanticcouncil.org/blogs/natosource/australia-deepens-engagement-with-nato-appoints-first-ambassador-to-the-alliance/.

missions in Afghanistan and Iraq).[87] In addition, Australia is also regularly involved in NATO military exercises. It is also one of the six countries that have enhanced opportunities for regular high-level political dialogue and cooperation with NATO under the latter's "Enhanced Opportunities Partners" scheme.[88] In 2019, the visit of the NATO Secretary-General to Australia resulted in the signing of a renewed partnership, followed, a year later, by Australia's first-time participation in a NATO Foreign Ministers Meeting scheduled to examine the rise of China and the shifts in the global balance of power.[89] In this context, it is also worth noting that in December 2019, former Foreign Minister Alexander Downer called for the inclusion of Australia, Japan and South Korea into the alliance, arguing that NATO could "be the catalyst to build a stronger, more global alliance of Western liberal democratic powers".[90] Although NATO has no plans to enlarge beyond Europe, Downer's remarks were symptomatic of a recurrent Australian desire for ever closer links with NATO. That said, since 1945, Australia has never committed to matters of European defence. Nor is NATO likely to become a global alliance of democracies. Nonetheless, closer cooperation with NATO could help Australia react more effectively to global crises.[91]

Conclusion: The Need for Greater Australian–Italian Cooperation

Italy and Australia share a strong commitment to democratic values and display similar attitudes to several international issues, from sustainable economic development, good governance and human rights to peace

---

[87] North Atlantic Treaty Organisation (henceforth NATO), "Relations with Australia", August 25, 2021, https://www.nato.int/cps/en/natohq/topics_48899.htm.

[88] NATO, "Relations with Australia"; William Leben, "Australia and NATO after Afghanistan", *Australian Defence Force Journal*, 2016, https://search.informit.org/doi/pdf/10.3316/ielapa.760670862404692. The other enhanced opportunity partners are Finland, Georgia, Jordan, Sweden and Ukraine.

[89] NATO, "Relations with Australia."

[90] Latika Bourke, "Let Australia Join NATO; Summit Beings with Plea of Change", *Sydney Morning Herald*, December 4, 2019, https://www.smh.com.au/world/europe/let-australia-join-nato-summit-begins-with-plea-for-change-20191204-p53glp.html.

[91] Leben, "Australia and NATO after Afghanistan."

promotion and counterterrorism.[92] As mentioned earlier, they also have a vested interest in the stability of each other's regions. In this context, both nations could collaborate more closely to promote their respective interests. Hence, as Gabriele Abbondanza has recently argued, negotiating a strategic partnership between the two governments would help deepen their bilateral relationship and act as a catalyst for enhanced collaboration in each other's region.[93] As one of the EU's "Big Three", Italy could play a valuable role in ensuring that Australian views and interests are not overlooked within the EU Council of Ministers, the Union's key decision-making body. For its part, Australia could help entrench a greater Italian political and economic presence in the Asia–Pacific. Furthermore, the two nations could also explore ways of cooperating more closely on the critical security challenges of each other's regions.[94] Although they both rely on their regional defence alliances (NATO in Italy's case and ANZUS in Australia's) to maintain peace and stability in their own neighbourhood, the current challenges presented by the emergence of increasingly aggressive Russia and China and their growing strategic alignment is likely to require far greater Western coordination across different strategic theatres. And while it is true, as former Australian foreign minister July Bishop once put it, that "Australia has little or no ability to impact the broad direction of NATO", it is equally true that "its partner status provides specific leverage and access relevant to its own strategic priorities".[95]

Furthermore, Australia could assist in "improving [NATO] member states' understanding of the vital Indo-Pacific and East Asian region".[96] In making these comments, Bishop specifically called for a less lopsided partnership in which NATO would display greater responsiveness to Australian views and interests. But while Bishop was voicing a legitimate Australian concern, it is important to note that it is precisely by fostering security dialogue and cooperation with key NATO members such as Italy that Australia could attain greater NATO responsiveness. To put it differently, an enhanced partnership with Italy could provide Australia with a

---

[92] For a detailed discussion on these issues see Abbondanza, "Time for a Strategic Partnership".

[93] Abbondanza, "Time for a Strategic Partnership".

[94] Abbondanza, "Italy and Australia".

[95] Julie Bishop cited in Leben, "Australia and NATO."

[96] Bishop cited in Leben, "Australia and NATO."

valuable channel to encourage NATO members such as Italy to take a greater interest in the Asia–Pacific and Australia's role in it. At the very least, it could increase Australia–NATO bilateral contacts beyond those already taking place in Brussels between Australian and European officials.[97] And while neither Italy nor Australia is likely to commit troops to the defence of each other's regions, both countries can nonetheless work to coordinate Western responses to Russian and Chinese revisionism in Europe and Asia, respectively. Australia and Italy share a genuine interest in a rules-based global order. As such, they should spare no effort to maintain world peace and stability through enhanced cooperation among like-minded nations.

BIBLIOGRAPHY

Abbondanza, Gabriele. "Italy and Australia: Time for a Strategic Partnership." *IAI Commentaries* 20, no. 87 (2020): 1–5.

Abbondanza, Gabriele. "The West's Policeman? Assessing Italy's Status in Global Peacekeeping." *The International Spectator* 55, no. 2 (2020): 127–141.

Abbondanza, Gabriele. "Time for a Strategic Partnership: The Scope for International Cooperation between Italy and Australia". In *Italy and Australia: Redefining Bilateral Relations for the Twenty-First Century*, edited by Gabriele Abbondanza and Simone Battiston, pp. 155–187. London: Palgrave Macmillan, 2024.

Abbondanza, Gabriele and Battiston, Simone. "Italy and Australia in the Twenty-First Century: Distant Connections or Close Partners?" In *Italy and Australia: Redefining Bilateral Relations for the Twenty-First Century*, edited by Gabriele Abbondanza and Simone Battiston, pp. 1–23. London: Palgrave Macmillan, 2024.

Allison-Reumann, Laura. "After Brexit: Australia's Relations with the EU and the UK." *Global Affairs* 5, no. 4–5 (2019): 567–573.

Andornino, Giovanni. "I Rapporti con la Cina." In *Rapporto sulla Politica Estera Italiana: Il Governo Renzi*, edited by Ettore Greco and Natalino Ronzitti, 113–116. Roma: Edizioni Nuova Cultura, 2016.

Andornino, Giovanni. "Gli Orizzonti della Politica Estera Italiana." *Torino World Affairs Institute*, undated, https://www.twai.it/articles/facciaafaccia-gli-orizzonti-della-politica-estera-italiana-in-asia-orientale/.

---

[97] For bilateral contacts within the NATO partnership framework see Leben, "Australia and NATO."

"Australia Deepens Engagement with NATO, Appoints First Ambassador to the Alliance." January 20, 2012, https://www.atlanticcouncil.org/blogs/natoso urce/australia-deepens-engagement-with-nato-appoints-first-ambassador-to-the-alliance/.

"Australia-NATO Relations." undated, https://belgium.embassy.gov.au/bsls/rel nato.html.

Benvenuti, Andrea. *Anglo-Australian Relations and the "Turn to Europe", 1961–1972.* Rochester, NY: Boydell & Brewer, 2008.

Benvenuti, Andrea. "Opportunity or Challenge? Australia and European Integration, 1950–57." *Australian Economic History Review* 51, no. 3 (2011): 297–317.

Benvenuti, Andrea. "Australia's Relations with the European Community in a Historical Perspective: An Elusive Partnership." *Australian Journal of International Affairs* 72, no. 3 (2018): 194–207.

Bourke, Latika. "Let Australia Join NATO; Summit Beings with Plea of Change." *Sydney Morning Herald*, December 4, 2019, https://www.smh.com.au/world/europe/let-australia-join-nato-summit-begins-with-plea-for-change-20191204-p53glp.html.

Brogi, Alessandro. "Ike and Italy: The Eisenhower Administration and Italy's 'Neo-Atlanticist' Agenda." *Journal of Cold War Studies* 4, no. 3 (2002): 5–35.

Butalia, Bela. "Indo-Italian Relations since 1947." *International Studies* 23, no. 2 (1986): 107–141.

Coralluzzo, Valter. "Italy's Foreign Policy toward China: Missed Opportunities and New Chances." *Journal of Modern Italian Studies* 13, no. 1 (2008): 6–24.

Clementi, Marco. "Domestic Constraints, Governmental Instability and Italian Foreign Policy." In *Italy and Japan: How Similar Are They? A Comparative Analysis of Politics, Economics, and International Relations*, edited by Silvio Beretta, Axel Berkofsky and Fabio Rugge, 260–275. Milan: Springer-Verlag Italia, 2014.

Dassù, Marta. "In Search of an Italian Policy towards Pacific Asia." *The International Spectator* 31, no. 3 (1996): 23–38.

Department of Foreign Affairs and Trade (Australia). "European Union Brief", https://www.dfat.gov.au/geo/europe/european-union/european-union-brief.

Department of the Prime Minister and Cabinet (Australia). "Speech by the Prime Minister of Australia at the International Press Centre in Brussels." December 18, 1974.

Documenti Diplomatici Italiani (DDI). 10th series, vol. 2, doc. 589, Quaroni to De Gasperi, September 30, 1945.

DDI. 10th series, vol. 6, doc. 386, Mingone to Sforza, August 27, 1947.

DDI. 10th series, vol. 6, doc. 802, Fransoni to Orsini Ratto, December 13, 1947.

DDI. 10th series, vol. 7, doc. 264, Gallarati Scotti to Sforza, February 13, 1948.

DDI. 10th series, vol. 7, doc. 497, Gallarati Scotti to Sforza, March 31, 1948.

Documents on Australian Foreign Policy (DAFP). vol. 21, doc. 47, Submission to Cabinet by Spender, February 15, 1951.

DAFP. vol. 27, doc. 444, Whitlam to Armstrong, March 1973.

European Council. "Indo-Pacific: Council Adopts Conclusions on EU Strategy for Cooperation." April 7, 2021, https://www.consilium.europa.eu/en/press/press-releases/2021/04/19/indo-pacific-council-adopts-conclusions-on-eu-strategy-for-cooperation/.

Ferraris, Luigi Vittorio. Manuale della Politica Estera Italiana, 1947–1993. Bari: Laterza, 1998.

Frühling, Stephan, and Benjamin Schreer. "Australia and NATO: A Deeper Relationship?" October 10, 2010, https://archive.lowyinstitute.org/the-interpreter/australia-and-nato-deeper-relationship.

Historical Archives of the European Commission (HAEC). vol. 1978/9021, COM(78)205 final, "Communication from the Commission to the Council on Relations between the Community and Australia." May 24, 1978.

HAEC. vol. 1978/9021, COM(78)205 final, annex 1 to COM(78)205 final.

"History of the Department of External Affairs: A Study Group." Australian Outlook 3, no. 3 (1949): 209–214.

Leben, William. "Australia and NATO after Afghanistan." Australian Defence Force Journal, 2016, https://search.informit.org/doi/pdf/10.3316/ielapa.760670862404692.

Lee, David. "Protecting the Sterling Area: The Chifley Government's Response to Multilateralism 1945–9." Australian Journal of Political Science 25, no. 2 (1990): 178–195.

Lowe, David. "Mr Spender Goes to Washington: An Ambassador's Vision of Australian-American Relations, 1951–58." Journal of Imperial and Commonwealth History 24, no. 2 (1996): 278–295.

Lowe, David. "Percy Spender's Quest." Australian Journal of International Affairs 55, no. 2 (2001): 187–198.

Mammarella, G., and P. Cacace. La Politica Estera dell'Italia. Bari: Laterza, 2006.

Markovic, Nina. "NATOs New Strategic Concept and Issues for Australia", December 17, 2010, https://www.aph.gov.au/About_Parliament/Parliamentary_Departments/Parliamentary_Library/pubs/BN/1011/NATO#_Toc280360894.

Mascitelli, Bruno. "Italy and Australia: A Relationship Made and Unmade by Immigration." Australian Journal of International Affairs 69, no. 3 (2015): 339–355.

Mariani, Lorenzo. "Il Pragmatismo di Draghi nei Rapporti con la Cina." In *Il Governo Draghi e il Nuovo Protagonismo Internazionale dell'Italia: Rapporto sulla Politica Estera Italiana*, edited by Andrea Dessì and Ferdinando Nelli Feroci, 57–61. Roma: Instituto Affari Internazionali, 2022.

Ministero degli Affari Esteri e della Cooperazione Internazionale (MAECI). "Rapporti con l'Asia Nord-orientale", https://www.esteri.it/it/politica-est era-e-cooperazione-allo-sviluppo/aree_geografiche/asia/rapporti-con-lasia-nord-orientale/.

Ministero degli Affari Esteri e della Cooperazione Internazionale. "L'Italia e le Organizzazioni Regionali e Multilaterali Asiatiche", https://www.esteri.it/it/politica-estera-e-cooperazione-allo-sviluppo/aree_geografiche/asia/organi zzazioni/.

Ministero degli Affari Esteri e della Cooperazione Internazionale. "Rapporti con l'Asia Meridionale", https://www.esteri.it/it/politica-estera-e-cooperazione-allo-sviluppo/aree_geografiche/asia/rapporti-con-lasia-meridionale/.

Ministry of External Affairs (India). "India-Italy Relations", https://www.mea.gov.in/Portal/ForeignRelation/Italy_09-02_2016.pdf.

Millar, T.B. *Australia in Peace and War: External Relations since 1788*. Canberra: ANU Press 1991.

Murray, Philomena, and Andrea Benvenuti. "EU-Australia Relations at Fifty: Reassessing a Troubled Relationship." *Australian Journal of Politics & History* 60, no. 3 (2014): 431–448.

Murray, Philomena, and Laura Allison-Reumann and Margherita Matera. "Brexit seen from Australia: Pragmatism Should Trump Nostalgia." *Friends of Europe*, April 25, 2017, https://www.friendsofeurope.org/insights/brexit-seen-from-australia-pragmatism-should-trump-nostalgia/.

Murray, Philomena. *Australia and the European Superpower: Engaging with the European Union*. Melbourne: Melbourne University Press, 2005.

Murray, Philomena. "EU-Australia Relations: A Strategic Partnership in all but Name." *Cambridge Review of International Affairs* 29, no. 1 (2016): 171–191.

Murray, Philomena. "Australia's Engagement with the European Union: Partnership Choices and Critical Friends." *Australian Journal of International Affairs* 72, no. 3 (2018): 208–223.

National Archives of Australia (NAA). A4940, C3368, part 1, Cabinet Submission 1183, June 26, 1961.

NAA. A3917, Volume 9, Cabinet Submission 1188, July 1, 1961.

NAA. A3318, L1948/3/34, Atlantic Pact—Australian Attitude: Statement by the Prime Minister, March 19, 1949.

National Archives of the United Kingdom (NAUK). PREM 16/300, Brussels to FCO, telegram 6051, December 17, 1974.

National Archive Records Administration (NARA). RG 59, Central Policy Files, Electronic Files 1974, Brussels to Washington, telegram 10050, December 20, 1974.

NARA. RG 59, Central Policy Files, Electronic Files 1977, The Hague to Washington, telegram 5306, October 18, 1977.

North Atlantic Treaty Organisation (NATO). "Relations with Australia." August 25, 2021, https://www.nato.int/cps/en/natohq/topics_48899.htm.

Nuti, Leopoldo. "Italian Foreign Policy in the Cold War: A Constant Search for Status." In *Italy in the Post-Cold War Order. Adaptation, Bipartisanship, Visibility*, edited by M. Carbone, 25–45. Lanham: Lexington Books, 2011.

Osti, Donatello. "Italy and Japan as Security Actors: Still Free Riding on the US?" In *Italy and Japan: How Similar Are They? A Comparative Analysis of Politics, Economics, and International Relations*, edited by Silvio Beretta, Axel Berkofsky and Fabio Rugge, 329–340. Milan: Springer-Verlag Italia, 2014.

"Roma e Hanoi Celebrano 45 Anni di Relazioni Diplomatiche", *AsiaNews*, March 23, 2018, https://www.asianews.it/notizie-it/Roma-e-Hanoi-celebrano-45-anni-di-relazioni-diplomatiche-43434.html.

Renard, Thomas. "Partnerships for Effective Multilateralism? Assessing the Compatibility Between EU Bilateralism, (inter-)regionalism and Multilateralism." *Cambridge Review of International Affairs* 29, no. 1 (2016): 18–35.

Reese, T.R. *Australia, New Zealand and the United States: A Survey of International Relations, 1941–1968.* London: Oxford University Press, 1969.

Romano, Beda. "La Ue Risponde alla Via della Seta Cinese e Va alla Conquista dell'Area Indo-Pacifico." *Il Sole 24 Ore*, September 17, 2021, https://www.ilsole24ore.com/art/la-ue-risponde-via-seta-cinese-e-va-conquista-dell-area-indo-pacifico-AE84lNj.

Spagnulo, Giuseppe. *Il Risorgimento dell'Asia: India e Pakistan nella Politica Estera dell'Italia Repubblicana (1946–1980).* Firenze: Le Monnier, 2020. Kindle.

Spender, Percy. "NATO and Pacific Security." *The Annals of the American Academy of Political and Social Science* 282 (1952): 114–118.

"Treaty of Friendship and General Relations between the Republic of the Philippines and the Italian Republic." July 9, 1947, https://web.archive.org/web/20150904011729/http://61.28.185.135/treaty/scanneddocs/571.pdf.

Vicari, Eros. "Il Problema Afro-Asiatico e la Visita di Sukarno in Italia." *Africa: Rivista Trimestrale di Studi e Documentazione dell'Istituto Italiano per l'Africa e l'Oriente* 11, no. 6/7 (1956): 147–149.

Zucconi, Paolo. "The Italy-China MoU: Opportunity or Risk for Rome?" *Foreign Brief*, May 21, 2019, https://www.foreignbrief.com/asia-pacific/china/the-italy-china-mou-opportunity-or-risk-for-rome/.

CHAPTER 9

Twenty-First Century Populism in Australia and Italy: A Comparative Analysis

Kurt Sengul and Francesco Bailo

INTRODUCTION

The proliferation of populist politics throughout the twenty-first century has presented Western democracies with both significant challenges and opportunities. A truly global phenomenon, populists throughout Europe, Asia, North and South America, and the Asia Pacific have challenged mainstream parties and squeezed liberal democracies.[1] Yet despite its global scale, the rise of populism has been uneven and varied in its expression around the world. This chapter presents a comparative review of two

---

[1] Cas Mudde and Cristóbal Rovira Kaltwasser, *Populism: A Very Short Introduction,* Very Short Introductions (New York, NY: Oxford University Press, 2017).

K. Sengul (✉)
Department of Media, Communications, Creative Arts, Language, and Literature, Macquarie University, Sydney, NSW, Australia
e-mail: kurt.sengul@uon.edu.au

F. Bailo
School of Social and Political Sciences, University of Sydney, Sydney, NSW, Australia
e-mail: francesco.bailo@sydney.edu.au

213

Global North countries with long and complex populist traditions, Italy and Australia. There is little doubt that populism has left an indelible mark on the political landscape of both countries, albeit in different ways. This chapter engages with key literature and electoral data from the two countries to interrogate the interaction between different forces—the media system, the party and electoral system, and the long-term decline in political trust—to explain why the expression of populism in Australia has been markedly different from that of Italy. The chapter first presents a contemporary history of populism in Italy and Australia. It then presents a comparative analysis of the state of political trust and instability in the two respective countries in order to understand the conditions that facilitate populist movements. Finally, the chapter explores the media systems in both countries, including the use of new media by populist politicians. The findings of this chapter reveal that despite a number of commonalities between the two countries, populism has manifested in markedly different ways. It is argued here that Italy has had a far stronger supply of charismatic populist leaders, a quality that has been lacking in the Australian populist radical right. The presence of populism in a democratic system represents a failure of representative politics to live up to its promises. The rise of populism should give democracies pause to consider why voters and citizens are turning away from mainstream politics. It is hoped that this chapter will serve to inform policymakers, scholars, and journalists about the conditions that facilitate populist politics, with a view to strengthening liberal democracies in both countries according to this book's broader goals.[2]

This chapter adopts an *ideational* view of populism as, first and foremost, a set of ideas that conceives politics as a 'Manichean struggle between a reified will of the people and a conspiring elite'.[3] In the populist worldview, "the people" are constructed as morally pure and virtuous who are being deprived of their sovereignty by an illegitimate

---

[2] Gabriele Abbondanza and Simone Battiston, "Italy and Australia in the Twenty-First Century: Distant Connections or Close Partners?", in *Italy and Australia: Redefining Bilateral Relations for the Twenty-First Century*, eds. Gabriele Abbondanza and Simone Battiston (London: Palgrave Macmillan, 2024), pp. 1–23.

[3] Kirk Hawkins and Cristóbal Rovira Kaltwasser, "Introduction: The Ideational Approach," in *The Ideational Approach to Populism: Concept, Theory, and Analysis*, eds. Kirk Hawkins et al. (Oxon: Routledge, 2019), 2–24.

and out-of-touch elite.[4] The ideational approach as described here has become increasingly dominant within the scholarship as scholars coalesce around the view that populism represents a container for ideas, discourse, or ideology.[5] Moreover, it is widely accepted within the literature that populism is almost exclusively found alongside a more dominant ideology. As noted by Mudde, 'populism is in itself neither left nor right, but most populist actors are…almost all successful populists combine populism with a host ideology'.[6] Populist parties and actors are said to be nominally in support of democracy but of an anti-liberal type of democracy.[7]

POPULISM IN AUSTRALIA

While the experience of populism in Australia has been relatively understated at the electoral level, its influence throughout the Australian socio-political landscape has been far more pervasive.[8] Indeed, although Australia has not experienced a ruling populist government at the federal level, it is widely accepted that minor populist parties have wielded disproportionate influence in Australia relative to their electoral presence.[9] The most successful and enduring of these parties has been the populist radical right (PRR) party *One Nation* which was formed in 1997 shortly after the election of its leader and founder Pauline Hanson at the 1996 Federal

---

[4] Cas Mudde and Cristóbal Rovira Kaltwasser, *Populism: A Very Short Introduction*.

[5] Sophia Hunger and Fred Paxton, "What's in a Buzzword? A Systematic Review of the State of Populism Research in Political Science," *Political Science Research and Methods* (September 20, 2021): 1–17, https://doi.org/10.1017/psrm.2021.44.

[6] Cas Mudde, "Populism in Europe: An Illiberal Democratic Response to Undemocratic Liberalism (The *Government and Opposition* /Leonard Schapiro Lecture 2019)," *Government and Opposition* 56, no. 4 (October 2021): 577–97, https://doi.org/10.1017/gov.2021.15.

[7] Tim Bale and Cristóbal Rovira Kaltwasser, eds., *Riding the Populist Wave: Europe's Mainstream Right in Crisis*, 1st ed. (Cambridge University Press, 2021), https://doi.org/10.1017/9781009006866.

[8] Kurt Sengul, "The Role of Political Interviews in Mainstreaming and Normalizing the Far-Right: A View from Australia," in *Adversarial Political Interviewing*, ed. Ofer Feldman (Singapore: Springer Nature Singapore, 2022), 357–75, https://doi.org/10.1007/978-981-19-0576-6_18.

[9] Giorel Curran, "Mainstreaming Populist Discourse: The Race-Conscious Legacy of Neo-Populist Parties in Australia and Italy," *Patterns of Prejudice* 38, no. 1 (March 1, 2004): 37–55, https://doi.org/10.1080/0031322032000185578.

Election. The success of One Nation reflects the broader reality that populism in Australia has almost exclusively manifested on the far-right. These parties have tended to focus on the core issues of immigration and asylum seekers, consistent with their contemporaries in the populist radical right parties throughout Europe and North America. However, notwithstanding sporadic moments of electoral success and their considerable influence on the Australian polity more broadly, populist radical right parties and actors in Australia have failed to achieve the level of success of similar parties internationally.[10] This, as argued by some, can be partly attributed to the mainstream political parties adopting the policy agenda of the populist radical right on issues such as asylum seeker policy.[11]

Described as the *quintessential* and *archetypal* populist radical right figure, Pauline Hanson was elected to the federal parliament as the member for Oxley in the 1996 Australian Federal election. Hanson, a *fish and chip* shop owner presented herself as a downtrodden 'Aussie battler' and a political outsider looking to take on the political establishment.[12] Hanson had previously been endorsed as the Liberal candidate for Oxley but was subsequently disendorsed due to racist comments directed towards First Nations people made to a Queensland newspaper. Hanson went on to contest the seat of Oxley as an independent and formed the populist radical right One Nation party in the following year.[13] Hanson's maiden speech to the House of Representatives was overtly nativist and generated significant controversy and media attention. Hanson claimed to represent "ordinary" and "mainstream" Australians, condemning so-called reverse racism, Indigenous rights, immigration, and multiculturalism. One Nation was immediately successful in electoral terms during that period, winning 11 seats (22.7% of the vote) in the 1998 Queensland State Election and 8.4% at the 1998 Federal

---

[10] Glenn Kefford and Shaun Ratcliff, "Populists or Nativist Authoritarians? A Cross-National Analysis of the Radical Right," *Australian Journal of Political Science* 56, no. 3 (July 3, 2021): 261–79, https://doi.org/10.1080/10361146.2021.1956431.

[11] Kurt Sengul, "'Swamped': The Populist Construction of Fear, Crisis and Dangerous Others in Pauline Hanson's Senate Speeches," *Communication Research and Practice* 6, no. 1 (January 2, 2020): 20–37, https://doi.org/10.1080/22041451.2020.1729970.

[12] Anna Broinowski, *Please Explain: The Rise, Fall and Rise Again of Pauline Hanson* (2018).

[13] Michael Leach, Geoffrey Stokes, and Ian Ward, eds., *The Rise and Fall of One Nation* (University of Queensland Press, 2000).

Election. However, Hanson personally went on to lose the 1998 election, unsuccessfully[14] After their initial surge, One Nation's fortunes quickly deteriorated as the party was plagued by fractured leadership, infighting, financial scandals, poor party management, and ill-advised political strategy.[15] Internal party issues would continue to beset One Nation into the twenty-first century.

The first decade of the twenty-first century was particularly poor for the radical populist right in Australia. After their strong performance at the 1998 Queensland Election, One Nation suffered a substantial swing against the party (−13.98%) in the 2001 election, retaining just three of the 11 seats won at the previous election (FN). In 2003 Pauline Hanson along with One Nation co-founder David Ettridge was convicted of electoral fraud and sentenced to three years' imprisonment. The decision was later overturned on appeal and Hanson was released from prison. The political conditions were challenging for the populist radical right for most of the decade as conservative Prime Minister John Howard adopted a punitive stance on immigration and border security in the wake of the *September 11 Terrorist Attacks* of 2001. This significantly muted the opportunity structures for right-wing populist movements as their core issues were effectively adopted by a mainstream conservative political party. Throughout this time Pauline Hanson transitioned from political leader to media celebrity, maintaining a consistent presence on Australian television programmes.[16] However, despite her growing status as a media star, Hanson made a number of failed bids at re-election at the federal and state levels throughout the 2000s and 2010s.

The political conditions became far more fertile for the populist radical right in Australia in the latter half of the 2010s. Globally, far-right anti-immigrant movements seized on the so-called "refugee crisis" of 2015, as well as several international terrorist incidents.[17] Domestically, anti-Muslim sentiments flourished after the 2014 *Lindt Cafe Siege* which led to the deaths of three people. The incident was exploited by an already stirring Islamophobic far-right movement in Australia. Indeed,

---

[14] Broinowski, 214.

[15] Curran, "Mainstreaming Populist Discourse," (March 1, 2004).

[16] Kurt Sengul, "'It's OK to Be White': The Discursive Construction of Victimhood, 'Anti-White Racism' and Calculated Ambivalence in Australia," *Critical Discourse Studies* (May 4, 2021): 1–17, https://doi.org/10.1080/17405904.2021.1921818.

[17] Cas Mudde, *The Far Right Today* (Cambridge, UK; Medford, MA: Polity, 2019).

in the absence of an electorally significant far-right presence, a range of heterogeneous anti-Islamic groups emerged throughout the 2010s, opposing the development of Islamic schools and mosques, the certification of Halal foods, and Sharia Law (FN). In 2015, dozens of anti-Muslim rallies were held in capital cities across Australia in the name of *Reclaim Australia*. One year later, Pauline Hanson would return to Australian politics after 18 years, along with three One Nation senators.

The election of Pauline Hanson and her One Nation party in the 2016 election was significant as it marked the return of the populist radical right to Australian federal politics. Hanson's return to politics occurred alongside several populist victories internationally, including the election of Donald Trump, Rodrigo Duterte, and the Brexit Referendum. Whereas her 1996 maiden speech warned that Australia was at risk of being 'swamped by Asians', her 2016 speech firmly cemented Muslims as the new Dangerous Other.[18] One Nation wielded significant legislative influence in the 45th Parliament of Australia (2016–2019), as one of several minor party and independent crossbench Senators to hold the balance of power. Unlike the 1990s, Hanson and One Nation returned to Australian politics with both considerable legislative *and* agenda-setting powers. As with their first iteration in the 1990s, Pauline Hanson and One Nation were initially very successful in the 45th Parliament, reaching a national polling high of over 10% and electing multiple representatives in state elections across Australia. However, the internal party issues and personal scandals that plagued One Nation in the 1990s eroded much of this early success, with Hanson struggling to gain traction in the 46th parliament (2019–2022).

The COVID-19 pandemic presented the populist radical right with an opportunity to exploit the dissatisfaction in certain sections of the community with mask and vaccine mandates, state border policies, and lockdowns. However, this vote was splintered across a number of populist and quasi-populist parties competing for this segment of the electorate. Competition from minor parties and independents such as Clive Palmer's United Australia Party (UAP) and the Liberal Democratic Party (LDP) resulted in a poor performance for One Nation and populists more generally at the 2022 Australian Federal Election.

---

[18] Sengul, "Swamped.".

POPULISM IN ITALY

Between 1991 and 1994, the Italian party system that had governed the country since 1948 collapsed and disappeared. That collapse opened the way not just to the emergence of new national actors (Bossi's *Northern League* in 1991, Berlusconi's *Forza Italia*, and Fini's *National alliance* in 1994) but also to a reconfiguration of political alliances between Italians and their national parties, with the old political identities of the post-war years fading into a mythological past. Three events—all endogenous to the party system—contributed to pushing the three major Italian parties—the Italian Socialist Party (PSI), the Italian Communist Party (PCI), and the Christian Democracy (DC) out of business: first in 1989, the end of the Cold War, second in 1992, the onset of the *Mani Pulite* anti-corruption investigation and, third also in 1992, the assassination with terrorist tactics by the Sicilian Mafia of prosecutors Giovanni Falcone and Paolo Borsellino.

The political system that emerged from the rubbles of the post-war Italian party system (and its style) was mostly shaped by chronically low levels of trust towards the political elites. Trust started to decline irreversibly already in the 1980s (see Fig. 9.3) as the economic growth of the country started to stagnate and the public debt ballooned, increasing from 59% of GDP in 1981 to 98% in 1991. A strong indication of the emergence of a new anti-establishment public mood was the result of the 1991 referendum to change the national electoral law, which passed against the voting indication of the two ruling parties: the PSI and the DC. The electoral law was further modified with another referendum in 1993 and then with the 1993 electoral law, which by introducing for the first time a majoritarian component into the repartition of seats contributed to transforming campaigning and political competition.

In March 1994, Silvio Berlusconi entered the Italian political scene, which he would dominate and shape for 17 years, by winning the general election in coalition with two other new anti-establishment parties: the Northern League in the Northern part of the country and the National Alliance in the Centre-South. All three parties were new also in the sense that their political identity was strongly associated with that of their leader, a first for the Italian party system. The election of 1994 was also the first election, after the 1993 electoral reform, in which coalitions could express a leader, implicitly the candidate for the premiership. The shift from *party* politics to *leader* politics in all the national electoral competitions ever since was a consequence of the erosion of trust towards representative institutions (i.e., parties and Parliament) but also of the emergence of new forms of televised political communication. It is of course not casual that the leader that most represents this shift is Silvio Berlusconi, owner of multiple media ventures, including the only three private nationwide TV channels. Berlusconi's political enterprise, in 1994 and in the following years, is unequivocally linked to his capacity to televise his image and his political message to the electorate, directly, without the intermediation of editors or commentators.

The period that runs from 1994 to 2011 is a period characterised by bipolar competition between a centre-right coalition led by Berlusconi and a centre-left coalition led by a series of short-lived leaders (Prodi, D'Alema, Amato, Rutelli, Prodi again, Veltroni, Bersani) and by crystallisation of populist elements into the political discourse. Overall, the electoral reform and the bipolar arrangement succeeded in slightly extending the average duration of cabinets. Yet, a more stable party system did not materialise and party rebranding was a constant feature of the bipolar period. This is associated with the continuation of very low levels of trust towards parties and political institutions, which were not perceived as capable of addressing social and economic structural issues. System stability in this period was mostly achieved by the continuous dominance of Berlusconi and by his capacity to control the national debate, shape the style and format of political communication, and, arguably, in defining through the opposition between *berlusconism* and *anti-berlusconism* both the centre-right and the centre-left coalitions. The importance of TV for the political system in this period derived not only from it being the most important source of political information for the public but also because its regulation was a constant subject of debate. The bipolar period ends at the peak of the European sovereign Debt crisis with Berlusconi's resignation from Prime Minister after losing his parliamentary majority in November 2011. But notably, the end of the bipolar period also corresponds to the emergence of the Internet as a source of political information in the media diet of the public and the relative decline of TV.

As Berlusconi used a populist repertoire and TV to socialise his new political project—not a party but a *movement*—in 1994, Beppe Grillo used the Internet to socialise and organise his movement (the Five Star Movement, M5S) after 2005. Between 2011 and the election of 2013, the party system was again transformed by the emergence of a new anti-establishment party, fuelled by political discontent and populist rhetoric, capturing one-fourth of the votes—the M5S. By entering Parliament in 2013, the M5S created a new political alternative to the centre-right and centre-left governments. By winning the election in 2018, and receiving almost one-third of the vote, the M5S created its first cabinet, headed by a Conte, a little-known law professor in the orbit of the M5S, but in coalition with another populist party, Salvini's Lega, the first party within the centre-right coalition. Yet the M5S-Lega coalition government did not survive the impact of the Covid-19 pandemic. In 2021, the leadership of both the M5S and Lega were both outmanoeuvred and Conte was replaced by an establishment figure, the former head of the European Central Bank, Mario Draghi.

POLITICAL TRUST AND POLITICAL INSTABILITY

Australia

Subsequent to the *1975 Australian Constitutional Crisis* whereby Labor Prime Minister Gough Whitlam was dismissed by then Governor-General Sir John Kerr, Australia entered into a period of relative political stability. From 1975 to 2007, Australia had four prime ministers, which included two of Australia's longest-serving prime ministers (John Howard and Bob Hawke). The election of Kevin Rudd in 2007 saw the Australian Labor Party return to office after 11 years of conservative rule. Running on a pro-climate agenda, Kevin Rudd enjoyed strong personal popularity in the opinion polls and maintained a large lead over the opposition in the early period of his administration. The *2008 Global Financial Crisis* precipitated a robust economic response from the Rudd Government who initiated multiple rounds of stimulus packages. Although criticised by the opposition and conservative media for their scale and administration, Australia largely avoided the worst of the financial crisis, aided by the strength of the mining and baking sectors.[19] However, the failure of Rudd to legislate his signature climate policy, a decline in public support, and criticism of his work style and temperament resulted in a challenge to

---

[19] John Quiggin, "Time for Rudd to Give a Full-Throated Defence of Keynesian Stimulus," *The Guardian Australia* (August 26, 2013).

his leadership in June 2010.[20] Having lost the support of his colleagues, Rudd did not contest the leadership vote and his deputy Julia Gillard was elected Labor leader unopposed. Gillard was sworn in and became the 27th Prime Minister of Australia in June 2010. The replacement of Kevin Rudd as Prime Minister was the first of a number of leadership challenges to occur over the following eight years. Indeed, from the period 2010–2018, Australia had four successful leadership challenges and five prime ministers.

The constant spate of leadership challenges and "revolving door" of prime ministers during this period had a corrosive impact on political trust, satisfaction in democracy, and trust in the major political parties. According to Cameron, "voters have largely disapproved of the leadership changes that have taken place from 2010 to 2018 from both sides of politics. Those who disapproved of the way parties handled the changes were more dissatisfied with the way democracy works in Australia".[21] On a number of key measures reported by the Australian Election Study (AES), democracy is seen to be underperforming in the minds of Australian citizens. In 2019, only 58% of Australians were satisfied with how democracy was working, down from 86% in 2007 (Fig. 9.1).[22] Moreover, in 2019, satisfaction with democracy plunged to its lowest level since the 1975 constitutional crisis. AES data also shows that a majority of citizens believe that government is run for a *few big interests*, with only 12% believing that government *serves all the people*. Trust in government has also steadily declined since 2007.[23] These indicators reveal an overall dissatisfaction with democracy and distrust in the political system.[24]

---

[20] Tim Leslie, "The Rise and Fall of Kevin Rudd," *ABC News*, November 14, 2013, https://www.abc.net.au/news/2013-11-14/the-rise-and-fall-of-kevin-rudd/5090194.

[21] Sarah Cameron, "Government Performance and Dissatisfaction with Democracy in Australia," *Australian Journal of Political Science* 55, no. 2 (April 2, 2020): 170–90, https://doi.org/10.1080/10361146.2020.1755221.

[22] Sarah Cameron and Ian McAllister, "Trends in Australian Political Opinion Results from the Australian Election Study 1987–2019" (ANU College of Arts & Social Sciences, 2019), https://australianelectionstudy.org/wp-content/uploads/Trends-in-Australian-Political-Opinion-1987-2019.pdf.

[23] Cameron and McAllister, 99.

[24] Ruth Dassonneville and Ian McAllister, "Explaining the Decline of Political Trust in Australia," *Australian Journal of Political Science*, (August 6, 2021): 1–18, https://doi.org/10.1080/10361146.2021.1960272.

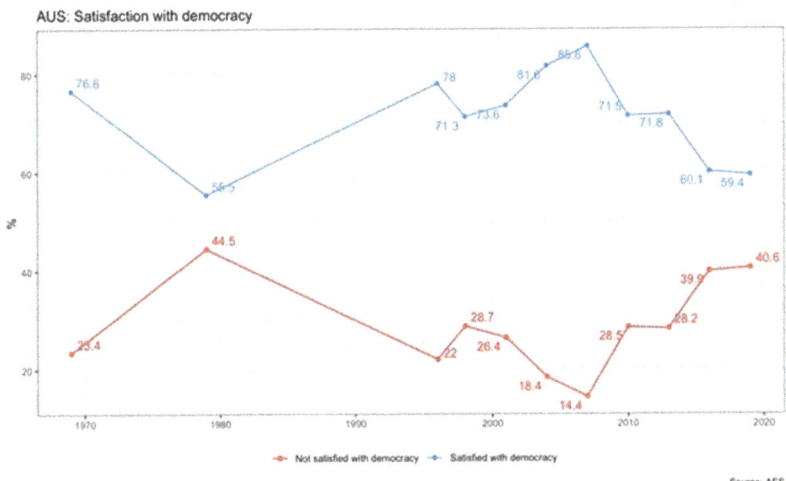

Fig. 9.1 Satisfaction in Australian Democracy (*Source* Australian Electoral Study AES)

This structural decline in satisfaction with democracy, institutions, and government has resulted in a significant shift away from the major political parties. An increasing proportion of voters are now casting votes for a range of heterogeneous minor parties and independents instead of the major parties. As suggested by Jiang and Ma, 'political distrust has...become a significant determinant of electoral support for minor parties'.[25] The vote share of non-major parties has steadily increased over the past 15 years in what appears to be a long-term trend away from the major political parties. These minor parties and independents are ideologically diverse and have had varying levels of success, longevity, and impact. While most of these parties and independents would not be technically characterised as populist under an ideational definition, many of them have embodied the performative, anti-establishment, and outsider qualities that we commonly associate with populist politics. In this sense, they may be considered quasi-populists who perhaps satisfy a particular

[25] Liang Jiang and Xiangjun Ma, "Political Distrust and Right-Wing Populist Party Voting in Australia," *Australian Journal of Political Science* 55, no. 4 (October 1, 2020): 362–77, https://doi.org/10.1080/10361146.2020.1799937.

demand for populist politics through their performative and communicative style.[26] Unsurprisingly, right-wing populist parties like Pauline Hanson's One Nation (PHON) and Bob Katter's Katter United Party (KAP) have to various degrees been the beneficiaries of this decline in political trust and drift away from the major parties. This, as further argued by Jiang and Ma, should be expected as "the underperformance of the government and major parties causes a decline in political trust, which, in turn, becomes one determinant of electors' decisions to vote for RPPs (right-wing populist parties)".[27] Moreover, found by Hoogh and Dassonneville, "voters with lower levels of political trust are more likely either to vote for populist or extremist parties".[28] However, given the fertile environment for populist politics, it is noteworthy that parties like One Nation have not been able to replicate the level of success of similar parties internationally. This, as will be argued later, can be attributed to a number of forces that have limited the effectiveness and success of populist parties in Australia.

Italy

Overall, we can observe two structural changes in the Italian party and political system after the end of the First Republic: while the life expectancy of cabinets increased (although governments still tended to be short-lived relatively to comparable countries), the stability of the party system decreased with new parties regularly entering the system. The new electoral law introduced in 1993 by configuring a bipolar competition between two coalitions of parties contributed to extending the duration of cabinets. If between 1946 and January 1994 the median duration of a cabinet was only 260 days between January 1994 and February 2021 the median duration increased by more than 70% to 444 days—still a significantly short period if compared to the five-year legislature cycles.

---

[26] Kefford, Glenn, Benjamin Moffitt, John Collins, and Joshua Marsh, "Populist Attitudes in Australia: Contextualising the Demand-Side," *Australian Journal of Political Science* (October 1, 2022): 1–17. https://doi.org/10.1080/10361146.2022.2122401.

[27] Jiang and Ma, 374.

[28] Marc Hooghe and Ruth Dassonneville, "A Spiral of Distrust: A Panel Study on the Relation Between Political Distrust and Protest Voting in Belgium," *Government and Opposition* 53, no. 1 (January 2018): 104–30, https://doi.org/10.1017/gov.2016.18.

Also, among the five longest-serving cabinets since 1946, four were inaugurated after 1994. And, finally, of the seven general elections called between 1972 and 1994 all but one were called before the constitutionally prescribed limit for the legislature of five years while between 1996 and 2019 that happened only twice. And yet if the electoral reform arguably increased the overall stability of Parliament, parliamentary coalitions, and as a consequence, cabinets, the stability of the party system actually declined.

Figure 9.2 compares turnout against the duration of cabinets (triangles) and the degree of party innovation measured in each general election. Party innovation is measured as the combined proportional success of new parties (if they reached at least 1% of the national vote) in a particular election.[29] If before 1992, party innovation was low or absent, after 1992 it increased dramatically. Specifically, we observed two critical waves of party innovations: the 1992–94 wave and the 2013 wave. It must be observed that populist parties were responsible for most of the electoral innovation both in 1992 and 1994, when the Northern League obtained 8.65% in 1992 while Forza Italia obtained 21% in 1994 (the National Alliance was likely a populist party but not formally a *new* party as it claimed a clear connection with the post-fascist Italian Social Movement) and in 2013 when the Five Star Movement obtained 25.56% of the vote.

One of the reasons for the success of populist parties is the persistently low level of political trust in Italy, which, arguably created a constant demand for anti-establishment, anti-party anti-politics electoral politics. According to Emanuele, between 1992 and 2018, 13 new parties entered the Italian party system obtaining at least 1% and capturing in total the year of their first election 83.9 percentage points.[30] Among these parties, five can be classified as populist (the Northern League in 1992, Forza Italia in 1994, Italy of Values in 2001, the Right in 2008, and the Five Star Movement in 2013). These five parties alone captured almost 73% of the votes going to new parties. Populist parties consistently demonstrated not only to be among the most successful new parties but also to be the

---

[29] Vincenzo Emanuele, *Dataset of New Parties and Party System Innovation in Western Europe Since 1945* (Rome: Italian Center for Electoral Studies, 2016), http://dx.doi.org/10.7802/1363.

[30] Emanuele.

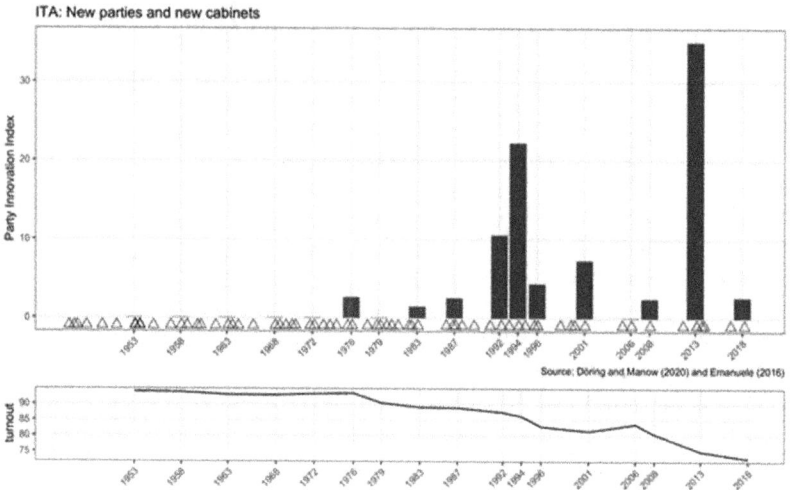

Fig. 9.2   Party innovation, cabinets, and turnout in Italy (1946–2018)

only type of new party able to have a disruptive and lasting effect on the party system.

It is interesting to note that the "anti-party sentiment"[31] and consequentially the demand (and the opportunity) for anti-party parties never receded after 1992 even following the emergence and electoral success of populist parties. Indeed, "anti-politics" became a structural component of the Italian political debate and competition. Even before the second populist wave of 2013 which brought both technocrats and populists and ended in the experiment of the Draghi Cabinet, Mete theorised the presence of different types of anti-politics in the Italian system.[32] To an *internal* form of anti-politics from populist parties such as Forza Italia, the Northern League, and Italy of Values, Mete added an *external* form of anti-politics from intellectuals and technocrats which will result in a long series of governments by experts (Amato, Ciampi, Dini, Monti, and

---

[31] Luciano Bardi, "Anti-Party Sentiment and Party System Change in Italy," *European Journal of Political Research* 29, no. 3 (1996): 345–63, https://doi.org/10.1111/j.1475-6765.1996.tb00656.x.

[32] Vittorio Mete, "Four Types of Anti-Politics: Insights from the Italian Case," *Modern Italy* 15, no. 1 (February 1, 2010): 37–61, https://doi.org/10.1080/135329409034 77872.

finally Draghi) but also two forms anti-politics "from below", that is, the *active* anti-politics of movements and party militants (the Five Star Movement between 2005 and 2018) and the passive anti-politics of "disaffected voters".[33]

POLITICS AND THE MEDIA

Australia's Media System

Australia has one of the most concentrated media systems in the world, resulting in a highly *mediatised* political environment.[34] Mediatisation refers to the long-term process of increasing influence, pervasiveness, and importance of media to political and social life.[35] As with many Western democracies, the media in Australia have become firmly embedded in the political process which presents significant implications, augmented by the scale of media concentration. A small number of highly influential media organisations dominate the media ecosystem across television, print, and radio markets. Arguably the most significant of these organisations is *News Corp Australia* which accounts for the majority of newspaper sales in Australia. News Corp Australia, founded and owned by Rupert Murdoch has typically adopted a conservative editorial stance and has been highly influential in the political process.[36] This combination of a highly concentrated media ecology and the dominance of conservative voices has presented favourable conditions for right-wing populist ideas and actors in Australia. The link between populism and the media has been well established in the literature, with some scholars going as far as suggesting that populism itself is a media-driven phenomenon.[37]

---

[33] Mete, 42.

[34] Tim Dwyer, "Is Australia's Media Market One of the World's Most Concentrated?," *The Conversation*, December 12, 2016, https://theconversation.com/is-australias-media-market-one-of-the-worlds-most-concentrated-68437.

[35] Jesper Strömbäck, "Mediatization and Perceptions of the Media's Political Influence," *Journalism Studies* 12, no. 4 (August 2011): 423–39, https://doi.org/10.1080/1461670X.2010.523583.

[36] Mitchell Hobbs and David McKnight, "'Kick This Mob Out': The Murdoch Media and the Australian Labor Government (2007 to 2013)," *Global Media Journal Australia* 8, no. 2 (2014): 1–3.

[37] S. Waisbord, "Populism as Media and Communication Phenomenon," in *Routledge Handbook of Global Populism*, ed. C de la Torre (Oxon: Routledge, 2019), 221–34.

It is argued that populists have proven to be particularly well suited to the contemporary mediatized environment.[38] A key reason for this is that the populist communication style is said to converge with the logic that governs commercial media. This *media logic* is characterised by tabloidisation, commercialisation, spectacularisation, and conflict-centred discourse.[39] As Cas Mudde notes, the commercial imperatives of the media have resulted in "mediagenic" far-right actors given disproportionate coverage and platforms because the media know they will provide controversy and spectacle.[40]

As Australia's most prominent populist politician, Pauline Hanson has benefited enormously from media attention throughout her political career, to the extent that some scholars have directly attributed this to her rise and fall.[41] Throughout the 1990s, Hanson and One Nation generated significant media coverage and controversy which was instrumental in the rise of the party. However, when this media attention started to wane, so too did Hanson's political profile.[42] The centrality of the media to Pauline Hanson's fortunes has led to some scholars describing her as a "media-fuelled phenomenon". However, despite the indisputable role that the media have played in Hanson's early rise and success, Hanson has largely been hostile to the media who, as with most populists, view them as part of the "corrupt elite". Yet, the media were not only vital to Hanson during her first iteration in politics in the late 1990s, but in the twenty-first century, Hanson transitioned from politician to media celebrity. Throughout this period, Hanson maintained a consistent media presence, including appearances on the *Sunrise* and *Today Show* breakfast programmes, and a number of reality programmes including *Dancing with the Stars* and *Celebrity Apprentice*. This constant presence in the

---

[38] Ruth Wodak, *The Politics of Fear: The Shameless Normalization of Far-Right Discourse*, 2nd ed. (Thousand Oaks: Sage, 2021).

[39] Gianpietro Mazzoleni, "Populism and the Media," in *Twentyfirst Century Populism: The Spectre of Western European Democracy*, eds. Daniele Albertazzi and Duncan McDonnell (Basingstoke: Palgrave, n.d.), 49–64.

[40] Mudde, *The Far Right Today*.

[41] Iva Ellen Deutchman and Anne Ellison, "A Star Is Born: The Roller Coaster Ride of Pauline Hanson in the News," *Media, Culture & Society* 21, no. 1 (January 1999): 33–50, https://doi.org/10.1177/016344399021001002.

[42] Giorel Curran, "Mainstreaming Populist Discourse: The Race-Conscious Legacy of Neo-Populist Parties in Australia and Italy," *Patterns of Prejudice* 38, no. 1 (March 1, 2004): 37–55, https://doi.org/10.1080/0031322032000185578.

media was critical in keeping Hanson in the public consciousness and laid the groundwork for her successful return to politics in 2016. Here we can see the alignment between the commercial media logic and Hanson's "controversial" political style.

Social media has also been a remarkably important communicative tool for Hanson and other far-right populist politicians in Australia. In Moffitt's analysis of the social media use of a number of populist leaders internationally, Hanson was categorised as having a *strong social media presence*.[43] Indeed, despite her relatively small electoral footprint, Hanson maintains a substantial presence on Facebook. *Pauline Hanson's Please Explain* Facebook page has over 440,000 followers and is one of the largest political accounts in Australia. Her social media presence can be scribed as very active, frequently updated, and often includes dialogic engagement with her followers.[44] Social media provides Hanson and other populist actors with a relatively unmediated form of communication with their followers and allows them to bypass the traditional gatekeeping role of the media.

Italy and the Media

The media played a critical role in the two populist waves that hit the Italian political system in 1994 and 2013. Indeed, both in 1994 and 2013 political outsiders used new media to bypass traditional gatekeepers, but notably until the 1990 law national TV broadcasting was limited to RAI, the public broadcaster, with strong limitations imposed on private channels. Only a few years before Forza Italia was created, the 1990 law replaced a public monopoly with a duopoly, with RAI's three TV channels now competing with Berlusconi's three TV channels for a national audience, with a minor role played by other private channels.[45] This duopoly

---

[43] Benjamin Moffitt, "Populism 2.0: Social Media and the False Allure of 'Unmediated' Representation," in *Populism and the Crisis of Democracy: Politics, Social Movements and Extremism*, eds. G. Fitzi, J. Mackert, and B.S. Turner (Oxon: Routledge, 2019), 30–46.

[44] Kurt Sengul, "Never Let a Good Crisis Go to Waste: Pauline Hanson's Exploitation of COVID-19 on Facebook," *Media International Australia* 178, no. 1 (February 2021): 101–5, https://doi.org/10.1177/1329878X20953521.

[45] Giuseppe Eusepi, "Broadcasting System in Italy: Evolution and Perspectives," *Public Choice (1986-1998)* 82, no. 3–4 (March 1995): 307–24.

was fundamentally never challenged: as of 2013 the two broadcasters still commanded 71% of the national audience.[46]

TV did not only give Berlusconi and his allies a net communicative advantage over political competitors. TV was central to Berlusconi's communication strategy as the format contributed to defining his political identity and his approach to politics and policies. Berlusconi entered the political area through a TV screen in January 1994 when in a pre-recorded video message first broadcasted by one of his TV channels he announced he would "take the field" and compete in the upcoming general election.[47] But TV always remained his medium of choice to communicate directly and intimately with his audience and electorate for the following 17 years. A signal of the strong politicisation of the medium is the very low level of trust towards the TV (see Fig. 9.4).

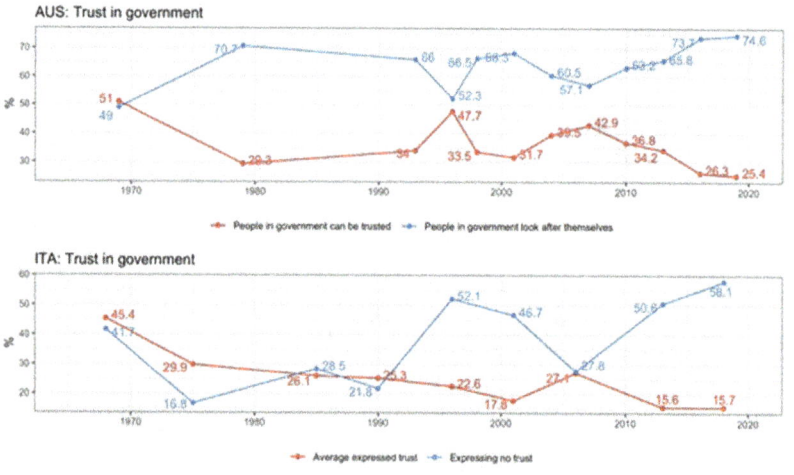

Fig. 9.3 Trust in Government in Italy and Australia

[46] Alessio Cornia, "TV-Centrism and Politicisation in Italy: Obstacles to New Media Development and Pluralism," *Media, Culture & Society* 38, no. 2 (March 1, 2016): 175–95, https://doi.org/10.1177/0163443715594035.

[47] Emanuela Poli, *Forza Italia: strutture, leadership e radicamento territoriale* (Bologna: Il mulino, 2001), 62.

What TV was for Berlusconi, a communicative as much as an identitarian tool, the Internet was for another charismatic political leader: Beppe Grillo. In a similar fashion, the Internet for Grillo represented the tool to reach out to his audience, to the people, bypassing traditional media captured and corrupted by the political, economic, and cultural elites. As in the case of Berlusconi in 1994, Grillo, who initiated his blog in 2005, had virtually no political competition on the Internet for a few years, until Facebook and social media started reaching mass audiences. The symbolism of the new medium (the Internet) against the old (TV) was so strong that not only the web address of Grillo's blog was added to the party's symbol but also during the electoral campaign for the 2013 elections, the M5S candidates were discouraged and then formally forbidden from to participate in talk shows (an extremely popular format in Italy).[48]

The direct, unmediated appeal to the people is of course critical for and a recurrent trait of populist leaders.[49] In particular, populist leaders would avoid as much as possible being interviewed by less than friendly journalists and instead prefer using a medium that offers a strong degree of control on the delivery of the message. A case in point is Berlusconi already mentioned the "take the field" message, which was recorded in his mansion by his staff and first aired in its entirety by a newscast on one of Berlusconi's TV channels.[50] Similarly, Grillo would avoid any formal interview setting until 2014, relying instead on his blog and YouTube channel (created in 2006) to distribute the message of his Movement,[51] a message amplified by the mainstream media reporting on his content often because of his aggressive and outrageous tones.

---

[48] Francesco Bailo, *Online Communities and Crowds in the Rise of the Five Star Movement* (Cham: Palgrave Macmillan, 2020), 27, https://doi.org/10.1007/978-3-030-455 08-8.

[49] Sven Engesser, Nayla Fawzi, and Anders Olof Larsson, "Populist Online Communication: Introduction to the Special Issue," *Information, Communication & Society* 20, no. 9 (September 2, 2017): 1279–92, https://doi.org/10.1080/1369118X.2017.1328525.

[50] Poli, *Forza Italia*, 62.

[51] Between 2009 and 2013 beppegrillo.it was likely the third most viewed non-sport news website in Italy, after the website of the two major newspaper—La Repubblica and Corriere della Sera. See Bailo, *Online Communities and Crowds in the Rise of the Five Star Movement*, 23.

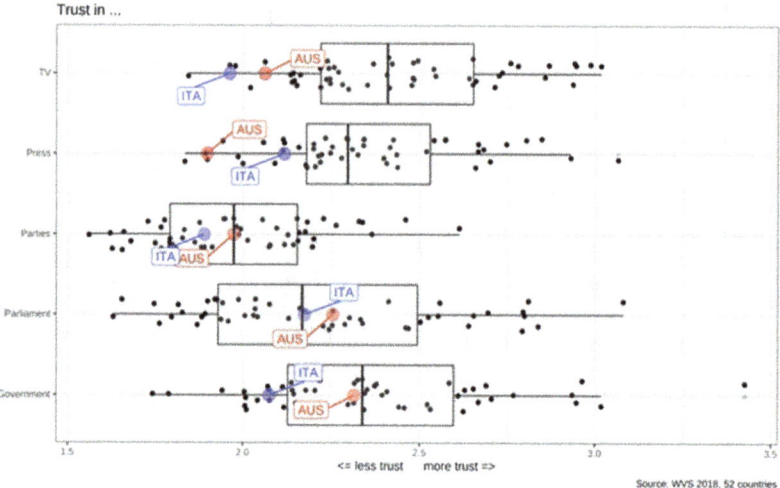

Fig. 9.4   Degree of trust in 52 countries

Conclusion

In this chapter, we have noted several strong similarities between the state of populism in Australia and Italy. First, we note that after emerging in the 1990s populist leaders and populist parties have been a constant presence within the two-party systems. Although further research is necessary to better understand the association between low political trust and the constant presence of populist actors in the political debate, we noted that the emergence of populist politics occurred during periods of low political trust. We also noted that both countries experienced structural levels of media concentration. It is possible that this concentration contributed to compressing in both countries the level of trust towards TV and the press (see Fig. 9.4) opening the way for a strong presence of populist leaders in the new media (see Fig. 9.5).

And yet, even while showing a similar profile, the electoral success of populist parties in the two countries is radically different: in Italy, populist parties have been the most successful parties to emerge over the last 30 years, while in Australia the populist vote has tended to split among several populist and quasi-populist parties and never reached any significant electoral mass while no populist leader succeeded in commanding

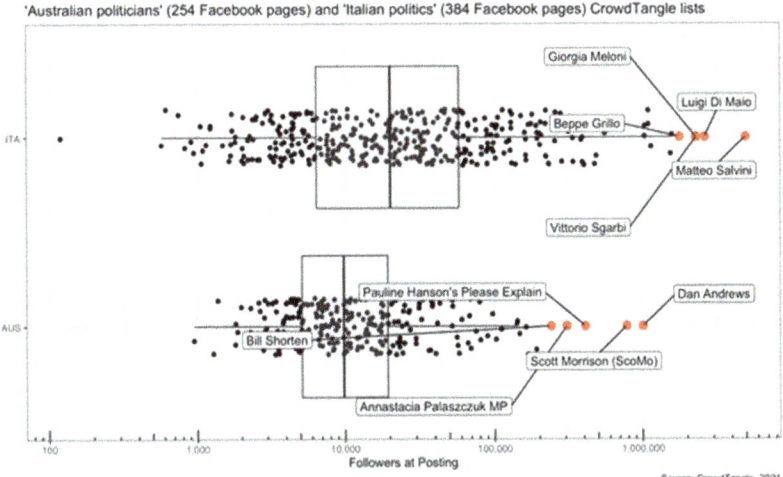

Fig. 9.5 Australian and Italian politician's Facebook pages (*Source* Crowd-Tangle)

large support. This can be partly attributed to a lack of supply of a strong and effective populist leader. As Australia's most prominent right-wing populist politician, Hanson has been unable to consolidate the strong demand for populism in Australia. As noted by Kefford and McDonnell, "the demand among the Australian public for parties with offers like that put forward by One Nation appears greater than One Nation has been able to mobilise".[52] Moreover, it is argued that "the relative lack of radical right populist success in Australia is not so much due to a lack of demand for populist ideas, but a lack of supply of [strong] populist leadership".[53] Thus, the inability of Hanson to consolidate the demand for populist and anti-establishment politics has resulted in the splintering of this vote across a number of heterogeneous minor parties and independents. Indeed, whenever Hanson has been included in the Australian Electoral Study's rating of political leaders, she has consistently been rated

[52] Glenn Kefford and Duncan McDonnell, "Submission to the National Identity and Democracy Inquiry" (Parliament of Australia, 2019), 5.

[53] Kefford and McDonnell, 5.

as the least popular political figure in Australia.[54] What this demonstrates is that Australia has lacked a populist leader with the charisma and political skills of Silvio Berlusconi or Matteo Salvini. Furthermore, research by Kefford and Ratcliff has found that nativism, rather than populism drives support for populist radical right parties.[55] In this context, voters wanting nativist politics have been well served by the mainstream political parties in Australia who have adopted hard-line policies on immigration and asylum seekers. Indeed, while PRR parties throughout Europe effectively exploited the so-called "refugee crisis" of 2015, it was the mainstream centre-right Liberal/National coalition that exploited refugee boat arrivals in the lead up to the 2013 Australian Federal Election.

In this sense, we can note that if Australia is not immune to populism, a number of features might have protected the party system from being dominated by populist parties as in the case of the Italian party system. First, in Australia, no media magnate decided to translate their media power into electoral power. If populist rhetoric is certainly present in the Australian media, these media have maintained formal independence from electoral politics. Second, compulsory voting in Australia may have muted the success of right-wing populist parties as noted by Malkopoulou.[56] Indeed we note that party innovation has been relatively low in Australia. Furthermore, populist parties in Australia have been plagued by poor internal party structures and disorganised organisational practices.[57] Indeed, this has been the case for One Nation in the 1990s and in their contemporary iteration. In contrast, successful Italian populist parties—the League, M5S, Forza Italia—have tended to have an effective party structure that likely helped in capturing political discontent and translating it into votes.

[54] Cameron and McAllister, "Trends in Australian Political Opinion Results from the Australian Election Study 1987–2019.".

[55] Kefford and Ratcliff, "Populists or Nativist Authoritarians?".

[56] Anthoula Malkopoulou, "Compulsory Voting and Right-Wing Populism: Mobilisation, Representation and Socioeconomic Inequalities," *Australian Journal of Political Science* 55, no. 3 (July 2, 2020): 276–92, https://doi.org/10.1080/10361146.2020. 1774507.

[57] McSwiney, Jordan. "Organising Australian Far-Right Parties: Pauline Hanson's One Nation and Fraser Anning's Conservative National Party." *Australian Journal of Political Science* (September 14, 2022): 1–16. https://doi.org/10.1080/10361146.2022.212 1681.

Thus, what the experience of populism in both Italy and Australia demonstrates is that low political trust and satisfaction in democracy create fertile conditions for populist parties, particularly those on the far-right. This should give policymakers, bureaucrats, academics and journalists pause to reflect on why voters are disengaging with political parties and institutions. To echo Cas Mudde, "contemporary populism is an illiberal democratic response to undemocratic liberalism".[58] The lesson for both countries is to strengthen liberal democracy and restore trust in political institutions and parties.

REFERENCES

Abbondanza, Gabriele and Simone Battiston. "Italy and Australia in the Twenty-First Century: Distant Connections or Close Partners?". In *Italy and Australia: Redefining Bilateral Relations for the Twenty-First Century*, eds. Gabriele Abbondanza and Simone Battiston, pp. 1–23. London: Palgrave Macmillan, 2024.

Bailo, Francesco. *Online Communities and Crowds in the Rise of the Five Star Movement*. Cham: Palgrave Macmillan, 2020. https://doi.org/10.1007/978-3-030-45508-8.

Bale, Tim, and Cristóbal Rovira Kaltwasser, eds. *Riding the Populist Wave: Europe's Mainstream Right in Crisis*, 1st ed. Cambridge University Press, 2021. https://doi.org/10.1017/9781009006866.

Bardi, Luciano. "Anti-Party Sentiment and Party System Change in Italy." *European Journal of Political Research* 29, no. 3 (1996): 345–63. https://doi.org/10.1111/j.1475-6765.1996.tb00656.x.

Bickerton, Christopher J., and Carlo Invernizzi Accetti. *Technopopulism: The New Logic of Democratic Politics*, 1st ed. Oxford: Oxford University Press, 2021. https://doi.org/10.1093/oso/9780198807766.001.0001.

Broinowski, Anna. *Please Explain: The Rise, Fall and Rise Again of Pauline Hanson*, 2018.

Cameron, Sarah. "Government Performance and Dissatisfaction with Democracy in Australia." *Australian Journal of Political Science* 55, no. 2 (April 2, 2020): 170–90. https://doi.org/10.1080/10361146.2020.1755221.

Cameron, Sarah, and Ian McAllister. "Trends in Australian Political Opinion Results from the Australian Election Study 1987–2019." ANU College of Arts & Social Sciences, 2019. https://australianelectionstudy.org/wp-content/uploads/Trends-in-Australian-Political-Opinion-1987-2019.pdf.

[58] Mudde, "Populism in Europe," 558.

Cornia, Alessio. "TV-Centrism and Politicisation in Italy: Obstacles to New Media Development and Pluralism." *Media, Culture & Society* 38, no. 2 (March 1, 2016): 175–95. https://doi.org/10.1177/0163443715594035.

Curran, Giorel. "Mainstreaming Populist Discourse: The Race-Conscious Legacy of Neo-Populist Parties in Australia and Italy." *Patterns of Prejudice* 38, no. 1 (March 1, 2004): 37–55. https://doi.org/10.1080/003132203200018 5578.

———. "Mainstreaming Populist Discourse: The Race-Conscious Legacy of Neo-Populist Parties in Australia and Italy." *Patterns of Prejudice* 38, no. 1 (March 1, 2004): 37–55. https://doi.org/10.1080/003132203200018 5578.

Dassonneville, Ruth, and Ian McAllister. "Explaining the Decline of Political Trust in Australia." *Australian Journal of Political Science*, August 6, 2021, 1–18. https://doi.org/10.1080/10361146.2021.1960272.

Deutchman, Iva Ellen, and Anne Ellison. "A Star Is Born: The Roller Coaster Ride of Pauline Hanson in the News." *Media, Culture & Society* 21, no. 1 (January 1999): 33–50. https://doi.org/10.1177/016344399021001002.

Dwyer, Tim. "Is Australia's Media Market One of the World's Most Concentrated?" *The Conversation*, December 12, 2016. https://theconversation.com/is-australias-media-market-one-of-the-worlds-most-concentrated-68437.

Emanuele, Vincenzo. "Dataset of New Parties and Party System Innovation in Western Europe since 1945." Rome: Italian Center for Electoral Studies, 2016. https://doi.org/10.7802/1363.

Engesser, Sven, Nayla Fawzi, and Anders Olof Larsson. "Populist Online Communication: Introduction to the Special Issue." *Information, Communication & Society* 20, no. 9 (September 2, 2017): 1279–92. https://doi.org/10.1080/1369118X.2017.1328525.

Eusepi, Giuseppe. "Broadcasting System in Italy: Evolution and Perspectives." *Public Choice (1986–1998)* 82, no. 3–4 (March 1995): 307–24.

Hawkins, Kirk, and Cristóbal Rovira Kaltwasser. "Introduction: The Ideational Approach." In *The Ideational Approach to Populism: Concept, Theory, and Analysis*, eds. Kirk Hawkins, Ryan. E Carlin, Levente Littvay, and Cristóbal Rovira Kaltwasser, 2–24. Oxon: Routledge, 2019.

Hetherington, Marc J., and Thomas J. Rudolph. "Priming, Performance, and the Dynamics of Political Trust." *The Journal of Politics* 70, no. 2 (April 2008): 498–512. https://doi.org/10.1017/S0022381608080468.

Hobbs, Mitchell, and David McKnight. "'Kick This Mob out': The Murdoch Media and the Australian Labor Government (2007 to 2013)." *Global Media Journal Australia* 8, no. 2 (2014): 1–3.

Hooghe, Marc, and Ruth Dassonneville. "A Spiral of Distrust: A Panel Study on the Relation between Political Distrust and Protest Voting in Belgium."

Government and Opposition 53, no. 1 (January 2018): 104–30. https://doi.org/10.1017/gov.2016.18.

Hunger, Sophia, and Fred Paxton. "What's in a Buzzword? A Systematic Review of the State of Populism Research in Political Science." *Political Science Research and Methods* (September 20, 2021): 1–17. https://doi.org/10.1017/psrm.2021.44.

Jiang, Liang, and Xiangjun Ma. "Political Distrust and Right-Wing Populist Party Voting in Australia." *Australian Journal of Political Science* 55, no. 4 (October 1, 2020): 362–77. https://doi.org/10.1080/10361146.2020.1799937.

Kefford, Glenn, Benjamin Moffitt, John Collins, and Joshua Marsh. "Populist Attitudes in Australia: Contextualising the Demand-Side." *Australian Journal of Political Science* (October 1, 2022): 1–17. https://doi.org/10.1080/10361146.2022.2122401.

Kefford, Glenn, and Duncan McDonnell. "Submission to the National Identity and Democracy Inquiry." Parliament of Australia, 2019.

Kefford, Glenn, and Shaun Ratcliff. "Populists or Nativist Authoritarians? A Cross-National Analysis of the Radical Right." *Australian Journal of Political Science* 56, no. 3 (July 3, 2021): 261–79. https://doi.org/10.1080/10361146.2021.1956431.

Krämer, Benjamin. "Media Populism: A Conceptual Clarification and Some Theses on Its Effects: Media Populism." *Communication Theory* 24, no. 1 (February 2014): 42–60. https://doi.org/10.1111/comt.12029.

Leach, Michael, Geoffrey Stokes, and Ian Ward, eds., *The Rise and Fall of One Nation*. Brisbane: University of Queensland Press, 2000.

Leslie, Tim. "The Rise and Fall of Kevin Rudd." *ABC News*, November 14, 2013. https://www.abc.net.au/news/2013-11-14/the-rise-and-fall-of-kevin-rudd/5090194.

Malkopoulou, Anthoula. "Compulsory Voting and Right-Wing Populism: Mobilisation, Representation and Socioeconomic Inequalities." *Australian Journal of Political Science* 55, no. 3 (July 2, 2020): 276–92. https://doi.org/10.1080/10361146.2020.1774507.

Manucci, Luca. "Populism and the Media." In *The Oxford Handbook of Populism*, eds. Cristóbal Rovira Kaltwasser, Paul Taggart, Paulina Ochoa Espejo, and Pierre Ostiguy, 1:467–92. Oxford: Oxford University Press, 2017. https://doi.org/10.1093/oxfordhb/9780198803560.013.17.

Mazzoleni, Gianpietro. "Populism and the Media." In *Twentyfirst Century Populism: The Spectre of Western European Democracy*, eds. Daniele Albertazzi and Duncan McDonnell, 49–64. Basingstoke: Palgrave, n.d.

McSwiney, Jordan. "Organising Australian Far-Right Parties: Pauline Hanson's One Nation and Fraser Anning's Conservative National Party." *Australian*

Journal of Political Science, (September 14, 2022): 1–16. https://doi.org/10.1080/10361146.2022.2121681.

Mete, Vittorio. "Four Types of Anti-Politics: Insights from the Italian Case." *Modern Italy* 15, no. 1 (February 1, 2010): 37–61. https://doi.org/10.1080/13532940903477872.

Moffitt, Benjamin. "Populism 2.0: Social Media and the False Allure of 'Unmediated' Representation." In *Populism and the Crisis of Democracy: Politics, Social Movements and Extremism*, eds. G. Fitzi, J. Mackert, and B.S. Turner, 30–46. Oxon: Routledge, 2019.

Mudde, Cas. "Populism in Europe: An Illiberal Democratic Response to Undemocratic Liberalism (The *Government and Opposition* /Leonard Schapiro Lecture 2019)." *Government and Opposition* 56, no. 4 (October 2021): 577–97. https://doi.org/https://doi.org/10.1017/gov.2021.15.

———. *Populist Radical Right Parties in Europe*. Cambridge: Cambridge University Press, 2007. https://doi.org/10.1017/CBO9780511492037.

———. *The Far Right Today*. Cambridge, UK ; Medford, MA: Polity, 2019.

Mudde, Cas, and Cristóbal Rovira Kaltwasser. *Populism: A Very Short Introduction*. Very Short Introductions. New York, NY: Oxford University Press, 2017.

Poli, Emanuela. *Forza Italia: strutture, leadership e radicamento territoriale*. Bologna: Il mulino, 2001.

Quiggin, John. "Time for Rudd to Give a Full-Throated Defence of Keynesian Stimulus." *The Guardian Australia*, August 26, 2013.

Sengul, Kurt. "'It's OK to Be White': The Discursive Construction of Victimhood, 'Anti-White Racism' and Calculated Ambivalence in Australia." *Critical Discourse Studies* (May 4, 2021): 1–17. https://doi.org/10.1080/17405904.2021.1921818.

———. "Never Let a Good Crisis Go to Waste: Pauline Hanson's Exploitation of COVID-19 on Facebook." *Media International Australia* 178, no. 1 (February 2021): 101–5. https://doi.org/10.1177/1329878X20953521.

———. "'Swamped': The Populist Construction of Fear, Crisis and Dangerous Others in Pauline Hanson's Senate Speeches." *Communication Research and Practice* 6, no. 1 (January 2, 2020): 20–37. https://doi.org/10.1080/22041451.2020.1729970.

———. "The Role of Political Interviews in Mainstreaming and Normalizing the Far-Right: A View from Australia." In *Adversarial Political Interviewing*, eds. Ofer Feldman, 357–75. Singapore: Springer Nature Singapore, 2022. https://doi.org/10.1007/978-981-19-0576-6_18.

Strömbäck, Jesper. "Mediatization and Perceptions of the Media's Political Influence." *Journalism Studies* 12, no. 4 (August 2011): 423–39. https://doi.org/10.1080/1461670X.2010.523583.

Waisbord, S. "Populism as Media and Communication Phenomenon." In *Routledge Handbook of Global Populism*, eds. C de la Torre, 221–34. Oxon: Routledge, 2019.

Wear, Rae. "Permanent Populism: The Howard Government 1996–2007." *Australian Journal of Political Science* 43, no. 4 (December 2008): 617–34. https://doi.org/10.1080/10361140802429247.

Wodak, Ruth. *The Politics of Fear: The Shameless Normalization of Far-Right Discourse.* 2nd ed. Thousand Oaks: Sage, 2021.

CHAPTER 10

Italian–Australian Scientific and Research Cooperation

Ilaria Stefania Pagani and Tiziana Torresi

INTRODUCTION

Scientific inquiry is a global endeavour and international by nature. It takes place, however, within the architecture of a world where nation-states remain the principal political actors and consequently, the main shapers of the work of researchers. The relationship between the international scholarly community and the community of states is co-constitutive

I. S. Pagani (✉)
South Australian Health and Medical Research Institute, Adelaide, SA, Australia
e-mail: Ilaria.Pagani@sahmri.com

Faculty of Health and Medical Sciences, Adelaide Medical School, University of Adelaide, Adelaide, SA, Australia

T. Torresi
School of Social Sciences, University of Adelaide, Adelaide, SA, Australia
e-mail: tiziana.torresi@adelaide.edu.au

© The Author(s), under exclusive license to Springer Nature Singapore Pte Ltd. 2023
G. Abbondanza and S. Battiston (eds.), *Italy and Australia*,
https://Doi.org/10.1007/978-981-99-3216-0_10

241

and can be one of mutual support and benefit.[1] But there are also tensions in the relationship that risk undermining the pursuit of the best outcomes for all. The global scientific community possesses its own aims and cultural norms which often tend to embrace cosmopolitan and progressive aims in the pursuit of knowledge for the common good of humanity. Moreover, it is partly because of these very attributes that researchers are so successful in international cooperation. On the other hand, states, while also often invested in international cooperation, mostly aim to advance their own national interests. States are also interconnected by a web of bilateral, multilateral and supranational structures which often extend to the regu-lation of scientific cooperation. But they in their turn have their own priorities and rationales. Further, there has been, in recent decades, signif-icant growth in the number of nongovernmental organisations interested in influencing the policies of governments and international organisations on science and technology issues.[2] Finally, public funding for fundamental research has been on a steady, relative decline since the latter half of the twentieth century. Private financing is, therefore, increasingly needed for the continued viability of scientific research. This has created a boom in academic entrepreneurship and a neoliberal marketplace for scientific knowledge, introducing private actors as more and more powerful players in the definition of research agendas and practices, often along with private and profit-driven interests.

No state, however, not even one with powerful scientific and technical capacities, can simultaneously conduct research in all the most important areas of scholarship effectively. Moreover, the pursuit of knowledge itself intrinsically suffers from any strictures imposed on intellectual freedom, whether in the name of national or corporate interests. Thus, the chal-lenges facing humanity—climate change as one of the most urgent—need states to effectively co-operate in all areas, including scholarship and

---

[1] While states shape research activities and cooperation though policy, the scientific community also has an influence on areas of state activity, such as foreign policy, and even impact national identity, see, for example, Fedoroff, Nina V. "Science diplo-macy in the twenty-first century." *Cell* 136.1 (2009): 9–11; Hamblin, Jacob Darwin. "Visions of international scientific cooperation: The case of oceanic science, 1920–1955." *Minerva* 38.4 (2000): 393–423; Strasser, Bruno J. "The coproduction of neutral science and neutral state in Cold War Europe: Switzerland and international scientific cooperation, 1951–69." *Osiris* 24.1 (2009): 165–187.

[2] Suttmeier, Richard P. "State, self-organisation, and identity in the building of Sino-US cooperation in science and technology." *Asian Perspective* 32.1 (2008): 5–31.

research, to find effective solutions for the benefit of all. The recent COVID-19 pandemic has shown us powerfully how both the pursuit of knowledge and the sharing of its benefits are at their best when global in scope. International scientific and scholarly cooperation is now more important than ever and reflections on how best to achieve it ought to be part of scholars' study of intentional politics.

Thus, within this complex framework of international research governance, this chapter explores Italian–Australian scientific cooperation with the aim of identifying its strengths and challenges. Italy and Australia are two countries with significant research capabilities and output, as well as scientific complementarity, yet research on their scientific cooperation is scant, a considerable gap in the literature that this chapter seeks to address. We begin, in Section I, by discussing scientific cooperation and its governance highlighting strengths and pitfalls. In Section II, we detail the specific bilateral framework which governs Italian–Australian research cooperation. Section III discusses the history and role of scholars' own role in the definition of the relationship by introducing ARIA, the Australian Association of Italian Researchers as a case study. We conclude our discussion in the final section with some recommendations noting that greater collaboration between institutions at the national and supranational level can effectively support research collaborations as long as the academic freedom, intellectual leadership and best values of the international scholarly community are recognised, respected and reinforced.

INTERNATIONAL SCIENTIFIC COOPERATION AND GOVERNANCE

International scientific cooperation has grown dramatically over the past three decades. Collaborations between researchers have been widely recognised as an increasingly common phenomenon, as evidenced by the significant growth in the number of co-authorships, agreements around cooperation, multilateral schemes as well as multinational mega-science programs.[3] The case is often made that science and research are becoming "de-nationalised" as research collaborations cross borders with

---

[3] Zitt, Michel, Elise Bassecoulard, and Yoshiko Okubo. "Shadows of the past in international cooperation: Collaboration profiles of the top five producers of science." *Scientometrics* 47.3 (2000): 627–657.

increasing frequency and ease.[4] From the perspective of liberal democratic theory, whose insights have been applied to international relations within the framework of normative international theory, increased international cooperation is, generally, to be welcomed. Global problems with strong dependence on scientific and technological factors have emerged in recent decades even more clearly, climate change and global pandemics as the most pertinent examples. These problems cannot be solved by any state acting individually nor can the advances in scientific knowledge needed to tackle them be achieved by single national scientific communities. Evidence shows that, through collaboration, partners in research projects can effectively share knowledge, skills, techniques and increase productivity.[5] Moreover, international collaborations are believed to generate even higher positive social impacts than domestic collaborations.[6] What factors, then, explain this growth in global research cooperation and what lessons can be learnt by observing current practices for best practices in scientific collaboration governance? Scholars have identified significant determinants of successful international scientific cooperation, which need not be considered mutually exclusive nor necessarily in competition, though we will note some tensions and potential issues in what follows.

The first factor to consider is the governments' own investment in scientific research. Many governments have increased absolute expenditures in this area in the pursuit of innovation, thus contributing to the growth and international diffusion of technical and scientific knowledge and capabilities. At the same time, the relative decline of public funding, particularly for primary research[7] combined with the increased numbers and global expansion of multinational corporations, especially high-technology companies, engaged in this field has been a concomitant powerful force for the global diffusion of research and knowledge.

[4] Suttmeier, Richard P. "State, self-organisation, and identity in the building of Sino-US cooperation in science and technology." *Asian Perspective* 32.1 (2008): 5–31.

[5] Wang, Lili, Xianwen Wang, and Niels J. Philipsen. "Network structure of scientific collaborations between China and the EU member states." *Scientometrics* 113.2 (2017): 765–781.

[6] Zitt, Michel, Elise Bassecoulard, and Yoshiko Okubo. "Shadows of the past in international cooperation: Collaboration profiles of the top five producers of science." *Scientometrics* 47.3 (2000): 627–657.

[7] Birch, Kean, Margaret Chiappetta, and Anna Artyushina. "The problem of innovation in technoscientific capitalism: Data rentiership and the policy implications of turning personal digital data into a private asset." *Policy Studies* 41.5 (2020): 468–487.

In short, we have witnessed significant public and private policy decisions and investment to enhance scientific and technological capabilities through increases in support for research that include the active encouragement of international scientific cooperation.[8] While obviously very positive in general, unfortunately both public and private investment in research has followed specific priorities and sought to shape research agendas to specific ends, with results that are not always most conducive to either best scholarship practices, public good outcomes or fairness to the actors involved in scientific research directly, as we argue later in this chapter.

A second factor that explains the growth of international scientific cooperation is known as the "specialisation" thesis.[9] This thesis focuses on the differentiation of scientific disciplines, which has increased in recent decades through the professionalisation of research.[10] Differentiation has resulted in the need to bring together complementary, specialised knowledge for scientific advancement, as we see, for example, in the mobilisation of different specialisations in support of "megascience projects". We identify here one area of concern where government policy can actually work to interfere and impede scholarly progress. This refers to the relationship between the so-called hard sciences, on one hand, and the social sciences and humanities on the other. Interdisciplinary collaboration between these fields is key to both advancing knowledge and to the successful application of knowledge to addressing global challenges.[11] But government policies that aim at fostering primarily STEM subjects—science, technology, engineering and mathematics—in preference to other disciplines, by dedicating funding and shaping education policy, can interfere with the successful and harmonious development of

---

[8] Suttmeier, Richard P. "State, self-organisation, and identity in the building of Sino-US cooperation in science and technology." *Asian Perspective* 32.1 (2008): 5–31.

[9] Suttmeier, Richard P. "State, self-organisation, and identity in the building of Sino-US cooperation in science and technology." *Asian Perspective* 32.1 (2008): 5–31.

[10] See, for example, Krishnan, Armin. "What are academic disciplines? Some observations on the disciplinarity vs. interdisciplinarity debate." (2009).

[11] See, for example, Miller, Thaddeus R., et al. "Epistemological pluralism: Reorganizing interdisciplinary research." *Ecology and Society* 13.2 (2008).

expertise in all fields by, for example, shaping student choices.[12] So while specialisation fosters collaborations, government interventions that aim at encouraging some forms of research at the expense of others distort scholarly activities in ways that may prevent optimal expertise development for interdisciplinary cooperation.

Third, some explanations for the growth of international scientific collaborations have emphasised various forms of affinity between co-operating countries. These may be based on history, such as colonial relationships, cultural, linguistic or geographical proximity, as well as economic complementarities. In fact, Breschi and Lissoni argue that connections in the social network (what they call *social* proximity) are of more importance than closeness in geography (known as spatial proximity).[13] This is confirmed by Autant-bernard et al. who argue that "social distance seems to matter more than geographical distance in discouraging cooperation".[14] The growth of information and telecommunications technologies to facilitate interactions also falls within this category, as a facilitator of communication and cooperation despite geographical distance.[15] Social proximity is arguably one of the key factors in explaining the successful cooperation between Italy and Australia. Another extra-scientific determinant, quite important in the Italian-Australia relationship is the role of diasporas in connecting countries.[16] The role of diasporas in facilitating transnational cooperation is amply

---

[12] For a critical take on Australia's STEM policies see, for example, Alan Sears and Penney Clark "Stop telling students to study STEM instead of humanities for the post-coronavirus world" The Conversation, September 29, 2020; see also, for a discussion of a more integrated approach, Madden, Margaret E., et al. "Rethinking STEM education: An interdisciplinary STEAM curriculum." *Procedia Computer Science* 20 (2013): 541–546.

[13] Breschi, Stefano, and Francesco Lissoni. *Mobility and social networks: Localised knowledge spillovers revisited*. Università commerciale Luigi Bocconi, 2003.

[14] Autant-Bernard, Corinne, et al. "Social distance versus spatial distance in R&D cooperation: Empirical evidence from European collaboration choices in micro and nanotechnologies." *Papers in regional Science* 86.3 (2007): 495–519.

[15] Suttmeier, Richard P. "State, self-organisation, and identity in the building of Sino-US cooperation in science and technology." *Asian Perspective* 32.1 (2008): 5–31.

[16] Gabriele Abbondanza and Simone Battiston, "Italy and Australia in the twenty-first century: Distant connections or close partners?", in *Italy and Australia: redefining bilateral relations for the twenty-first century*, eds. Gabriele Abbondanza and Simone Battiston (London: Palgrave Macmillan, 2024), p. 1.

evidenced in numerous fields, including business, and it has a significant role in fostering international scientific cooperation.[17] One of the most interesting explanations for the growth of international collaboration is the role of researchers themselves and points to networks of scientists which are truly global. While a real force behind scientific cooperation, as we will see also in the discussion of the Italy–Australia relationship later in the chapter, the activity of this international scientific community reveals some of the tensions inherent within current frameworks of scientific governance. Paradoxically, the very characteristics of scientists and researchers that make them so capable of fostering international cooperation, also mean that these key actors find themselves at odds with ideas and priorities of "national" research policies that often shape governance frameworks.[18] Researchers are committed to the pursuit of knowledge for knowledge's sake. They communicate with ease because of shared knowledge and values, thus creating an international community with common interests and experiences. They work within a strong tradition of internationalism and are committed to the meritocratic nature of the scientific enterprise that recognises talent regardless of other identities, for example, national ones, as well as possessing what we may call social conscience, a desire to find solutions for outstanding problems for the benefit of all.[19] These characteristics, key to facilitating international cooperation, sometimes mean scientists fit awkwardly with states' own understandings of the direction scholarly research and science and technology-related policy should take to fit in with national priorities and interests.[20] We saw an example of these tensions in the recent

[17] The literature on diasporas is very extensive, but see, for example, Tejada Guerrero, Gabriela. "Mobility, Knowledge and Cooperation: Scientific Diasporas as Agents of Change." *Migration and Development* 10 (2012): 59–92; Burns, William J. "The potential of science diasporas." *Science & Diplomacy* 2.4 (2013); Séguin, Béatrice, et al. "Scientific diasporas as an option for brain drain: re-circulating knowledge for development." *International Journal of Biotechnology* 8.1–2 (2006): 78–90.

[18] Wagner, Caroline S., and Loet Leydesdorff. "Network structure, self-organisation, and the growth of international collaboration in science." *Research policy* 34.10 (2005): 1608–1618.

[19] Skolnikoff, Eugene B. "The political role of scientific cooperation." *Technology in Society* 23.3 (2001): 461–471.

[20] In one example of direct conflict, this tension came clearly to the fore in Australia recently when the Morrison government used their veto powers to prevent a number of research projects that had been selected for funding by the Australian Research

COVID-19 pandemic where the scientists involved in the creation of the vaccine strongly advocated for its fair distribution globally, rather than nationally.[21]

This is not to say that there are no issues in the academic community that contradict this vision of scientists as idealistically committed to progressive values and the common good. Issues around representations and inequality in academia are well known and similar to trends true of communities at large. Discrimination and under-representation concern most minority groups in academia, and is evident along gender, sexuality, race, class, caste and ethnic and linguistic lines.[22] Similarly, in the production of knowledge itself, certain groups are privileged while some groups' knowledge remains excluded from academic discourse.

These patterns are repeated at the level of international cooperation. Scientists, in fact, still identify with and work within nations and domestic institutions, even though they see themselves as integrally part of an international community.[23] Thus, given the dominance of actors in the Global North in international cooperation large portions of the Global South remain excluded from global networks.[24] These issues are exacerbated by the contemporary prevalence of what has been termed "technoscientific

Council on the basis of their not serving the national interest, a decision that was criticized by many and remains very controversial (see, Daniel Hurst "Federal government's Christmas Eve veto of research projects labelled 'McCarthyism'". *The Guardian*, 24/12/ 2021 https://www.theguardian.com/australia-news/2021/dec/24/federal-governments-christmas-eve-veto-of-research-projects-labelled-mccarthyism accessed on June 6th, 2022).

[21] Sarah Boseley "Leading scientists urge UK to share Covid vaccines with poorer nations" *The Guardian*, 28 Apr 2021, https://www.theguardian.com/world/2021/apr/ 28/leading-scientists-urge-uk-to-share-covid-vaccines-with-poorer-nations (accessed June 6, 2022).

[22] See, for example, Casad, Bettina J., et al. "Gender inequality in academia: Problems and solutions for women faculty in STEM." *Journal of neuroscience research* 99.1 (2021): 13-23; Bunda, Tracey, Lew Zipin, and Marie Brennan. "Negotiating university 'equity' from Indigenous standpoints: a shaky bridge." *International Journal of Inclusive Education* 16.9 (2012): 941–957; Hyland, Ken. "Academic publishing and the myth of linguistic injustice." *Journal of Second Language Writing* 31 (2016): 58–69.

[23] Skolnikoff, Eugene B. "The political role of scientific cooperation." *Technology in Society* 23.3 (2001): 461–471.

[24] Kreimer, Pablo, and Jean-Baptiste Meyer. "Equality in the Networks? Some are more equal than others: International Scientific Cooperation: An approach from Latin America." *Universities as Centres of Research and Knowledge Creation: An Endangered Species?*. Brill Sense, 2008. 121–133.

capitalism", the dominance of private financing of research. This dominance creates the consequent need, on the part of researchers, to generate returns for investors, over and above other considerations, for example, societal benefits for all.[25] A fair governance framework for international cooperation ought to address these issues.

BILATERAL COOPERATION BETWEEN ITALY AND AUSTRALIA

Italy and Australia have a long history of bilateral relations, driven by shared values and common strategic interests.[26] The two countries established their first diplomatic relations in 1959 and are highly developed and complementary G20 economies, with robust international engagement.[27] Italy has the world's eighth-largest Gross Domestic Product (GDP) valued at US$2.1 trillion in 2022. Despite an unemployment rate of 8% and a government debt-to-GDP ratio of 150.2% (2022), Italy has important economic strengths.[28] Before World War II, Italy's economy depended primarily on the agricultural sector, but it has now transformed into one of the most advanced economies with a highly developed manufacturing sector. Italy is the second-largest exporter in the European Union, after Germany. With a total export of US$481 billion in 2020, Italy ranked seventh worldwide.[29] Australia ranked thirteen worldwide with a GDP valued at US$1.75 trillion in 2022, an unemployment rate of 3.8% and a debt-to-GDP of 24.8%.[30] Australia's goods and services trade with Italy was valued at $7.9 billion, with the balance strongly in

[25] Birch, Kean, Margaret Chiappetta, and Anna Artyushina. "The problem of innovation in technoscientific capitalism: Data rentiership and the policy implications of turning personal digital data into a private asset." *Policy Studies* 41.5 (2020): 468–487.

[26] https://www.dfat.gov.au/geo/italy/italy-country-brief, Last accessed, March 19, 2023.

[27] https://ambcanberra.esteri.it/ambasciata_canberra/en/i_rapporti_bilaterali/ Last accessed, March 19, 2023.

[28] https://tradingeconomics.com/italy/government-debt-to-gdp Last accessed, March 19, 2023.

[29] https://tradingeconomics.com/italy/exports; https://oec.world/en/profile/bilateral-country/ita/partner/aus Last accessed, March 19, 2023.

[30] https://tradingeconomics.com/australia/government-debt-to-gdp Last accessed, March 19, 2023.

Italy's favour.[31] Australia and Italy have the basis to be good partners for collaborations, because they engage on equal terms, especially in terms of GDP per capita, indicating that both countries are at a similar stage of economic development, avoiding therefore, some of the pitfalls and inequities that may derive from collaborations between countries with different economic and political capacities.

Italy is an important partner for Australia especially in the area of scientific and technological cooperation, highlighting the importance of social rather than simply geographical proximity as predicted by studies of the determinants of successful collaboration internationally. The importance of Italy as a partner for collaborations with Australia lies also in the opportunity it provides for Australia to join the European Union's (EU) Research Framework Program,[32] with its very significant funding and cooperation opportunities.[33] Interestingly, the first, treaty-level, science and technology agreement signed by the EU with an industrialised country was with Australia in 1994.[34] Australia has more research collaborations with the EU than with any other single country in the world, with an average of 13.000 co-publications per year during the period 2011–2015.[35] Because of this partnership, Australian researchers have access to Horizon Europe, the largest EU research and innovation programme with

[31] https://www.dfat.gov.au/geo/italy/italy-country-brief. In 2020, Italy exported goods for a total value of US$4.28 billion to Australia. The main products exported included packaged medicaments ($188M), blood, antisera, vaccines, toxins, and cultures ($118M), and washing and bottling machines ($107M). In 2020, Australia exported $419M to Italy. The main products exported from Australia to Italy were Coal Briquettes ($72.8M), Wool ($60.2M), and Hot-Rolled Iron ($31.8M). During the last 25 years the exports of Italy to Australia have increased at an annualized rate of 4.07%, from $1.58B in 1995 to $4.28B in 2020, while the exports of Australia to Italy have decreased at an annualized rate of 3.67%, from $1.07B in 1995 to $419M in 2020. Data from BACI HS6 REV. 1992 (1995–2020).

[32] https://ec.europa.eu/info/research-and-innovation/strategy/strategy-2020-2024/europe-world/international-cooperation/australia_en. Last accessed, March 19, 2023.

[33] https://ec.europa.eu/info/research-and-innovation/strategy/strategy-2020-2024/europe-world/international-cooperation/australia_en. Last accessed, March 19, 2023.

[34] https://ec.europa.eu/info/research-and-innovation/strategy/strategy-2020-2024/europe-world/international-cooperation/australia_en. Last accessed, March 19, 2023.

[35] https://ec.europa.eu/info/research-and-innovation/strategy/strategy-2020-2024/europe-world/international-cooperation/australia_en It is worth noting that this figure refers to EU-28 (UK included). Last accessed, March 19, 2023.

more than €90 billions of funding available over 7 years (2021–2027).[36] An access opportunity whose importance cannot be underestimated if one bears in mind the bilateral relation between Italy and Australia. On the Australian side of this equation, the Global Innovation Strategy (GIS) fosters Australia's national industry, innovation and science cooperation.[37] All EU countries are eligible to apply, albeit with an Australian partner, for the GIS Global Innovation Linkages programme and the Global Connection Fund providing more opportunities for cooperation. An additional two implementing arrangements have been signed between the National Health and Medical Research Council (NHMRC) in 2018, and the Australian Research Council (ARC) in 2019 for research collaborations with the EU.[38]

Bilaterally, the research relations between Italy and Australia are regulated by the Cultural Cooperation Agreement signed in 1975, which encourages the development of collaborations in the scientific, social, artistic and cultural fields, and by the Agreement for the Antarctic signed in 1992.[39] This latter encouraged scientific research on projects of mutual interest and provided opportunities for the exchange of ideas and personnel.[40] Subsequently, the treaty-level Agreement on Scientific, Technological and Innovation Cooperation, entered into force in 2021. The objective of this agreement was to promote and establish a high-level framework for the technological and scientific cooperation between the two countries, underscoring how both countries are committed to this partnership.[41]

---

[36] https://euraxess.ec.europa.eu/worldwide/australia-nz/horizon-europe-australia-new-zealand. Last accessed, March 19, 2023.

[37] https://www.industry.gov.au/data-and-publications/global-innovation-strategy. Last accessed, March 19, 2023.

[38] https://ec.europa.eu/info/research-and-innovation/strategy/strategy-2020-2024/europe-world/international-cooperation/australia_en. Last accessed, March 19, 2023.

[39] https://ambcanberra.esteri.it/ambasciata_canberra/en/i_rapporti_bilaterali/cooperazione%20scientifica/politica_ricerca_e_sviluppo/bilateral-scientific-cooperation.html. Last accessed, March 19, 2023.

[40] https://ambcanberra.esteri.it/ambasciata_canberra/resource/doc/2016/11/antarctic_ita_aus_science.pdf. Last accessed, March 19, 2023.

[41] https://internationaleducation.gov.au/internationalnetwork/europe/PolicyUpdatesEurope/Pages/Article-Australia-Italy-MOU-2013.aspx. Last accessed, March 19, 2023.

Australia and Italy have a strong record of research and scholarly cooperation. In science and technology, as well as in general economic terms as noted above, Italy and Australia are comparable actors. According to the Scopus's International Science Ranking, Italy and Australia rank 7th and 10th respectively worldwide, in the number and frequency of citations of publications.[42] More precisely, in select fields, Italy ranked 12th in biological and agricultural science and Australia 9th; in Arts and Humanities, Italy was 8th and Australia 9th; and in biochemistry, genetics and molecular biology, Italy ranked 7th and Australia 11th.[43]

The importance of the relationship is evidenced, amongst other indicators, by the significant number of high-impact, joint research publications. Moreover, there are solid indications that the relationship is increasing in significance. The number of joint publications has in fact more than tripled over the past decade, reaching almost 8.000 peer-reviewed publications.[44] The top research fields for co-authored articles are, in order, astronomy and astrophysics; particles and fields physics; oncology; genetics and clinical neurology, indicating a particularly strong pattern of cooperation in the hard and medical sciences, while cooperation in the social sciences and humanities field, also significant, lags behind, a point to which we will return later in this chapter. Over the period 2011–2015, Italy was Australia's eighth-highest publication partner, while Australia was Italy's eleventh-highest collaborator.[45]

In the past 25 years, 215 international agreements have been signed between Italian and Australian universities and research institutes, of which 25 are still active.[47] They provide opportunities for staff and

---

[42] https://www.scimagojr.com/countryrank.php. Last accessed, March 19, 2023.

[43] Gabriele Abbondanza, "Italy and Australia: Time for a strategic partnership", *IAI Commentaries* 20(87) (2020): 1–5; Gabriele Abbondanza, "Time for a strategic partnership: The scope for international cooperation between Italy and Australia", in *Italy and Australia: redefining bilateral relations for the twenty-first century*, eds. Gabriele Abbondanza and Simone Battiston (London: Palgrave Macmillan, 2024), pp. 1–23.

[44] https://www.science.org.au/news-and-events/events/international-events/italy-aus tralia-science-and-innovation-forum. Last accessed, March 19, 2023.

[45] https://www.science.org.au/news-and-events/events/international-events/italy-aus tralia-science-and-innovation-forum; https://accordi-internazionali.cineca.it; https://ambcanberra.esteri.it/ambasciata_canberra/en/i_rapporti_bilaterali/cooperazione%20scie ntifica/politica_ricerca_e_sviluppo/bilateral-scientific-cooperation.html; https://www.sci ence.org.au/news-and-events/events/international-events/italy-australia-science-and-inn ovation-forum. Last accessed, March 19, 2023.

student exchange and foster research collaboration.[46] An important field of cooperation regards aerospace. On 21 October 2021, the Australian Space Agency signed a Memorandum of Understanding in Canberra with the Italian Space Agency (ASI)—an Italian government agency established in 1988 to fund, regulate and coordinate space exploration activities— to explore cooperative projects, including space science and technology, small satellites, earth observations, space weather and education, health, and remote asset management.[47] ASA is a leading actor in space research and security and—together with the German and New Zealand Space Agencies, aimed to triple the size of the space sector in Australia to AUD$ 12 billion, as well as creating 20,000 new jobs by 2030.[48] Moreover, Australia needs a skilled workforce to grow the local space industry and take advantage of global opportunities, aims that can perhaps be facilitated by collaborating with Italian industries and research centres. On this point, at the time of writing, discussions for an Italian expansion in the Australian aerospace market are unfolding between the "Officine Meccaniche Segni (OMS)" and the Australian CUAVA (ARC Centre for CubeSats, UAVs and their applications).

In this context, there are additionally important cooperation agreements in strategic areas such as hypersonics, a sector in which Italy and Australia are both global leaders. The University of Queensland Centre for Hypersonics and the Italian Centre for Aerospace Research (CIRA) signed a Memorandum of Understanding in 2009. This aims to provide the legal and organisational framework for the development of mutually beneficial cooperation in hypersonics and propulsion relating to the future development of vehicles for access to and return from, space, as

---

[46] There are also several institutions that operate within a broader mandate to foster academic relations between the two countries. For example, ACIS (Australasian Centre for Italian Studies, headquartered at the University of Melbourne), the Cassamarca Foundation, which funds Italian Studies departments across Australia. Also, there are two Italian Cultural Institutes (funded by the Italian Ministry of Foreign Affairs), ten Dante Alighieri Societies in Australia (private entities), and several Com.It.Es, Commitees for Italians abroad. They all promote Italian culture in Australia in a more general way, yet they also provide funds for research projects and organise scientific seminars.

[47] https://www.industry.gov.au/news-media/australian-space-agency-signs-with-italian-space-agency. Last accessed, March 19, 2023.

[48] https://forum.andythomas.foundation/wp-content/uploads/HS030-13ASF-Program-Book_web_210222.pdf. Last accessed, March 19, 2023.

well as hypersonic civil transport.[49] In 2008, another Memorandum of Understanding was signed between the Australian Synchrotron and the "Sincrotrone ELETTRA" in Trieste, with the aim of combining expertise to achieve common scientific goals, share facilities and mutual support in general.[50] Additionally, both Italy and Australia are founding members, out of only 10 full members, of the Square Kilometre Array global science project. This is an international effort to build the world's largest radio astronomy observatory to be located in Australia and in South Africa.[51] The importance of this cooperative project cannot be underestimated as this powerful instrument, is widely believed, will produce data that will profoundly change our understanding of the Universe. This project is a powerful reminder of how scientific research is inherently global and cooperative, especially when at its most powerful. Italy and Australia are both key players in this endeavour. Italy signed the first Memorandum of Understanding in Manchester, UK, to establish the steering committee to oversee the project, this was followed by other agreements signed in 2006, 2010 and 2011. Italy also holds two seats on the board of directors. The Australian Commonwealth Scientific and Industrial Research Organisation (CSIRO) and the Italian National Institute for Astrophysics signed a cooperative agreement in February 2012 related to this particular project.[52]

Australia and Italy have also a strong collaboration in the area of physics, especially in the sub-field of studies of dark matter and gravitational waves. In 2014, the Australian and Victorian governments awarded funding of almost AU$5 million for the construction of the Stawell Underground Physics Laboratory in Victoria, the first of its kind in the Southern Hemisphere.[53] This project is a collaboration between six international partners, including the Italian National Institute of Nuclear Physics. It is expected that the laboratory in Victoria will work closely with the Gran Sasso laboratory in Italy, the largest underground

[49] https://ambcanberra.esteri.it/ambasciata_canberra/resource/doc/2016/11/cira-uq_collaboration.pdf. Last accessed, March 19, 2023.

[50] https://ambcanberra.esteri.it/ambasciata_canberra/resource/doc/2016/11/mou_elettra_australian_synchrotron_may_2008.pdf. Last accessed, March 19, 2023.

[51] https://italy.skatelescope.org/welcome/. Last accessed, March 19, 2023.

[52] https://www.atnf.csiro.au/the_atnf/annual_reports/2012/2012_AnnualReport.pdf. Last accessed, March 19, 2023.

[53] https://www.supl.org.au. Last accessed, March 19, 2023.

research laboratory in the world.[54] Another notable collaboration in this area is the LIGO–VIRGO international collaboration on gravitational waves detection.[55] There is a longstanding collaboration between the University of Western Australia, the University of Adelaide and the European Gravitational Observatory, which is hosted by Italy and where the VIRGO gravitational wave detector is located, near Pisa.[56] This large-scale research infrastructure was visited on the 26th of September 2016 by Australia's Chief Scientist, Dr. Alan Finkel. In 2014, a Memorandum of Understanding for cooperation in the mathematical sciences was signed between the Istituto Nazionale di Alta Matematica (National Institute for High Mathematics) and the Mathematical Sciences Institute, to promote the development of the field of mathematics amongst members of the two institutes.[57] Moreover, additional and significant cooperation exists in other fields too. Amongst the many, in ophthalmology, with Dr. Marco Abbondanza and his team (Italy) and Prof. Stephanie Watson and her team at the Save Sight Institute/University of Sydney (Australia) producing numerous joint innovative publications for the treatment of a degenerative corneal pathology called keratoconus. In biomedical engineering, we see Prof. Alberto Avolio, from Macquarie University, collaborating with the University of Perugia. In orthopaedics, the firsthand transplant was carried out by a team comprising also Italian and Australian surgeons, including Prof. Marco Lanzetta Bertani, who was Director of the Microsearch Foundation in Sydney from 1996 to 2006.[58] The full list is, of course, much longer.

Formal agreements have also been signed between the Accademia Nazionale dei Lincei,[59] the Australian Academy of Science and the

---

[54] https://spaceaustralia.com/news/stawell-underground-dark-matter-lab-nears-comple tion. Last accessed, March 19, 2023.

[55] https://ambcanberra.esteri.it/ambasciata_canberra/resource/doc/2016/11/mou_ elettra_australian_synchrotron_may_2008.pdf. Last accessed, March 19, 2023.

[56] https://www.news.uwa.edu.au/archive/2017100410009/gravitational-waves-bin ary-black-hole-merger-observed-ligo-and-virgo/. Last accessed, March 19, 2023.

[57] https://ambcanberra.esteri.it/ambasciata_canberra/resource/doc/2016/11/indam_ msi.pdf. Last accessed, March 19, 2023.

[58] We thank the editors of this volume and the anonymous referees for alerting us to these collaborations.

[59] The Accademia dei Lincei, which was founded in 1603 by Federico Cesi, is the oldest scientific academy in the world; see https://www.lincei.it/en/institution.

Australian Academy of the Humanities.[60] In September 2014, a Memorandum of Understanding was signed between Italy's National Research Council and the CSIRO to develop relationships between scientists from both organisations.[61] The Australian Nuclear Science and Technology Organisation and Italy's National Hadron Therapy Centre, signed in 2013 a Memorandum of Understanding on a cooperative programme to use nuclear science and technology in the areas of hadron therapy and tumour diagnosis. The aim was to develop a mutually beneficial cooperative programme of research, to improve therapies and foster greater innovation.[62]

This review of bilateral projects makes no pretence of comprehensiveness, yet it shows the level and potential for future beneficial cooperation between the two countries. In sum, Italy-Australia scientific cooperation is shaped by a complex web of bilateral agreements and cooperation with industry which have created some important synergies for the advancement of scientific discovery in key areas. However, some of the areas of most intense cooperation are clearly market-led, and while cooperation with industry is a key aspect of scientific and research work, strong government leadership is needed to ensure that development of research capacity happens in all areas of human interest. Cooperation between researchers and public institutions is key in advancing research agendas that are shaped by curiosity and the disinterested pursuit of knowledge for the benefit of all. According to the Australian Academy of Science,[63] the bilateral scientific cooperation between Italy and Australia has been enhanced by the many young and talented Italian scientists who have either temporarily or permanently migrated to Australia to pursue their careers, underlying the fundamental role of scientific diasporas in this context.[64] The role researchers themselves play in creating those links

[60] https://humanities.org.au. Last accessed, March 19, 2023.

[61] https://www.cnr.it/it/memorandum-understanding/documento/50/mou-cnr-csiro-australila.pdf. Last accessed, March 19, 2023.

[62] https://ambcanberra.esteri.it/ambasciata_canberra/resource/doc/2016/11/signed_mou_cnao_ansto_10_october_2013.pdf. Last accessed, March 19, 2023.

[63] https://www.science.org.au/news-and-events/events/international-events/italy-australia-science-and-innovation-forum. Last accessed, March 19, 2023.

[64] However, the recent COVID-19 pandemic, and the closure of the Australian national borders, had a negative impact on mobility, reducing the number of Italian visitors in Australia to 1,800 in 2021, nearly halving the number from the pre-pandemic level.

of cooperation as members of a global, cosmopolitan community ought to be recognised and facilitated by public institutions and agreements if the benefits of the free pursuit of knowledge are to be enjoyed by all. To explore some of these dynamics in the context of the bilateral relationship we are examining, in the next section, we consider the role that Italian researchers in Australia have played in building such cooperation with public authorities by exploring the history and activities of the organisation that has, in Australia, brought together and represented Italian researchers: the Association of Italian Researchers in Australasia.

THE ASSOCIATION OF ITALIAN RESEARCHERS IN AUSTRALASIA

Promoting the activities of Italian scientists and scholars abroad and the exchanges of knowledge and expertise between research institutes in Italy and other countries is one of the main priorities of the Italian Government. For this aim to be pursued effectively, the active bottom-up cooperation and work of researchers themselves is necessary, particularly if the most progressive aims of such cooperation are to be safeguarded. For this purpose, the "First Conference on Italians Abroad" was held on 11–15th December 2000, in Frascati, Rome, with the participation of the highest public authorities: the President of the Italian Republic, His Excellency Carlo Azeglio Ciampi, the then Prime Minister of Italy, His Excellency Giuliano Amato, then Ministry of Foreign Affairs and International Cooperation, the Ministry for University and Research and the General Council of Italians Abroad (CGIE). Subsequently, the Australian delegation, which included Prof. Marcello Costa, Prof. Antonio Cantoni and Prof. Anna Maria Arabia, with the support of the scientific attaché of the Italian Embassy in Australia, Prof. Nicola Sasanelli, created the "Association of Italian Researchers in Australia and New Zealand, ARIA". On 26 March 2001, a committee of 30 scientists from all over Australia had

---

Resident returns also dropped by almost 99% by the end of 2021, compared to 2019 and the number of Working Holiday Maker visas granted up to the 30th of June 2021 fell by 68.1%, to 2619 in 2021 (https://www.dfat.gov.au/sites/default/files/italy-country-fact-sheet.pdf). Australia had one of strictest COVID-19 travel policy worldwide, with the international borders closed for most of 2020 and 2021. This resulted in a reduction of enrolment in 2021 as international student number fell by 17% in 2021 compared to 2020. What the long-term effects of this policy will be on researchers' and students' mobility and for research cooperation more in general remains to be seen.

a first discussion regarding the creation of ARIA in the presence of the Ambassador of Italy in Australia, His Excellency Giovanni Castellaneta and of Dr. Luciano Criscuoli and Dr. Gioacchino Fonti from the Ministry of Education, University and Research.[65]

From the beginning it was clearly stated by the participants that all researchers from every field should be part of ARIA. This is an important example of how researchers self-organising can work to correct policy-makers' overreaching, such as the attempt to foster STEM education and research which, as we have argued, can create artificial imbalances in the academy and therefore undermine necessary interdisciplinary collaborations.

It was believed that the parallel creation of separate associations in each state of Australia would be more feasible and probably more effective. Thus, the first ARIA Association was launched in Canberra in November 2002 by the Hon. Peter McGauran, Minister for Science and the Italian Ambassador H.E. Dino Volpicelli. The role of the Association was to foster research cooperation between Italy and Australia, promoting collaboration between Italian and Australian researchers, research organisations, Australian and Italian government institutions and private companies. A few years later, in 2004, ARIA-South Australia was founded, with Prof. Enzo Lombi as President, followed by Professor Costa in 2006.[66] ARIA-South Australia was, unfortunately, the only such chapter formed in Australia, under the alternating presidency of Prof. Marinella Marmo and Dr. Antonio Dottore, no other ARIA associations were created in any other Australian States and the ACT chapter did not survive.[67]

In 2020, ARIA-South Australia saw the beginning of a new era. Under the leadership of Dr. Ilaria Pagani (President) and Dr. Tiziana Torresi (Vice-President) ARIA expanded to all Australasia, including all of Australia, New Zealand and the Pacific Islands, realising the vision of a united group of Italian researchers down-under. ARIA also launched special projects, including ARIA-women and ARIA-young. The objective of ARIA-women is to connect women across every professional

[65] Prof. Marcello Costa, personal communication to the authors, June 2, 2022. Text of the original communication on file with the authors.

[66] Prof. Marcello Costa, personal communication to the authors, June 2, 2022. Text of the original communication on file with the authors.

[67] A. Prof. Marinella Marmo and Dr. Antonio Dottore personal communication to the authors, June 4, 2022. Text of the original communication on file with the authors.

sector: education, research, industry, academia and government. The aim is to promote women in research by offering tailored workshops, promoting the work of female Italian researchers, networking events aimed at empowering women and promoting a more balanced representation in every field which, as we noted above, is a serious equity issue in academia and research. This initiative shows how researchers autonomously organising can begin to address some concerns around fairness in the field, attempts that can and ought to be supported by equivalent policy initiatives.

Another initiative is ARIA Young to provide mentorship and support to students interested in a career in research. The new board of ARIA, with Dr. Caterina Selva (secretary 2021), Mario Calabro (secretary 2022), Dr. Pina D'Orazio (treasurer 2021–2022) and Clizia Restivo (Special Engagement 2021), is fostering bilateral cooperation on research between Italy and Australia in all the areas of human interest. This is testified by events organised on the occasion of the Italian Research Day in the World, celebrated around the 15th of April for the birthday of Leonardo Da Vinci. In 2022, ARIA organised four events in three Australian States, with the participation of the Italian Human Technopole and the Italian Institute of Technology at two events in Adelaide, South Australia. These events were supported by Italian institutions in Australia, in particular by the Italian Embassy, the Italian Consulates, the Italian Chamber of Commerce and Industry Sydney, and the Italian Institutes of Culture of Sydney and Melbourne, showing, again, how researchers bottom-up self-organisation works at its best when supported by appropriate policy and regulatory frameworks.

Italy and Australia have built a successful and longstanding relationship of cooperation which is for the most part advantageous to all involved. Some issues remain, however. Italian researchers abroad, with their high level of expertise and prestigious positions, represent a wealth of knowledge, skills, collaborative potential and reference of immense value for Italy. This valuable heritage is dispersed around the globe and is difficult to quantify. The reticence of Italian researchers resident abroad to be surveyed and counted, as clearly is the wish of the Italian government, could be attributed to a common distrust of Italian public institutions. This could be due to personal negative experience with regards to funding and recognition, often resulting from the perception of a modus operandi judged to be inefficient and penalising.[68]

The Scientific Technological Laboratory more than twenty years ago ascertained the inadequacy of resources allocated to research, science and technology in Italy, including an insufficient use of the researcher experiences gained by Italians abroad. One of the main problems, still present today, is the lack of "brain gain", which is the attraction of foreign researchers, including the return to Italy of Italians working abroad. Solutions for the return of high-skilled Italian researchers from abroad are therefore recommended. They could range from the right support to the returning researchers for starting their independent line of research in Italy, to assistance to find a position in Italy for young researchers who studied abroad. Other solutions could include fellowship or seed grants to promote an exchange of researchers between Institutions. In this context, ARIA could play a critical role, fostering collaborations between Countries and engendering the kind of collaborative dynamic between researchers and institutions we have suggested is best practice in this context.

Conclusion

The relationship between states and the international community of scholars and researchers is one that, well managed, can result in positive outcomes for all actors concerned as well as the global community at large. Some issues remain however in relation to equity both within the scientific community and in relation to how the advantages that flow from scientific enquiry are shared around the world. In this chapter, we have attempted to explain some of the drivers of increased international cooperation but also to point out some of these issues from the perspective of normative international relations theory. We have suggested, on the basis of an analysis of the Italian–Australian relationship that public institutions, at the national and supranational level, can work to support research collaborations to great positive effect. They may also work to

[68] https://www.esteri.it/mae/resource/pubblicazioni/2015/01/atti%20e%20docu menti%20del%20cgie.pdf?TSPD_101_R0=081e1ab290ab2000b376b3d6fe59fe7b04a5108 359bfe97831a310474f027a0e7f6f10a10f78f33608d8905a1c14300055a204da7f290e2e24 4e467c69a976a39e9c72645c169e8505cf6a6bae6e48086b70076813317a91cef953e86d 2fdac3. Last accessed, March 19, 2023.

correct some of the imbalances we have detailed as long as the academic freedom, intellectual leadership and best values of the international scholarly community are recognised, respected and reinforced. This could be achieved by greater involvement and cooperation between public institutions and the global scientific and scholarly community in a combined bottom-up/top-down approach, as our case study detailing the history and activities of ARIA has attempted to illustrate.

BIBLIOGRAPHY

Abbondanza, Gabriele and Simone Battiston. "Italy and Australia in the twenty-first century: Distant connections or close partners?". In *Italy and Australia: Redefining bilateral relations for the twenty-first century*, edited by Gabriele Abbondanza and Simone Battiston, pp. 1–23. London: Palgrave Macmillan, 2024.

Abbondanza, Gabriele. "Time for a strategic partnership: The scope for international cooperation between Italy and Australia". In *Italy and Australia: redefining bilateral relations for the twenty-first century*, edited by Gabriele Abbondanza and Simone Battiston, p. 155. London: Palgrave Macmillan, 2024.

Abbondanza, Gabriele. "Italy and Australia: Time for a strategic partnership". *IAI Commentaries* 20(87) (2020): 1–5.

Accademia dei Lincei. https://www.lincei.it/en/institution.

Ambasciata d'Italia, Canberra. https://ambcanberra.esteri.it/ambasciata_canberra/en/i_rapporti_bilaterali/.

Ambasciata d'Italia, Canberra. https://ambcanberra.esteri.it/ambasciata_canberra/en/i_rapporti_bilaterali/cooperazione%20scientifica/politica_ricerca_e_sviluppo/bilateral-scientific-cooperation.html.

Ambasciata d'Italia, Canberra . https://ambcanberra.esteri.it/ambasciata_canberra/resource/doc/2016/11/antarctic_ita_aus_science.pdf.

Ambasciata d'Italia, Canberra. https://ambcanberra.esteri.it/ambasciata_canberra/en/i_rapporti_bilaterali/cooperazione%20scientifica/politica_ricerca_e_sviluppo/bilateral-scientific-cooperation.html.

Ambasciata d'Italia, Canberra. https://ambcanberra.esteri.it/ambasciata_canberra/resource/doc/2016/11/cira-uq_collaboration.pdf.

Ambasciata d'Italia, Canberra. https://ambcanberra.esteri.it/ambasciata_canberra/resource/doc/2016/11/mou_elettra_australian_synchrotron_may_2008.pdf.

Ambasciata d'Italia, Canberra. https://ambcanberra.esteri.it/ambasciata_canberra/resource/doc/2016/11/mou_elettra_australian_synchrotron_may_2008.pdf.

Ambasciata d'Italia, Canberra. https://ambcanberra.esteri.it/ambasciata_canb erra/resource/doc/2016/11/indam_msi.pdf.

Ambasciata d'Italia, Canberra. https://ambcanberra.esteri.it/ambasciata_canb erra/resource/doc/2016/11/signed_mou_cnao_ansto_10_october_2013. pdf.

Andy Thomas Space Foundation. https://forum.andythomas.foundation/wp-content/uploads/HS030-13ASF-Program-Book_web_210222.pdf.

Australian Academy of the Humanities. https://humanities.org.au.

Australian Academy of Science. https://www.science.org.au/news-and-events/ events/international-events/italy-australia-science-and-innovation-forum.

Australian Academy of Science. https://www.science.org.au/news-and-events/ events/international-events/italy-australia-science-and-innovation-forum.

Australian Government. https://www.industry.gov.au/data-and-publications/ global-innovation-strategy.

Australian Government. https://internationaleducation.gov.au/international-network/europe/PolicyUpdatesEurope/Pages/Article-Australia-Italy-MOU-2013.aspx.

Autant-Bernard, Corinne et al. "Social distance versus spatial distance in R&D cooperation: Empirical evidence from European collaboration choices in micro and nanotechnologies." *Papers in regional Science* 86, n. 3 (2007): 495–519.

Breschi, Stefano, and Francesco Lissoni. *Mobility and social networks: Localised knowledge spillovers revisited*. Università commerciale Luigi Bocconi, 2003.

Birch, Kean, Margaret Chiappetta, and Anna Artyushina. "The problem of innovation in technoscientific capitalism: data rentiership and the policy implications of turning personal digital data into a private asset." *Policy Studies* 41.5 (2020): 468–487.

Bunda, Tracey, Lew Zipin, and Marie Brennan. "Negotiating university 'equity' from Indigenous standpoints: a shaky bridge." *International Journal of Inclusive Education* 16.9 (2012): 941–957.

Casad, Bettina J., et al. "Gender inequality in academia: Problems and solutions for women faculty in STEM." *Journal of neuroscience research* 99.1 (2021): 13–23.

Centro Nazionale Ricerche, Italia. https://www.cnr.it/it/memorandum-unders tanding/documento/50/mou-cnr-csiro-australila.pdf.

Cineca. https://accordi-internazionali.cineca.it.

Consiglio generale degli italiani all'estero. https://www.esteri.it/mae/resource/ pubblicazioni/2015/01/atti%20e%20documenti%20del%20cgie.pdf?TSPD_ 101_R0=081e1ab290ab2000b376b3d6fe59fe7b04a5108359bfe97831a310 474f027a0e7f6f10a10f78f33608d8905a1c14300055a204da7f290e2e244e4 67c69a976a39e9c72645c169e8505cf6a6bae6e48086b70076813317a91cef9 53e86d2fdac3.

CSIRO Astronomy and Space Science, Annual report 2012. https://www.atnf. csiro.au/the_atnf/annual_reports/2012/2012_AnnualReport.pdf.
Department of Foreign Affairs and Trade, Australian Government. https://www. dfat.gov.au/geo/italy/italy-country-brief.
Department of Foreign Affairs and Trade, Australian Government. https://www. dfat.gov.au/geo/italy/italy-country-brief.
Department of Industry, Science and Resources, Australian Goverment. https:// www.industry.gov.au/news-media/australian-space-agency-signs-with-italian-space-agency.
Euraxess. https://euraxess.ec.europa.eu/worldwide/australia-nz/horizon-eur ope-australia-new-zealand.
European Commission. https://ec.europa.eu/info/research-and-innovation/str ategy/strategy-2020-2024/europe-world/international-cooperation/austra lia_en.
European Commission. https://ec.europa.eu/info/research-and-innovation/str ategy/strategy-2020-2024/europe-world/international-cooperation/austra lia_en.
European Commission. https://ec.europa.eu/info/research-and-innovation/str ategy/strategy-2020-2024/europe-world/international-cooperation/austra lia_en.
European Commission. https://ec.europa.eu/info/research-and-innovation/str ategy/strategy-2020-2024/europe-world/international-cooperation/austra lia_en.
European Commission. https://ec.europa.eu/info/research-and-innovation/str ategy/strategy-2020-2024/europe-world/international-cooperation/austra lia_en.
Fedoroff, Nina V. "Science diplomacy in the 21st century." *Cell* 136.1 (2009): 9–11.
Hamblin, Jacob Darwin. "Visions of international scientific cooperation: the case of oceanic science, 1920–1955." *Minerva* 38.4 (2000): 393–423.
Daniel Hurst. "Federal government's Christmas Eve veto of research projects labelled 'McCarthyism'." *The Guardian*, 24/12/2021. https://www.thegua rdian.com/australia-news/2021/dec/24/federal-governments-christmas-eve-veto-of-research-projects-labelled-mccarthyism accessed on June 6, 2022.
Hyland, Ken. "Academic publishing and the myth of linguistic injustice." *Journal of Second Language Writing* 31 (2016): 58–69.
Kreimer, Pablo, and Jean-Baptiste Meyer. "Equality in the Networks? Some are More Equal than Others: International Scientific Cooperation: An Approach from Latin America." *Universities as Centres of Research and Knowledge Creation: An Endangered Species?*. Brill Sense, 2008. 121–133.
Krishnan, Armin. "What are academic disciplines? Some observations on the disciplinarity vs. interdisciplinarity debate." (2009).

Madden, Margaret E., Marsha Baxter, Heather Beauchamp, Kimberley Bouchard, Derek Habermas, Mark Huff, Brian Ladd, Jill Pearon, and Gordon Plague. "Rethinking STEM education: An interdisciplinary STEAM curriculum." *Procedia Computer Science* 20 (2013): 541–546.

Miller, Thaddeus R., Timothy D. Baird, Caitlin M. Littlefield, Gary Kofinas, F. Stuart Chapin III, and Charles L. Redman. "Epistemological pluralism: reorganizing interdisciplinary research." *Ecology and Society* 13.2 (2008).

Scimago Journal & Country Rank. https://www.scimagojr.com/countryra nk.php.

Sears, Alan and Penney Clark. "Stop telling students to study STEM instead of humanities for the post-coronavirus world." The Conversation, September 29, 2020.

Séguin, Béatrice, Leah State, Peter A. Singer, and Abdallah S. Daar. "Scientific diasporas as an option for brain drain: re-circulating knowledge for development." *International Journal of Biotechnology* 8.1–8.2 (2006): 78–90.

SKA Observatory. https://italy.skatelescope.org/welcome/.

Skolnikoff, Eugene B. "The political role of scientific cooperation." *Technology in Society* 23.3 (2001): 461–471.

Space Australia. https://spaceaustralia.com/news/stawell-underground-dark-matter-lab-nears-completion.

Stawell Underground Physics Laboratory. https://www.supl.org.au.

Strasser, Bruno J. "The coproduction of neutral science and neutral state in Cold War Europe: Switzerland and international scientific cooperation, 1951–69." *Osiris* 24.1 (2009): 165–187.

Suttmeier, Richard P. "State, self-organisation, and identity in the building of Sino-US cooperation in science and technology." *Asian Perspective* 32.1 (2008): 5–31.

Tejada Guerrero, Gabriela. "Mobility, knowledge and cooperation: Scientific diasporas as agents of change." *Migration and Development* 10 (2012): 59–92; Burns, William J. "The potential of science diasporas." *Science & Diplomacy* 2.4 (2013).

Trading Economics, Italian Government. https://tradingeconomics.com/italy/government-debt-to-gdp.

Trading Economics, Italian Government. https://tradingeconomics.com/italy/exports; https://oec.world/en/profile/bilateral-country/ita/partner/aus.

Trading Economics, Italian Government. https://tradingeconomics.com/australia/government-debt-to-gdp.

University of Western Australia. https://www.news.uwa.edu.au/archive/201 7100410009/gravitational-waves-binary-black-hole-merger-observed-ligo-and-virgo/.

Wagner, Caroline S., and Loet Leydesdorff. "Network structure, self-organization, and the growth of international collaboration in science." *Research policy* 34.10 (2005): 1608–1618.

Wang, Lili, Xianwen Wang, and Niels J. Philipsen. "Network structure of scientific collaborations between China and the EU member states." *Scientometrics* 113.2 (2017): 765–781.

Zitt, Michel, Elise Bassecoulard, and Yoshiko Okubo. "Shadows of the past in international cooperation: Collaboration profiles of the top five producers of science." *Scientometrics* 47.3 (2000): 627–657.

Where to from Here? The Need for a Long-Term Strategy in Italian–Australian Relations

Simone Battiston and Gabriele Abbondanza

INTRODUCTION

In the past two decades, the decline of traditional multilateralism has paved the way for a resurgence of bilateralism, minilateralism, and to a lesser extent regionalism. For both Italy and Australia, bilateral ties with

S. Battiston (✉)
History and Politics, Department of Humanities and Social Sciences, Swinburne University of Technology, Hawthorn, VIC, Australia
e-mail: sbattiston@swin.edu.au

G. Abbondanza
Complutense University of Madrid, Madrid, Spain

School of Social and Political Sciences, University of Sydney, Sydney, NSW, Australia

Istituto Affari Internazionali (IAI), Rome, Italy

G. Abbondanza
e-mail: gabriabb@ucm.es

© The Author(s), under exclusive license to Springer Nature Singapore Pte Ltd. 2023
G. Abbondanza and S. Battiston (eds.), *Italy and Australia*,
https://doi.org/10.1007/978-981-99-3216-0_11

267

like-minded countries may at times be seen as a faster way of safeguarding their interests, while minilateralism (briefly explored in the third section of this chapter), regionalism, and multilateralism have offered a platform where great powers that often employ middle power-like diplomacy (Italy[1]), or traditional middle powers (Australia[2]), could more effectively exert their influence. The renewed importance of bilateralism, in particular, has encouraged the authors of this edited volume to critically review the existing country-to-country connections between Italy and Australia from a multidisciplinary perspective. The aim is twofold: to identify areas of strengths and areas for improvement and to articulate a long-term strategy, which would sustain this bilateral relation in the coming decades.

This chapter is divided into three core sections. In the first section, Italian–Australian relations are contextualised with three frameworks: diplomatic history, geopolitics, and migration, and mobility. Challenges and opportunities to Italian–Australian relations are the topics of section two, where diverse areas such as populism, decolonial discourses, language, and scientific and research cooperation are explored. The task of the third section is to explore the need for a long-term strategy to elevate twenty-first-century Italian–Australian relations. By doing so, the chapter delves into the main findings of this volume, seeks a potential "red thread" transcending disciplinary boundaries, and echoes calls for closer bilateral relations as a result.

[1] See Congyan Cai, "New Great Powers and International Law in the 21st century", *European Journal of International Law* 24, no. 3 (2013): 755–795; Gabriele Abbondanza, "The odd axis: Germany, Italy, and Japan as awkward great powers", in *Awkward powers: Escaping traditional great and middle power theory*, eds. G. Abbondanza and T. Wilkins (London: Palgrave Macmillan, 2021), 43–71.

[2] Andrew F. Cooper, Richard A. Higgott, and Kim R. Nossal, *Relocating middle powers: Australia and Canada in a changing world order* (Vancouver: UBC Press, 1993); Gabriele Abbondanza, "Australia the 'good international citizen'? The limits of a traditional middle power", *Australian Journal of International Affairs* 75, no. 2 (2021): 178–196.

CONTEXTUALISING ITALIAN–AUSTRALIAN RELATIONS

Italy and Australia share a long history of diplomatic relations, as Robert Pascoe has painstakingly reconstructed,[3] which can be fully appreciated if one bears in mind the domestic context (e.g. a federated Australia gradually developing its own foreign policy) as well as the international context (e.g. Italy being a large European country which is seen by Australia as a potential gateway into Europe). Since the early twentieth century, these relations have undergone through different stages, including a period of formal hostility during the Second World War, which negatively affected not only diplomatic ties but also the local Italian–Australian community.[4] Relations quickly resumed after the war, when Italy and Australia found common ground and mutual interests in key portfolios such as immigration—which led to a bilateral immigration agreement (1951)—and trade. Yet, cooperation has at times proven to be problematic and rife with hurdles. For instance, Australia's relative inexperience in treaty-making may in part explain the temporary suspension of the immigration agreement following the employment crisis of 1952. Some five decades later, a Working Holiday Maker arrangement between the two countries—which allowed thousands of young adults (by and large Italians, and to a lesser extent Australians) to travel and visit each other's country in a working-holiday capacity since the mid-2000s—was only reached after years of negotiations and delays, due to different bureaucratic approaches stifling efforts to attain reciprocity.[5]

Italian–Australian relations have grown gradually since the post-war period. In the late 1950s, the Australian Legation in Rome was upgraded to Embassy, and the "Minister" elevated to "Ambassador", reflecting Italy's key status as Australian partner in the newly created European

---

[3] Robert Pascoe, "A historical overview of Italian-Australian bilateral relations", in *Italy and Australia: Redefining bilateral relations for the twenty-first century*, eds. Gabriele Abbondanza and Simone Battiston (London: Palgrave Macmillan, 2024), pp. 25–48.

[4] See, for example, Gerardo Papalia, "The Italian "fifth column" in Australia: Fascist propaganda, Italian-Australians and internment", *Australian Journal of Politics and History* 66, no. 2 (2020): 214–231; Evan Smith, "Shifting undesirability: Italian migration, political activism and the Australian authorities from the 1920s to the 1950s", *Immigrants & Minorities* 40, nos. 1–2 (2022): 106–131.

[5] Bruno Mascitelli, Rory Steele, and Simone Battiston, *Diaspora parliaments: How Australia faced the Italian challenge* (Ballan, VIC: Connor Court Publishing, 2010), 104–105.

Economic Community (later the European Union). Relations became more symmetrical in the course of the 1960s and the 1970s when political, cultural, and commercial ties deepened and high-level visits took place more frequently. Yet, the diplomatic history in the last quarter of the twentieth century suggests that a decrease in significance has been unfolding for some time, since Australia turned its attention to the Asia–Pacific (later the Indo-Pacific) and Italy's destiny became ever more entwined with that of Europe, the EU, NATO, and the "Enlarged Mediterranean" (*Mediterraneo Allargato*). Geopolitical priorities of both Australia and Italy notwithstanding, several attempts have been made to broaden and deepen bilateral cooperation between Italy and Australia in terms of trade, mobility, social security, cultural exchanges, and research and scientific cooperation in the past decades, which have led to new or renewed agreements and partnerships. Past and recent high-level visits and high-profile diplomatic appointments are further proof that efforts to strengthen bilateralism have never been lacking. The current post-Brexit era, as Pascoe has underscored, allows for a fresh start for both Italy and Australia to invigorate their relations and to leverage each other's geopolitical position, viewed as a getaway into the EU and a stepping-stone into the Asia–Pacific/Indo-Pacific respectively.[6]

Indeed, Italy and Australia have increasingly shown interest in each other's regions, as examined by Andrea Benvenuti in his chapter.[7] Historically, Italy's interest in what used to be the "Asia–Pacific" has advanced slowly and has experienced periods of both high and low intensity. While Italy quickly established diplomatic relations with most of the post-colonial states in the region and sought to expand trade and commercial links with emerging markets, its overall engagement with this region has nonetheless remained low-key for most of the second part of the twentieth century, if benchmarked with that of the comparable European states. The reasons are manifold and can be chiefly found in Italy's different foreign policy priorities, but also in its lively domestic politics, which have curbed the country's foreign policy ambitions, as well as external commitments and constrains, such as the emergence of a

---

[6] Pascoe, "A historical overview of Italian-Australian bilateral relations", pp. 25–48.

[7] Andrea Benvenuti, "The Australian interest in the European Union and the Italian interest in the Asia–Pacific", in *Italy and Australia: Redefining bilateral relations for the twenty-first century*, eds. Gabriele Abbondanza and Simone Battiston (London: Palgrave Macmillan, 2024), pp. 189–212.

more unified European foreign policy strategy. Despite that, in the last two decades or so, Italy's interest in this macro-region has experienced a renewed push, which occurred bilaterally, multilaterally, and at the European level, as Benvenuti has emphasised. Not only has Italy's trade relationship with major Asian economies—not only China—significantly increased of late, but Italy's broad engagement has expanded too, through several multilateral initiatives and different fora, whether under the aegis of the European Union, the United Nations, other major intergovernmental bodies, or unilaterally (as in the case of Rome's growing Indo-Pacific approach).

Australia's interest in Europe, on the other hand, has traditionally been multifaceted and spread across different areas, from defence to trade to immigration. In the post-war period, Canberra viewed a stable, peaceful, and prosperous Western Europe as a stronghold of world stability, a containment wall against Soviet expansionism and a lucrative market for Australian products. But a stronger Europe, and in particular a raising and expanding European Economic Community (EEC), has generated anxieties too. The British membership of the EEC in the 1970s, which was thought to undermine the longstanding close Anglo-Australian partnership in different areas, and the detrimental effects of the Common Agricultural Policy (CAP) to Australian exports to Europe in particular, cooled down Australian-European relations for years. Differences notwithstanding, both Australia and the now European Union (EU) have continued to engage and seek ways to foster greater political and economic cooperation, which allowed not only the thorny agricultural question to be largely resolved by the late 1990s but also to venture into an Agenda for Cooperation (2003), a Framework Agreement (2017) for deeper cooperation, and eventually to start negotiations on a Free Trade Agreement (2020) which is now close to a positive outcome. By collaborating more closely, given the shared interest in democratic values and stability of each other's regions, Italy and Australia could ultimately play a valuable role in ensuring that each other's views and interests are not only noted but also valued within the EU and in the Indo-Pacific respectively.

Besides diplomatic history and broad geopolitical matters, migration and mobility offer a further lens for probing Italian–Australian relations. In the immediate post-war period, the two countries shared "common destinies in relation to migration" with Australia seeking migrant labour and settlers beyond the British and Irish diaspora for its post-war strategic objectives, while Italy "encouraged its impoverished rural population to emigrate" abroad.[8] Historically, migration has constituted a common thread responsible for the making of the modern relationship between Italy and Australia, according to Bruno Mascitelli, but equally for its unmaking in the post-1970s period due to strategic repositioning and pursuing of different national interests by both countries.[9]

Yet, the complexity of contemporary mobility and migration—whose trajectories often display transnational, circulatory, and short-term patterns—suggests paying close attention to recent flows of citizens in each other's countries. For instance, the latest "wave" of Italian arrivals in Australia, although chiefly characterised by its non-permanent, skilled, and transnational nature, has nonetheless injected new blood into the historical Italian-background community and wider Australian society at large.[10] Such recent developments have also provided significant insights into Italians' voting patterns abroad, including in Australia, as argued by Simone Battiston.[11] Even though Italian–Australian migration and mobilities have almost exclusively been studied so far from the point of view of successive waves of Italians moving to and settling in Australia, movements in the opposite direction have recently attracted attention. As documented by Giulia Marchetti and Loretta Baldassar in their chapter, Italy has been a magnet for Australians for quite a long time.[12] Italy is indeed one of the most preferred destinations for Australian tourists, but also one that entices Global North elite mobility (often scarcely noticeable in the context of comparable countries and thus somewhat hidden from view) and migration of different kinds (return, roots, retirement, sentimental, and even virtual). Although less than 2000 Australian citizens live permanently in Italy, the Australia-born residents in Italy are

---

[8] Bruno Mascitelli, "Italy and Australia: A relationship made and unmade by immigration", *Australian Journal of International Affairs* 69, no. 3 (2015): 339.

[9] Mascitelli, "Italy and Australia", 353.

[10] Simone Battiston, "Italians in Australia in the twenty-first century", in *Italy and Australia: Redefining bilateral relations for the twenty-first century*, eds. Gabriele Abbondanza and Simone Battiston (London: Palgrave Macmillan, 2024), pp. 49–80.

[11] See Simone Battiston, Stefano Luconi, and Marco Valbruzzi (eds.), *Cittadini oltre confine: Storia, opinioni e rappresentanza degli italiani all'estero* (Bologna: Il Mulino, 2022).

[12] Giulia Marchetti and Loretta Baldassar, "Australians in Italy in the twenty-first century", in *Italy and Australia: Redefining bilateral relations for the twenty-first century*, eds. Gabriele Abbondanza and Simone Battiston (London: Palgrave Macmillan, 2024), pp. 81–111.

almost ten times as much, a tangible legacy of the significant history of Italian migration to Australia.

CHALLENGES AND OPPORTUNITIES

The rise of populism in liberal democracies like Italy and Australia presents both significant challenges and opportunities for bilateral relations. Populism in these two countries, which have experienced structural levels of media concentration, has typically flourished during periods of low political trust. By looking into how populism has manifested in these two Global North case studies, Kurt Sengul and Francesco Bailo encourage policymakers, scholars, and experts to examine the conditions that have facilitated the advent of populist politics in the hope of finding solutions that would strengthen (and improve) liberal institutions in both countries.[13] Another area that also offers both challenges and opportunities for bilateral relations is decolonisation, discussed by Francesco Ricatti and Matteo Dutto in their chapter.[14] By acknowledging the existence and significance of Indigenous sovereignty debates, State actors could meaningfully engage with the process of decolonisation. As far as Italy is concerned, non-State actors, influential individuals, associations, and in part cultural institutions, have mostly been at the forefront of engagements with Indigenous people, lands, and cultures. Historically, Italian artists and activists have been leading a proactive role in documenting Indigenous activities and communities across Australia (see the works of the Cavadini brothers, in particular). It is therefore not surprising that interesting developments are now emerging in the broader field of visual and performing arts, including the rise of *artivists* of mixed Indigenous and Italian background, such as Paola Balla. More recently, academic works, transnational film, and media productions have offered new insights into contemporary encounters of Italians with

---

[13] Kurt Sengul and Francesco Bailo, "Twenty-first century populism in Australia and Italy: A comparative analysis", in *Italy and Australia: Redefining bilateral relations for the twenty-first century*, eds. Gabriele Abbondanza and Simone Battiston (London: Palgrave Macmillan, 2024), pp. 215–241.

[14] Francesco Ricatti and Matteo Dutto, "First nations sovereignty: Towards a decolonial approach to Italy–Australia relations", in *Italy and Australia: Redefining bilateral relations for the twenty-first century*, eds. Gabriele Abbondanza and Simone Battiston (London: Palgrave Macmillan, 2024), pp. 113–136.

Indigenous Australians, while critiquing the historical role of migrants in settler-colonial societies.

If we move our attention to the fields of language, as well as scientific and research cooperation, there is ample scope for advancing Italian–Australian relations. Italian is among the most studied foreign languages in the world, whose teaching abroad has long been recognised as "an instrument of cultural diplomacy and soft power".[15] Cristiana Palmieri has underscored that several factors "contribute to the appeal of Italian in Australia", including "the presence of a large and well-established Italian migrant community" which "plays a pivotal role in attracting learners to various aspects of the culture of Italy".[16] In her studies, Palmieri suggests that learning Italian is seen as the quintessence of European refinement, supported by the longstanding tradition of Italophilia in Australia and by unwavering passion of the Italian cultural heritage, broadly defined. For Italians seeking to learn English or further their studies in English, on the other hand, Australia offers plenty of opportunities too, as the data outlined in Palmieri's chapter attest.

Additionally, Italy and Australia share a long-standing history of fruitful relations in terms of scientific and research collaboration, as Ilaria S. Pagani and Tiziana Torresi have pointed out.[17] In particular, a recent treaty-level scientific cooperation agreement has officialised years of productive scientific cooperation at the institutional, academic, and private levels. Yet, much potential remains untapped. Indeed, there is much to be gained by furthering collaboration in key areas of research for both Rome and Canberra, should national and supra-national actors step up their level of reciprocal engagement as well as their interaction with private actors that are already involved or would like to be.

[15] Roberto Dolci, "Language teachers and textbooks as cultural ambassadors and mediators", *Teaching Italian Language and Culture Annual* (2021): 27–45.

[16] Cristiana Palmieri, "Connecting Australia and Italy through language", in *Italy and Australia: Redefining bilateral relations for the twenty-first century*, eds. Gabriele Abbondanza and Simone Battiston (London: Palgrave Macmillan, 2024), pp. 137–154.

[17] Ilaria Stefania Pagani and Tiziana Torresi, "Italian-Australian scientific and research cooperation", in *Italy and Australia: Redefining bilateral relations for the twenty-first century*, eds. Gabriele Abbondanza and Simone Battiston (London: Palgrave Macmillan, 2024), pp. 243–267.

A LONG-TERM STRATEGY:
FROM BILATERALISM TO MULTILATERALISM

The current state of bilateral relations, recounted above, allows for some considerations on how to strengthen Italian–Australian ties in the context of a global order in flux. Conceptually rejoining the initial premise of this chapter, this can occur bilaterally, minilaterally, and multilaterally. Starting with *bilateral* relations—noticeably understudied, and thus the focus of this volume—Rome and Canberra may examine their key priorities and discover that many of them are mutually shared, which could warrant the decision to elevate their relationship to the strategic partnership level. As already argued in think tank circles, the increasing convergence of strategic interests, and the remarkable level of complementarity the two countries have in a number of significant fields, would strongly support such as a diplomatic advancement in Italian–Australian relations.[18]

More specifically, research included in this volume by Gabriele Abbondanza has explicitly examined the strengths and limitations of existing bilateral relations, therefore outlining what could be done to improve the former and ameliorate the latter.[19] On the one hand, a strategic partnership would address the unexpressed potential in terms of shared international goals, defence capabilities, trade, scientific cooperation, and people-to-people links. On this point, it is worth remembering that Italy already has strategic partnerships with key Indo-Pacific nations such as Japan, India, South Korea, Vietnam, and others, and that Australia has done the same with France and Germany, which are comparable to Italy under a variety of relevant criteria. On the other, a strategic partnership would address existing issues currently curbing stronger ties, which include a number of well-known industry-specific challenges.

Second, stronger ties between Rome and Canberra could also strengthen existing *minilateral* fora. To wit, minilateralism stems from the recent trend of "alignment" (as opposed to "alliance") and refers to states' groupings with only a few members, which allows them to

---

[18] Gabriele Abbondanza, "Italy and Australia: Time for a Strategic Partnership", *IAI Commentaries* 20, no. 87 (2020): 1–5.

[19] Gabriele Abbondanza, "Time for a strategic partnership: the scope for international cooperation between Italy and Australia", in *Italy and Australia: redefining bilateral relations for the twenty-first century*, eds. Gabriele Abbondanza and Simone Battiston (London: Palgrave Macmillan, 2024), pp.155–187.

more swiftly respond to fast-paced challenges and concurrently avoid the inevitable internal differences and oppositions of larger blocs.[20] In the context of an increasingly volatile security landscape, especially in the Indo-Pacific, a few interrelated examples stand out. These include the enhanced strategic partnership between Australia, the UK, and the US (AUKUS); Italy's new key role in India's Indo-Pacific Oceans Initiative (IPOI); the Quadrilateral Security Dialogue between India, Japan, the US, and Australia (the Quad); the Global Combat Air Program developed by Italy, the UK, and Japan (GCAP); and several others. As can be seen, both Italy and Australia are actively engaged with the same key Indo-Pacific states, with which they share similar goals and compatible means. Consequently, strengthened bilateral relations would support the broader objectives of these minilateral fora, and would therefore be welcomed by the other member states.

Third, all of the above would ultimately help to promote *multilateralism*, by supporting the wide-scoped aims of relevant international organisations such as the United Nations (UN), the European Union (EU), the Association of Southeast Asian Nations (ASEAN), the Indian Ocean Rim Association (IORA) and, to a more circumscribed extent, the North Atlantic Treaty Organization (NATO) too, among the many. With the international law as one of the pillars of these organisations, which embody the concept of multilateralism itself, the maintenance of the status quo, the liberal order, and the rules-based order becomes a shared priority. To that extent, the presence of like-minded and aligned countries, as well as that of related minilaterals, cannot but support the commitment towards an international society of states centred on the primacy of the international law, diplomacy, and multilateralism as a just and sustainable pathway to common prosperity.

Italy and Australia represent two highly significant case studies in this respect, and more closely aligned goals and means would therefore play a tangible role in supporting the values they both stand for and the interests they both pursue. As the contributors of this innovative volume have attested, the remarkable cooperation in the fields of history, migration, Indigenous Australian voices, culture, language, politics, trade, international relations, and science is a strong and valuable point of departure, if an understudied one. To that end, we hope to have fostered a renewed

---

[20] Bhubhindar Singh and Sarah Teo, *Minilateralism in the Indo-Pacific* (London: Routledge, 2020).

debate on Italian–Australian relations in the disciplinary literature, policy circles, and beyond.

Bibliography

Abbondanza, Gabriele. "Italy and Australia: Time for a strategic partnership". *IAI Commentaries* 20, no. 87 (2020): 1–5.

Abbondanza, Gabriele. "Australia the 'good international citizen'? The limits of a traditional middle power", *Australian Journal of International Affairs* 75, no. 2 (2021): 178–196.

Abbondanza, Gabriele. "The odd axis: Germany, Italy, and Japan as awkward great powers". In *Awkward powers: Escaping traditional great and middle power theory*, edited by G. Abbondanza and T. Wilkins, 43–71. London: Palgrave Macmillan, 2021.

Abbondanza, Gabriele. "Time for a strategic partnership: The scope for international cooperation between Italy and Australia". In *Italy and Australia: Redefining bilateral relations for the twenty-first century*, edited by G. Abbondanza and S. Battiston, pp. 155–187. London: Palgrave Macmillan, 2024.

Battiston, Simone. "Italians in Australia in the twenty-first century", in *Italy and Australia: Redefining bilateral relations for the twenty-first century*, edited by G. Abbondanza and S. Battiston, pp. 49–80. London: Palgrave Macmillan, 2024.

Battiston, Simone, Stefano Luconi, and Marco Valbruzzi (eds.). *Cittadini oltre confine: Storia, opinioni e rappresentanza degli italiani all'estero*. Bologna: Il Mulino, 2022.

Benvenuti, Andrea. "The Australian interest in the European Union and the Italian interest in the Asia-Pacific", in *Italy and Australia: Redefining bilateral relations for the twenty-first century*, edited by G. Abbondanza and S. Battiston, pp. 189–212. London: Palgrave Macmillan, 2024.

Cai, Congyan. "New Great Powers and International Law in the 21st Century". *European Journal of International Law* 24, no. 3 (2013): 755–795.

Cooper, Andrew F., Richard A. Higgott, and Kim R. Nossal, *Relocating middle powers: Australia and Canada in a changing world order* (Vancouver: UBC Press, 1993).

Dolci, Roberto. "Language teachers and textbooks as cultural ambassadors and mediators", *Teaching Italian Language and Culture Annual* (2021): 27–45

Gerardo Papalia, "The Italian "fifth column" in Australia: Fascist propaganda, Italian-Australians and internment", *Australian Journal of Politics and History* 66, no. 2 (2020): 214–231.

Mascitelli, Bruno. "Italy and Australia: A relationship made and unmade by immigration", *Australian Journal of International Affairs* 69, no. 3 (2015): 339–355.

Marchetti, Giulia and Loretta Baldassar, "Australians in Italy in the twenty-first century", in *Italy and Australia: Redefining bilateral relations for the twenty-first century*, edited by G. Abbondanza and S. Battiston, pp. 81–111. London: Palgrave Macmillan, 2024.

Mascitelli, Bruno, Rory Steele, and Simone Battiston, *Diaspora parliaments: How Australia faced the Italian challenge* (Ballan, VIC.: Connor Court Publishing, 2010).

Pagani, Ilaria S. and Tiziana Torresi, "Italian-Australian scientific and research cooperation", in *Italy and Australia: Redefining bilateral relations for the twenty-first century*, edited by G. Abbondanza and S. Battiston, pp. 243–267. London: Palgrave Macmillan, 2024.

Palmieri, Cristiana. "Connecting Australia and Italy through language", in *Italy and Australia: Redefining bilateral relations for the twenty-first century*, edited by G. Abbondanza and S. Battiston, pp. 137–154. London: Palgrave Macmillan, 2024.

Pascoe, Robert. "A historical overview of Italian-Australian bilateral relations", in *Italy and Australia: Redefining bilateral relations for the twenty-first century*, edited by G. Abbondanza and S. Battiston, pp. 25–48. London: Palgrave Macmillan, 2024.

Ricatti, Francesco and Matteo Dutto, "First Nations sovereignty: Towards a decolonial approach to Italy-Australia relations", in *Italy and Australia: Redefining bilateral relations for the twenty-first century*, edited by G. Abbondanza and S. Battiston, pp. 113–136. London: Palgrave Macmillan, 2024.

Sengul, Kurt and Francesco Bailo, "Twenty-first century populism in Australia and Italy: A comparative analysis", in *Italy and Australia: Redefining bilateral relations for the twenty-first century*, edited by G. Abbondanza and S. Battiston, pp. 215–241. London: Palgrave Macmillan, 2024.

Singh, Bhubhindar and Sarah Teo, *Minilateralism in the Indo-Pacific* (London: Routledge, 2020).

Smith, Evan. "Shifting undesirability: Italian migration, political activism and the Australian authorities from the 1920s to the 1950s", *Immigrants & Minorities* 40, nos. 1–2 (2022): 106–131.

INDEX

Printed in the USA
CPSIA information can be obtained
at www.ICGtesting.com
LVHW021448100224
771434LV00005B/533